CRIPPLED GIANT: NIGERIA
SINCE INDEPENDENCE

To the two teachers who moulded me:
my father
CHRISTOPHER OSAGIEDE OSAGHAE
who found fulfilment in being a teacher
and
MISTER OLOYEDE
the teacher God sent to raise me

EGHOSA E. OSAGHAE

Crippled Giant
Nigeria since Independence

INDIANA UNIVERSITY PRESS
BLOOMINGTON AND INDIANAPOLIS

First published in North America in 1998 by

Indiana University Press
601 North Morton Street
Bloomington, Indiana 47404

Copyright © 1998 by Eghosa E. Osaghae

Manufactured in India

Library of Congress Cataloging-in-Publication Data

Osaghae, Eghosa E.
    Crippled Giant: Nigeria since independence / Eghosa E.
Osaghae.
       p.   cm.
    Includes bibliographical references (p.   ) and index.
    ISBN 0-253-33410-1. —ISBN 0-253-21197-2 (pbk.)
      1. Nigeria—Politics and government—1960–   I. Title.
DT515.8.075   1998
966.905—dc21   97-32892

1 2 3 4 5   03 02 01 00 99 98

CONTENTS

v

TABLES

PREFACE

Following the killings of the Ogoni minority activists on 10 November 1995, world attention focused on Nigeria as it had not done since the country's civil war. Underlying the condemnations that greeted the killings was a range of pertinent questions which observers and scholars of the Nigerian political scene had continuously asked over the years: what exactly is the trouble with Nigeria? Why did a country once regarded as the giant and hope of Africa because of its immense human and material resources founder so badly? How did a country which many called an exception to the tragedy that had befallen post-colonial states in Africa become like 'any other African country?' With the killings, these questions became more pertinent. Many commentators and scholars then began to refer to the country's descent into decline. A few less optimistic ones talked of the final eclipse of the troubled state.

What is really the trouble with Nigeria? It is arguably one of the most complex countries in the world and belongs to the genre of the most troubled complex societies called deeply divided societies. Could this be the problem? Others talk of the pervasive corruption and gross mismanagement that made a country which was on a par with Malaysia and Indonesia in 1960 one of the world's poorest fifteen countries in 1995, according to World Bank Statistics. Could this be the problem? Still others consider Nigeria's inability to determine its fate in the global system and its susceptibility to the crisis of extraversion (i.e. crisis which follows from external forces outside the control of the state) which reduce even the most stable and seemingly wealthy rentier state (i.e. a state which derives its revenue from taxes or rents on production of minerals by multinational corporations rather than from productive activity) to impotent anger, a major factor. Could this be the problem?

Obviously each one of these viewpoints, which together approximate a rough summary of the efforts of scholars to explain the trouble with Nigeria, has validity. Yet they need to be proved, and it is dangerous to accept them at face value. The present book is an attempt to address the sort of questions presented above within these perspectives. It has the advantage of tracing Nigeria's history from the present, meaning that its major objective is to analyse why the country has found itself in the present predicament or what Joseph

ix

(1996) has called the dismal tunnel. The major argument in the book may be summarised as being that Nigeria is a crippled state. It was crippled from the beginning by the nature of its colonial creation and integration into the global economy, and has remained crippled by corrupt and authoritarian regimes, the inability to overcome its divisions, and the inability to determine its manifest destiny in the face of a hegemonic world order. The major effect of the crippling of the state has been its failure to realise its vast potential. Against this background, the decline of the 1980s and 1990s has in fact been long in coming, and the events of these years culminating in the Ogoni killings – the political turbulence, the stepping up of authoritarian rule, the economic recession and the conflict generating and exacerbating economic reforms, and the manipulations of a hostile international milieu – only served to accelerate it.

The book is divided into eight chapters. The first provides the historical background and analytical framework for the more substantive chapters. The second examines the major events and issues which cumulatively led to the collapse of the First Republic (1960-66). The third examines the initial phase of military rule (1976-9), the fourth the rise and fall of the Second Republic (1979-83), the fifth the Buhari regime (1983-5), the sixth the eventful Babangida years (1985-93) which saw the accentuation of the crisis that accelerated the country's descent into the abyss, and the seventh the Abacha regime (1993-6). The final chapter presents the conclusion and ends with a brief look at possible ways out of Nigeria's crippled state. A few comments on the approach and organisation of the main body of these chapters. The approach is analytical, empirical and interpretive and, as spelt out in Chapter 1 which presents the analytical bases of Nigeria's politics, is guided by a number of broad and general explanatory categories. The attempt is to provide a comprehensive analysis of Nigeria's post-independence political history. This necessarily includes the economy and foreign relations, which are examined in every chapter for the period covered. The emphasis throughout is on identifying and accounting for political trends and tendencies. Although issues and events are located within the periods in which they occur, they are not treated in isolation. In a sense, therefore, the entire book is a single continuous history.

I want to thank Michael Dwyer of the publishers C. Hurst & Co. for offering me the opportunity to write a book on Nigeria's post-independence history, and for prompting me at every stage of the period it took to complete the work. From the period of my brief stay in Uppsala, where work for this book started, right through to my return to Ibadan and finally my move to Umtata, I have received tremendous support and encouragement all the way. As usual, my family has been in the thick of it all, making the sacrifice of being without me. Would Osahon, Noyo, Esosa and our one and only Amen see their imprint here? It is in the thanks which I offer, but it is also in this product of our collective will. I am grateful to the Nordiska Afrikainstitutet in Uppsala for offering me the window to this work, and for the warmth of the Director and staff that made my winter stay very fruitful. I thank Ade Isumonah, Osasu Osaghae, Uyilawa Usuanlele, Dr Chris Oche, Professor Tunde Lawuyi and Professor Bayo Adekanye who contributed in various ways to the completion of this work. I also thank A.H.M. Kirk-Greene, the doyen of Nigerian studies in Britain, who read through the entire manuscript and gave insightful critical comments and suggestions. The last word is for Dr Solomon Yirenkyi-Boateng who gave me Solomon's words.

Umtata, January 1998   EGHOSA E. OSAGHAE

ABBREVIATIONS

ABN	Association for Better Nigeria
ABU	Ahmadu Bello University
ACP	African-Caribbean-Pacific (countries)
ADB	African Development Bank
ADP	Agricultural Development Programme
AFRC	Armed Forces Ruling Council
AG	Action Group
ANC	All-Nigeria Congress
ANC	African National Congress (South Africa)
ANPP	All Nigeria People's Party
APPA	African Petroleum Producers Association
ASUU	Academic Staff Union of (Nigerian) Universities
BBC	British Broadcasting Corporation
BDPP	Benin-Delta People's Party
BECGD	British Export Credit Guarantee Department
BLP	Better Life Programme
BP	British Petroleum
bpd	barrels per day
BPE	Bureau for Public Enterprises
BYM	Bornu Youth Movement
CA	Constituent Assembly
CAN	Christian Association of Nigeria
CARIA	Cross River-Abia-Rivers-Imo-Anambra (states)
CBN	Central Bank of Nigeria
CD	Campaign for Democracy
CDC	Constitution Drafting Committee
CDS	Centre for Democratic Studies
CGS	Chief of General Staff
CLO	Civil Liberties Organization
CNC	Committee for National Consensus
CNUP	Committee for National Unity and Progress
COR	Calabar-Ogoja-Rivers
CRC	Constitution Review Committee
CRP	Civil Rights Project

DFRRI	Directorate of Food, Roads and Rural Infrastructure
DP	Dynamic Party
DPA	Distributable Pool Account
DPN	Democratic Party of Nigeria
DSM	Directorate of Social Mobilization
ECOWAS	Economic Community of West African States
ECOMOG	ECOWAS Monitoring Group (peace-keeping force)
EEC	European Economic Community
EIU	Economist Intelligence Unit
EMIROAF	Ethnic Minorities Rights Organization of Africa
EU	European Community
FSP	Family Support Programme
FCDA	Federal Capital Development Authority
FCT	Federal Capital Territory
FEDECO	Federal Electoral Commission
FESTAC	(Second) World Black and African Festival of Arts and Culture
FGN	Federal Government of Nigeria
FNLA	Frente Nacional de Libertacão de Angola
GDM	Grassroots Democratic Movement
GDP	Gross Domestic Product
GNPP	Great Nigeria People's Party
HOA	(state) House of Assembly
HOR	House of Representatives
IGR	Inter-governmental Relations
IMF	International Monetary Fund
ING	Interim National Government
IPP	Ideal People's Party
ITT	International Telegraph and Telephone (Corporation)
JMB	Johnson Matthey Bank
LC	Liberal Convention
LNG	Liquified Natural Gas
LOOBO	Lagos, Ogun, Ondo, Bendel and Oyo (UPN states)
MAD	Movement for the Advancement of Democracy
MAMSER	Mass Mobilization for Economic Recovery, Self Reliance and Social Justice
MDF	Mid-West Democratic Front
MORETO	Movement for Reparation to Ogbia

MOSIEND	Movement for the Survival of Izon Ethnic Minority in the Niger Delta
MOSOP	Movement for the Survival of Ogoni People
MPLA	Movimento Popular de Libertacão de Angola
MSM	Mid-West State Movement
NAA	Nigeria Airports Authority
NADECO	National Democratic Coalition
NAM	Non Aligned Movement
NANS	National Association of Nigerian Students
NAP	Nigeria Advance Party
NARD	National Association of Resident Doctors
NBA	Nigeria Bar Association
NCCC	National Constitutional Conference Commission
NCNC	National Council of Nigerian Citizens
NCPN	National Centre Party of Nigeria
NDC	Niger Delta Congress
NDE	National Directorate of Employment
NDIC	National Deposit Insurance Corporation
NDLP	National Democratic Labour Party
NDP	National Democratic Party
NDSC	National Defence and Security Council
NEC	National Electoral Commission
NECON	National Electoral Commission of Nigeria
NEPA	National Electric Power Authority
NEPU	Northern Elements Progressive Union
NIPSS	National Institute for Policy and Strategic Studies
NITEL	Nigeria Telecommunications Limited
NLC	Nigeria Labour Congress
NLP	Nigeria Labour Party
NMA	Nigerian Medical Association
NNA	Nigerian National Alliance
NNC	Nigerian National Congress
NNDP	Nigerian National Democratic Party
NNOC	Nigerian National Oil Corporation
NNPC	Nigerian National Petroleum Company
NPA	Nigeria Ports Authority
NPC	Northern People's Congress
NPC	National Population Commission

NPN	National Party of Nigeria
NPP	Nigeria People's Party
NPWP	Nigerian People's Welfare Party
NRC	National Republican Convention
NSPA	National Solidarity People's Alliance
NSO	National Security Organization
NUC	National Union Council
NUP	National Unity Party
NUPENG	National Union of Petroleum and Natural Gas Workers
OAPEC	Organization of Arab Petroleum Exporting Countries
OAU	Organization of African Unity
OECD	Organization of Economic Cooperation and Development
OFN	Operation Feed the Nation
OIC	Organization of Islamic Countries
OMPADEC	Oil Mineral Producing Areas Development Commission
OPEC	Organization of Petroleum Exporting Countries
PAC	Pan African Congress (South Africa)
PAC	Presidential Advisory Committee
pb	per barrel
PCP	Peoples Consensus Party
PENGASSAN	Petroleum and Natural Gas Senior Staff Association of Nigeria
PFP	People's Front of Nigeria
PLOs	Presidential Liaision Officers
PNP	Patriotic Nigerian Party
PPN	Progressive Party of Nigeria
PPP	People's Patriotic Party
PPP	People's Progressive Party
PRC	Provisional Ruling Council
PRP	People's Redemption Party
PSP	People's Solidarity Party
PTF	Petroleum Trust Fund
RPN	Republican Party of Nigeria
SAP	Structural Adjustment Programme
SDP	Social Democratic Party
SGN	Solidarity Group of Nigeria
SMC	Supreme Military Council
SPP	Social Progressive Party
SSS	State Security Service

SWAPO	South West African People's Organization (Namibia)
TAC	Technical Aid Corps
TC	Transitional Council
TCPC	Technical Committee on Privatisation and Commercialisation
UAC	United African Company
UBA	United Bank for Africa
UK	United Kingdom
UMBC	United Middle Belt Congress
UMEOA	West African Economic and Monetary Union
UN	United Nations
UNCP	United Nigeria Congress Party
UNDP	United Nigeria Democratic Party
UNIP	United National Independents Party
UNITA	União Nacional para a Independencia Total de Angola
UPGA	United Progressive Grand Alliance
UPN	Unity Party of Nigeria
UPP	United People's Party
USA (US)	United States of America
VAT	Value Added Tax
WAI	War Against Indiscipline
WAIC	War Against Indiscipline and Corruption
WIN	Women in Nigeria

POLITICAL MILESTONES IN NIGERIA, 1960-96

1960
1 October. Independence from Britain.
1962
May. State of Emergency declared in Western region; Abortive census exercise.
1963
August. Mid-West region created.
1 October. Nigeria becomes a Republic.
November. Fresh census: 55.67 million.
1964
December. Election crisis.
1965
October-December. Political crisis deepens after Western regional elections.
1966
15 January. First military coup, overthrow of First Republic, Ironsi regime.
24 May. Decree abrogates federal system, establishes unitary system.
29 July. Second military coup, Gowon regime.
8 August. Decree restores federal system.
September-October. *Ad Hoc* Constitutional Conference.
1967
January. Aburi meeting to forestall imminent civil war.
27 May. Creation of twelve states to replace four regions.
30 May. Ojukwu announces secession of Eastern region and declares Republic of Biafra.
6 July. Start of civil war.
1970
12 January. End of civil war.
1 October. Gowon announces 9-point programme for return to civil rule in 1976.
1972
February. First Indigenization decree.
1973
November. Provisional population census results announced: 79.76 million, later annulled.
1974
1 October. Gowon postpones return to civilian rule indefinitely.
1975
29 July. Third military coup, Mohammed regime.
1 October. Mohammed announces 5-stage programme for return to civilian rule in 1979.

18 October. CDC inaugurated.

1976

3 February. Twelve states replaced by nineteen states.
13 February. Fourth military coup (abortive), Mohammed assassinated.
14 September. CDC submits report.
December. Local government reforms.

1977

January. Second Indigenization decree.
6 October. CA inaugurated.

1978

March. Land use decree.
29 August. Constitution presented to head of state.
21 September. 1979 Constitution promulgated, ban on politics lifted.

1979

July-August. Elections into state and federal legislative and executive bodies.
1 October. Inauguration of Shagari as civilian president, Second Republic.

1980

December. Fundamentalist Muslim uprising in Kano (Maitatsine riots).

1981

22 June. Governor Balarabe Musa of Kaduna state impeached.

1983

13 August-3 September. Federal and state elections.
31 December. Fifth military coup, Buhari regime.

1984

Arrests, detention and selective trials of former political office holders.

1985

27 August. Sixth military coup, Babangida regime.
1 October. State of national economic emergency declared.
20 December. Seventh coup (Vatsa coup) announced.

1986

January. Return to civil rule by 1 October announced, Political Bureau appointed.
February. Nigeria joins OIC.
July. SAP formally announced.

1987

March. Christian-Muslim clashes in Kafanchan, Kaduna, Zaria, Katsina.
11 July. White paper on Political Bureau Report, timetable for return to
    civilian rule on 1 October 1992 announced.
September. Two more states (Akwa Ibom and Katsina) created.
12 December. Local government elections without parties.

1988

11 May. CA inaugurated.

1989

May. Constitution promulgated, two-party system adopted.
5 October. NEC recommends six out of thirteen political associations.

7 October. AFRC dissolves all thirteen political associations and 'manufactures' two parties: NRC and SDP.

1990

22 April. Eighth military coup led by Major G. Orkar (abortive).

August. ECOMOG moved into Liberia.

December. Local government elections on party basis.

1991

April. Muslim-Christian conflicts in Bauchi.

27 August. States increased to thirty.

12 December. Federal capital moved from Lagos to Abuja.

14 December. State assembly and gubernational elections.

1992

2 January. Presidential election shifted to 5 December 1992, and date of hand-over to civilians to 2 January 1993.

19 March. Census returns announced: 88.5 million.

4 July. National Assembly elections.

August-September. Party presidential primaries.

October. AFRC annuls presidential primaries, dissolves NRC and SDP executive committees and appoints caretaker committees.

November. Presidential election postponed to 12 June 1993, and date of hand-over to civilians to 27 August.

5 December. National Assembly inaugurated.

1993

2 January. Transitional Council headed by Ernest Shonekan appointed; NDSC replaces AFRC.

January. 'Option A4' adopted, over 250 presidential aspirants emerge.

29 March. Presidential candidates nominated: NRC – Bashir Tofa, SDP – M.K.O. Abiola.

10 June. Abuja High Court grants ABN an injunction to stop presidential election.

12 June. Presidential election still held.

16 June. ABN secures another injunction to stop further release of election results by NEC.

23 June. Presidential election annulled, NEC and transition programme suspended.

27 August. Babangida 'steps aside', ING named, with Ernest Shonekan as head of state.

10 September. 19 February 1994 announced as date for new presidential election.

24 September. Abiola returns from self-exile.

10 November. Lagos High Court declares ING illegal.

17 November. Ninth military coup, Abacha regime, all democratic and transition structures dissolved.

1994

14 January. Commission for Constitutional Conference appointed.

May. National Constitutional Conference elections: NADECO issues ultimatum to the Abacha regime to relinquish power by 31 May.

June-July. Abiola proclaims himself president, paralyzing anti-government restoration of 12 June presidential election; strikes and demonstrations by oil workers and other civil society constituents.

July. Constitutional Conference begins.

December. 'First Phase' of Transition to civil rule programme which stipulated. 17 January 1995 as date of lifting of ban on politics, announced.

1995

March. Coup plot involving former head of state, General Olusegun Obasanjo and forty-four others 'uncovered'.

27 July. Report of Constitutional Conference submitted.

1 October. 'Comprehensive' timetable for return to civil rule on 1 October 1998 announced.

10 November. Ken Saro-Wiwa and eight other Ogoni minority rights activists executed; world-wide condemnation.

11 November. Nigeria expelled from Commonwealth.

1996

30 September. Five new political parties announced.

1 October. Six more states and 138 local government areas created.

Location of major ethnic groups

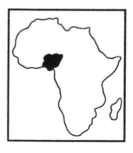

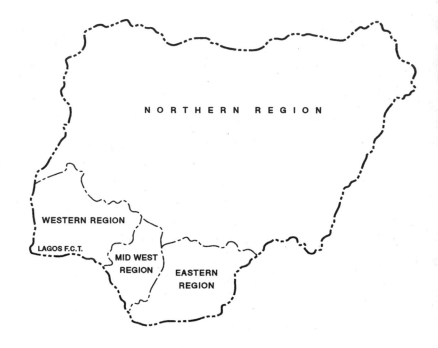

NORTHERN REGION

WESTERN REGION

LAGOS F.C.T.

MID WEST
REGION

EASTERN
REGION

Four Regions, 1963

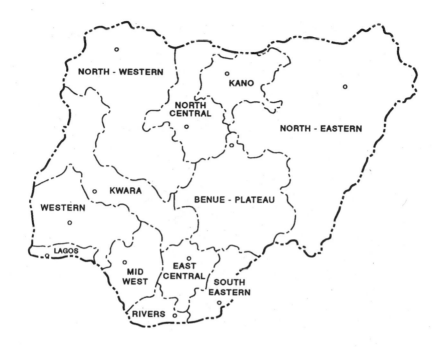

Twelve States, 1976

Nineteen States, 1976

Thirty States, 1991

1. ENUGU
2. ANAMBRA
3. EBONYI
4. ABIA
5. CROSS RIVER
6. AKWA IBOM
7. RIVERS

Thirty-six States, 1996

1

HISTORICAL AND
ANALYTICAL OVERVIEW

The roots of Nigeria's post-independence politics are deeply entrenched in its colonial history. Like most other modern African states, the country was created through the expedient acts of British colonial administration. In a profound sense, many of the post-independence socio-political and economic formations and malformations are a direct consequence of the state-building and economic integration processes begun under colonial rule.

This is not to heap all the problems of the post-colonial state and society on colonial rule, although Nigerians disenchanted with the inadequacies of power and resource allocation in the country have, following the late Ahmadu Bello, continued to refer to 'the mistake of 1914', i.e. the decision by the British colonial authorities to amalgamate the North and South, whose groups had little in common. Rather, the point is that, given the deep roots of post-independence structures and processes, as well as the continuities between colonial and post-colonial formations, an historical background is necessary to provide the context and point of departure for analysing post-independence politics. The first task of this chapter is to present and discuss this background. Its other task is to examine the underlying bases of politics in Nigeria as a framework for the analysis undertaken in this book. What counts as politics in Nigeria? What forms does it take and why? How may we account for political formations? Answers to these and other pertinent questions which are attempted in the second part of the chapter will provide the necessary conceptual handle for subsequent chapters.

HISTORICAL OVERVIEW

The main elements of Nigeria's pre-independence history and, in particular, political developments of consequence are well covered in the literature (cf. Coleman, 1958; Crowder, 1962; Schwarz, 1965;

1

Mackintosh, 1966; Arikpo, 1967; Okonjo, 1974; Nicolson, 1977; Ikime, 1977, 1980). At the risk of repeating what is well known, we shall attempt to sketch the essentials of this historical background and examine how it shaped the character and dynamics of Nigerian politics. January 1, 1914, the day when Lord Lugard effected the amalgamation of the Protectorate of Northern Nigeria and the Colony and Protectorate of Southern Nigeria which were previously administered as separate though related territories, is generally regarded as the birthdate of the Nigerian state. Before it – indeed, before the advent of colonial conquest and rule – there was no Nigeria, and the likelihood that a state like it could have evolved was quite remote. What existed in the period before the establishment of colonial rule was a motley of diverse groups whose histories and interactions, interlaced as they were by external influences – principally trade with Europeans and with the Arab world – had nevertheless crystallised in three clearly discernible regional formations by the end of the nineteenth century.

To the North of the country was an Islamic push which was the outcome of long-established trans-Saharan trade and migrations which linked the Hausa states, Kanem Bornu empire and the Fulanis mainly to North Africa, the Mediterranean and the rest of the Arab world (Adamu, 1978; Dusgate, 1985; Takaya, 1987). The apogee of this Islamic ascendancy was the Fulani *jihad* launched in 1804 which more or less succeeded in bringing most parts of Hausaland and portions of so-called 'pagan' groups of the Middle Belt region under the centralised and hierarchical theocratic rule of the Sokoto Caliphate (Usman, ed. 1979).

The Islamic push had two consequences which received reinforcement and elaboration under colonial rule and shaped inter-group relations in Nigeria in the post-independence period. First, by establishing Muslim groups and adherents as the 'core' of an emergent Northern formation, it pushed to the periphery the non-Islamic segments who were also numerically inferior. Not even the influence of important non-Islamic empires like the Igala, whose Niger-Benue confluence formations some historians regard as the fulcrum of modern-day Nigerian groups, could counteract this peripheralisation. This 'internal colonialist' pattern was more visible after the *jihad*, when attempts to subjugate the so-called pagan groups of the Middle Belt were pursued more vigorously (cf. Tseayo, 1975, 1981). Under British rule, appointees of the Caliphate and Emirates were imposed as rulers on the non-Muslim groups in pursuance of the indirect rule policy. Second, by attaining the most advanced form of political, administrative and military organisation in the Sokoto Caliphate including its Emirates, which for the British were the hallmarks of African civilisation, the 'core' North was easily accepted by the colonisers as the model whose superior civilisation was to be extended, if possible by force, over the rest of what later became Nigeria.

To the West was a group of closely related empires, states and kingdoms, the most notable of which were Oyo and Benin (cf. Smith, 1988). At the height of their respective glories, these two empires between them controlled almost the entire regional formation. The vast majority of the groups in the West spoke dialects of the Yoruba language, in addition to laying claims to a myth of common origin through the legendary Oduduwa. The non-Yoruba groups – including the various Edo sub-groups: Urhobo, Isoko and some Igbo states – were mostly subjugated by the Benin empire. By the end of the nineteenth century, the Oyo and Benin empires were in decline, and the region witnessed internecine wars, mostly among the Yorubas, which were marked by the emergence of new states and political alliances (Ijebu, Ibadan, the Egba confederation and Ekiti *parapo*, among others, rose to prominence at this time). The wars and crises in the West were instigated and fuelled by the meddling of Fulani jihadists whose sphere of influence spread to Oyo and other northernmost parts of the West, and European traders and colonialists who, particularly since the era of the slave trade, pursued manipulative and divisionist strategies to gain trade advantages and retain political-cum-military control in the region. In terms of political organisation, the groups in the West ranked next to the centralised theocracies of the Islamised parts of the North.

Finally, to the East were scores of segmented Igbo, Ijaw, Efik Annang, Kalabari and other city (or village)-states whose political organization was highly non-centralist though not, as earlier anthropologists like Fortes and Evans-Pritchard thought, 'stateless'. From the mid-nineteenth century, a few city-states like old Calabar and Opobo rose to prominence largely due to privileges they enjoyed in trade in slaves and other commodities with Europeans, and approximated to the category of centralised states in the North and West. There were also the Arochukwu (*long juju*, lit. masquerade) who attempted to exert political and religious overlordship over several Igbo sub-groups. But by and large, the Eastern region had a proliferation of segmentary, non-centralized and autonomous city-states. With the notable exception of the Onitsha, who traced their origins from Benin, the preponderant Igbo sub-groups whose members spoke dialects of a generic Igbo language and therefore had the potential of large-scale political organisation failed to evolve any major centralised political system.

Given the scenario presented above, it is most unlikely that anything similar to the present state of Nigeria could have evolved without external intervention. The relationships – trade, conquest, political association and familial ties based on myths of common origin – among the pre-colonial groups tended to be limited to the geographical regions, although Dudley (1982) has advanced a counterfactual argument that these ties could still have provided the basis for a state like Nigeria. A more weighty counterfactual, well articulated by the late powerful premier of the former Northern region and Sardauna of Sokoto, Sir Ahmadu Bello (1962), is that if the colonisers had not intervened, the southern extension of the *jihad* could have brought into being a state with approximately the present shape of Nigeria. But even this plausible argument remains no better than what it is: a counterfactual.

So it was that Nigeria was a British colonial creation. Through a piecemeal and combined process of trade monopoly, military superiority, 'divide and rule' and outright conquest, the various groups were brought together under the aegis of colonial authority. The nature of this bringing together requires elaboration because of the far-reaching implications it had for state- and nation-building. British acquisition of territory in Nigeria had three different strands which roughly approximated to the regional formations described above: the colony of Lagos and hinterland (Western) protectorate; the oil rivers and later Niger Delta protectorate (Eastern); and the Northern protectorate. The question of how to structure and administer the colony and protectorates of the future Nigeria led to the setting up of the Selborne committee in 1898. Partly in line with the recommendation of the committee that the territor(ies) be unified but administered as the 'Soudan' (Northern) and 'Maritime' (Southern) provinces, the colony and hinterland protectorate and the Niger Delta protectorate were brought together in 1906 as the Colony and Protectorate of Southern Nigeria, which existed alongside the Protectorate of Northern Nigeria until the amalgamation of the two territories in 1914. With amalgamation came

> the partial abolition of customs frontiers existing between the 'two countries', the unification of the railway system, adoption of a standard currency..., universalization and systemization of taxation, a unified judicial system and integrated bureaucracy, extension of indirect rule to the south, the abolition of separate northern and southern regiments, and ... the adoption of a ... uniform time of 71/20 meridian and single weekly Gazette. (Ngou, 1989: 81)

In spite of these, the two parts of the new state continued to develop along different lines. This has been attributed mainly to the attitudes of a few diehard British administrators in the north who were determined to keep the region apart from the 'corrupt' South. To this end the entry of Southerners to the North was kept in check through policies like that which vested ownership of land in the region in government hands and prohibited freehold titles (by contrast, traditional practices of land tenure were retained in the South), and the practice of settling 'strangers', who were mostly Southern and Christian, apart from the Muslim indigenes in major towns and cities.

Furthermore, while most parts of the North were shielded from Western influences, especially education and Christian missionary activities, in accordance with a pact Lugard was said to have signed with the emirs, they were allowed free rein in the South. This gave a headstart to Southern groups not only in education but also in political development. The gap between the two parts in Western education was very wide largely because most of the schools in the country were established by Christian missions. By 1912 there were only thirty-four primary schools in the North to the South's 150 primary, and ten secondary schools (the first in the North was established in 1922).[1] The wide gap also extended to tertiary education: in 1950, while Southern graduates and professionals with university degrees ran into scores of hundreds, there was only one Northern university graduate. These gaps had grave consequences for political competition as well as competition for socio-economic goods like employment in the public service and admission to government-owned secondary and tertiary institutions in the latter part of colonial rule and the post-independence period.

The gap in political development was equally serious. Whereas nationalist movements emerged in the early twentieth century in Lagos and a few other Southern towns, and political parties like Herbert Macaulay's Nigerian National Democratic Party (NNDP) were formed to contest the elective legislative seats for Lagos and Calabar introduced by the Clifford constitution in 1922, political and nationalist activities were discouraged in the North where the first political association only emerged in the 1940s. The evolution of the print media in the North also lagged far behind the South. A newspaper was started in Lagos as early as 1890, but the first one in the North did not appear till 1935 by which time there were eleven newspapers in Lagos and five in other parts of the South. By 1950 there were thirty-five newspapers in the South and only five in the North.

---

[1] By 1957 when many of the restrictions on Christian missionary activities in the North had been relaxed, especially in the Middle Belt areas, the number of schools increased to 2,080 primary with 185,484 pupils and eighteen secondary with 3,643 students. Comparative figures for the South were: 13,473 primary with 2,343,317 pupils and 176 secondary with 28,208 students (Ngou, 1989: 84).

Furthermore, while Southern politicians and nationalists had gained considerable experience being members of the central legislative council, their Northern counterparts did not sit in this council until 1947 when the principle of regional representation was introduced by the Richards constitution. That was when Northern and Southern politicians met for the first time as citizens of the same country which had been amalgamated in 1914. Afraid that their educational and political headstart gave the Southerners an advantage that could easily be translated into political domination after independence, nationalists from the North refused to agree to self-government in 1953 when Southern parties sponsored a motion to that effect. They seized on Northern preponderant size and population to insist on certain counter-measures designed not only to nullify the grounds for fear of Southern domination but also pave the way for Northern domination as the minimum conditions for agreeing to remain in the country and to eventual self-government.

These counter-measures which were forcefully articulated at the Ibadan General Conference of 1950 included demands that the Northern region be allocated 50 per cent of the seats in the House of Representatives at the centre; that allocation of nationally collected revenue be based on population; that no part of the Northern region should be joined to the Western region as was being demanded by the Yorubas in the Kabba and Ilorin areas; and that ministerial responsibility should only be introduced when the North was ready for it. To these was later added the demand for regional autonomy which was the fulcrum of the eight-point programme the Northern delegation took to the 1953 London Constitutional Conference which was convened after the region threatened to pull out of the colonial union. All these demands were granted, and accelerated the adoption of a federal constitution in 1954 to accommodate the unevenly developed regions (for the historical background of Nigerian federalism, see Ezera, 1964; Ballard, 1971; Osuntokun, 1979; and Afigbo, 1991). The granting of the demands conferred political advantages on the Northern region in the federation which emerged, and underlay the problem of Northern domination which was a major source of the country's political problems after independence. In particular, granting the Northern region 50 per cent of the seats in the House of Representatives (this was later increased to 52 per cent) and leaving its preponderant size and population which were more than those of the Southern regions put together intact, meant that the region could single-handedly obtain the dominant position under the majoritarian system the country inherited at independence.

North-South separation was not the only structural flaw of colonial rule that had grave consequences for post-independence politics. There were also regionalism, the question of minorities, the nature of the country's economic development and integration into the global system, and the character of the state. We shall leave discussion of the last aspect which is one of the building blocks of our conceptual framework, to the next section. Regionalism may be defined as a system in which citizens who are not originally from a region are discriminated against in, and excluded from, the provision and enjoyment of public goods. In other words, the government of the region makes public goods exclusive to citizens whose origins are from the region. Regionalism evolved under colonial rule in Nigeria, and remained a central problem of post-independence politics.[2]

Its deeper origins lie in the discriminatory practices encouraged by the differentiated governance of the North and South of the country and the uneven levels of development of the various parts, but, in more concrete and immediate terms, regionalism began with the administrative restructuring of the country based on what the governor, Arthur Richards, regarded as the 'natural divisions' of the country. The process started in 1939 with the division of the Southern protectorate into the Eastern and Western groups of provinces. This was followed by the establishment of regional assemblies by the Richards' Constitution of 1946. This was done primarily to link the Native Authorities, the particularistic units of local administration, to the central government in Lagos. In effect, the regions were half-way houses, and the assemblies served as colleges for elections to the central legislative council. This enabled Nigerian nationalists from the North to sit together with their counterparts from the South.

Meeting together for the first time brought to light the marked imbalances in political and socio-economic development and differences in orientation between the Northern and Southern regions, and convinced the leaders that the country could only remain together on the basis of the federal principle and regional autonomy – a conclusion long since reached by Azikiwe (1945) and Awolowo (1947). As Tafawa Balewa, a Northern delegate who later became prime minister, put it in one of the sessions of the legislative council in 1948,

> I am beginning to think ... that Nigeria's political future may only lie in federation because so far as the rate of regional progress is concerned, some of the other groups appear to be more developed than

---

[2] The creation of 12, 19, 21, 30 and 36 states to replace the regions did not destroy regionalism as was hoped. Regionalism was reinforced by the emergence of an ancilliary and more particularistic form of discrimination – statism.

others and I think that no region should be denied self-government because others are not prepared for it.

During the debate on the matter, a motion was proposed calling for the unity of Nigeria on the basis of a federation of autonomous regions. The clamours for regional autonomy led to the collapse of the Macpherson Constitution which gave the central government veto power over regional legislation and was therefore considered too unitarist by the regional leaders. The clamours were championed by regional political parties which emerged in 1949-50 to contest the regional seats provided for by the Macpherson Constitution and ultimately control the regions (cf. Sklar, 1963). This was the origin of the regionalised party system which later resulted in one-party regions (and later states).

The major regional parties which emerged in 1949-50 were Action Group (AG, Western region); the National Council of Nigeria and the Cameroons (later National Council of Nigerian Citizens, NCNC), which was the foremost nationalist coalition in the country but was forced to become an Eastern regional party after its leader Nnamdi Azikiwe, who had won a seat in the Western regional assembly, was prevented from going to the centre by the newly formed AG (representation in central institutions was determined by regional assemblies); and the Northern Peoples Congress (NPC), the dominant party in the North which, under the majoritarian political system also became the dominant party in the country. However, these were not the only parties that emerged in the period. Largely because the dominant parties derived the bulk of their membership and support from the major ethnic groups in the regions and in general worked to advance the interests of these groups, the minority ethnic groups that were thereby excluded from power in both the regions and the centre formed their own parties (or, in most cases, promotional groups), to advance their demands for separate states.[3]

The main minorities' parties were the United Middle Belt Congress (UMBC), Bornu Youth Movement (BYM), and Ilorin Talaka Parapo in the North; the United National Independents Party (UNIP) and the Niger Delta Congress in the East; and the Benin-Delta Peoples Party (BDPP), Mid-West State Movement (MSM), and Otu-Edo-NCNC in the West. These second-order parties functioned as opposition parties in the regions, and favoured strong federation based on the creation of more states. By contrast, the dominant parties, especially the NPC, advocated regional autonomy and weak federation. It was the latter

---

[3] This was because regional representation in central executive bodies, notably the Council of Ministers, was determined by the party in power in the region.

parties that negotiated a federal system with strong regions at the 1953–4 constitutional conferences which followed the collapse of the Macpherson Constitution (the only minority party at the conference – UNIP – which opposed strong regions was forced to withdraw in protest).

The 1954 Constitution created full-fledged regional governments, public services, judiciary and, later, marketing boards. These became the pedestal for regionalism, as each region sought to 'protect' its interests. The majority of regionalism was discrimination against non-indigenes, especially in regional public service employment, but it also involved intense rivalry among the regions to outdo each other in socio-economic development,[4] maximise their shares of the federation's resources,[5] and control federal power. This rivalry reached its height with the opening of regional consulates abroad at independence, which made the regions, according to Dudley (1973), members of 'a primitive inter-national system'. The Northern region, for fairly obvious reasons was the champion of regionalism, but it also applied to the two Southern regions.

References to the 'South', usually in contradistinction to the North, do not mean that the South is monolithic or more united than the North (more or less the same thing can be said of the 'North'). The major cleavages in the South, which were reinforced by the marked differences in the levels of socio-economic development among the groups,[6] were between the Igbos (Eastern region) and Yorubas (Western region), and between these major groups and the minorities in the regions. Of these the most serious was that between the Igbos and Yorubas whose rivalries and conflicts began from Lagos, where they were exacerbated by the ethnicisation and regionalisation of nationalism beginning from the late 1930s (Coleman, 1958). Igbo-Yoruba rivalry remained a major theme of Nigerian politics after independence, as we see in later chapters.

---

[4] This form of rivalry was considered 'healthy', as the bulk of the revenue for development projects came from the regions themselves and led to the development of all sections of the country. Nevertheless, it resulted in sometimes wasteful duplication of institutions.

[5] Rivalry over sharing federal resources made political considerations, rather than feasibility and economic costs, the major determinant of where federal industries and agencies were to be sited. A good example was the iron and steel industry which was stalled for a long time by disagreements among the regions, and had eventually to be regionalised (see Ohiorhenuan and Onu, 1989).

[6] The Yorubas were clearly ahead of all the other groups, especially in Western education. The fact of Lagos, the hub of political activities, being in Yorubaland also made them more politically sophisticated and effective than others. This partly explains why the West was the centre of 'opposition' civil society activities. The Igbos ranked next, followed by the minorities.

The other problematic structural feature of colonial rule was the problem of minorities. This derived from the anomalous constitution of the regions whereby each had a core major ethnic group – Igbo (Eastern region), Yoruba (Western region), and Hausa/Fulani (Northern region) and a 'periphery' of numerical minorities (in the North, in addition to being numerically inferior, the minorities were also non-Muslim and had long been engaged in the struggle to overthrow feudal Muslim overlords). These minorities, which make up the bulk of the country's 250 or more ethnic groups, occupied distinct territories apart from the majority groups, and this encouraged the development of separatist agitations (Tamuno, 1970; Ikporukpo, 1986). However, it was the emergence of majoritarian nationalism on the part of the majority groups which led them to seek exclusive control of the regions, that stirred and heightened agitations for separate states. These demands were based on claims of discrimination, neglect and political as well as cultural domination by the majority groups (Osaghae, 1986a, 1991a).

The agitations were generally peaceful, and involved the formation of alliances between minority opposition parties and dominant parties which supported their demands, typically those from other regions,[7] but there were a few violent agitations, especially by the Tiv of the North (cf. Okpu, 1977; Anifowoshe, 1982). In 1956 a commission headed by Sir Henry Willink was instituted to enquire into the fears of the minorities and the means for allaying them. The commission found evidence of discrimination and other problems alleged by the minorities, and acknowledged the genuineness of their fears and anxieties, but believed that the solution to the problem of minorities lay in the political process rather than the creation of separate states for them. It accordingly recommended, among other things, the constitutional entrenchment of a bill of rights and the creation of a special commission to address the peculiar environmental problems of the Niger Delta minorities, and hoped that the emergence of national political parties after independence would help to allay the fears of the minorities (Willink Report, 1957; also Osaghae, 1996a).

The failure of the Willink Commission to recommend the creation of new states, the opposition of British colonial authorities to a policy of states creation, and the selfishness and hurry of the regional leaders to become independent (the colonialists made the creation of new states dependent on postponing the date of independence) meant that the structural anomalies of Nigerian federalism were carried over

---

[7] The UMBC aligned at various times with the NCNC and AG, BDPP, MSM and Otu-Edo with NCNC, UNIP with AG, and NDC with NPC.

into independence. In retrospect the last British governor-general, Sir James Robertson, believed that the creation of new states, especially from the North, would have helped to ameliorate the problems of Northern domination and minority agitations which catalysed the collapse of the First Republic (Robertson, 1974). The greatest danger to the stability of the emergent state was however the regionalised party system, and the contradictions that developed shortly before and immediately after independence between the forces of regionalism and those of centralisation (Sklar, 1965). The years 1954-9 were used to prepare the country for independence. In deference to the demand by the Northern political leaders that every region should be allowed to become self-governing at its own pace, the two Southern regions became self-governing in 1957, and the Northern region in 1959. In 1958, the principle of North-South parity in the allocation of seats in parliament (House of Representatives) gave way to a population-weighted principle which gave the Northern region 52 per cent of the seats. This became the main basis for the fear of Northern domination which was a major theme of post-independence politics. Meanwhile, in 1957, the office of Prime Minister was created at the centre, and predictably went to the NPC, whose deputy leader, Tafawa Balewa, occupied the office from the inception until the fall of the First Republic in 1966 (given the enormous powers of the regions, the NPC leader Ahmadu Bello preferred to remain as regional premier). In the run-up to independence, during which the leaders needed to demonstrate their ability to work together as members of one country, the regional parties put aside their differences to form a government of national unity which comprised ministers from all the main regional parties. Perhaps the continuation of this practice after independence would have saved the country from its quick plunge into the political crisis of the 1960s and beyond.

The final aspect of pre-independence history which we must briefly consider was the nature of the colonial economy and the implications this had for post-independence politics. The first point to be made is that, in contradistinction to the political dynamics which encouraged centrifugal tendencies, the colonial economic imperatives worked in the opposite direction of centralisation and the integration of the country as a single economic unit (which in the first place was the main reason for the amalgamation of 1914). This had implications for the process of national integration as a whole. Thus, although the development of the railway, roads and other infrastructure was mainly to facilitate the exploitation of resources, it opened up the whole country to its diverse peoples, and enabled migrations across regional lines, particularly from the South to the North. The expansion of economic activities and urbanisation also facilitated the coming together of peoples from different groups. In addition, the fiscal policies of the colonial regime as embodied in the development plans, which were the main instruments of economic development, were centralist. But the graver implications and consequences of the colonial economic structure lay in the fact that its primary motive was to exploit the resources of the country and link it to metropolitan Britain and other international capitalist centres as a periphery. Accordingly, the colonial state was an *extractionist* state, as is evident in the activities of the commodity marketing boards. The emphasis was on the law and order functions of the state which facilitated the smooth exploitation of resources and expropriation of surplus. The welfare functions of the state were almost non-existent, as the social sector was dominated by missionaries and voluntary agencies. Secondly, the economy was import-export driven, and very little effort was made to build an industrial or manufacturing sector. Thirdly, and closely related to this, there was a stimulation of a desire for European manufactured goods which was crucial to dependence.

Fourthly, the private sector of the colonial economy was dominated by European firms, particularly the United African Company (UAC), which handled the bulk of the import-export trade – in the late 1940s these firms established a consortium called the Association of West African Merchants. The development of local or indigenous capitalism was hampered, and the few Nigerian entrepreneurs were agents of the big trading companies. Finally, only the major trading centres, port towns, and areas which produced cash crops or minerals, and which were the main beneficiaries of infrastructural development, were integrated into the modern economy. Communal and rural economies were not, and remained outside the mainstream of economic development. For this reason, Nnoli (1978: 124-6) concludes that there was no national economy under colonial rule. The consequences of this colonial economy are considered in the next section.

THE BASES OF NIGERIAN POLITICS

We next turn to conceptual issues. How can political tendencies, behaviour and problems of a country as diverse and complex as Nigeria be understood? Several approaches and perspectives have been advanced. These include ethnicity, ethnic pluralism and ethnopolitics (cf. Nnoli, 1978; Diamond, 1988b; Osaghae, 1986b; Otite, 1990); institutional or structural and process perspectives, including federalism and more recently governance and democratisation (cf. Awa, 1964; Oyediran, 1979; Mahwood, 1980; Oyovbaire, 1985; Jinadu,

1985; Ayeni and Soremekun, 1988; Diamond, 1988a; Dent, 1989;
Ekeh and Osaghae, 1989; Bach, 1989; Elaigwu, 1979, 1991; Elaigwu
and Olorunsola, 1983; Adamolekun and Kincaid, 1991; Eleazu, 1977;
Olowu, 1990; Williams, 1992; Olagunju *et al.*, 1993); the political
economy approach, with emphasis on class and materialist forces,
the role of oil in the economy, as well as dependency-underdevelopment
perspectives which search for explanations in terms of Nigeria's location
as a peripheral capitalist formation in the global system (cf. Panter-Brick,
1978; Nnoli, 1981, 1993; Ake, 1985; Onimode, 1982, 1988; Bienen,
1985; Biersteker, 1987; Forrest, 1993; Soremekun and Obi, 1993);
civil-military perspectives (cf. Adekanye, 1981; Dudley, 1973, 1982;
Miners, 1971; Luckham, 1971; Odetola, 1978, 1980; Agbese, 1991);
and statist and state-society perspectives, including political culture
perspectives like clientelistic/patronage politics, prebendalism and the
system of values (cf. Okpaku, 1972; Oyovbaire, 1987; Williams, 1980;
Ekeh, 1975, 1989a; Dudley, 1973, 1982; Ajayi and Ikara, 1985; Joseph,
1987, 1996; Lewis, 1996).

Whichever of these perspectives or combinations of them are
employed will of course depend on the writer's interests and focus.
For a macro-level study like ours, the appropriate conceptual framework
will be one which provides the most basic and generalisable explanations
for politics in the country. We do this by examining the bases of
politics, i.e. the forces which underlie political behaviour and structural
formations. But first, a working definition of politics is necessary.
In general, it has to do with power relations. In more specific terms,
it involves how individuals and groups organise to pursue their divergent
and often conflicting interests, why the state is crucial to this process,
how and why domestic and external economic, social, cultural and
other forces shape or influence this process, what major issues ensue
from power relations, and how conflicts are managed and resolved.
This operational definition of politics assumes that it takes place
within states, and that most of its forms are state-centred, though
it does not preclude non-state or inter-state politics.

Providing a working definition of politics is not all that is required
for a meaningful discussion of the bases of politics. There is also
a need to characterise post-independence Nigerian politics so as to
know what exactly one is to explain or analyse. What has been
the character of Nigerian politics since independence? It may be
summarised as a long-drawn-out decay or decline, whose empirical
elements are political instability, a low level of national cohesion,
and economic crisis, all of which are mutually reinforcing. Decline
in this sense is not to be understood as the opposite of sustained
progress or growth or political stability, none of which the country

has really enjoyed. Rather it refers to the empirical fact that Nigeria has since independence moved away from – rather than towards – the actualisation of its vast potential. The main indices of political instability include the high turnover of governments (regime, structures, institutions and personnel) occasioned by military coups, inconclusive and contested electoral outcomes, frequent changes in policy, political violence and the crisis of legitimacy. Between 1960 and 1996 there were no less than ten officially known coups. Six of these – two in 1966 and one each in 1975, 1983, 1985 and 1993 – were successful and involved the government being overthrown, two were unsuccessful but bloody (1976, 1990), and three were nipped in the bud and the officers involved were jailed or executed (1986, 1995). These were in addition to rumours of unreported coup plots and executions of convicted officers.

Within the same period, the country had three civilian (Tafawa Balewa, Shehu Shagari, Ernest Shonekan) and seven military (Generals Ironsi, Gowon, Mohammed, Obasanjo, Buhari, Babangida and Abacha) heads of state, an average of one head of state every three and a half years (General Ironsi and Ernest Shonekan, who headed the interim national government of 1993, held the position for six months and less). The situation in the state and local governments – whose numbers increased respectively, from three to thirty-six and 301 to over 750 in the same period – was even more unstable. For example, before it was split into two states in 1991, the old Bendel state, from its creation as the former Mid-West region in 1963, had a total of three civilian and seven military governors; Edo and Delta states, which were carved out of the state in 1991, had between then and 1996 one civilian governor and four military governors each. Oyo state, between 1975 when it was carved out of the former Western state and 1991 when it was split into Oyo and Osun states, had two civilian and six military governors. The trend is the same for all the other states. As for local governments, between 1991 and 1996, each council had at least five chairmen, making an average of one chairman per year.

Regime change at the federal, state and local levels have been attended by massive structural, institutional and policy changes. Government ministries, departments, agencies, parastatals and other institutions were in an almost permanent state of restructuring with their executive heads constantly changed (the judiciary was perhaps the only slight exception). One of these, the Nigerian National Petroleum Company (NNPC) – which supervised oil exploration and production in the country and, given the reliance on oil, was the life-line of the country – had eight chief executives between 1985 and 1996. Policies were also in flux, as each regime and chief executive saw new beginnings and discontinuity with previous dispensations as part of its legitimation process. Particularly notable in this regard were frequent changes in the revenue allocation system, taxation, monetary and financial regulations announced in the annual budgets. Foreign policy tended to be somewhat more stable, but it was often incoherent. The indices of a low level of national cohesion are fairly obvious and well known. They have been well summarised by Graf (1988: 13) thus: 'Harmony, cooperation and "unity" have manifestly not characterised social and political life in post-independence Nigeria. No effective formulas have been found to bring ethnic competition, class conflict, social diversity and the like into a "higher" productive synthesis.' Politics in the country, especially contestation for state power and resources, tended to be organised around regional, ethnic and religious interests. The centrifugal pulls emanating from this pattern of politics made resolution of what Nigerian social scientists refer to as the 'national question' difficult. Fundamental issues of minority rights, resource distribution and power-sharing remain volatile and even became greater in the late 1980s and 1990s. The result is that even in the fourth decade after independence, and after a civil war provoked by unresolvable issues of the national question, the country's continued existence as one unit was not assured and could not be taken for granted. Indeed, the schisms that followed the annulment of the 12 June 1993 presidential election threatened the very foundations of the country, and there were widespread fears of it breaking up or another civil war erupting.

The third element of our characterisation of post-independence Nigerian politics is economic crisis. With abundant resources – oil, natural gas, solid minerals and agricultural resources, as well as high-level manpower produced by over 100 tertiary institutions of which thirty-seven were universities by 1996 – Nigeria had the potential of becoming a highly developed country. Indeed, it was regarded in the 1960s as a potential African *tiger*, but by 1995, according to World Bank sources, it had slipped far behind Malaysia, with which it was roughly on a par in that decade, to the status of one of the world's most indebted and fifteen poorest countries. This decline was attributed to mismanagement of the national economy, itself attributable to regime instability; the disenablement of rational planning and deployment of resources by centrifugal politics; primitive accumulationist inclinations of state officials; pervasive corruption and the absence or ineffectiveness of institutions of oversight. But, as we shall see, the fundamental cause of the crisis lay in the larger crisis of disarticulation and extraversion which resulted from the country's peripheral location in the global system. How do we analyse and account for the character of Nigerian politics? It follows from the characterisation outlined above that to reduce explanation even at the micro level to all-purpose popular constructs like ethnicity, regionalism or religious divisions or even class is an obvious over-simplification. No matter how real and central to politics these variables may be – Graf (1988: 13) argues that break-downs in the Nigerian political system have *'always* occurred within a context of inter-ethnic controversy' and that, consequently, ethnicity is 'a focal point of national politics' – they provide only part of the explanation and usually have, themselves, to be explained. For example, to say that the civil war was a consequence of ethno-regional differences is to discount the character of the Nigerian state and the economic considerations which underlay the war. Similarly, those who explain the events leading up to and following the annulment of the June 12, 1993 presidential election only in ethnic terms fail to see the dimensions of (military) institutional interests, elite fac-tionalisation and international dynamics. Given the complexity of Nigerian politics, therefore, even where explanation rests heavily on a core variable, cognisance has to be taken of how that variable relates to other relevant and recurring variables.

It is against this background that the bases of Nigerian politics are discussed here. The objective is to pull together important and related explanatory variables into a logically coherent framework. The bases will be discussed in terms of four core variables: the nature of society and its relations with the state; the character of the state itself; the character of the contestation for power; and the consequences of the country's location in the global system.

The nature of society. Politics, as students of political culture tell us, is grounded in the nature of the society in which it takes place. Thus the nature of politics in Nigeria is largely determined by the nature of the society, especially the values which govern behaviour in the public realm. What, for example, is the implication of the premium placed on wealth (material possession) and status in politics? What are the consequences for politics of the highly plural and divided nature of the Nigerian society? Extant perspectives on Nigerian politics which relate political tendencies and formations to the character of the society and the interface between state and society are relevant here.

One of the most elaborate of these is the attempt by Dudley (1982) to explain political behavioural and institutional patterns in terms of Weberian themes, i.e. individual and collective values. Given the differentiation of values in a heterogeneous society like Nigeria, he recognises the elite-mass, ethno-regional and inter-generational nuances of the value system, although he emphasises the elite determinism of values (in the Gramscian sense of *hegemonia*) and the gradual evolution of a Nigeria-wide value system. The core of Dudley's perspective is the impact on politics of the country-wide premium placed on wealth and status and the need to guard against personal and collective future insecurity, as well as the state of belonging to the (sub-national) community defined in terms of the moral obligations of the individual to the sustenance of his kith and kin (what Göran Hyden (1980) calls the 'economy of moral affection'). These linkages help to explain the prevalence and ambivalence of corruption in Nigerian politics: 'insecurity is guarded against not just by safeguarding the present but also by insuring against the future which, in practice, means the use of one's office to enrich one's self ... in so far as a successful individual is seen to contribute to the welfare of his community, he is not seen as corrupt' (Dudley, 1982: 28-9).

The Weberian themes were elaborated on earlier by Ekeh (1975): in his theory of the two publics in Africa, he argued that, by the very nature of the grafting of the colonial state, the progenitor of the post-colonial state, on to the Nigerian society an amoral milieu was entrenched as the code for behaviour in the public realm. This happened because the public realm in colonial Africa, unlike in the West from which the state was imported, developed as two publics rather than one. One was the civic public, which is roughly coterminous with the sphere of government, and the other was the primordial public, comprising ethnic and regional promotional associations, which was nurtured by the values of the indigenous society or private realm. While the former public operated in an essentially amoral milieu, the latter retained an abiding morality which emphasized the obligations of the individual to his extended family and community. Problems of corruption, ethnicity and their like are then attributed to the fact that the same individuals operate in the two publics working at cross-purposes. Elsewhere, the present author has argued that these disjunctures between state and society underlie the legitimacy crisis which debilitates the state in Africa (Osaghae, 1989; also 1995e).

Finally, there is Joseph's (1987) prebendalist perspective which also draws from Weber and explains the abuse of government positions and resources for personal ends in terms of patron-client relations, which constitute 'the common thread underlying ethnic, regional and religious identities' (p. 55). However, Forrest (1993: 6-7) has criticised the prebendalist and patrimonialist perspectives for undermining the (autonomous) administrative and economic functions of the state, for giving scant attention to the political and social space that is autonomous of the state, and for neglecting political conflicts not focused on the struggle for material benefits and access to state power. Forrest's criticisms are valid to the extent that Joseph's focus is on the state, but he underplays the search for the antecedents of prebendalism in the larger value-system.

What Dudley, Ekeh and Joseph all share is the assumption that an amoral value-system, which Ekeh attributes to disjuncture between the state and society under colonial rule, prevails in the public realm, and this gives rise to corruption, abuse and exploitation of public office to serve private ends, ethnicity and reliance on patron-client networks for legitimacy. However, what they all fail to emphasise is the dynamic nature of values, and in this case that the pervasiveness of amoralism does not make it a monolith acceptable to all segments of society. It is certainly contested by the more nationalistic elements of civil society, who struggle to set new moral rules for behaviour in the public realm. The wide support usually given to 'strong' 'corrective' governments in fact suggests that the amoral value system is not a settled terrain as is often assumed. This is not to deny the explanatory power of 'Weberian themes', but to establish the point that values are contested.

The other aspect of the nature of the society is the country's plurality. Nigeria belongs to the category of problematic states that have been labelled 'divided' (or 'deeply divided') societies. It has more than 250 ethnic groups identified on the basis of distinct languages, dialects and insider-outsider perceptions, two or three historically entrenched regional divisions (North-South; North, East, West) depending on the circumstances, and serious religious divisions, especially between Muslims and Christians, all of which were accommodated by 1996 within a federal structure of thirty-six states, a federal capital territory, and over 750 local government councils. What makes these cleavages problematic for politics is that, on the one hand, they are mutually reinforcing and, on the other, they tend to coincide with the major lines of socio-economic and political inequalities.

However, it is erroneous to describe Nigeria's plurality only in terms of primordial cleavages or to assume that only these cleavages are of political consequence. As scholars of the civil society and governance perspectives emphasise, class categories as well as non-governmental, non-primordial and cross-cutting organisations proliferate in the civil society landscape, and act as countervailing forces to the centrifugal pulls of primordial formations. In this pro-democracy, human rights and civil liberty organisations, labour unions, student bodies, women's organisations, alumni associations, professional associations, and political movements and parties were important actors, especially after the global democratic revolution of the 1980s, although their national orientations were often threatened by primordial proclivities during periods of intense political crisis. Nevertheless, the civil society, especially its press section, was in the forefront of the search for, and entrenchment of, a new code of public conduct which hinged on nationalism, morality, transparency and accountability. The turmoil and struggles for democracy of the 1980s and 1990s gave a big boost to this transformed public realm project and established civil society as the engine-room of future national development.

As can be seen from the foregoing, focus on the nature of the society is an important element in explaining core aspects of Nigerian politics: why politics is important to individuals and groups (this is what makes Nigeria a highly politicised society), why competition for state power is so fierce, why the (ab)use of the state power is so pervasive, why patron-client relations and elite-directed actions form the hub of political relationships, why the state finds difficulty in enforcing its policies (in effect, why the state is 'soft'), why 'strong' governments with 'corrective' inclinations are more likely to succeed, and why civil society has played a crucial role in political development.

The character of the state. This can be broken down into three elements: the colonial nature of the state, its lack of relative autonomy, and the federal system of government. The basic points about the post-colonial state in Nigeria are that it originated under colonial rule, and that the perceptions and attitudes which attended the latter subsist in disturbing ways in the post-colonial period despite the structural transformations that have taken place since independence, and the fact that Nigerians themselves rather than colonisers now controlled the reins of power.

The post-colonial state, like its colonial progenitor, is primarily a law and order state, and this has remained its most abiding attribute, as fledgling welfarist and socialist schemes designed sometimes as legitimation stratagems have failed to endure. This law and order orientation underlies the reliance on instruments of coercion to sustain state power, and authoritarian tendencies on the part of rulers; both of which are conducive to military governance, and seem to invite it (it should be remembered that the colonial state was an authoritarian one *par excellence*). To facilitate its regulatory and extractive roles, the post-colonial state centralises the 'production' and distribution of national resources, and in the context of state capitalism this encourages the perception of the state as an instrument of accumulation and the patron-client ties as the dominant mode of political relations. Control over production of oil and revenue from it, the mainstay of the country's economy (Table 1.1 shows how oil climbed to become the country's principal revenue-earner), over commodity marketing boards before they were abolished under the Structural Adjustment Programme (SAP), and over major taxes facilitated this process. Beginning from the era of the oil boom in the 1970s, the federal government gradually took over many of the responsibilities that previously belonged to the states, especially in the area of education (cf. Oyovbaire, 1985).

Table 1.1. CONTRIBUTION OF OIL TO FEDERAL GOVERNMENT REVENUE, 1958-90

	Total Federal Government revenue (N000)	Revenue from oil	Oil share of total revenue %
1958-9	154,632	122	0.08
1959-60	177,648	1,776	1.00
1960-1	223,700	2,452	1.10
1961-2	228,962	17,070	7.46
1962-3	231,638	16,938	7.31
1963-4	249,152	10,060	4.04
1964-5	299,132	16,084	5.38
1965-6	321,870	29,175	9.06
1966-7	339,196	44,976	18.26
1967-8	300,176	41,884	13.95
1968-9	299,986	29,582	13.95
1969-70	435,908	75,444	17.31
1970-1	755,605	196,390	25.99
1971-2	1,410,811	740,185	52.46
1972-3	1,389,911	576,151	41.45
1973-4	2,171,370	1,549,383	71.36
1974-5	5,177,370	4,183,816	80.81
1975-6	5,861,600	4,611,700	78.70
1976-7	7,070,400	5,965,500	77.20
1977-8	8,358,900	5,965,500	71.40
1978-9	7,252,400	4,809,200	66.30
1979-80	12,273,400	10,100,400	82.30
1980-1	15,813,100	14,936,900	81.20
1981-2	10,143,900	8,847,800	67.50
1982-3	10,811,400	7,253,000	67.00
1983-4	11,738,500	8,209,700	69.93
1984-5	15,041,800	10,915,100	72.65
1985-6	12,302,000	8,107,300	65.90
1986-7	25,099,800	19,027,000	75.80
1987-8	27,310,800	20,933,800	76.65
1988-9	50,272,100	41,334,400	82.22
1989-90	47,657,000	46,244,000	97.24

Source: NNPC Annual Statistical Bulletin, 1994.

Another attribute of the post-colonial state with deep roots in the colonial past is the negative attitude to government and its operators. Largely because the colonial state was imported from metropolitan Europe, grew apart from the society and was made to serve the interests of the colonisers, the nationalists who led the anti-colonial movements mobilised support on the strength of an interest-begotten idea that the state was 'alien'. This perception became ingrained in the popular consciousness, with the result that society at large refused to develop any serious stake or interest in the state's well-being and sustenance, such as would have emphasised accountability, transparency, responsiveness and other aspects of a moral ethos. Rather, the state and government which animated it were approached as alien institutions which belonged to the *oyibo* (white man), was not deserving of the citizen's obligations or duties, could be plundered to feather private nests, and whose survival only the few who benefited directly from it were prepared to fight for.

It is a popular Nigerian saying, which took root under colonial rule, that 'government's business is no man's business'. There was thus nothing seriously wrong with stealing state funds, especially if they were used to benefit not only the individual but also members of his community. Those who had the opportunity to be in government were expected to use the power and resources at their disposal to advance private and communal interests. While they may have served the needs of the anti-colonial situation, negative attitudes toward the state and government became the Achilles heel of the post-colonial state, and many of the problems which afflicted and disabled it (the 'soft state' variables) – corruption, scant regard for constitutional rule or, in effect, arbitrary rule, the absence of a national society governed by common moral, cultural and behavioural norms and, indeed, political stability – can be explained in terms of these attitudes.

Operators of the post-colonial state tried to change the debilitating perception and attitudes, with little success. Among the notable efforts to this end, which were basically admonitory and mobilisatory, were the famous 'Jaji Declaration' by General Obasanjo in 1977, the 'ethical revolution' launched by the Shagari administration in the Second Republic, and the anti-corruption and patriotism-, discipline- and self-reliance-mobilising programmes launched by the military regimes of the 1980s and 1990s – War Against Indiscipline (WAI), Mass Mobilization for Economic Recovery, Self-Reliance and Social Justice (MAM-SER), and the War Against Indiscipline and Corruption (WAIC) (for an analysis of the theoretical underpinnings of these social mobilisation projects in a comparative African perspective, see Osaghae, 1989a, 1990a). The following, said in a budget speech in April 1972 by

Ukpabi Asika, administrator of the then East Central State, aptly summarises the overall concern and goal of the operators of the post-colonial state:

'We must now reject for all time the conception of the state as a foreign institution standing outside the community and whose money, property and goals are not the direct responsibility and concern of the community. The community is the government, and the government is the community. It is no longer *olu oyibo* [whiteman's business]. Government business is truly and property *olu obodo* [community's business].' (cited in Oyediran and Gboyega, 1979: 178)

A major consequence of government (and political elite) initiatives in bridging state-citizen ties has been the encouragement of the equally counter-productive perception of the state singly in terms of its allocative and distributive roles. The state is presented and approached by the vast majority of the citizens as a benevolent 'Father Christmas' who distributes the 'national cake'. This perception, which was also encouraged by the anti-colonial nationalists, distorts and stultifies the development of the necessary social and political correlates of public finance (for an excellent analysis of the problematic aspects of the political culture of public finance in Africa in general, see Ekeh, 1994). Most people not only believe that government is a reservoir of what, for lack of a more appropriate term, can be called 'free money', but also fail to see or realise that a significant part of the country's wealth comes from the taxes and levies they pay. Since the entry of oil as the main revenue-earner, this notion of free money has become even more pronounced and problematic. The failure of most citizens to realise that government revenue and public funds are collectively owned, and that all citizens have contributed to it by one way or another, largely explains the virtual absence of demands for accountability in the political culture of public finance. It also explains why plunderers of the government treasury are excused on the grounds that they have only 'taken their share of the national cake'.

The pulls of these conceptions and perceptions make the reciprocity between the citizen's rights and duties which are necessary for sound governance problematic, and detract from the entrepreneurial ethos required for transforming the state from a rentier state to a truly productive capitalist one. One reason why state operators have so far found it difficult to change these perceptions and attitudes to the state is that they are themselves guided by the same codes and reap huge benefits of political legitimacy from them. Thus attempts to entrench a moral code for public service through agencies like the Code of Conduct Bureau, provided for in the 1979 Constitution, have not helped. In effect, the state continues to exist in an amoral and disabling milieu which permits actions which would otherwise be reprehensible to society. The demands for accountability, probity and transparency on the part of public officials by elements of the fledgling civil society (referred to earlier) have served to counteract this amorality.

In addition to being post-colonial, the state in Nigeria, as explained by Ake (1985), lacks autonomy in the sense that its apparatuses are not well developed, and not insulated from private capture. This means that the legal-rational and bureaucratic ethos of impersonality, impartiality and rationality has not been entrenched, making it possible for the state to be captured by hegemonic classes and groups as well as ambitious rulers. The consequences of the lack of autonomy are best described in Ake's own words:

> In the absence of autonomizing mechanisms in the post-colonial state, the resources of physical coercion become the tools of particular groups, especially the hegemonic factions of the ruling class... Also, the only effective check on the use of the coercive resources becomes merely the prudence of enlightened self-interest of those who control them. So we have essentially relations of raw power in which right tends to be coextensive with power and security depends on the control of power. *The struggle for power, then, is everything and is pursued by every means.* (Ake, 1985: 4, emphasis added)

The third and final element of the character of the state to be considered here is federalism which, many argue, accords well with the highly diversified nature of the political society. Indeed, 'it is a truism of Nigerian politics that the country's continuing existence as a nation-state hinges on its capacity to evolve and maintain an adequate system of federalism' (Graf, 1988: 133). The federal system, adopted in 1954 but in decline since the late 1970s, underlies some of the peculiar features of politics in Nigeria. Chief among these is the legitimation of accommodationist demands which are intolerable in most other African states. Demands for local political autonomy and for more equitable methods of power and resource sharing, which frequently involve extra-parliamentary tactics by aggrieved groups, are not uncommon. Another of these features is the 'live-and-let-live' political culture which moderates political competition in a way that makes exclusivist domination of state power by a single group unacceptable. The federal character principle, introduced in the 1979 Constitution to ensure that the composition of government institutions should be representative of the country's kaleidoscopic diversity, has emboldened this culture. It is precisely the attempt by hegemonic ruling classes to violate this unwritten code that provokes serious conflicts. A third feature is the deflection of communal conflicts and other conflicts of a local nature to the states and local governments, leaving only conflicts of national significance to the centre. The multilayer configuration of power in the federation which has been enhanced by the increased powers granted to local governments since the late 1970s has enhanced this dispersal of conflicts. Finally, federalism has made democracy and individual and group rights important factors of stability in the country's political process.

Although prolonged military rule, with its nation-centredness, has desecrated core federal principles, the basic tenets of a federalist political culture which underlie the features described above remain. This explains why the federal system has survived in spite of the principles of unity of command and hierarchical authority which contradict federal principles of non-centralisation and shared power. Indeed, 'military federalism' has been rationalised as an integral part of the pragmatic military approach to nation-building by retired Admiral Aikhomu, vice-president in the Babangida administration:

'... we thought it more patriotic and expedient to strengthen the powers and status of the national government, provided that Nigeria avoided the dangers of disintegration. Our own understanding of a pragmatic approach to Nigerian federalism has been to use the advantages of centralized military administration to weaken the prospects of a confederation and thus strengthen Nigerian federalism.' (Aikhomu, 1994: 11)

While the need for a strong centre in a divided society which lacks a unifying set of goals or ideology is self-evident, over-centralisation, as military federalism entails, had the danger of raising the stakes of contestation among groups for control of central power, thereby negating the dispersal of conflicts – an advantage inherent in the federal system. The essence of the federal system for the character of the state is that it provides a relatively peaceful context for preserving the plurality of the society and managing the conflicts within it. Scholars like Graf in fact think that Nigeria is unlikely to survive without the federal framework, and for similar reasons successive military governments have insisted that federalism is an unchangeable basis of the country's structuration – Ironsi, who tried to change it, paid dearly and plunged the country into crisis. The fact that even the unitarist colonial regime found it expedient to apply federal principles in governing the country is an indication of how central federalism is to the Nigerian state.

The character of contestation for power. Power relations and competition for power constitute the core of politics. How do individuals and groups organise to contest for power? The first point to be made is that, like most other countries in the world, the elites dominate the struggle for power in Nigeria. This is not to belittle the importance of peasant-based state-challenging struggles such as the Agbekoya (1968) and Bakolori (1981) revolts against excessive taxation and forcible removal from land, and the sporadic outbursts by the urban poor, which can be interpreted as part of the struggles for state power, but to emphasise that the elite are in the forefront of political competition, and that it is they who invariably constitute the political and ruling classes. The key to understanding the contestation for power therefore lies in knowing the character of the elite whom Dudley (1982: 28) has defined simply as 'the rich and the powerful'.

The elite in Nigeria is factionalised mainly along ethnic, regional, religious and institutional lines, being the product of the uneven development and rivalry which British colonial administration fostered among the different segments. It has accordingly built its support constituencies from communal, ethnic, religious and regional groups depending on the level of contestation, and has sought to manipulate and exploit the differences and anxieties arising from unequal size and population to further its interests. At the macro national level, powerful ethno-regional elite blocs have emerged at various times to forge constitutive interests in competition with others. Examples of such blocs include the Egbe Omo Oduduwa and Jamiyyar Mutanen Arewa in the past and, in the 1980s and 1990s, Northern Elders Forum, Afenifere and Ohaneze.

While ethno-regional blocs like these tend to be most active during periods of civilian rule and political transition, there are others, equally powerful, which mostly operate underground as the powers behind the throne under both military and civil rule. Perhaps the most talked about and controversial of these is the 'Kaduna mafia' whose existence and membership, though a subject of speculation, nevertheless has a concrete political connotation. The mafia is said to comprise core Northern elites, 'old brigade' and 'newbreed' alike – intelligentsia, serving and retired military officers and bureaucrats, and members of the business and political classes – and its objective is believed to be the defence and advocacy of Northern interests, the most important of which is to sustain Northern political domination of the federation.

Joseph (1987: 134) articulates the most critical attribute and weapon of the mafia as ' "an embryonic state class"[8] to emphasise the political

---

[8] Graf, 1988: 129 refers to this sort of class as 'state-bourgeois class'.

base of its members within the expanding institutions of the Nigerian state'. In other words, the main objective of the mafia is to capture state power on which its members depend in order to flourish and continue. It is as such that the mafia has been seen as the moving force for all core-North-dominant military and civilian regimes since General Mohammed (for an exhaustive analysis of the mafia, including whether it is a myth or not, see Takaya and Tyoden, 1987; Joseph, 1987; and Othman, 1989; Olukoshi, 1995c). Other mafias that have been talked about but which, relative to the Kaduna mafia, are ephemeral and less powerful, include that of Ikenne, which controlled power in the West of the country in the Second Republic, and that of Langtang (a town in Plateau state), believed to be behind the preponderance of officers from Langtang town in the military governments of the 1980s.

While the Kaduna mafia constitutes an 'embryonic state class', these other mafias could be described as 'aspiring state classes' to emphasise the fact that their members do not have the advantage of state control – in fact, apart from their narrow spheres of political control, their members are either excluded from federal power or constitute a dependent mafia. For example, one reason given in 1983 by many commentators who expected Chief Obafemi Awolowo's party (UPN) to improve on its 1979 performance was the presumed support of the Kaduna mafia. Apart from these mafias, secret societies whose members are obliged by religio-social ties to help one another have also been used to further bloc interests. Membership of these societies has been known to secure electoral victories, contracts from government, appointments and promotions in public service, and so on. Examples of such societies which successive administrations have tried unsuccessfully to proscribe include the Ekpe, Owegbe and Ogboni.

Old boys' or alumni associations, many of which reinforce ethno-regional elite ties, are also critical in inter-elite competition. Old students' associations of Barewa College (attended by most Northern military, bureaucratic and academic elites), Baptist Academy Abeokuta, and Government Colleges in Bida, Ibadan, Ughelli and Umuahia, and the various university alumni associations, are notable. One alumni association which was the major recruiting ground for political appointments and other patronages in the Babangida administration, and played a crucial role in the circulation of elites in military administrations, is that of the National Institute for Policy and Strategic Studies (NIPSS), Kuru. Founded in 1979 as a policy school for top military officers, bureaucrats, academics and private sector chief executives, NIPSS has helped to forge strong, though largely instrumentalist, links among an emergent national elite which, as already indicated, dominated the Babangida administration, and played key roles in the political transition programme.

The other characteristic of the elite is its dependence on the state which, in the circumstances of peripheral capitalism, and the state's domineering tendencies, provides the most important access to accumulation. This largely explains the collaborative and extractive disposition of the elite towards the state, a disposition which has colonial antecedents. Indeed, the combination of coercive and regulatory power as well as patronage control available to the state means that very few elites are able to reproduce their privileges and wealth outside the state or in opposition to it. Thus, in civilian dispensations, most businessmen join the party in power to gain access to contracts and other forms of accumulation. All this explains the desperation and opportunism with which political power is sought and used because, as Ake (1985a: 5) puts it, 'Power is everything, and those who control the coercive resources use it freely to promote their interests, including the appropriation of surplus.' In particular, reliance on patronage networks for retention of political power and legitimacy means that any segment of the elites or political party in the case of civilian regimes which loses control of political power at the federal, state or local levels, loses the wherewithal to compete for power. Parties which do not control any state (such as the NAP in 1983) simply stand no chance of winning elections.

This is the major explanation for the warlike approach to elections. As Graf (1988: 108) explains in relation to the 1983 elections, the emergence of the NPN as a virtually hegemonic party led the other party elites to see 'their chances for access to patronage, clientelism and state office greatly diminish. At this point, protests, violence, lawsuits and hence a process of *delegitimation* set in.' As it is for the elites, so it is for members of the groups which they lead, for whom the struggle for power is enmeshed in the 'politics of anxiety':

Contending groups struggle on grimly, polarizing their differences and convinced that their ability to protect their interests and to obtain justice is coextensive with their power. In this type of politics, there is deep alienation and distrust among political competitors. Consequently, they are profoundly afraid of being in the power of their opponents. This fear in turn breeds a huge appetite for power which is sought without restraint and used without restraint. (Ake, 1985: 10)

The final aspect of the intra-elite contest for power is that it involves a struggle among various institutions and segments: military, bureaucracy, academia, the political class (or politicians), the business class and so on. The military emerged as the most critical segment of all in the struggle for power. It had two major advantages over the other elite segments. First, its national cohesion orientation as opposed to the divisive orientation of the political class made it assume the dual role of custodian and saviour of the nation. Successive military regimes also pursued a deliberate policy of destroying the credibility of the political class by exposing the moral bankruptcy, corruption and deficiencies in government of its members. The second advantage was the barrel of the gun. The military used these advantages to dominate the political process, and to build a comprador elite from the other elite segments. Nevertheless, the exposure of the paucity of military regimes and, in particular, its emergence as an instrument of divisive politics and the attempts by successive regimes to perpetuate themselves in power, running counter to the accepted 'fire brigade' role, led to an intensification of the contesting of military claims to power by displaced elites and other segments of civil society.

THE CONSEQUENCES OF NIGERIA'S LOCATION IN THE GLOBAL SYSTEM

The consequences of the structure of the colonial economy on the post-colonial formations are fairly well known. The state remained primarily extractionist, and its situation is aptly captured by Graf's characterisation of it as a rentier state, the essential feature of which

....is that it severs the link between production and distribution. State revenues accrue from taxes or 'rents' on production, rather than from productive activity. This production depends, however, on techniques, expertise, investments – and markets generated outside the territory controlled by the state. For this reason, practically all aspects of exploration, production and marketing are dominated by international capital, typically in the form of the multinational corporation. (Graf, 1988: 219)

The rents in the post-independence period came initially from agricultural products, but from the 1970s, oil became virtually the only major source of rents. The implications of the rentier state for Nigeria's global location are clear. In broad terms, it underlies the country's peripheral or dependent status. The other implications are well summarized by Graf's (1988: 220ff) characteristics of the rentier state. These are, first that the economy is susceptible to crisis and shocks in the prices of commodities in the world market, and hence tendentially unstable – this is referred to as the crisis of extraversion; secondly, the economy is dependent on north-south trade patterns; and thirdly, dependence on oil disarticulates the economy, discourages agricultural development which is the mainstay of the dominant rural economy, and stultifies the growth of non-state capitalism. These factors seriously limited the scope of the state's autonomous economic action and largely explain the externalisation of the efforts to arrest the economic decline of the 1980s and 1990s, after a period of boom.

In terms of the domestic economy, state capitalism, import substitution industrialisation, the rapid expansion of the public sector, development of local capital in collaboration with foreign capital, indigenisation, and diversification were the main themes of the attempts to correct the anomalies of the colonial structures and, in particular, to transform the economy from its externalised orientation to a welfarist and development-driven formation. But the structural creations of the colonial economy, which were a part of what led to the rentier state and sustained the forging of close ties between local and international capital, proved to be quite formidable obstacles to this transformation. The economic mismanagement of the successive post-independence governments, which was closely connected to the prebendalisation of the state (i.e. conversion of public office into an instrument of private accumulation) and the expansion of patronage networks, was also a major factor, as we find out in subsequent chapters.

Nigeria's situation as the most populous country in Africa and the black world also had important implications for its post-independence politics. This is especially true of its foreign policy which has been informed by a perception of leadership (what Nigerian scholars refer to as the country's 'manifest destiny') which emphasises the country's responsibility for the liberation and development of Africans and the entire black race. It is for this reason that Nigeria was among those which spearheaded the African part in the liberation of southern African countries, established a trust fund in the African Development Bank, initiated the integration of the West African sub-region, and has been involved in peacekeeping operations in the continent – to mention a few instances. The country's wealth and vast human resources encouraged the leaders to play this leadership role, even in the worst stages of its economic decline. Otubanjo (1989) has also pointed out that the unity of the country after the civil war and the emergence of oil as a weapon of foreign policy were the major factors for the actualisation of this manifest destiny, which had remained latent in the first decade of independence. This perception of leadership also underlies the fierce nationalism and anti-imperialist attitudes of most Nigerian leaders and ordinary people. The attempts to indigenise the economy, Nigeria's persistent demands for a new world order which led it to collaborate with other third world 'powers', and the insistence on autonomy in its internal affairs are remarkable products of these attitudes. However, these were severely limited by its rentier status, and some commentators attribute the West's hostility towards Nigeria to its resistance to neo-colonial control.

This chapter has attempted to provide a background for the rest of the chapters in which more substantive issues of Nigeria's post-independence history are examined. As was indicated at the beginning, the historical background is important because in many ways post-independence politics derives its roots from the colonial history. On the other hand, the bases of politics discussed in the second section are the analytical lens through which the issues and events in the following chapters are to be interpreted.

2

THE FIRST REPUBLIC, 1960-1966

On October 1 1960, Nigeria was granted independence as part of 'Her Majesty [the Queen of Great Britain's] Dominion'. The period between that date and 15 January 1966, when the first post-independence civilian administration was violently overthrown by the military, is generally referred to as the First Republic, although the country did not become a Republic until 1 October 1963 when its dominion status came to an end. The focus of most studies of the First Republic is on why the newly-independent country, with all the promise it held of political stability, turned out to be no better than a 'typical case'. Explanations advanced for this include institutional inadequacies and failures, especially the lack of congruence between institutional forms and the political culture; the corruption of the political class, and the failure to respect basic rules of the game in the zero-sum contest for power reinforced by the system of 'government' and 'opposition'; irreconcilable ethnic and regional differences articulated by the sectional political parties; and the failure of the political leaders to meet the expectations of independence, including the hopes of minority groups for separate states (cf. Vickers and Post, 1973; Dudley, 1973, 1982; Oyewole, 1987; and Diamond, 1988). Hopefully, the strengths (and weaknesses) of the different perspectives will become clear as the conflicts and crises that underlay the collapse of the Republic are analysed.

But there was more to the First Republic than its collapse. The patterns and directions of post-independence politics were established in the short-lived Republic, and this has made it the reference point for discussing the country's political problems and searching for solutions. It is as such that the major political events and issues in the Republic, as they cumulatively led to its collapse, are discussed in this chapter. There is also consideration of the Republic's political economy and external relations in the period.

31

BACKGROUND

The setting for the Republic was provided by the 1959 federal elections whose outcome determined the nature of post-independence government, and the structural framework within which the Republic was to be operated.

THE 1959 ELECTIONS

Dudley (1973) has described the 1959 election as a critical election because it was to decide which parties were to control the federal government after independence. Given the background of intense regionalism and mutual fears and suspicions among the ethno-regional leaders which characterised the final phase of colonial rule, every major party was anxious not to lose out in the power-game. However, the NPC had a headstart advantage as the Northern region was allocated more than half of the seats in the House of Representatives.[1]

All the party needed to do to control the federal government alone was to win enough seats in its Northern region to give it the necessary majority in parliament. Knowing this, NCNC and AG, the two major Southern parties, tried to counteract NPC hegemony in the North by entering into alliances with the main Northern opposition parties: the NCNC with the NEPU and the AG with the UMBC. This strategy yielded dividends, as the NPC failed to secure the majority required to form the government alone. It nevertheless had enough seats and other advantages to make it 'a favoured partner to any winning coalition' (Dudley, 1973). The position of the parties is presented in Table 2.1. As the table shows, no party won enough seats to form the government alone, which meant that a coalition government had to be formed. Although they remained essentially regional parties, the NCNC and AG had much more national spread through coalition partners than the NPC, which refused to be drawn out of its regional shell despite the token votes it got in the West and Lagos. If therefore nationalness was a major consideration, then the NCNC and AG (together with their alliance partners) were in the best position to form a coalition. Moreover, the assumptions of rationality, as embodied in the notion of minimum winning coalitions, favoured such a coalition (Dudley, 1973).

---

[1] The Northern region, with 174 seats, had more than half the seats in the 312-member house. The Eastern region had 73, the Western region 62, and Lagos federal capital territory 3.

Table 2.1. REGIONAL DISTRIBUTION OF SEATS WON BY MAJOR
PARTIES IN THE 1959 ELECTIONS

Party	North	West	East	Lagos	Total
NPC	134	0	0	0	134
NCNC/NEPU	8	21	58	2	89
AG	25	33	14	1	73
Others	7	8	1	0	16
Total	174	62	73	3	312

Source: Ngou (1989: 100).

But this was not to be. In the manner of 'politics' taking precedence over 'rationality' or what Essien-Udom once described as "politics without vision" – which characterised much of Nigerian politics in later years – it was a coalition of the NPC and NCNC which was formed. Dudley has tried to show that this coalition was not as non-rational as it appeared at first sight, especially given the fact that a coalition of the NCNC and AG would have been essentially a southern coalition, something the NPC was most unlikely to accept. This was ostensibly why, even before the results of the elections were announced (but presumably when they were already known), the governor-general, Sir James Robertson, invited the leader of the NPC to form the government. It was feared that the Northern leaders would not agree to independence if they did not control the federal government, or were not, at the very least, part of it.

For the colonial authority, this consideration was more important than any other. So once the favoured status of the NPC was made clear, the question of coalition was no longer a theoretical one; it was simply which – the AG or the NCNC – the NPC leaders were willing to work with. The obvious choice was the NCNC, not only because leaders of both parties had forged close links in the course of national governments of the late 1950s, but also because NPC leaders resented what they considered the anti-Northern and radical inclinations of the Awolowo-led AG.

The NCNC's decision to enter a coalition with the NPC had less to do with its avowed commitment to national unity than with the 'aspectival' calculations that it would be better assured of government patronage and other privileges associated with Northerners than it would in partnership with rival Westerners. The pay-offs reaped by the NCNC shortly after the coalition came into being justified this calculation: in addition to Nnamdi Azikiwe becoming first president of the Senate and later governor-general and president of the country, party stalwarts got plum ministerial and ambassadorial posts, and appointments to boards of federal institutions and parastatals, and there was enhanced entry and promotion for Easterners in the public service and armed forces into the bargain. In spite of this, the NPC and NCNC were strange bedfellows and even serious rivals, as later events were to show. Much of the tension that dogged the coalition in its later years has been attributed by Dare (1989) to a basic contradiction in the horizontal and vertical levels of the coalition: the fact that cooperation at the centre was not extended to the regions, so that supposed coalition partners at the federal level seriously opposed one another at the regional level. This was more on the part of the NCNC which not only continued to ally itself with opposition parties in the Northern region – to the consternation of the NPC – but also played the role of opposition party in parliament, especially from 1963 when the AG was thrown into disarray following the imprisonment of its leaders. Later, after the demise of the AG government in the Western region, the two coalition parties were engaged in a desperate struggle to enhance their chances of becoming single majorities. These rivalries naturally weakened the fragile coalition.

THE STRUCTURAL FRAMEWORK

The structural framework of the Republic was defined by the 1960 independence and 1963 Republican constitutions, which had essentially the same features (for a comparative analysis of the two constitutions see Ojo, 1989). The salient elements of the framework included the following.

First, Nigeria was a federation of three largely autonomous regions each of which had its own constitution, public service, judiciary and marketing boards alongside those of the federation. Residual powers – i.e. powers over matters not on the exclusive and concurrent legislative lists, and which students of federalism consider an index of where the balance of power lies in a federation – belonged to the regions which were, in effect, very powerful. From 1954, when the federal constitution which gave regions wide-ranging powers was introduced, they had continually been 'the principal arena of politics, the field "where the action is"' (Dudley, 1982: 52). This was why party chieftains like Ahmadu Bello chose to remain regional premiers rather than prime minister or president at the centre. The federal government nevertheless had a leverage over the regions in terms of the provisions in section 70 of the 1963 Constitution which empowered it to declare a state of emergency in the federation or any part thereof; control of the police and armed forces; and the determination of fiscal relations and economic planning. This leverage was exploited to the full by the coalition parties in their attempt to assert federal power and to further their hegemonic interests. This changed the complexion of politics by effectively transferring the arena of politics and action from the regions to the centre.

Secondly, the country operated the Westminster parliamentary system. This meant that executive power derived from legislative majority (of the NPC and NCNC at the centre); there was a tension- and conflict-laden dual headship of the executive, which had a titular head of government – called governor-general at independence and president after 1963 – and a prime minister who was the effective head of government (in the regions these were the governor and premier); and there was an officially designated opposition party in parliament: the AG. The legislature at the centre was bicameral. In addition to the House of Representatives (HOR), there was the Senate which had a balancing function to counterbalance the gross inequalities in representation in the HOR, as it was composed on the basis of equal representation for the regions. But the Senate had very limited legislative powers; it had delaying powers only and lacked jurisdiction over financial matters. Moreover, the upper house appeared 'to have been transformed by politicians into a dumping ground for those who failed to win seats at popular elections but who ha[d] ambition to become ministers' (Azikiwe, 1965: 451).

And thirdly, the same structure of party government existed in the regions but in important ways this presented a different complexion. In the first place, all the regions were one-party systems. Following the patterns established during the nationalist phase of the colonial era, the majority ethnic group-based regional parties held firm sway in the regions – the NPC in the North, the NCNC in the East and the AG in the West.[2] The opposition consisted of the ethnic minority parties, whose mainspring was agitation for separate states, and several other parties representing ethnic, religious, professional and ideological interests (a good example of the last was Aminu Kano's Northern Elements Progressive Union, NEPU). By the time the military intervened in January 1966, there were seventy-eight minor 'opposition' parties operating in the regions, although some of these were no more than ethnic 'progressive' unions. The minor or what Dudley calls 'second-order' parties derived their main strength from their electoral alliances with major parties from other regions which, in ethnic minority parties, supported their separatist agitations (while at the same time opposing and repressing the agitations within their own regions). The major

---

[2] The only exception was of course the AG whose control of the Western region was weak, a situation made more precarious by the attempts by the federal coalition partners to take over control of the region as part of their strategies to become single winning parties.

parties exploited the plight of the minorities to extend their electoral strengths beyond the immediate boundaries of their regions, although in the case of the Mid-West minorities the NCNC and NPC used their federal strength to create a new region for them in 1963 as part of the strategy of eliminating the AG and taking over its Western region.

The structural framework of the short-lived Republic had flaws which were the source of some of the conflicts and crises which catalysed its collapse. The most serious of these was the preponderant size and population of the Northern region which, contrary to the 'Mill's law of federal stability', made it possible for the region perpetually to dominate the federation (the majoritarian principle of the Westminster system, which gave the region more than half of the seats in parliament, facilitated this anomaly). Such a federation, Mill (1948) argues, will be conflict-ridden and unstable, and the Nigerian experience (like Jamaica's domination of the West Indian federation and Singapore's of the Malaysian federation, among others) has clearly demonstrated this.

Closely related to the anomaly of Northern domination was that of an insufficient number of federating units. In a two- or three-unit (or even four-unit) federation – as the country was in the First Republic – perpetual face-to-face conflicts cannot be avoided. What exacerbated the Nigerian case was not only the gross inequality among the regions but the dissatisfaction of the ethnic minority groups in the regions with the number and composition of the regions and their subsequent agitation for more states.

The creation of more states to satisfy the clamour of the minorities, especially those from the Northern region, would at once have attenuated the danger of Northern preponderance, and it was for this reason that the NPC leaders were vehemently opposed to the creation of any new state from the region. Not even the violent agitations by the Tiv (the so-called Tiv riots, which were suppressed by military force in the early 1960s) could change this instance of politics without vision, at least from the standpoint of national cohesion. Ostensibly it was difficult to create new states because the process of doing so as laid down in the constitution was near-impossible, yet when it served to further their hegemonic interests, the NPC and NCNC were able to manipulate the process to create the Mid-West region. Unfortunately, apart from heightening the NCNC's hope of successfully challenging the NPC because the new region easily fell under its control, the creation of the Mid-West did little to ameliorate the structural anomalies of the federation.

Another structural problem was extreme regionalism which was oiled by the substantial powers and relative autonomy the regions enjoyed from the adoption of the federal constitution in 1954. The history of the First Republic is replete with examples of discrimination against citizens from other regions, especially in employment in regional public services and in the provision of public goods, and the intense inter-regional rivalry extended to the imposition of tariffs and restrictions on inter-regional trade. Regionalism of this kind was of course championed by the major ethno-regional parties, which exploited the unevenness in socio-economic development among the regions to mobilise fears of possible domination by rival regions, thereby making regionalism and ethnicity cardinal points of their legitimisation strategies.

A good example of this was the publication in 1965 of a document by Akintola's fledgling NNDP government in the Western region which sought to mobilise support of Yorubas in the region by cataloguing Igbo domination of federal institutions based in 'Yorubaland', and how this was a prelude to an Igbo take-over of the region. However, this negative form of regionalism is distinct from that which Chief Obafemi Awolowo regarded as the type of positive, healthy rivalry, which led the regions to establish universities and other educational institutions, industries, media houses, hospitals and so on in a bid not to be lagging behind the others.[3]

Then there was the parliamentary system itself whose core elements were detrimental to the stability of the federation. The first-past-the-post electoral system, clearly favoured majoritarianism, and thus engendered Northern domination. An electoral system giving more emphasis to achieving balance, like proportional representation, would have been less destabilising, as some of the formulators of the 1979 Constitution later argued. The other problem was with the dual-headed executive. Although Dennis Osadebey, premier of the former Mid-West region, pointed out (1978) that this arrangement allowed for political balancing among the major sections of the federation and regions, it was the source of major tensions and friction, especially at the federal level where there was a coalition government (in the regions, the arrangement did not cause so much friction, largely because the party governments were based on one-party systems).

The rivalry and mistrust between the NPC and NCNC easily degenerated into a power struggle between President Nnamdi Azikiwe and Prime Minister Tafawa Balewa over who would actually exercise

---

[3] In addition to duplication and other uneconomic consequences of the 'healthy' rivalries pointed to in Chapter 1, it is difficult to draw the line between positive and negative regionalism because some of the examples of so-called positive regionalism actually inspired the attempts by NPC leaders to employ federal power to extend regional advantages, a development which seriously heightened the contest for federal power.

executive power, including control of the armed forces. As Azikiwe himself admitted:

> Nigeria [was] not ready to have a constitutional head of state with hollow power working parallel with a power-loaded head of government. No matter what may be the good relations between the two persons involved, as [was] the case between me and Sir Abubakar, external factors are bound to provoke feelings and sow seeds of misunderstanding. (Azikiwe, 1965: 461)

Relations between Azikiwe and Balewa were badly strained after the 1964 general elections (which the NCNC and its electoral alliance members boycotted), when Azikiwe refused to call on Tafawa Balewa to form the government after the NPC had secured a parliamentary majority from the elections in the Northern region. Matters came to a head when the two leaders engaged in a struggle to gain the support of the armed forces, and were resolved only after the 'Zik-Balewa pact' had been negotiated by elder statesmen, led by the then Chief Justice Adetokunboh Ademola. These frictions were a major ground for the rejection of the Westminster system by constitution-makers who in 1976 opted for the executive presidential system. They argued that a division between real authority and formal authority 'is meaningless in the light of African political experience and history ... No African head of state has been known to be content with the position of mere figurehead' (FGN, 1976: xxix).

POLITICAL DEVELOPMENTS AND BUILD-UP TO THE COLLAPSE OF THE REPUBLIC

The history of the First Republic consists of the bitter rivalry among the major regional parties in their struggle for supremacy at the centre. The crises provoked by this rivalry cumulatively led to the collapse of the Republic. At the heart of the problems were the tension and mistrust in the NPC-NCNC coalition – generated by, among other things, the NPC's attempts to use its control of the federal government to extend political and economic domination by the Northern region, as well as attempts by the NCNC to wrest power from the NPC by counteracting its political advantages and extending its own power-base. Strains in the coalition appeared soon after independence, especially when sixteen of the independent members of parliament joined the NPC in 1961 to give it a working majority in parliament.

However, the strains did not become open till the publication of the 1962-8 development plan which showed that the bulk of federal capital expenditure was to be concentrated in the North, suggesting that the NCNC had lost its 'pivotal role' and therefore its 'extractive capability' (Dudley, 1982: 63). Apart from projects connected with coastal waterways, Lagos affairs, information and communication – with a total cost of approximately 68.1 million pounds – the major capital projects went to the North:

> The Niger dam, estimated at 68.1 million pounds [it eventually cost more than 88 million pounds] represented more than 10 per cent of total federal government spending; almost all of the 29.7 million pounds scheduled for defence; the major proportion of 39.2 million pounds to be spent on health and education, and the bulk of the 35.3 million pounds to be spent on roads. (Dudley, 1982: 63)

This plan, as well as the accelerated appointments of less qualified Northerners in place of Southerners to top political, military and bureaucratic positions (apparently to provide the necessary support base for Northern control of political power), dashed the hopes of the NCNC that its partnership with the NPC would enhance the extractive capacity of its Eastern region. The party was then forced to seek alternative ways of securing control of the federal government which, with the dwindling revenues of the regional governments, had become the most critical extractive instrument.

THE ACTION GROUP CRISIS AND ITS AFTERMATH

Meanwhile, the AG – the opposition party in parliament and the party in power in the Western region – was falling apart, a development which at first favoured NCNC designs. The AG's role as opposition party, which extended beyond parliament, did not enjoy the support of important members of the party including Chief Ladoke Akintola, then premier of the Western region, who, like their counterparts in the NCNC, had established strong links with NPC leaders when they served in the national government headed by Tafawa Balewa in 1957. These members believed that the AG should seek ways of joining the coalition government because being in opposition meant that the elites of the Western region were excluded from privileges and benefits in the federation. Many felt that the Yorubas were losing their pre-eminent economic and bureaucratic position to the Igbos due to opposing the NPC-led federal government. Moreover, elements within the party were opposed to attempts by Chief Awolowo to transform the party into a radical nationalist-democratic socialist party for which purpose the chief had sent young party members to Winneba in Ghana for training at Nkrumah's Ideological Institute.

The party split along these lines at its 1962 congress in Jos.

From that point, matters degenerated rapidly. An attempt to remove Chief Akintola as premier and replace him with Chief Adegbenro precipitated a parliamentary crisis in May 1962. This gave a pretext for the NPC-led federal government, which was bent on weakening the AG and installing a puppet government in order to further consolidate its chances of holding on to federal power, to declare a state of emergency in the region (the NCNC's complicity in this could be inferred from the fact that earlier in 1961 Dr Michael Okpara, leader of the party and premier of the Eastern region, had called for the declaration of a state of emergency in the Western region on the grounds of a breakdown of law and order; what happened in 1962 could then be taken to mean that the AG played into the NCNC's hands). The declaration of a state of emergency was followed by the suspension of the AG party government, and in its place an interim government was appointed, headed by Chief M.A. Majekodunmi. Subsequently a commission of inquiry (the Coker Commission) found Chief Awolowo guilty of misuse of Western regional funds – specifically, that he diverted funds from the regional government-owned National Investment and Properties Corporation, totalling N4.4 million in cash and N1.3 million in overdraft, from the National Bank (also owned by the Western region) to finance the AG and publish newspapers supporting the party – and indicted him for trying to build a financial empire through abuse of his official position. At the same time as the Coker Commission was indicting him, the Chief, and other party leaders including Chief Anthony Enahoro, Alhaji Lateef Jakande and Joseph Tarka (UMBC leader) were tried, convicted and imprisoned for treasonable felony. After six months of the state of emergency Chief Akintola was reinstated as premier, this time under the banner of a new party – the United Peoples' Party (UPP) – which formed a coalition government with the Western regional NCNC.

The weakening of the AG was completed when the Mid-West region was carved out from the Western region in 1963. The new region immediately fell under the control of the NCNC, and this, together with the party's foothold in the Western regional government, increased its hope of posing a formidable challenge to the NPC. But the NCNC's advantage in the Western region was short-lived because, once Chief Akintola consolidated his hold on power with the backing of the NPC (which realised the dangers of the increasing strength of its coalition partner), he dissolved the UPP-NCNC coalition government and co-opted several leaders of the Western NCNC to form a new party – the Nigerian National Democratic Party (NNDP) – which then controlled power in the region. Still all hope was not lost for the NCNC: the 1964 general elections were to provide the opportunity for challenging the NPC, especially as the party believed Akintola's NNDP was not popular and could be easily defeated in an election.

THE CENSUS CRISIS

Perhaps the best opportunity for the NCNC and indeed all the Southern parties which resented so-called Northern domination to try to remove its basis was presented by the census of 1962. Since its preponderant population (based on the census) was the reason for its domination, the calculation was that, if it were possible to change the population balance in favour of the South, then the basis of Northern domination would be permanently removed (there was, and continues to be, a suspicion that the preponderance of the Northern population is the result of a gross inflation of the actual figures). But this was not the only reason why the census was a major political issue. The use of population figures for revenue allocation among the regions in particular and resource distribution in general, for assessing the viability of new states, for allocating quotas in recruitment into the armed forces, and so on, made the census as important as (if not more important than) elections for villages, provinces, state creation movements, political parties, and the regional governments (for a good account of the problems of the census in historical perspective, see Aluko, 1965).

Table 2.2. CENSUS FIGURES, 1962 AND 1963

Region	1962	1963
North	29,777,986	29,758,875
East	12,388,646	12,394,462
West	10,278,500	10,265,846
Mid-West	2,533,337	2,535,839
Lagos	675,352	665,246
Total	55,653,821	55,620,268

These considerations help to explain the fraudulent inflation of figures (livestock were reported to have been counted in some places as human population), and the controversies which followed the publication of the census results. In particular, as the figures confirmed Northern preponderance (see Table 2.2), the NCNC Eastern regional government spearheaded a Southern rejection of the results (unfortunately, the reaction of the West was compromised by Akintola's dependence on the NPC – he could not afford to bite the hand that fed him!). This was despite the fact that, as verificatory tests carried out to check the validity of the results showed, the inflation of figures and other fraudulent acts were more prevalent in the East, the West and Lagos (the first headcount suggested that while the population of the North had increased by only 30 per cent since 1952-3, those of the East and West increased by an incredible 71 and 70 per cent respectively). A fresh census was ordered in 1963 but the results, published in February 1964, differed little from those of 1962, as Table 2.2 shows. The NCNC once again opposed the new figures and the premier of its Eastern regional government even went to court to seek the nullification of the census exercise, but failed, partly because the party did not get the support of the two other Southern premiers. While, for reasons already given, Akintola readily accepted the results, Chief Dennis Osadebey, premier of the newly created Mid-West region, decided to accept the results after initially rejecting them, 'for the sake of national unity'. However, the Mid-West's decision was forced by the NPC's threat to withdraw federal aid on which the young fledgling region depended.

THE 1964 ELECTIONS

This left the 1964 elections as the final opportunity for the NCNC and its allies to unseat the NPC and possibly stop the threat, now virtually a fact, of Northern domination. The stakes in the elections were therefore very high: there was the NCNC hoping to turn the table at all costs; the NPC confident of consolidating its Northern hegemonic hold and possibly extending its sphere of influence to include the West where its protégé Akintola had to defeat the AG once and for all; and there was of course the badly battered AG which hoped, through its alliance with the NCNC, to regain control of the Western region at least. The volatile political situation and the realignment of forces produced two alliances for the elections. One was the Nigerian National Alliance (NNA) comprising the NPC and its client-parties: Akintola's NNDP, the Niger Delta Congress (NDC), the Mid-West Democratic Front (MDF) and the Dynamic Party. The main campaign theme of the NNA was national unity through the representation of all ethnic groups in a national government, a theme informed by the NPC's expected reassertion of federal control. The other was the United Progressive Grand Alliance (UPGA) formed by the NCNC and AG as well as their Northern allies, NEPU, UMBC, Zamfara Commoners' Party and Kano People's Party which had joined forces in the Northern Progressive Front formed in January 1964. The UPGA campaigned on a promise to restructure the federation and create new regions reflecting the common purpose of its members to halt Fulani-directed Northern hegemony of the federation. The character of these alliances set the parameters for the party political alignments which have endured – indeed, in the Second Republic alliances closely resembling those of 1964 emerged to contest the 1983 elections, and the two-party system which was decreed by government in the aborted Third Republic was justified by the Political Bureau which made the recommendation as an acknowledgement of a two-party tendency begun in the First Republic. Certain observations can be made about the character of the alliances.

First, in spite of the national, cross-regional appearance of the alliances – the two camps presented a North versus South constellation of forces. The mainstay of the NNA was the NPC, whose motive force was the consolidation of Northern hegemony – indeed, the party concentrated its efforts on winning in the North, and did not bother to campaign outside its region, since it was assured of federal control if it could win all or almost all of the Northern seats. However, the NPC leaders recognized the expediency of extending their sphere of influence to the South in pursuit of this objective, especially to counteract the efforts of the NCNC, but whatever alliance resulted from this had to be forged on terms determined by the Northern hegemonic class. The UPGA, on the other hand, was a Southern coalition whose primary objective was to halt Northern hegemony, an objective that could only be realised through alliance with formidable opposition parties in the Northern region itself.

The other point to be highlighted was the attempt by elements within the AG and the Northern opposition parties to forge a 'progressive' ideological unity. The notion of 'progressive' here related more to a counter-movement to Northern conservatism than anything else. Chief Awolowo and his supporters in the AG saw this so-called progressive movement as the surest way of mobilising support among members of the opposition minority and marginalised groups in the North. But it was precisely because they championed this movement that the Awolowo camp was highly resented by the hegemonic Northern class. The NCNC did not have any such 'progressive' pretensions, preferring a more conciliatory approach involving a détente with the Northern hegemonic class. Nevertheless, given the pragmatism of its leaders, the realisation of ends was a far more important criterion of success than the means used, which largely explains the 'pragmatic' switch from détente to progressive confrontation as the 1964 elections drew closer. Their divergence on strategy, and underlying mutual suspicion and rivalry, made a strong alliance between the two Southern parties unlikely. Indeed, the electoral alliance was basically one of expediency for both of them. While they 'cooperated' at the centre, they were rivals in the regions, and more or less sought to fight the election alone rather than as members of an alliance.

These elements governed subsequent political alliances in Nigeria. In the Second Republic, for example, the emergence of the Progressive Parties Alliance in 1983 was a resurrection of the UPGA with more or less the same actors and objectives: to stop Northern hegemony, by then championed by the NPN. In all this it was believed that unity of the progressive front (which included the heirs to the NCNC) was the only antidote to the perpetuation of Northern hegemony (the victory of Chief M.K.O. Abiola in the annulled presidential election of 1993 seemed to vindicate this 'thesis'). This perception was shared by members of the Northern hegemonic class who accordingly used their control of the state's coercive and patronage apparatuses to divide the progressive camp. In his analysis of the 'political manipulation and scheming by the Kaduna mafia', Ochoche (1987) shows that the fight against the progressive front extends to the military which, more than political parties, became the critical instrument of power relations, and attributes the frequent execution of minority-Christian, especially Middle-Belt military officers to the determination of the Northern cabal to sustain the hegemonic agenda.

Let us now return to the 1964 elections, which were scheduled for December. With the high stakes involved the run-up to the election was conflict-ridden. There were claims and counter-claims of intimidation of opponents, involving the use of thugs to disrupt and prevent campaigns, and to harass candidates and electoral officials, making it impossible in many cases for nomination papers to be filed. These incidents and other acts of political violence were more in the Northern and Western regions, which were the focus of competition to control the centre. To arrest the drift towards lawlessness and provide a modicum of order necessary to make the conduct of the elections possible, a peace meeting of all political parties was held in October, where they resolved to ensure that the elections should be free and fair.

But in face of the desperation of the parties, such interventions were insufficient to arrest the descent into anarchy. Employing violent tactics which sometimes involved the physical elimination of opposition candidates, the parties sought to reduce the uncertainties of the electoral process by working to ensure that wherever possible candidates were returned unopposed, without a vote. At the close of nominations, eighty-eight of the total 174 NPC candidates in the Northern region and about 30 per cent of the NNDP candidates in the Western region and NCNC candidates in the Eastern region were returned unopposed. Thus, even before the elections the position of the parties was clear. Feeling frustrated by the strong-arm tactics of the NPC to retain control of the North and of the NNDP to consolidate its hold in the West, UPGA decided to boycott the elections. However, the announcement of this decision came too late to stop its candidates and supporters taking part in the elections. In the event, it was only in the Eastern region, where the NCNC government deployed its machinery to stop the election, that the boycott was effective; in the Mid-West and West elections were held (in part because AG members feared a boycott would give the NNDP a field day). In the Northern region, the effect of the boycott was nil. The results of the elections released by the Federal Electoral Commission (which itself was badly divided at this time, thanks to the decision of some regional representatives to resign in protest at a farcical election) showed that the NPC lost only five of the 174 seats allocated to the North, while the NNDP won the majority of seats in the West and NCNC in the Mid-West (see Table 2.3).

Table 2.3. SEATS WON BY PARTIES IN THE 1964/65[*] ELECTIONS

Region	NPC	NNDP	NCNC	AG	NPF	IND	Total
North	162	—	—	—	4	1	167
West	—	36	5	15	—	1	57
Mid-West	—	—	13 (1)	—	—	—	14
East	—	—	15 (49)	4	—	2	70
Lagos	—	—	(1)	(2)	—	1	4
Total	162	36	84	21	4	5	312

[*] 1965 figures are in brackets.

With a clear NNA majority, Tafawa Balewa called on President Azikiwe to reappoint him Prime Minister. Swayed by his loyalty to the NCNC/UPGA, whose leaders rejected the conduct and outcome of the elections, Azikiwe refused to do so, thereby precipitating a constitutional stalemate. What followed was a struggle for power between the president and prime minister, a struggle which at one stage involved competition for control and support of the armed forces. The recourse to the military at the height of the power struggle

.... only succeeded in making the armed forces ultra-conscious of the blurred boundary lines separating the 'military' from the 'civil' and the 'legal' from the 'political'.[...] The armed forces [became] aware they had a political role to play and so paved the way for the military coup which followed in 1966.... (Dudley, 1982: 71)

The constitutional impasse ended only after a truce mediated by the chief justice of the Supreme Court (Sir Adetokunboh Ademola) and the chief justice of the regional high courts. Under the 'Zik-Balewa pact' Azikiwe agreed to invite Balewa to form a new government provided

(1) such a government was a 'broad-based government', and included, wherever possible, representatives of the two competing alliances;
(2) the boycotted elections in the Eastern region were to be rescheduled for March 1965 after which NCNC members would be appointed to the government; and
(3) there should be elections to the Western regional assembly in October (cited in Dudley, 1982: 69-70).

Balewa was then invited to form a new government which included members of the NNDP. After the rescheduled Eastern regional elections in which the NCNC lost only six of the seventy seats (four of these to UNIP, the AG's Eastern regional ally), the broad-based federal cabinet was enlarged to the unprecedented size of eighty ministers. But the aftermath of the events of 1964-5 could only, at best, produce a fragile peace. The frustrations felt by the NCNC (and AG) at being unable to halt the extension of Northern hegemonic rule provoked deep hostility in many Eastern leaders, and there were talks of confederation and secession as possible solutions to the Northern problem. But worse was still to come, when the 1965 Western regional election turned out to be the final Waterloo for the young Republic.

The setting for the election in the West made it a matter of high risk for the Republic. After the tensions and conflicts generated by the 1964 elections, the struggle to control the region was of critical importance for all the parties. Thus, although the NNDP (desperate to hold on to power in the region by every means) and the AG (equally desperate to shame the NNDP for being a usurper that sold out to the Northern cabal) were the direct contestants, their performances were crucial to the game plans of the NPC and NCNC. The campaigns and preparations for the elections were violent, as the NNDP deployed the coercive forces at its disposal against the more popular AG. The election was massively rigged and manipulated by both parties, but NNDP's incumbency gave it the edge.

Both parties claimed victory in the election and each actually tried to swear in its own leader as Premier. The supposed victory of the NNDP was greeted with violent protests and demonstrations by AG supporters. Lives and property were destroyed in 'Operation Wetie' (literally, 'wet with petrol and burn') which extended to attacks on Hausa settlers in Sagamu and other parts of the West. There was a complete breakdown of law and order which made the 1962 crisis in the region seem like child's play, but unlike on that earlier occasion, Balewa refused to declare a state of emergency in the region because of the NPC's support for Chief Akintola. Balewa also rejected the option of calling in the military because it was believed that many soldiers stationed in the region favoured the UPGA. It was while the West burned (which was not enough to stop Balewa from hosting the Commonwealth leaders' conference in Lagos) that the military struck in January 1966. This marked the end of the ill-fated Republic.

THE ECONOMY

The main objective of economic policy during this period was economic growth, and fiscal, monetary and development policies were geared to fostering this objective. Industrial policy was geared towards the encouragement of import substitution industrialization under a free enterprise system. Fiscal incentives including high tariff protection were designed to encourage private domestic and foreign investment. Agriculture was consistently neglected and the rural sector based on agriculture was deprived of development funds in favour of the urban areas ... (Iwayemi, 1979: 51)

Nigeria's economy in the First Republic exhibited the characteristics of a peripheral capitalist formation. Chief among these were its domination by foreign multinational and trading companies, reliance on foreign capital and investment as the key to economic development, and dependence on a few cash crops and minerals for foreign exchange. Given the country's colonial legacy, the dominant foreign capital was British. Before the civil war, British capital investment, the bulk of which was in the lucrative extractive industry (petroleum, coal and tin), manufacturing, trading and financial (banking and insurance) sectors, was estimated at 1 billion pounds. The major investments included 49 per cent ownership of Shell-BP, the main oil-exploiting company in the country, and 60 per cent ownership of Amalgamated Tin Mining (Nig) Ltd which dominated tin, iron and cobalt mining. The two largest trading companies in the country, which between them dominated the trading, import-export, distribution and manufacturing sectors – John Holt and the United Africa Company (UAC), with their subsidiaries – were British. The UAC controlled 41.3 per cent of Nigeria's import and export trade. Britain also assisted in securing foreign aid from multilateral donor agencies for Nigeria. In its first eight years of independence, for example, British initiative and support got Nigeria about US$273 million in technical and capital assistance from the Organization of Economic Cooperation and Development (OECD).

Britain's dominance of Nigeria's economy has been attributed by Akeredolu-Ale (1975) to its colonial policy which stunted the growth of indigenous entrepreneurship. Osoba (1987: 223) has also alluded to the role of 'an elite which, conditioned by the colonial educational system and persuaded by the substantial political and economic advantages that would accrue to it from power sharing with the colonial authorities, was broadly committed to protecting this colonial economic bequest'. In the absence of strong indigenous capital, the state assumed the role of entrepreneur and 'control' of commanding heights of the economy at independence; this placed it in a position to alter radically the inherited structure of the Nigerian economy as was done in some other newly-independent African states (Tanzania for example). But rather than establish a productive base, the federal government continued with the extractive policies of the colonial regime and the externalisation of the economy. Externalisation informed the adoption of the strategy of import substitution industrialisation, which led to a proliferation of assembly plants mainly for the local production of consumer items like soft drinks, beer, tyres, paints, car batteries, sweets and confectionary, bicycles, radios, and so on. Import substitution did not end the reliance on imports; it in fact reinforced it, as the local industries depended on imported technology and raw materials, and reinforced foreign tastes. Thus, in the early 1960s manufactured (consumer) goods, machinery and equipment made up an average of 60 per cent of imports (food imports accounted for about 11 per cent). But by and large, the manufacturing sector was neglected (cf. Teriba and Kayode, 1977). Between 1960 and 1966, the share of manufacturing in GDP averaged 5.5 per cent, a marginal increase over the share of 4.7 per cent in 1959 (Adeboye, 1989).

Foreign investment was regarded as the key to economic growth and development. Local private and pseudo-private participation involved federal and regional commercial ventures, including mainly commodity marketing boards and local partners and clients of international capital. By 1963, 68 per cent of invested paid-up capital in the country was in foreign hands; federal and regional governments held 22 per cent and private Nigerians only 10 per cent. Adeboye (1989: 22) gives a clearer picture of the extent of foreign capital domination:

> As at 1965, there were 110 wholly-owned foreign firms with a total paid up capital of nearly N28 million. There were 52 Nigerian wholly-owned firms with paid up capital of less than N4 million. The Nigerian

government owned only 14 firms wholly and invested almost N11 million in them. On the other hand, there were 115 joint ventures of which expatriate interests held controlling shares in 73 firms ....

To attract foreign capital, the federal and regional governments introduced tax reliefs, protective tariffs and other incentives. Largely, for similar reasons, the federal government failed to repeal the mineral oil ordinance and the petroleum tax ordinance of 1959, the generous conditions of which attracted the oil majors, led by British Petroleum, to invest in the country at the country's expense: 'While Nigeria obtained royalties that ranged between 8 and 12 per cent, countries like Libya, Saudi Arabia and Venezuela were able to secure levels like 12½ per cent, 20 per cent and 16½ per cent respectively' (Soremekun, 1987: 278). This did not, however, mean that the government was not concerned about the underdevelopment of local or indigenous capital. The 1962-8 National Development Plan stated, for example, that direct government investment was to be sold to private Nigerian investors in the long run (this was obviously to enable state power holders to build a comprador bourgeoisie). This was the nature of the bogus mixed economy policy to which the federal government committed itself (see Ohiorhenuan, 1989).

Foreign domination of the economy attracted the criticism of the opposition AG, whose leader Chief Awolowo, an advocate of democratic socialism, advanced nationalization as the best strategy for economic development. In November 1961 he moved in the HOR that the policy of nationalizing strategic and commercial enterprises – including mining, marine insurance and foreign-owned plantations – be approved in principle. The motion was opposed by the federal government whose finance minister, Chief Festus Okotie-Eboh, argued that such a policy was not in the national interest, since it was likely to scare away foreign investment. According to the finance minister, the extant nationalization of air and rail transport, electric power, communications, shipping, agricultural commodity marketing boards and public utilities was sufficient to protect the national economy.

The country did manage to attract foreign capital, although this never matched the expected levels. For example, 50 per cent of the resources needed to implement the 1962-8 development plan was expected from foreign sources, but by the time the civil war broke out in 1967, only 14 per cent had been invested by the World Bank, other international financial institutions and private foreign capital. Failure to attract sufficient foreign investment was largely caused by the unstable and unpredictable political situation. For example, it has been estimated that the political crisis between 1964 and 1966 reduced the volume of foreign investment by up to 20 per cent (Iwayemi, 1979).

Alongside foreign control was the fact that the state played a largely extractive role in the economy. Through the produce marketing boards established under colonial rule, it appropriated the surplus from agrarian production of so-called cash crops, which it used to finance the rapid expansion of the public sector and the development of local capitalism, although a significant portion of the earnings disappeared into private pockets. The bulk of government revenue was derived from a few cash crops – cocoa, rubber, oil palm and groundnut (and minerals). Cocoa was the chief foreign exchange earner, and Nigeria was the world's largest exporter of oil palm. At independence in 1960 and all through the First Republic, agriculture accounted for over 50 per cent of GDP and, on average 75 per cent of export earnings. By 1965, however, crude oil had become a major source of revenue as Table 1.1 shows. In terms of foreign trade Britain was the centre of the country's imports and exports, although its shares of trade fell as Nigeria expanded its relations with the United States and some West European countries. Between 1960 and 1965, the volume of exports to Britain decreased from 47.6 to 37.8 per cent, and imports from 42.3 to 30.9 per cent.

FOREIGN POLICY

Nigeria's foreign policy in the First Republic has often been described as conservative and timid. The colonial legacy which restricted the policy options of the immediate post- independence leaders, the relative poverty of the country at the time, the lack of experience in international affairs, the conservative outlook of the prime minister Tafawa Balewa and other members of his cabinet, and serious domestic divisions which led the regions to open different consulates abroad are some of the reasons that have been advanced for the low-profile foreign policy (cf. Idang, 1973; Akinyemi, 1974; Aluko, 1981). The distinctive feature of foreign policy under Balewa was its pro-Western orientation. This was most obvious in the premium the regime placed on the maintenance of colonial-type relations with Britain and the Commonwealth group. The pro-Western posture was in spite of an avowed policy of non-alignment – that is, neutrality in relations between the cold war combatants – which was the vogue among newly-independent third world countries. Nigeria pursued a policy that bordered on hostility towards the USSR and other members of the Eastern bloc – this was partly informed by Balewa's personal fears of the dangers of communism. Among other anti-East actions, the Nigerian government refused to open an embassy in Moscow and only reluctantly allowed the Soviet Union to open its mission in Lagos; it also placed restrictions on travels to the Eastern bloc countries and communist literature, refused to recognise the People's Republic of China and Mongolia, and rejected aid and bilateral agreements with communist countries, including Soviet scholarships for Nigerian students. Trade relations with the East were insignificant.

By contrast, relations with Britain and the West were conducted in a manner that sometimes cast doubts on the country's independence. It took protests from university students, the AG and other opposition and progressive elements for the federal government to abrogate its defence pact with Britain. Nigeria defied African opposition to British policy on Rhodesia, and after Ian Smith unilaterally declared the independence of Southern Rhodesia in 1965, tried to discourage African countries from breaking diplomatic ties with Britain. Over the Congo crisis Balewa's government actively supported the West. Nevertheless, on a few occasions when the federal government was forced to defer to populist demands at home or when Nigeria's strategic interests were at stake, the Balewa regime showed flashes of delinked policies. (It should also be remembered that one of the avowed guiding principles of foreign policy under Balewa was 'the defence and promotion of Nigeria's sovereignty, territorial integrity and national independence'.) Thus, in 1963 it broke diplomatic ties with France over that country's nuclear testing in the Sahara, despite reassurances from Britain that the tests would have no effects on Nigeria. In 1961 it defied Britain to champion the expulsion of South Africa from the Commonwealth. The Balewa regime also tried to reduce its dependence on Britain by diversifying its trade relations and strengthening relations in other spheres with the United States and other Western powers. But by and large Nigeria's foreign policy in the First Republic remained pro-Western and was greatly influenced by its relations with Britain.

In its dealings with the outside world, the conservatism of the Balewa regime led it to emphasise the legal principles of international relations. This was evident in the country's participation in the international organisations to which it belonged – the United Nations (UN), the Commonwealth, the Non-Aligned Movement, the Group of 77 and the Organization of African Unity (OAU) – where it insisted on the principles of non-interference in the internal affairs of other countries, peaceful resolution of conflicts, inviolability of national boundaries, and so on. The use of these organisations as the main channels of foreign policy was also a mark of the regime's legalistic approach to foreign relations. Nevertheless, the Balewa administration also favoured the formation of powerful Third World commodity organisations as a way of improving the terms of trade with the capitalist centres. To this end it sponsored the meeting of the Africa Primary Agricultural Producers in 1962, and was a founding member of both the Cocoa Producers Alliance and the African Groundnut Council.

These attitudes also influenced Balewa's African policy. In his speech at the UN's General Assembly on the occasion of Nigeria's admission to the body, he articulated the Afrocentricity of the country's foreign policy which showed clear signs of a readiness to assume the 'manifest destiny' of African and black leadership. He referred to

'.... the creation of the necessary economic and political conditions to secure the government, territorial integrity and national independence of other African countries and their total liberation from imperialism and all forms of foreign domination; ... creation of the necessary conditions for the economic, political social, and cultural development of Africa; ... promotion of the rights of all black and oppressed peoples throughout the world;... [and] promotion of African unity.' (cited in Otubanjo, 1989: 4)

But the regime lacked the progressive or radical orientation required to play these roles. On apartheid in South Africa, for example, Nigeria was one of the very few countries on the continent which favoured dialogue with the Pretoria regime (it surprised other Africans by inviting South Africa to its independence celebrations), although it never had a consistent policy on the matter. Thus, at the same time as it advocated dialogue, Nigeria championed the expulsion of South Africa from the Commonwealth and the International Labour Organization and, following the Sharpeville massacre of 1960, the ultra-conservative government of the Northern region, whose position on issues determined that of the federal government, established a trust fund for the victims and banned further employment of white South Africans in the regional public service.

Nigeria was also a foundation member of the OAU, but favoured the functional approach to unity as opposed to the more radical political approach championed by President Nkrumah of Ghana, who advocated a United States of Africa. This and several other disagreements, like backing anti-Lumumba forces in Congo in opposition to Ghana, were manifestations of a rivalry between Nigeria and Ghana for the leadership of Africa. Nkrumah's radical, pro-communist inclination and support for radical opposition groups in Nigeria also underlay the rivalry. Nnoli (1989: 258) points out that anti-Nkrumahism was a major theme of Nigeria's foreign policy in the First Republic.

But this rivalry only made Nigeria more determined to assert its leadership in other spheres. Thus technical assistance in the form of manpower was given to several African countries, a military contingent was sent to assist Tanzania in putting down a mutiny, and Nigeria played a frontline role in the UN peacekeeping mission in the Congo. It also initiated the establishment of the Chad Basin Commission and the Niger Basin Authority in 1964, though these were directed more at sustaining a policy of good relations with immediate neighbours.

On balance, despite the criticisms of Balewa's conservative policies and his failure to assert Nigeria's rightful role as an independent country and the leader of Africa, which are oblivious of the inexperience of the regime and the divided domestic terrain,[4] most of the so-called guiding principles of foreign policy in the post-independence period were established under the First Republic. These were principally the commitment to the total liberation and development of Africa, a largely pro-Western orientation despite non-alignment, and the defence of Nigeria's core interests.

---

[4] Divisions within the regions, especially opposition from the predominantly Muslim Northern region, long prevented Nigeria from opening diplomatic ties with Israel.

3

THE FIRST PHASE OF MILITARY RULE, 1966-1979

THE CHARACTER AND CONTEXT OF MILITARY INTERVENTION AND RULE

The post-independence political history of Nigeria has largely been one of military intervention in politics as well as the modes and consequences of this intervention: coups, counter-coups, a civil war and military governance. The military ruled the country for twenty-seven of the thirty-six years covered in this study, and did much to shape the political, economic and social formations of the post-independence period. It is as such that the military phenomenon has been central to analyses of Nigerian politics. But in spite of being deeply embedded in the country's political process, military intervention and rule are regarded even by military leaders themselves – as both an aberration and a key indicator of political instability. This perception underlies the problem-solving, stability-restoring and nation-saving roles assumed by so-called 'corrective' military regimes.

Typically, the military intervenes to 'save' the country from collapse, disintegration and economic mismanagement where civilian regimes are overthrown or, in the case of military regimes, from misdirection. Either way, therefore, the military has carved for itself the role of *saviour* and *guardian* of the nation, and has indeed been invited to play this role by vocal sections of the aggrieved public during periods of serious national crisis, such as those which marked the collapse of the First Republic and which followed the annulment of the 12 June 1993 presidential election.

These contexts define military 'interregnum' as a (necessary) stopgap or fire-brigade measure which is not expected to last longer than the period it takes to set things right, after which state power should be handed over to the civilians. The notion of impermanence, Hutchful (1986) says, is central to the legitimacy of 'corrective' military governments. So is commitment to what are called in Nigeria transition-to-civil rule programmes. The underlying premise of transition programmes is that instability-generating issues have to be dealt with before power

54

can be handed over to civilians (how else could military intervention be justified?). A transition programme typically involved attempts to resolve critical issues of democratic stability such as the party system, a census, revenue allocation, the creation of more states, public sector representativeness, and how, through constitution-making and other institutional processes, to assure access to state power for all groups. Military regimes which did not have a transition programme or failed to carry through their transitions (Ironsi, Gowon, Buhari, Babangida) provided a justification for their own later overthrow.

The flaw in the foregoing way of looking at military intervention in general is that it assumes neutrality, altruism and nationalism on the part of the military. These assumptions fly in the face of personal ambition, professional and institutional interests, as well as partisan considerations which attend military interventions. For example, programmes for transition to civilian rule have sometimes been aimed more at prolonging the life of military regimes than at the stated objective, which is to reform the polity. In Nigeria every military regime with the exception of Buhari's engaged in one form of transition or another, but the Mohammed/Obasanjo regime was so far the only one that successfully handed over power to civilians. The other point is that the military is not insulated from the political cleavages which afflict the larger society: 'It is impossible for military men, who are part and parcel of the society, to be entirely unaffected by or unconcerned with politics' (Adekanye, 1989a: 188). This often makes military intervention and rule the continuation of politics by military means.

In the case of Nigeria, apart from specific calls for military intervention, the politicisation of the institution made an apolitical military intervention unlikely. There were two major sources of politicisation. First was concern with the representativeness of the institution whose initial composition was lopsided, due largely to the 'warrior tribe' policy pursued by colonial authorities and disparities in socioeconomic opportunities available to different groups (Miners, 1971; Adekanye, 1979; 1989b). By 1966, for example, Middle-Belt minorities – Angas, Birom, Idoma, Igbirra and Tiv – accounted for 60 per cent of the soldiers and officers from the North, and 40 per cent of the entire Nigerian army (Adekanye, 1989a: 189). Increasing concern among members of the political class over the potential political roles of the military, given the trends in developing countries, led to the introduction of the quota system of recruitment (and later promotion) to the non-commissioned ranks in 1958 and the officer corps in 1961. This had 'the inherent tendency of dragging [soldiers] willy-nilly into the acute political controversies or conflicts raging in the wider society' (Adekanye, 1989a: 190). The second source of politicisation was the political uses to which the military was put in times of peace, which gave the soldiers a measure of political effectiveness. In the First Republic the use of soldiers to quell the Tiv riots, to man and provide essential services during the workers' general strike of 1964, and the struggle between Azikiwe and Balewa to secure support of the military all suggested an important political role for the military.

This underlying character of the military's intervention and rule – namely their interface with political society provides the conceptual lights for analysis of military rule in this book. We elaborate further on the character of military intervention and rule in Chapters 5, 6 and 7. This chapter is concerned with the first phase of military rule which spanned thirteen unbroken and eventful years, 1966-79. There were three military governments in this period: General Ironsi's, which lasted only seven months, January-July 1966; General Gowon's, which lasted nine years, 1966-75, punctuated by the three-year civil war (1967-70); and the government of Generals Mohammed/Obasanjo, which lasted from 1975 till 1979 when it voluntarily handed over state power to a civilian democratic regime. Analysis of the first phase now follows.

THE IRONSI REGIME

On the morning of 15 January 1966, the 'five majors' – as Major Kaduna Nzeogwu and his colleagues Majors E. Ifeajuna, D. Okafor, C.I. Anuforo and A. Ademoyega,[1] who planned and executed the coup came to be known – struck. The lingering crisis which followed the violent elections of 1964-5 provided the immediate grounds for the intervention by the young, idealistic officers who wanted to 'stamp out tribalism, nepotism and regionalism' and fight the enemies of progress – the ten percenters, homosexuals, feudal lords and so on. But bad planning, sabotage and lapses in execution made the bloody coup only partly successful in the Northern region, where Major Nzeogwu himself was in charge; in Lagos and the Western region it was also partly successful to the extent that the prime minister and some ministers, as well as the premier of the Western region and top military officers were assassinated; in the East and Mid-West the arrest of the premiers (quickly followed by their release) was

---

[1] Other key actors in the coup were Majors I.H. Chukuka and T. Onwuatuegwu, Captains E.N. Nwobosi, Oji and Gbulie, and Lieutenants N.S. Wokocha, B.O.O. Oyewole, Azubuogu and Ojukwu.

the only evidence of the coup. In effect the coup was not successful, but since the leaders of the federal, Northern and Western regional governments had all been killed, it plunged the country into a deep crisis. The coup also led to a temporary split within the army between Southern and Northern formations.

Under the circumstances, it was easy for General Aguiyi-Ironsi, general officer commanding the Nigerian army whose links to the coup remain a matter of speculation,[2] to 'persuade' what was left of the federal cabinet to hand over the reins of power to him. In his inaugural speech on 16 January, Ironsi alluded to this 'voluntary' transfer of power, and to the temporary nature of his government:

'The military Government of the Republic of Nigeria wishes to state that it has taken over the *interim* administration of the Republic of Nigeria following the *invitation* of the Council of ministers of the last Government for the army to do so.' (emphasis added)

He referred to the political disturbances and crisis of confidence which rocked party politics and posed a threat to the nation which, by implication, necessitated the coup, and stated the purpose of his government as 'maintaining law and order ... and essential services ... until such a time when a constitution is brought out [*sic*] according to the wishes of the people'. The regime also committed itself to a corrective agenda, which included preservation of the unity of the nation, eradicating regionalism, tribalism, corruption and dishonesty in public life, and accelerating economic development. In pursuit of some of these objectives, it issued decree 33 which prohibited eighty-one political parties (most of these were actually interest groups) and twenty-six tribal and cultural organisations, and instituted commissions of inquiry into major parastatals – the Electricity Corporation of Nigeria, Nigeria Railway Corporation and Nigerian Ports Authority – and the 'corrupt' Lagos City Council.

The regime also set up transitional study groups to examine and make recommendations on problematic areas of national life: on economic planning and national unity; on restructuring of the public service; and on constitutional review. The last study group, which indicated the likelihood of a return of power to civilians was asked,

---

[2] Why, for example, was he not killed like other senior officers, mostly of Northern origin? There are popular accounts of how he managed to escape the killing squads in Lagos, but official sources released subsequently suggested that he was party to the coup. It was assumed that his movement of the commanders of the five army battalions to ensure that four of those outside the Eastern region were controlled by Igbo officers on the eve of the coup was meant to facilitate its success.

among other things, to examine factors which militated against national unity and the emergence of a strong centre. Although the committee never really got started on its task before Ironsi took the impolitic step of abrogating the federal system (see below), its terms of reference, especially those which required it to examine how the centre could be made stronger than the regions, were, according to Gboyega (1979: 238), merely an indication of Ironsi's preferences which crystallised in the unitary system he later introduced. Finally, the regime established the parameters of military government which were followed by subsequent regimes. The most important of these was Decree 1 (Constitution, Suspension and Modification Decree) which vested executive and legislative powers in the federation in the hands of the head of state, and in the hands of military governors in the regions. The decree also established the supremacy of military decrees which could not be challenged in courts of law – the so-called ouster clauses.

The coup and subsequent military take-over of government were at first welcomed all over the country – there had been calls for the military to intervene at the height of the crisis of 1964-5. But this welcome was quickly replaced by apprehension, resentment and then hostility in the Northern region, where the leaders began to read anti-Northern motives and attempts at Igbo domination in the take-over. (By contrast, although there was apprehension over possible Igbo domination in the Western region, UPGA supporters were at least satisfied with the ouster of the unpopular NNDP regime led by the slain Premier, Ladoke Akintola – especially as Colonel Adekunle Fajuyi, who was appointed regional governor, was known to have UPGA sympathies).

The ethnic interpretation of the coup was reinforced by several factors. First was the pattern of killings of political leaders and military officers. With the exception of Lt.-Col. Arthur Chinyelu Unegbe, quartermaster general of the army, who was Igbo, all the senior military officers killed were Northerners and Westerners.[3] Furthermore, none of the political leaders killed was Igbo; while the Northern and Western regional premiers were assassinated, the two Igbo premiers – of the Eastern and Mid-Western regions – were spared. The North suffered the greatest losses with the killing of its two most powerful politicians, Premier Sir Ahmadu Bello and federal Prime Minister

---

[3] Those killed included Brigadier S.A. Ademulegun (Westerner), commander first brigade, Kaduna; Brigadier Z. Maimalari (Northerner), commander second brigade, Lagos; Colonel K. Mohammed (Northerner), chief of staff at army headquarters; Colonel R.A. Shodeinde (Westerner), deputy commandant, NDA, Kaduna; Lt. Col. Y. Pam (Northerner), adjutant-general at army headquarters, Lagos; and Major S. Adegoke, (Westerner) deputy adjutant and quarter-master general, first brigade, Kaduna.

Tafawa Balewa, and its leading military officers. Accounts by some of the surviving major actors in the coup deny ethnic considerations in execution (cf. Ademoyega, 1981; Gbulie, 1981), but Northern accounts insist on anti-Northern motives (Mainasra, 1982; Muffett, 1982; Mohammed and Haruna, 1979). The second factor had to do with the actions of Igbos in the North, who carried on with an exuberant air of conquest. Posters appeared in Kaduna showing Nzeogwu standing over a fallen Ahmadu Bello. Third was the ethnic interpretation of the military take-over through the networks of the British Broadcasting Corporation (BBC), whose Hausa service enjoyed wide patronage in Northern Nigeria. The fourth, and perhaps most important of all, had to do with the actions of the Ironsi regime itself, which seemed to confirm the suspicion of an Eastern-Igbo agenda to dominate the country. It is these actions which ultimately led to the overthrow of Ironsi in a bloody counter-coup.

Being the country's first military leader with no precedents to learn from, General Ironsi was said to have been too politically naive and inexperienced (and, perhaps, also too military) to respond properly to the exigencies of the crisis situation in which he found himself. His rather simplistic perception of national unity is a case in point. On the other hand, he probably also acted in furtherance of a contradictory but overriding agenda to enthrone Igbo hegemony, something which the NCNC had failed to do on the open political battlefield – in which case, his was the continuation of an Igbo political agenda by other means. It is reasonable to assume that the two factors combined explain what he did and failed to do (how else does one explain the contradiction of a general pursuing an anti-Northern agenda while at the same time surrounding himself with Northern personal security staff?).

First, he failed to put Major Nzeogwu and his collaborators on trial, as was demanded by sections of the army (the Supreme Military Council [SMC] actually took a decision to try the officers in May 1966). Secondly, the promotion of Igbo officers was accelerated – he is said to have promoted twenty-one officers, eighteen of them Igbo, to the rank of colonel against SMC advice (Mohammed and Haruna, 1979: 28) – and effected postings that placed Igbo officers in charge of strategic command positions. Thirdly, he surrounded himself with a caucus of Igbo bureaucrats and intelligentsia. Fourthly, and most fatal of all, he abrogated Nigeria's federal system: by Decree no. 34 of May 24 1966 the country ceased to be a federation, and the regions were thenceforth to be called 'Groups of Provinces'. In the administrative restructuring which followed, regional public services were abolished, and there was now to be one public service for the entire country. The provisions of Decree 34 were 'provisional', pending the outcome of the work of the study group on constitutional review (why could the decision not wait until the group had completed its job?). But Gboyega (1979: 239) points out that, at the same time, 'the meetings of the Supreme Military Council and Federal Executive Council preceding the announcement of these measures had also approved the outline of a 25-year "perspective development plan" and a 5-year "medium term plan" '. This implied that the changes were unlikely to be provisional.

These sweeping changes were consistent with Ironsi's persistent argument that a military government could not pretend to be run federally (it should be noted that right from when he took over power, he deliberately avoided referring to his government as 'federal military government' or 'federal government'; rather it was called 'military government of the Republic of Nigeria'). They were also consistent with his avowed commitment to 'national unity' and a strong centre. According to him, Decree 34 was meant to remove 'the last vestige of intense regionalism, and to produce that cohesion in government structure which is so necessary in achieving and maintaining the paramount objective of the National Military Government...national unity' (cited in Elaigwu, 1991).

But all this failed to impress the already apprehensive Northern elites for whom federalism was, and remains, a device to protect differences and ensure that each segment of the country progresses at its own pace. Northern students and academics in Ahmadu Bello University and public servants spearheaded the violent demonstrations and riots which greeted the promulgation of the decree in the North. For two months the riots continued, involving the massacres of Igbos in the North and the destruction of their property. While General Ironsi was at Ibadan to open a conference of traditional rulers, a group of Northern soldiers abducted and killed both him and his host, the military governor of the West, Col. Adekunle Fajuyi.

This was the culmination of a revenge coup planned mostly by Northern NCOs and a few officers, including the then Major Murtala Mohammed and Captain T.Y. Danjuma. The coup had been in the offing since the January coup that brought Ironsi to power. The main objective was to avenge the deaths of the Northern officers killed in January. This was achieved as, besides Ironsi and Fajuyi, only one of the ten officers whose deaths were officially announced was not an Igbo-Easterner.[4] Other than the revenge killings, there

---

[4] The ten were Lt. Col. I.C. Okoro, commanding officer, 3rd battalion, Kaduna; Lt.-Col. G. Okonweze, garrison commander, Abeokuta; Major T. Nzegwu, air force staff officer; Major B. Nnamani, company commander, 2nd battalion; Major C.C. Emelifonwu, quarter-

was no clear-cut plan to take over power; in fact many of those who executed 'Operation Araba' (literally, secession) as the counter-coup was code-named, favoured the secession of the Northern region from the federation, and had embarked on the repatriation of their families from the South to the North. Under the circumstances, discipline was difficult to enforce, as was manifest in the inability of Brigadier Ogundipe, the most senior ranking army officer, to assume control. It took the intervention of the British high commissioner, Francis Cumming- Bruce, as well as the US ambassador, Elbert Matthews, to convince the Northern secessionist officers to drop their plans. For three critical days while all this was going on, 29-31 July, the country drifted along without a head of state, a situation only (temporarily) brought under control by the assumption of office by the then Lt.-Col. Yakubu Gowon who announced on 1 August that he had been brought to 'shoulder the great responsibilities of this country and the armed forces, with the consent of the *majority* of the members of the Supreme Military Council' (note emphasis on majority which shows that there was no unanimity within the military on Gowon's accession to the office of head of state).

THE GOWON REGIME

General Yakubu Gowon assumed office at the climax of a deep national crisis. In addition to the unsettled terrain in Lagos and the continuing furore over the abrogation of the federal system, the counter-coup resonated in the Northern region in the form of renewed genocidal killings of Igbos and Easterners. The military governor of the Eastern region, Col. Odumegwu Ojukwu, also refused to accept Gowon's accession to power; he insisted on knowing what had happened to General Ironsi (whose assassination was not officially announced till 14 January 1967!), and that Brigadier Ogundipe, the next most senior officer, should take over the reins of power. Faced with such a complex situation, Gowon was sensible enough to begin tackling it by first trying to sort out the issue of an acceptable political arrangement (or 'national standing', as he called it). Meanwhile, to increase his popular support, he released Chief Obafemi Awolowo and other top politicians who had been in prison or detention since the First Republic or the coup of January 1966. In this inaugural

master-general, 1st battalion, Kaduna; Major J.I. Obienu, inspector of recce, Abeokuta; Major Ibanga Ekanem, provost marshal, Apapa; Major P.C. Obi, Nigerian air force; Major A. Drummond; Major V.A. Ogunro, chief instructor, NDA, Kaduna; and Major O.U. Isong, commanding officer, 1 Recce squadron.

speech, Gowon suspended the unitary decree, arguing that the basis of unity did not exist (this was deliberately misrepresented at the time by Easterners seeking to justify their planned secession to read 'There is no basis for Nigerian unity'!). Soon afterwards, in September, he convened an '*Ad Hoc* Constitutional Conference' at which the regions, including the aggrieved East, were represented by delegations that comprised politicians, academics, lawyers, bureaucrats and traditional rulers. Gowon asked the delegations to rule out either the break-up of the country or a unitary state, and reduced their choices to four: a federal system with a strong centre; a federal system with a weak centre; a confederal system; and an entirely new arrangement peculiar to Nigeria.

The proposals presented by the regional delegations showed the extent to which the country had drifted apart, and was on the brink of disintegration. The Northern and Eastern regional delegations, representing the major protagonists in the crisis, demanded a confederal system in which, among other things, the central government would function as determined by the regions (the Northern region proposed that chairmanship of the central executive council should rotate from year to year among the regions); each region would retain its revenue and contribute equally as others to finance the central government; would have its own army, air force, navy and police; would issue its own currency notes and coins; and would be free to secede from the union.

The Western and Lagos delegations proposed a 'true' federation on the basis of a restructuring of the four regions into eighteen states, and control of the armed forces by the states. If agreement could not be reached on this, they proposed, as an alternative, a 'commonwealth' of Nigeria based on the existing regions each of which would then be completely sovereign in all matters except the few delegated to the central authority. The other details of the proposed commonwealth showed that it was no different from the confederal system favoured by the North and East. By contrast to the foregoing proposals, the Mid-West delegation demanded a federation based on the creation of more states, with a strong centre committed to correcting the injustices of the past and resolving basic conflicts, and in which no state would be allowed to secede. As the only minorities' region and representatives at the conference, the Mid-West was influenced in its position by the historical experience which continually led minorities in Nigeria to favour a strong centre as a guarantee against majority oppression in the regions. Such preferences provided the middle ground which saved the country from breaking up as the majority groups demanded (it probably also helped that Gowon himself was a minority Angas and not from one of the major groups).

By the time the conference adjourned on 3 October 1966,[5] the Northern delegation, after persuasion by the British high commissioner, the US ambassador and federal government officials, retracted its confederal proposals, and favoured not only a federation but also the creation of new states based on consultations with the groups concerned. On these points, it reached agreement with the Lagos, Western and Mid-Western delegations. The Eastern delegation rejected them, arguing that not only was the time not opportune for the creation of new states, but that it was a matter for individual regions to decide. However, Gowon did secure a major political victory: the five regional delegations (including Lagos) unanimously agreed that the country should remain one political entity. This was the 'mandate' that guided him throughout the period of national crisis, especially the civil war that eventually ensued.

But while he made progress on this front, Gowon had serious and irreconcilable problems with Ojukwu's Eastern regional government. The personal conflicts between the two leaders, and Ojukwu's political ambitions were well known, but it was the genocide against Igbos in the Northern region which had gone on since the unitary decree was promulgated in May, and the revenge killings of Eastern officers, including the head of state, in the July counter-coup, that provided the grounds for Ojukwu's secessionist plans. Ojukwu argued that these actions had cast serious doubts on whether the people of Nigeria could ever sincerely live together as members of the same country. Between May and September 1966, an estimated 80-100,000 Easterners were killed and several thousands more wounded in different parts of the North.

By the end of September, Ojukwu concluded that the safety of Easterners living outside the region could no longer be guaranteed, and asked them to return home. He also asked non-Easterners to leave the region. This order, combined with the revenge massacres of Northerners in Port Harcourt, Enugu and other Eastern cities, led to a counter-exodus of non-Easterners from the region. Secessionist sentiments and feelings grew strong among Igbo elites, and pressure mounted on Ojukwu to act. It is necessary to stress that although secession was proposed in the name of the Eastern region, it was primarily an Igbo affair. Minorities had also tended to suffer the same fate as the Igbos in the Northern massacres and some of their

[5] The *Ad Hoc* Conference could not reconvene because of the deterioration in relations between the federal and Eastern regional governments, and the resumption of killings of Easterners in the North.

leaders supported secession, but the fear of Igbo domination and the desire to be free from Igbo control influenced their half-hearted and reluctant involvement in the war that later ensued. The decision by Gowon to carve out separate states for them in May 1967 strengthened their resolve to be free. The story of secession and civil war is also the story of the persecution of the minorities by the 'Biafrans', who accused them of supporting the federal side.

From October 1966, relations between the Eastern government and the federal government/Northern region deteriorated rapidly, and all attempts to find a solution failed as Ojukwu insisted that neither he nor any other representative of the Eastern region any longer felt safe attending meetings outside his region. This was the background to the 'peace summit' of the Supreme Military Council held in Aburi, Ghana, on 4-5 January 1967 under the auspices of the military government in Ghana. The meeting was partly successful in that it afforded the opportunity for Gowon, Ojukwu and other military and police leaders to meet in a collegial though tense atmosphere for the first time since the counter-coup of July, and it was possible for the Eastern region (and other regions as well) to join issues and reach agreement on how to allay mutual fears and distrust, and keep the country together.

Whatever gains were made at Aburi vanished soon afterwards, following fundamental differences in the interpretations of the agreements reached by the federal government on the one hand and the Eastern regional government on the other. While Ojukwu argued that the agreements in effect established a confederal system which, among other things, allowed each region to have its own military formation, to keep its revenue and to secede if it chose to, the federal government believed that they upheld federation, and in particular reiterated the supremacy of the Supreme Military Council on matters affecting the whole country. The federal government subsequently promulgated decree 8 which embodied its interpretation. Ojukwu promptly rejected the decree and proceeded to implement his own interpretation which suited the secession agenda. 'On Aburi we stand' became the motto of Eastern secessionists.

In March Ojukwu announced the take over, from 1 April, of all federal departments and parastatals in the Eastern region by the regional government and the witholding of all federal taxes and revenue in the region. The federal government responded by declaring the actions illegal and unconstitutional and later suspended port operations in the region and postal services and Nigeria Airways flights to and from it, and imposed various economic sanctions. Several last-minute efforts were made to prevent the imminent civil war. Most notable were the efforts of the conciliation committee composed of eminent persons like Chief Justice Adetokunboh Ademola, Chief Obafemi Awolowo and Chief Jereton Mariere. These leaders managed to get Ojukwu to repeal three edicts he promulgated based on his interpretation of the Aburi agreements – on revenue allocation, legal education and the court of appeal – which would virtually make the Eastern region autonomous, on condition that the federal military government would lift the embargo on foreign exchange transactions and communications imposed on the East. But while the federal government agreed to do this, and actually announced a lifting of the embargo, Ojukwu failed to reciprocate.

THE CIVIL WAR

On 27 May the decision of the Eastern regional consultative assembly mandating Ojukwu to declare as soon as practicable an independent state to be called the 'Republic of Biafra' was announced. Gowon's response, in a broadcast to the nation later that day, was to declare a state of emergency throughout the federation, create twelve new states (including three from the East, apparently to divide the region and weaken support for secession especially by the Calabar-Ogoja Rivers minorities) to replace the regions, and (re)impose economic sanctions against the Eastern region. He concluded the broadcast with the statement that the federal government was prepared to 'fight to keep Nigeria one':

'If it were possible for us to avoid chaos and civil war merely by drifting apart as some people claim, that easy choice may have been taken. But we know that to take such a course will quickly lead to the disintegration of the existing regions in condition of chaos and to disastrous foreign interference.'

The die was cast. In a dawn broadcast on 30 May, Lt.-Col. Odumegwu Ojukwu proclaimed what had long been in the offing: the 'Independent Republic of Biafra'. The federal government declared this a rebellion and promised to crush it. Fighting broke out between federal and Biafran forces on 6 July 1967, with Gowon ordering 'police action' in a war which he and other top federal military officers believed would not last long. The civil war turned out to be protracted, and raged on for thirty months largely because of foreign involvement and support for Biafra. Stremlau (1977) reminds us that with only 10 million pounds in foreign reserve, Ojukwu could not have waged a war for as long as he did without external support. French supplies of arms, which averaged 300 tons per week in September-October

1968, gave the life-line to a practically defeated Biafra. External support also neutralised the devastating effect of the decision by the federal government to change currency notes at the height of the war in January 1968.

The external support and sympathy obtained by Biafra was partly the result of campaigns by relief organizations like Oxfam, the Red Cross and Caritas, which had pro-Biafra sympathies. But it was more the result of a well organised and effective propaganda machinery which was handled internally by the 'Biafra Directorate of Propaganda' headed by Uche Chukwumerije (who in the 1990s became federal minister for information under the Babangida administration), and coordinated externally by the Geneva-based Mark Press. The war was presented as a genocidal one waged by the Muslims of Northern Nigeria who had declared a *jihad* to exterminate Igbos from the face of the earth (the massacres of Igbos in the North, as well as the strategies of economic blockade and starvation pursued throughout the war, seemed to lend credence to this). In Italy, for example, pro-Biafra sympathies were strong, and Ojukwu protested in letters to the Pope and the prime minister over the sale of arms by 'Catholic' Italy to Muslim Northern Nigeria to be used in killing the 'Catholic' Igbos of Eastern Nigeria. Thus,

> The Italians were made to believe that Col. Ojukwu's secession attempt ... represented the manifestation of 'the very progressive, intelligent, Westernized and hard working Roman Catholic Igbos' to live their own existence in peace and prosperity, free from domination and annihilation by the 'backward Hausa/Fulani Moslems of the North'. Not a few Italians often saw a parallel between Nigeria and the Sudan where the Christians of the south were in conflict with the Muslims of the north. (Garba, 1989: 291, 293)

The same picture was painted by the Igbos, and had more or less the same effect, all over the world.

The issues in, and story of, the Nigerian civil war – including detailed accounts of the battles on various fronts and efforts by the OAU, the Commonwealth, the United Nations and other members of the international community to broker peace – has been well documented in several sources (cf. St Jorre, 1972; Kirk-Greene, 1971; Nzimiro, 1979; Obasanjo, 1981; Tamuno, 1984, 1989), and will not detain us here. But the war had important implications and consequences for post-independence politics. First, the international context within which the war was fought produced a mix of forces which led to fundamental changes in Nigeria's foreign policy. It led to improved relations with the Soviet bloc and a review of relations with Britain, the rest of the Western bloc and African countries. To this extent the civil war marked a watershed in the development of Nigerian foreign policy.

However, the major consequences of the war were internal to the country, and mostly to do with inter-group relations. First, although the main protagonists in the war were 'Northerners' and the federal government on the one hand and Igbos-Easterners on the other, and actual fighting was restricted more or less to the Eastern region, all groups in the country were involved. The patterns of involvement generally followed those that had been established since colonial times, with minorities being the spearheads of the fight to save the federation. As we have seen, the Mid-West delegation to the ad hoc constitutional conference of 1966 was unequivocal in its support for the continuation of the federation.

Powerful Southern minority top bureaucrats – or super-permanent secretaries, as they were called: notably Allison Ayida, Ime Ebong and P.C. Asiodu – used their positions of vantage as Gowon's chief advisers and confidants to work for a strong centre. Also, federal delegations at the various peace meetings during the war contained key minority leaders – Anthony Enahoro, Okoi Arikpo, Joseph Tarka and the super-permanent secretaries. The creation of twelve states – which greatly favoured the minorities, as the states demanded by them since the 1950s were finally created – brought them firmly to the federal side, as Gowon had calculated. In particular, by dividing the Eastern region into three states and creating two – Rivers and South-Eastern states – for minorities in the region, the federal government undercut Eastern solidarity, and this accelerated Biafra's collapse.

Hopes for a 'Southern' united front which were brightened by talk before the war broke out by Yoruba leaders, notably Awolowo, to follow the example of Biafria if it 'was allowed' to secede were quickly dashed as soon as the war began. Efforts made by Biafran leaders to reach out to the Yorubas came to nought. The religious card of Southern Christian solidarity was played without success (the fact that Islam is not really a minority religion among the Yorubas was seemingly not reckoned with). An even more painful and costly move to Biafra, in that it gave federal troops time to recoup, was the delay of the advance of Biafra troops who had overrun the Mid-West and were heading for Lagos at Ore, by Colonel Victor Banjo, himself a Yoruba and Biafran by choice, for the purpose of striking a deal with Yoruba leaders.

Many Igbos felt betrayed by the failure of the Yorubas to support their cause, which in one sense was in the interest of the whole 'South' (perhaps the only notable exception was Wole Soyinka, who was detained by Gowon throughout the period of the war for his pro-Biafra position). This and the fact that Yorubas then joined the federal side – and, in particular, the role Awolowo was perceived to have played as federal commissioner for finance and vice-chairman of cabinet in the defeat of Biafra – continue to have an adverse effect an Igbo-Yoruba relations in the country. In the Second Republic elections some of Awolowo's worst results were in the Igbo-speaking states, and efforts to forge a viable political coalition to challenge the Northern-based NPN failed. The reluctance of Igbos to support the Yoruba-led struggle to 'actualise' the annulled 12 June 1993 election which was won by M.K.O. Abiola, a Yoruba, also had a streak of 'vengeance'.

But by far the most serious consequence of the war for Igbos was their marginalisation in post-war military regimes. This, as many Igbo leaders believed, was why they lagged behind the other ethnic majority groups. For example, it explained why their demands for more states were ignored for a long time. But a more serious problem, given the persistence of military governments, was Igbo 'under-representation' in the armed forces. Although some middle-ranking officers of Igbo origin who ostensibly did not play active roles in the secession bid were re-absorbed into the army (with loss of service seniority) to join a few others who remained on the federal side during the war, there was a dearth of senior Igbo officers in the post-war period. Some Igbo leaders also alleged that there was an official policy to limit the recruitment of Igbos into the army. For example, Arthur Nwankwo, one of the leaders of the Eastern Mandate Union, referred to the patterns of intake into the Nigerian Defence Academy regular courses nos. 29 and 31: of 153 entrants for course no. 29, forty-nine were Hausa/Fulani, forty Yorubas and only thirteen Igbo; similarly, of 172 entrants in course no. 31 only fourteen were Igbo, while Hausa/Fulani and Yorubas were seventy-two and thirty-one respectively (*Newswatch*, 12 September 1994: 26). However, beginning with the Babangida regime, during which Ebitu Ukiwe, an Igbo, served briefly as chief of the general staff, the lot of Igbos in military regimes gradually improved. Beginning with retired Major-General Ike Nwachukwu, a few Igbos were promoted to major-general and equivalent ranks in other services, and Rear-Admiral Allison Madueke served briefly as chief of naval staff under Abacha. But, in general, Igbos continued to allege marginalisation in the 'federal power equation' (cf. Igbokwe, 1995).

POST-WAR DEVELOPMENTS

On 12 January 1970 the civil war ended with the announcement of the surrender of Biafra by Lt.-Col. Phillip Effiong, to whom Ojukwu handed over a virtually vanquished 'Republic' when he fled to Ivory Coast the day before. The devastation of the war was enormous. In economic terms, although the exact costs of the war remain unknown, Chief Awolowo, then federal commissioner of finance, estimated them to be 230.8 million pounds in local currency and 70.8 million pounds in foreign exchange. The war also affected revenue from oil (the oil fields and refineries were concentrated in the East): this dropped from US$257 million in 1966 to US$164 million in 1968. Overall value added in oil and mining fell from 38 per cent in 1966 to a mere 8 per cent in 1969 (Mohammed and Haruna, 1979).

The number of deaths, mostly of Easterners, was estimated at between 1 and 3 million, while another 3 million became displaced persons and refugees. The Eastern economy was in ruins, with infrastructure and utilities destroyed and severe shortages of shelter, food, clothing and medicine. Gowon took the reconciliatory step of declaring an amnesty for all who had fought for Biafra (disproving the last-gasp propaganda by Biafran leaders that genocide awaited Biafrans at the end of the war), saying there was no 'victor' or 'vanquished' from the 'war of brothers'. The federal government embarked on a vigorous policy of reintegration and rehabilitation built around the 'three Rs' – Reconstruction, Rehabilitation, Reconciliation. The result of all this was an amazing recovery within a very short time, although the oil boom which the country enjoyed right after the war aided the recovery process. Perhaps the only issue of reconciliation and reintegration of Easterners on which Gowon was not forthcoming was that of the so-called 'abandoned' properties, that is properties left behind by displaced Easterners, many of which had been taken over by wartime owners. The issue was finally dealt with, albeit in a manner unsatisfactory to the Easterners, by the Mohammed regime which in February 1976 announced a N14 million grant to state governments to pay five years' arrears of rent to certified owners. The federal and state governments acquired some of the properties for their use, and the remaining ones were sold to indigenes of the states where they were located.

THE TRANSITION THAT NEVER WAS

With the war over, the Gowon regime had to tackle other serious and urgent matters that were pending. Chief among these was the question of return to civil rule – in fact, while the war raged on, there were calls on the regime to hand over power to civilians. Jakande (1979) points to the *Nigerian Tribune* editorial of 19 March

1969 which demanded a return to civilian rule while the military 'concentrated all its human and other material resources on winning the war'. For this he, as editor of the newspaper, was detained for seventeen days. Shortly after the war, Gowon indicated that he would hand over power to civilians within two years. This was later amended when, in his 1 October independence anniversary broadcast, he announced that it would be done in 1976. He issued a nine-point programme for transition to civilian rule which outlined the major issues and problems to be resolved before it would be realised: census, a system for revenue allocation, a new constitution, the organization of genuinely national as opposed to regional political parties, the creation of states, eradication of corruption, implementation of the 1970-4 National Development Plan (later extended to 1976), reorganisation of the armed forces including demobilisation of soldiers whose number had swelled from about 10,000 before the war to about 250,000 at its end and finally elections at state and federal levels.

The promise of a return to civilian rule generated considerable excitement among old and aspiring politicians, though some – like Chief Awolowo, who resigned from the Federal Executive Council in anticipation of an early return – preferred a shorter transition. The excitement increased from 1972, when the ban on politics was partly lifted to enable discussion of what form a new constitution should take. Gowon and the intellectuals who surrounded him, including the 'super-permanent secretaries',[6] toyed with the idea of a military-led one-party system with a civilianised Gowon continuing as head of state. This proposal was defended in 1973 by Allison Ayida, one of the most influential super-permanent secretaries, on the grounds that the military could no longer be left out of governance:

> 'Nigeria no longer has a ceremonial army. We are building a large modern army of well trained, self-conscious and intelligent young men who will not be content to be relegated to the barracks ... The military leadership in the new set up is of necessity obliged to conceive an interventionist role for itself. The constitutional settlement must take into account this new and crucial factor.' (Ayida, cited in Dudley, 1982: 96)

Another proposal which generated considerable debate, and was well

---

[6] Dudley (1982: 90) underlines the influential role of super-permanent secretaries in the Gowon regime by pointing to the high dependence on them by Gowon: 'Over the monitoring of the *ad hoc* constitutional conference, the Aburi meeting and its aftermath, the division of the country into twelve states, and the initial moves towards mobilization for the civil war, it was the top bureaucrats who defined the political position for Gowon.'

received by top-ranking military officers, was Azikiwe's for a diarchy, which involved power sharing between military and civilian leaders. Although the debate was stymied by the failure of Gowon to energise the process of constitution–making, it is unlikely that a one-party system, least of all one led by the military, could have been adopted except by imposition. For one thing, Chief Awolowo and other politicians were already making moves and renewing political contacts all over the country preparatory to forming new parties, and for another, there was increasing impatience with the military. However, the failure to embark on writing a new constitution, which was one of the key items on the transition agenda, prevented the matter from ever getting beyond the level of debate.

With the exception of the National Development Plan and the reconstruction of war-damaged areas which proceeded relatively well, Gowon failed to deliver on most other items on the transition agenda or, where he did, resolution of the problems was at best tentative. Let us examine some of the issues and steps taken to deal with them. First, there was revenue allocation. The Dina Commission was set up in 1970, among other things to review the existing system and make recommendations on how to make it better and more acceptable. In its report the Dina Commission rejected the historical approach to revenue allocation as a constitutional exercise and instead sought to establish it as an instrument of development planning and national integration. This approach emphasised the centrality of the federal government in this area by giving it jurisdiction over disbursements of the expanded Distributable Pool Account (DPA) and all principal taxes and receipts, and increasing its powers over and share of royalties from oil. As for oil revenue, a distinction was made between onshore and offshore oil, which was to be a major blow to oil-producing states in the federation. They were to be precluded from any share in offshore royalties (60 per cent was to be retained by the federal government, 30 per cent to DPA, and 10 per cent to a special contingency account), and were to get 40 per cent less than previously under the principle of derivation from onshore royalties. Other principles of horizontal revenue allocation, i.e. allocation among the states, recommended by the Dina Commission were basic needs, balanced development and a minimum national standard. The commission also recommended the establishment of a permanent national planning and fiscal commission and expansion of the role of the federal government in the social sector to be facilitated by, among other things, a system of grants-in-aid.

Although the report of the commission was rejected, as recommended by a meeting of federal and state commissioners of finance, on the grounds that the commission went beyond its terms of reference, most of the changes in fiscal relations and revenue allocation between 1970 and 1975 were directly derived from it. As Oyediran and Olagunju (1979: 199) put it, 'Dina [was] rejected yet implemented'. The commission's recommendations were apparent in the take over by the federal government of social sector responsibilities which previously belonged to the states, especially in the areas of education and health. In other areas where the federal government did not take over state responsibilities, it used a system of grants-in-aid introduced in 1971 'to encourage states to devote more resources to agriculture, industry, health, education, housing, and water supply' (Phillips, 1991: 105).

Burgeoning federal financial might and centralisation were largely the consequence of the oil boom of the early 1970s which increased federal revenue (see Table 1.1). According to Dudley (1982: 80-1), the revenue rose from 170 million pounds (roughly N340 million at the time) in 1966/7 to N5,514.7 million in 1974/5. The boom encouraged heavy spending on defence and prestige projects, which included financial aid to various African countries. Defence expenditure rose steadily between 1972 and 1975, when it hit N1 billion for the first time, although a large proportion of this went into salaries and administrative costs – in 1972, an average of N17.8 million was spent per month on salaries (Adekanye, 1981). According to Akinyemi (1979), Nigeria gave aid to the following African countries for various purposes: Guinea-Bissau, Cape Verde, São Tomé and Principe, and Mozambique at independence; Mali, Senegal, Upper Volta (later Burkina Faso), Chad, Mauritania, Niger, Ethiopia, Sierra Leone and Somalia for drought and natural disasters; and Niger, Zambia, Sudan, and São Tomé and Principe for other purposes. Total estimated expenditure for the country as a whole rose from N2 billion in the second National Development Plan (1970-4) to N33 billion, later revised to N43 billion in the third development plan (1975-80). As the oil boom was expected to last into the 1980s, the planners of the latter plan footnoted that 'finance is unlikely to be a major problem during the third national development plan period'.

The views of the Dina Commission were also apparent in the changes to revenue allocation outlined in decree 13 of 1970:

(a) The 100 per cent export duties that went to the states of origin was reduced to 60 per cent, while 40 per cent was retained by the federal government; (b) the 100 per cent duty on fuel paid to the states of consumption was reduced to 50 per cent; the balance of 50 per cent went to the federal government; (c) The 50 per cent mining rents and royalties formerly paid to the states of origin were reduced to 45 per cent, while the DPA was credited with 50 per cent and the federal government retained 50 per cent; (d) excise duties were to be divided between the federal government and the DPA; (e) DPA was to be distributed 50 per cent on the basis of equality of all states and 50 per cent proportionately according to the population of each state; [and (f) decree no 9 of 1971 transferred rents and royalties on offshore petroleum from states of origin to the federal government].[7] (Oyediran and Olagunju, 1979: 200-1)

The new structure of revenue allocation had far-reaching implications for the polity. It strengthened the federal government's role as the sole allocative and distributive authority and gave it a domineering fiscal position. In the short run, this was justified, as Emenuga (1993: 85) suggests, on the grounds that the federal government needed more resources to undertake post-war reconstruction. The problem however was that it was the beginning of a trend consistent with the essentially centrist 'military federalism', rather than a short-term device.

The ascendancy of the federal government, it goes without saying, heightened concern and anxiety over its control. The new structure also introduced the problem of inadequate compensation to oil-producing states which were the country's gold mine. As most of these were minorities' states, this was seen as a deliberate design to oppress minorities, especially as the principle of population (which clearly favoured the ethnic majorities) took precedence over that of derivation. This became a highly contentious issue, and took a new turn in the 1990s when the Ogoni, Ijaw, Urhobo and other minorities became more militant and anti-state in demanding adequate compensation. Finally, the new revenue allocation structure encouraged the demand for more states. By allocating revenue to states on the basis of 50 per cent equality and making states more dependent on the federal government for their revenue, the new structure effectively abolished the criterion of viability for states creation which required an aspiring state to possess at least a good measure of fiscal autonomy.

States creation generated much hope and excitement among agitators for new states, but Gowon did not create new states as he had promised to. The twelve states created in 1967 were inspired, among other criteria stated by Gowon, by the need to balance the federation and remove any basis for fears of domination. Indeed the 12-state structure went a long way to allay the two principal fears: minorities'

---

[7] More changes were introduced to the structure of revenue allocation in 1975. These included a further reduction of the 45 per cent of mining rents and royalties due to the states to 20 per cent; and increase in the share of import duties (except on motor spirit, diesel oil, tobacco, wine, spirit and beer, which went to the DPA) retained by the federal government to 65 per cent, and the standardisation of personal income tax throughout the country.

fears of oppression in the old regions and Southern fears of Northern domination. By splitting up the old Northern region and creating an equal number of states from the North and South (six each), the exercise dealt in one fell swoop with the basic structural flaw which created so much tension in the federation. Also, minorities' fears which historically revolved around alleged domination and oppression by the majority groups in the regions were also allayed by the creation of six separate states for them (which, in a way, also ensured majority-minority balance).

In spite of these, there were still unresolved and emergent problems with the creation of states. The circumstances under which the twelve states were created in 1967 did not allow for consultation with the groups concerned – apart from the minorities' states which had long been demanded, other states were created mostly on the advice of the super bureaucrats. In creating twelve states, Gowon had promised that a state delimitation commission would be set up to enable groups not satisfied with the new states to seek redress, but this was not done. Thus the exercise left many questions unasked or unanswered, and many groups dissatisfied. Advocates for the majority groups, for example, saw the minorities as the main beneficiaries of the exercise, and questioned the implicit attempt to make minorities equal to majorities. They accordingly demanded more states for the majorities to reflect the population differences. Then problems emerged from the new state structures, and chief among these were the appearance of new majorities and minorities and new fears of domination. For these reasons Gowon promised to revisit the issue and create more states where necessary. This (and the changes in the revenue allocation structure) heightened the tempo of demands for new states in the post-war period, but no concrete step was taken to address the agitations.

Next was the census issue, which was an explosive one in Nigeria. Population figures were highly controversial because of the political uses to which they were put: determination of representation in the legislature, (under the majoritarian system of the First Republic this was the main determinant of political power); revenue allocation; provision of social services, including siting of parastatals, industries, schools, post offices, electricity, police stations and so on; and determination of the viability of new states. These uses made census a difficult exercise for partisan civilian regimes, as experience of the 1962-3 exercise had shown. It was therefore believed that a 'neutral' military government was in a better position to conduct a census. This belief underlay the census exercise of 1973 (see Adepoju, 1981).[8] Efforts

---

[8] However, Oluleye (1985: 158) believes the exercise was more likely to succeed when

were made to depoliticise the issue through public enlightenment campaigns (in which the technical uses of the census for planning purposes rather than its political dimensions were emphasised). Other precautions taken to ensure a less controversial exercise included ethnic and regional balancing in the composition of the census commission, use of computers to process results, posting of enumeration officers outside their home states, and the deployment of unarmed soldiers to accompany the officers. But these measures did not prevent the controversies which greeted the publication of the provisional results (see Table 3.1).

Table 3.1. 1973 CENSUS PROVISIONAL RETURNS COMPARED WITH 1963 RETURNS (*millions*)

State	1963	1973	+/–
Southern States			
Lagos	1.44	2.47	+1.03
Western	9.49	8.92	−0.52
Mid-Western	2.54	3.24	+0.7
Rivers	1.54	2.23	+0.69
East Central	7.23	8.06	+0.83
South Eastern	3.62	3.46	−0.16
Total	25.86	28.32	+2.52
Northern States			
Benue-Plateau	4.01	5.17	+1.16
Kwara	2.40	?	
North-Western	5.73	8.50	+2.77
North-Central	4.10	6.79	+2.69
Kano	5.77	10.90	+5.13
North-Eastern	7.79	15.38	+7.59
Total	29.80	51.38	+21.58
Grand Total	55.66	79.76	+24.10

Source: Adapted from Campbell (1976: 247).

There was suspicion that the figures were inflated all over the country, but this was not the reason for the controversy they provoked.

conducted by a civilian regime because, as he says, politicians could manage to reach a compromise on the results as they did in 1963. The problem is not one of regime as such but of how to reduce the political sensitivity of the census. In fact, contrary to Oluleye's assumption, a population headcount is more unlikely to succeed in a civilian dispensation because the political uses of population figures are more pronounced.

The main reason was the 'confirmation' of Northern preponderance, which showed an increase from 53.7 per cent in 1963 to 64 per cent. What Southern leaders found unacceptable was the idea that only Northern states recorded major increases. For example, while the three key Northern states showed astronomical increases over 1963 – Kano, from 5.77 million to 10.90 million; North-East, from 7.79 to 15.38 million, and North-West, from 5.73 to 8.50 million – the population of the Yoruba heartland, which had hardly been affected by the violence in 1966/7 declined from 9.49 to 8.92 million.

The figures resurrected old fears of domination and were promptly rejected by Western-Yoruba leaders (including the military Governor of Lagos state), who were now 'protectors' of Southern interests because the Igbos were not in a position to engage in any serious political contest so soon after the war. Gowon explained that the results were only provisional, but the final results were never published. Another reason for the controversy generated by the census was that it was part of a transition to civil rule programme which rekindled old fears and all the political calculations that went into previous exercises. The failure of the census – which was Gowon's barometer for measuring the success of his corrective agenda, especially the aspect of national unity – convinced him that the country had not yet reached the point where stable civilian rule could be guaranteed. The announcement in 1974 that return to civilian rule in 1976 was no longer realistic therefore had much to do with the outcome of the census.

Other transition items were unattended to. Because the state of emergency imposed in 1967 and the ban on political activities were not lifted, no political parties were formed, and there were no elections. Gowon also vacillated over the reorganisation of the armed forces. He carefully avoided demobilisation, a politically loaded issue: for one thing, there were officers who, afraid that a repeat of the ethnic-based wars in the name of coups of 1966 was still possible, resisted postings outside their states or ethnic areas of origin (Oluleye, 1985: 154), and for another, Northern war commanders opposed demobilisation because they believed that it would affect Northern soldiers most (Othman, 1989: 122; Oluleye, 1985: 161). Moreover, the involvement of soldiers in the increasing wave of violent crime, especially armed robbery, that followed the civil war meant that demobilisation had to be handled with caution. Adekanye (1981: 11) believes there was also a moral angle to demobilisation: 'It was unfair and ungrateful of the nation to throw onto the tight job market without adequate preparation, thousands of Nigerians who had sacrificed their lives in the precious war fought to keep Nigeria one.' Whatever Gowon's reasons may have been, he preferred to be silent on the issue of reorganisation and demobilisation, and this heightened tension within the armed forces.

All along, there were doubts about the sincerity of Gowon's promise to hand over power. His prevarication on many transition issues seemed to reinforce these doubts, and his popularity steadily waned, but many still hoped that he would make good his promise. These hopes were dashed when, in his independence anniversary broadcast on 1 October 1974, he announced that the 1976 hand-over date was no longer realistic. He alluded to 'a high degree of sectional politicking and intemperate utterances and writings' which implied that Nigerians had not learnt any lessons from past events. To hand over power under the existing circumstances he said, would, amount to 'a betrayal of trust.'

To pre-empt the anticipated consequences of his decision, Gowon announced some damage-limitation measures. He promised to appoint a panel to draft a new constitution; broaden the scope of civilian participation at the state and federal levels by setting up advisory councils; create more states and release the census results once post-enumeration checks were completed; release all political detainees; continue the fight against corruption; appoint new federal commissioners in January 1974; and reassign his powerful Governors after launching the new (1975-80) development plan. By July 1975, when he was overthrown, only the appointment of new commissioners had been effected. The shock and indignation that followed the abrogation of the hand-over date were such that his overthrow was only a matter of time.

A BALANCE SHEET ON GOWON'S REGIME

Historians are not agreed on how to judge the place of Gowon's regime in Nigeria's history because of the mixed fortunes which made the regime both 'good' and 'bad' (see, for example, Gowon's biography (Elaigwu, 1986)). Thus, despite the palpable shortcomings of his regime, corruption and all, a newspaper editorial still thought Gowon was a good administrator ruined by absolute power:

> Let it be said in fairness to him that General Gowon [was] a sincere and well-meaning man; the creation of twelve states, the indigenization of foreign businesses, and the formation of the Economic Community of West African States are all credits to his administration. But power is delightful and absolute power is absolutely delightful. (*Daily Times* editorial, 2 August 1975)

Gowon took over power at a point when the country was on the brink of collapse, and fought successfully to keep it united. His magnanimity at the end of the civil war and the seriousness of purpose with which his regime tackled the three Rs, which led to the speedy reintegration of Easterners, were gestures of rare statesmanship. The regime pursued the national cohesion project on other fronts, especially at the level of the youths. More 'unity' schools (federal government colleges) were established, with students from all states of the federation on a quota basis. In 1973 the regime introduced the National Youth Service Corps (NYSC) programme, under which graduates of universities and polytechnics (and for a time, graduates of colleges of education) did a compulsory one year of national service outside their states of origin to further national integration. The same year also saw the introduction of the national sports festival, which complemented the national festivals of arts and culture in promoting greater understanding among the various groups in the country.

Gowon was unable to control, much less discipline, his corrupt and powerful governors, commissioners and super-bureaucrats. He is said to have depended on these lieutenants to the point of becoming hostage to them. For example, he retained the services of Joseph Gomwalk, the police officer governor of Benue-Plateau state, after Aper Aku had sworn to alleged corrupt practices on his part, and did not dismiss Joseph Tarka as commissioner despite allegations of corruption by Godwin Daboh – this in defiance of popular demands for the dismissal of these and other functionaries. Meanwhile anti-corruption crusaders like Tai Solarin and Air Iyare were detained without trial.

Gowon also failed to manage the enormous wealth brought by the 'oil boom' of the early 1970s. Rather than invest in the productive sector, he approved stupendous salary increases for public servants (the famous Udoji awards) which brought about steep inflation, and engaged in profligate spending on prestige projects like the second World Black and African Festival of Arts and Culture (FESTAC), which was later scaled down and hosted by the Mohammed-Obasanjo administration. The regime lacked the discipline to curtail the huge appetite among its members for imported luxury and food items, especially the urban dwellers (Gowon was said to have once boasted that Nigeria's problem was not money but how to spend it!). Agriculture, the mainstay of the economy before the boom, was left to decline, as people migrated from the 'squalor' of the villages to the 'Eldorado' of the towns, and a country that once enjoyed a good measure of food security came to depend increasingly on imports. The overall effect of the boom was therefore to discourage expansion of productive capacity – the manufacturing share of GDP decline from 9.4 per cent in 1970 to 7.0 per cent in 1973/4.

Increased revenue from the boom led the federal government to engage in massive infrastructural development (especially of urban roads and highways), a rapid expansion of federal government competence in the social sector, and efforts to indigenise the economy, but the overall effect of the boom on the standard of living of the masses of the people was negligible, especially in the rural areas. Rather, through the indigenisation programme (discussed below) and the expansion of opportunities for 'rent-seeking' (i.e. kickbacks) in the public sector, it was the bourgeoisie – a loose coalition of military officers, bureaucrats, political office holders and commissioned agents of foreign capital – who were the main beneficiaries of the boom. According to Dudley (1982: 116)

> ...with no constituents to conciliate and no electorate to be accountable to ... the effect of the oil boom was to convert the military political decision-makers and their bureaucratic aides into a new property-owning, rentier class working in close and direct collaboration with foreign business interests with the sole aim of expropriating the surpluses derived from oil for their private and personal benefit.

The poor management of the economy under Gowon extended to congestion in the ports and acute scarcity of petrol (in an oil-rich country) which characterised the final months of the regime.

THE MOHAMMED/OBASANJO REGIME

We begin this section with a necessary conceptual clarification. The Mohammed/Obasanjo regime involved two heads of state – General Murtala Mohammed (July 1975-February 1976) and General Olusegun Obasanjo (February 1976-October 1979) – but it was essentially a continuous regime. When it came to power following the overthrow of Gowon, Mohammed was head of state and Obasanjo his deputy (chief of staff supreme headquarters). After Mohammed was assassinated in an abortive coup in February 1976, Obasanjo succeeded him, retained the same structures and key members of the administration, and faithfully stuck to the agenda of the regime outlined in the transition to civil rule programme. Because of this continuity the administrations of the two heads of state are treated here as one regime rather than two.

The bloodless coup that brought General Mohammed to power was planned and executed by a group of officers mostly of the rank of lieutenant-colonel and colonel, notably Col. Joseph Garba, who as commander of the brigade of guards was Gowon's chief of security (he made the broadcast announcing the coup), and Lt.-Col. Musa Yar'Adua who became chief of staff supreme headquarters after the assassination of Mohammed. The coup was welcomed throughout the country as people had become disenchanted with the increasing ineptitude of the Gowon regime. Its bloodless execution was hailed as indicating the 'maturity' of the military, as if military coups had become another form of party politics. A newspaper editorial even went as far as to say that 'The swiftness of the latest change in our government gives us cause to be proud' (*New Nigerian*, 1 August, 1975).

Intra-military problems and factionalisation were believed to be the main reasons for the coup. These had to do with resentment against Gowon on the part of the too powerful governors, dissatisfaction of war-time commanders who felt left out of the administration of the country and hounded by Gowon and his supportive generals (Othman, 1989), and increased opposition to Gowon's policies and appointments from then Brigadier Mohammed, who was clearly Gowon's main adversary. This explains why 'Strategic military and political posts went to officers who had brought Gowon to power, fought in the civil war, were Mohammed's proteges, and also organised Gowon's removal' (Othman, 1989: 125). Othman also suggests that there was a streak of Northern nationalism that held together the key figures of the new regime, a point which came to the fore after Mohammed's assasination in 1976 (see below).

The coup was nevertheless presented as having been aimed at restoring the 'dignity' of the military which had been badly rocked by the corrupt Gowon regime, and putting the so-called corrective mission of the military back on course. In his maiden broadcast to the nation, Mohammed gave the background to the 'inevitable' change:

> 'After the civil war, the affairs of state, hitherto a collective responsibility, became characterized by lack of consultations, indecision, indiscipline and even neglect. Indeed the public at large became disillusioned and disappointed by these developments. *The trend was clearly incompatible with the philosophy and image of our corrective regime.* [...] Things got to a stage where the head of the administration became virtually inaccessible ... and when advice was tendered it was often ignored. [...] The nation was thus plunged inexorably into chaos. It was obvious that matters could not ... be allowed to continue in this matter.' (*Daily Times*, 30 July 1975 – emphasis added)

The remedial and corrective mission explains why 'untainted' officers with a reputation for professional commitment and moral uprightness were the first choice as members of the new government. However, this has to be qualified since Mohammed himself had supported Northern secession and actually led the group of secessionists following the 29 July 1966 coup. But he still enjoyed wide respect and confidence in the army, and had the reputation of being a bold and fearless officer, the kind many felt was what the country needed at the time. He acquitted himself creditably well during his short period as head of state, thereby transforming himself from 'a secessionist to a Nigerian patriot' (Elaigwu, 1991: 138).

To gain popular support, the regime sought to distance itself as much as possible from the Gowon regime. It compulsorily retired General Gowon himself and other generals in the armed forces, the Inspector-General of police and his deputy, and military governors, and dismissed all federal and state civilian commissioners. The structure of the federal military government was reorganised into three organs, namely the Supreme Military Council which remained the highest legislative and executive body; the Council of States, a new subordinate organ composed of state governors; and the Federal Executive Council.

One of the objectives of this reorganisation was to stop the practice of state governors being members of the Supreme Council, which was believed to have made those in Gowon's administration too powerful. The principle of posting officers to states other than their own as governors was also partly aimed at this end. Bureaucrats were also excluded from these bodies except when specifically invited to attend meetings, ostensibly to prevent the re-emergence of Gowon's super bureaucrats. The need for intellectual input which these bureaucrats supplied under Gowon nevertheless led to the creation of a cabinet office political department, which became a powerful policy think-tank. Young and innovative technocrats and academics including Yaya Abubakar, Gidado Idris, Babagana Kingibe, Tunji Olagunju and Patrick Cole, most of whom, according to Othman (1989: 126), had firm links with the Kaduna mafia, were appointed to this body.

The regime embarked on structural reforms in other areas, aimed at underlining the centralisation of power in the federation, and the extension of state control over civil society. The federal government took over control of universities, and created six new ones bringing the number to twelve. Primary education, previously a state matter, was also brought under federal control. Government control of the press was tightened. In addition to bringing all television and radio broadcasting under federal control, the regime established the News Agency of Nigeria and bought controlling share holdings in the country's two largest newspapers, the *Daily Times* and *New Nigerian*. The regime also created the National Security Organization (NSO) which 'was supposed to be the "watchdog" of public "security" but [became] the "para-political" organ of the Mohammed/Obasanjo administration, geared more to the intimidation of ... alleged critics of the administration than to ensuring the "security" of the nation' (Dudley, 1982: 103). Its 'reforms' also extended to labour unions. It reorganised the unions, numbering over 250, into eight organisations under the umbrella national union, the Nigerian Trade Union Congress (later called Nigeria Labour Congress). This reorganisation made it possible for government to monitor the unions more closely and manipulate them when necessary. Finally, panels were instituted to investigate, among other things, the issue of abandoned properties (discussed below), the operation of the indigenisation decree, and revenue allocation.

The regime took decisive steps on issues over which the Gowon regime proved too weak to act. The controversial 1973 census was cancelled, and for purposes of planning the 1963 figures were to continue in use. The regime promised to address the question of creating more states for which the Irikefe panel was set up, as well as the suitability of Lagos to continue as the federal capital because of its congestion; for this the Aguda Panel was set up. The third national development plan was to be reviewed, and a reorganisation was to be carried out, including demobilisation of the armed forces. By 1979, over 50,000 officers and soldiers had been demobilised. The anchor for all this, which also became the rallying point of the regime's dynamism, was the transition to civil rule programme to which we return shortly.

The regime next turned its corrective lenses on 'cleansing' the public sector and society at large of corruption and other ills. Panels set up to probe former state governors and top government officials found massive corruption, mostly involving embezzlement of public funds; this resulted in the seizure of hundreds of ill-gotten assets all over the country, their value estimated at over N10 million. Next, more than 10,000 public officers of all cadres were compulsorily retired or dismissed from the civil service, the judiciary, the armed forces, the police, the universities, parastatals, media organisations and other government departments and agencies. Similar retrenchments or 'purges', as they were called, were carried out in the states. The objective was not to rationalise the public service but to rid them of 'deadwoods', as corrupt officials were called, and their like.

Thus criteria for retrenchment ranged from old age, absenteeism and drunkenness to fraud and corrupt practices, although the exercise was accompanied by many personal vendettas and animosities. The 'great purge', which lasted from August to 21 November when it was formally ended, enjoyed popular acclaim and made people 'sit up', but the subsequent decline of civil service morale, productivity and efficiency has been attributed to the purges of 1975-6 which marked the end of the security of tenure and *esprit de corps* previously enjoyed by civil servants (cf. Asiodu, 1979). It is also uncertain how the purge was expected to check corruption, since the vast majority of those retrenched were people from the lower rungs – messengers, cleaners, drivers, clerks and such like – whose share in the corrupt practices of the past was nowhere near that of their bosses who recommended them for retrenchment.

The cleansing process also extended to the creation of anti-corruption and public morality and protector institutions, notably the Assets Investigation Panel, Corrupt Practices Investigation Bureau and Public Complaints Commission (Ombudsman). To complement these and 'lead by example', public officers, including the head of state and members of the Supreme Military Council, were directed to declare their assets – of which those owned in excess of legitimate earnings were to be forfeited to the state. The new government also encouraged a 'low profile' orientation to counteract the profligate ostentation which the oil boom era had made a way of life. As part of the new orientation (and to demonstrate transparency and accessibility), the head of state decided to do away with the elaborate security paraphernalia of the Gowon era – a decision that was to cost him his life.

These largely *ad hoc* and unsustained measures were insufficient to change the fundamental social antecedents of prebendalism and corruption, and in any case did not prevent corruption. Even the head of state was accused of under-declaring his assets, for which Obarogie Ohonbamu, the radical University of Lagos lecturer who made the allegation, was put in detention. Instances like this, reminiscent of the Daboh-Tarka affair, led the government to issue the Public Officers (Protection against False Accusation) Decree (1976) which made it an offence for anyone to propagate false allegations of corruption against any member of the Supreme Military Council, National Council of States and Federal Executive Council (this was a precedent to the widely criticised Decree 4 of the Buhari regime). Notwithstanding these shortcomings, the corrective measures at least suggested a new direction in social relations and public sector behaviour, with important implications for the incoming politicians of the Second Republic. The dramatic departure from the Gowon days made the new orientation appear significant, and Nigerians responded positively to the 'dawn of a new era'.

The Mohammed administration moved quickly to consolidate its popularity. Even before the new government had had a chance to settle down, demands were made by politicians and the press for an early return to civilian rule, with some calling for a return to the October 1976 date originally promised by Gowon. Chief Awolowo, whose preparations for a re-entry to party politics were cut short by Gowon's turnaround, called for a lifting of the ban on political activities in October 1975 and the hand-over to civilians in 1977. He warned: 'A date longer than this would arouse deep suspicion and detract from the goodwill which the military now enjoys among our people', and urged the regime to refrain from engaging in 'the massive and never-ending task of rebuilding or reconstructing our body politic' (Awolowo, cited in Oyediran, 1981: 8). Obviously commitment to a recivilianisation programme was necessary for the regime's legitimacy, and a prolonged transition would require justification. These considerations informed the regime's programme for a four-year transition to civilian rules which was announced on 1 October 1975. Specific dates and deadlines were attached to the items on the transition agenda, and the precision with which these were approached buoyed up confidence in the process and support for it. The timetable of the five-phase transition programme is presented in Table 3.2.

Table 3.2. TIMETABLE FOR TRANSITION TO CIVILIAN RULE, 1975-79

Programmes

Phase I	Creation and establishment of new states *(August 1975-April 1976)*
	Constitution drafting (October 1975-September 1976)
Phase II	Local Government reorganisation, reforms and elections; Constitutional Assembly to deliberate on draft constitution (September 1976-October 1978)
Phase III	Electoral constituency delimitation; lifting of the ban on political party activities (October 1978)
Phase IV	Holding of legislative and executive elections at state level
Phase V	Holding of legislative and executive elections at the federal level; handing over of power by 1 October 1979

Source: Adekanye (Adekson), 1979: 220.

The transition timetable was strictly adhered to. On August 9, a panel headed by Mr Justice Ayo Irikefe (later Chief Justice of the federation) was inaugurated to study and make recommendations on the question of states creation (other members of the panel were A.D. Yahaya, S.D. Lar, C. Audifferen, Brigadier G.G. Ally, and

P.D. Cole, who served as secretary). Based on the memoranda submitted to it by various groups demanding states (there were demands for at least thirty-two new states), and evidence collected from a tour of the country, the Irikefe Panel recommended the creation of new states, on the basis of which, with some modifications,[9] the federal government increased the number of states to nineteen on 3 February 1976 (see Table 3.3). Only seven old states were retained with minor boundary adjustments (Lagos, Kano, Kwara, Rivers, North Central renamed Kaduna, Mid-West (Bendel), and South Eastern (Cross River). It was decided that, 'to erase memories of past political ties and emotional attachments', states should no longer have names which bore reference to regional divisions, and so the nineteen states were named after rivers and other historical landmarks of the area. A boundary adjustment commission was set up to look into inter-state boundary disputes identified by the Irikefe Panel.

Table 3.3. THE 1976 STATES CREATION EXERCISE

12-state structure, 1967	*19-state structure, 1976*
Lagos	Lagos
Western	Ogun
	Ondo
	Oyo
Mid-Western	Bendel
South-Eastern	Cross-River
East-Central	Anambra
	Imo
Rivers	Rivers
Kwara	Kwara
Benue-Plateau	Benue
	Plateau
North-Eastern	Borno
	Bauchi
	Gongola
North-Western	Sokoto Niger
Kano	Kano
North-Central	Kaduna

[9] For example, the panel recommended that Ijebu and Abeokuta provinces be merged with Lagos, but instead a separate Ogun state was created for these provinces. It is widely believed that Obasanjo, an indigene of Abeokuta, was behind this. Also the recommendation that Borgu and Igala divisions be separated from Kwara state and merged with Niger and Benue states respectively was rejected, although this was eventually done in 1991.

The report of the Irikefe Panel had important implications and consequences in later years for the states in question. In recommending that more states be created, the panel pointed to one factor which 'outweighed' all others, namely that political stability could not be guaranteed if this was not done. In its articulation of the principles for states creation – even development, bringing government nearer to the people, minimising minority problems (though it rejected the ethnic criterion for creating states), a balanced federation – the report marked a final departure from a federal system in which states were to have a relatively autonomous role as centres of development to one in which states were peripheries of the centre and functioned as administrative agents and distribution outlets for federal resources. This diluted the viability criterion which had kept down the number of states in the past and ensured a measure of fiscal autonomy for existing ones. The demonstrable effect of this development was the phenomenal rise in demand for new states as various groups struggled to maximise their shares of the 'national cake'. In other words, the question of states, like party politics and the census, became a continuation of 'warring' politics. The Igbos were to argue later that a situation where they had only two states (Imo and Anambra) from the 1976 exercise while Yorubas and Hausa/Fulani, the other majority groups, had about five each, was unjust and unacceptable. Indeed, after the Irikefe report, states creation was no longer simply a response to minorities' problems, but a contest among majority groups struggling to square up. Not to be outdone, tiny minority groups also demanded new states for the same reasons. By 1982 the total number of new states demanded reached an unprecedented fifty-eight. Underlying these demands were the constitutive interests of members of the privileged classes, for whom states creation had become an avenue for multiplying rent seeking and other prebendalist accumulation opportunities (cf. Ekekwe, 1986). Thus, although General Mohammed announced that the nineteen states were the 'last' to be created, and that his administration would not reopen the state's question, this did no more than shelve the problem; it was far from being resolved.

The next item was constitution-making. On 4 October 1975 a fifty-member Constitution Drafting Committee (CDC) was set up to 'produce an initial draft of a constitutional arrangement which would provide a sound basis for the continuing existence of a united Nigeria'. The composition of the all-male committee reflected a technicist rather than political approach: with the exception of a few politicians – Chief Awolowo (who declined to serve on the grounds of not having been consulted before his appointment), Aminu Kano, Richard Akinjide, K.O. Mbadiwe, Sule Gaya and I.I. Murphy – membership, which was 'representative' of the states (at least two persons were appointed to represent each one), was drawn from professions and academic disciplines relevant to constitution-making (political science, law, history, economics) and from the ranks of administrators with relevant experience. It was headed by Chief Rotimi Williams, the renowned constitutional lawyer who had earlier been appointed to head the constitution review committee under Ironsi.

At the inauguration of the committee, General Mohammed outlined certain 'principles' reflecting the regime's views on how to ensure political and democratic stability through constitutional engineering. Broadly, the regime was committed to a federal system of government, a free democratic political system guaranteeing human rights, and the creation of viable political institutions to ensure maximum political participation, consensus and orderly succession to power. The head of state pointed to the requirements of democratic stability, which were informed by the need to avoid the pitfalls of the First Republic:

1. elimination of 'cut-throat' political competition based on a system of winner-takes-all;
2. discouragement of institutionalised opposition to the government in power, and encouragement of consensus politics and government based on a community of interests;
3. decentralisation of power;
4. establishment of the principle of public accountability;
5. free and fair elections; and
6. depoliticisation of the census.

To meet these requirements of stability, the constitution makers were asked to consider embodying the following in the constitution:

1. the formation of genuine and truly national political parties whose number, because of the harmful effects of a proliferation of parties, could be limited according to criteria to be determined (if the CDC found some means by which government could be organized without the involvement of political parties, it should make it recommendation accordingly);
2. an executive presidential system of government in which the president and vice-president were elected and brought into office in a manner that reflected the 'federal character' of the country;
3. an independent judiciary, guaranteed by appropriate constitutional provisions as well as the establishment of institutions like the judicial service commission;
4. the institutionalisation of corrective organs like the corrupt practices tribunal and public complaints bureau; and

5. restriction on the number of further states to be created.

The CDC's final draft constitution embodied these points, though Dudley (1982: 129), who was himself a member of the committee, says this was more because of a 'coincidence' of views than because the parameters set by the military 'dictated' the provisions of the draft. This may well have been the case because the head of state's speech at the CDC's inauguration could have been written by one or more members of the committee, as is often the case in Nigeria.

THE ASSASSINATION OF GENERAL MOHAMMED

On 13 February 1976 General Mohammed was killed in an unsuccessful coup organised by a group of officers mostly from the Middle Belt, which called itself the 'young revolutionaries', led by Col. Bukar S. Dimka.[10] The (alleged) motives for the coup were mixed. It was said to have originated from intra-military institutional problems and involved the grudges of certain officers in the army over promotion, and opposition to the appointment of General T.Y. Danjuma as army chief of staff. The coup plotters allegedly planned to assassinate most of the generals and top officers connected with the regime in addition to the head of state. This was the part of the coup that implicated the then commissioner for defence, General I.D. Bisalla, who was allegedly incensed not only by the promotion over him of his former course mates Mohammed and Obasanjo and his junior Danjuma, but was also said to nurse the ambition of becoming head of state.

A second motive was the possible restoration of General Gowon, who was at the time a student at Warwick University in England, as head of state. Investigations later revealed that Dimka met Gowon in London, that most officers (including retired police officer Joseph Gomwalk, governor of the former Benue-Plateau state under Gowon) involved in the coup were from the same Middle Belt as Gowon, and that Dimka himself and civilians involved were related to the Gowon family, and these facts were cited as evidence of Gowon's complicity.[11] However, entreaties made to the British authorities to

---

[10] Others killed were Lt. Tunde Akinsehinwa, Mohammed's aide-de-camp, and his driver and orderly, who were all caught in the ambush on the head of state's unescorted car in a traffic hold-up, and Col. Ibrahim Taiwo, military governor of Kwara state.

[11] Dimka's elder brother, who was the Kwara state police commissioner at the time, was married to Gowon's elder sister; Abdulkarim Zakari, the only civilian executed, who worked at the then Nigerian Broadcasting Corporation and provided the martial music tapes used for the coup broadcast, was Gowon's wife's elder brother.

get Gowon extradited from Britain to face trial along with other arrested officers were turned down. Although Gowon denied any knowledge of the coup, his retirement was meanwhile promptly changed to dismissal from the army.

Yet a third motive related to the complicity of Western powers – the United States and Britain were specifically mentioned – which did not approve of Mohammed's radical or 'communist' inclinations. The United States was still licking its wounds from the diplomatic battle it lost to Nigeria over Mohammed's support for the Marxist Agosthino Neto's MPLA in Angola, which it saw as a dangerous indication of a possible challenge to its strategic interests in Southern Africa. Suspected foreign power complicity was reinforced by Col. Dimka's visit to the British high commission in Lagos, allegedly to arrange for the return of Gowon to take over power. Although the involvement of any Western power could not be proved, Nigerians strongly believed that the American and British were guilty, and demonstrators attacked the embassy and high commission of the two countries.

The coup and assassination of General Mohammed, whose short period as head of state was hailed as the best in the country's history, were strongly condemned by Nigerians. There were demonstrations especially by university students who, even before the outcome of the coup was known, had taken to the streets in solidarity with the Mohammed regime. Following the assassination, General Olusegun Obasanjo, chief of staff at supreme headquarters, became head of state – by his account, against his personal wish and desire (Obasanjo, 1990), while Lt.-Col. Shehu Yar'Adua, commissioner for transport, and one of the core plotters in the coup which overthrew Gowon, was promoted to brigadier and appointed to Obasanjo's former No. 2 position. The unprecedented accelerated promotion of Yar'Adua and his appointment to the *de facto* position of deputy head of state were meant to pacify the Kaduna mafia and powerful Hausa/Fulani Sultan, Emirs and other leaders who felt strongly about Mohammed's assassination and its implications for the locus of political power in the country. Indeed, it took visits to the North by General Obasanjo to reassure the Hausa/Fulani leaders that their interests were still well protected, and for the tension generated by Mohammed's assassination to subside. The extreme caution taken by Obasanjo not to offend Northern (Hausa/Fulani) interests, is believed to have made him something of a 'hostage' head of state whose degree of freedom was limited.

Over fifty officers were tried by a military tribunal headed by General Emmanuel Abisoye (its other members were Adamu Suleiman, deputy inspector-general of police, Navy Captain Olufemi Olumide, and Lt.-Cols M.I. Vatsa, M. Mohammed and J. Dogonyaro). Thirty-two of these, including Major-General I.D. Bisalla, were found guilty and executed on 11 March. Seven others, including Col. Dimka, were executed on 15 May. Other guilty officers and men were sentenced to life imprisonment.

RETURN TO TRANSITION

In his inaugural broadcast as head of state, General Obasanjo promised to continue with policies laid down by the Supreme Military Council under General Mohammed. At the heart of this, of course, was the transition programme. The CDC completed its task – the work of the committee and its various sub-committees is well documented in two volumes of *Reports of the Constitution Drafting Committee* (FGN, 1976; also see Mohammadu and Haruna, 1989) – and submitted a final draft of the constitution to the head of state n 14 September 1976. The main recommendations of the CDC, most of which were embodied in the 1979 Constitution, are analysed in the next chapter.

Next, a Constituent Assembly (CA), headed by a supreme court judge, Mr Justice Udo Udoma, was inaugurated to consider, amend and ratify the draft constitution. Of the Assembly members 190 were elected as state representatives based on local government areas as constituencies, twenty were nominated by the federal government to represent special interests including students and labour, and chairmen of the various CDC sub-committees were co-opted. Deliberations in the CA, as a more politically partisan and representative body, were more controversial than those in the more technical CDC – all the more because of the partisan views of the political associations and alliances forged in the CA in anticipation of the ban of politics being lifted (Omoruyi, 1989).[12] Controversial issues which generated heated debates in the Assembly included revenue allocation, the establishment of a federal *Sharia* court of appeal, age requirements and limits for political office-holders, a rotational presidency, the scope of the executive president's powers, freedom of the press, and creation of states.

Of these the most controversial and the one which brought the

---

[12] Thus the importance of the CA in the transition process was not restricted to the production of a final constitution. It also provided a forum for the formation and consolidation of political alliances and coalitions (which shaped positions taken on most issues) around which political parties were later formed. Although this was not one of the roles spelt out for the assembly, it helped to fill a vacuum in the process of party formation created by the continued ban on political party activities.

Assembly to a halt was the *Sharia* issue (cf. Laitin, 1982). The draft constitution (s. 184) made provision for a federal court of appeal with appellate jurisdiction on matters of Islamic personal law, which Muslims, especially from the Northern parts of the country which had *Sharia* courts, had demanded for some time. The anti-*Sharia* group in the CA, a loose coalition of Southern and Middle-Belt Christians, moved to expunge this provision, which created a deep division within the Assembly and led to a walk-out by ninety-two members of the pro-*Sharia* group on 5 April 1978. It took the personal intervention of the head of state to get the Assembly working again. The provision in the draft constitution was expunged, but a compromise clause, worked out by a special sub-committee of the Assembly headed by the late Simeon Adebo, which allowed three judges versed in Muslim law to sit in appeal cases referred from state *Sharia* courts was finally adopted.

Notwithstanding the controversies that rocked its proceedings, the CA completed its assignment in record time, and submitted a 'clean' copy of the constitution to the head of state on 29 August 1978. The Supreme Military Council further deliberated on the new constitution, and amended, added or deleted some clauses. These included the removal of capital expenditure from the consolidated fund; deletion of the clause on admission of another state or part of another state as part of Nigeria, which was said to be at variance with the country's foreign policy; extension of the application of the federal character principle to the composition of the officer corps of the armed forces; and use of Hausa, Igbo and Yoruba as additional languages in the National Assembly. Finally, by Decree 25 of 1978, the 1979 Constitution was enacted.

Long before the constitution-making process was finalised in 1976, the system of local government was reformed. The basic objectives of the reforms were to empower local governments to perform the tasks of modern government at the local level with greater efficiency, and to streamline local government practice in the country. The main points of the reforms, which were outlined in the *Guidelines for Local Government Reform*, included the introduction of a uniform system to replace the different systems which had been practised in the country since colonial times. Local government units were to have populations of between 150,000 and 800,000, and be democratically administered by elected councils. To accommodate traditional leaders who, since colonial times, held sway over local government administration in several parts of the country, especially the North, traditional councils were instituted with purely advisory powers.

The other highlight of the reforms, which became the point of departure for subsequent ones, was the institution of local government as the third tier of government in the federation. This meant that local government was now entitled to revenue allocation and, more important, that it had its own areas of legislative competence, which made it a relevant tier of the federal grid with 'guaranteed' powers. The matters assigned to local government under the reforms were enshrined in the Fourth Schedule of the 1979 Constitution. They included collection of rates, radio and television licenses; markets, motor parks, public conveniences and cemeteries; registration of births and deaths; and refuse disposal. Local governments were also granted 'concurrent' powers with state governments on primary education, agriculture and natural resources, other than exploitation of minerals, and health services, and were to make recommendations to state governments on economic planning. These powers marked a significant departure from the 'boreholes' theory which relegates local government to garbage collection and local taxes (Gboyega, 1987). This development made Nigeria one of the few three-tier federations in the world, though in practice federal and state control and intervention prevented local governments from being the autonomous units they were in theory.

Also in 1976, the Federal Electoral Commission (FEDECO) was established, with Michael Ani as chairman. The commission comprised five federal appointees (including the chairman), and nineteen appointed by the states. The commission conducted the transition elections, which began with the reformed local government elections on a non-party basis, delimited electoral constituencies, and registered political parties according to the criteria laid down in the electoral decree (see next chapter). On the issue of revenue allocation, the Aboyade Technical Committee (named after the renowned professor of economics, Ojetunji Aboyade, who headed the committee) was appointed in 1977. Like the drafting of the constitution, a technicist approach to revenue allocation was apparent in the appointment of professionals to the committee (hence the 'technical' in the title of the committee); this was expected to depoliticize revenue allocation. The committee was asked, among others things, to try and establish a means of ensuring that each government in the federation, including local government, had adequate revenue to discharge its constitutional responsibilities (the correspondence factor) and to balance the imperatives of population, equality, even development, derivation, geographical peculiarities and national interest in allocating revenue among states.

In its report the committee recommended replacing the DPA with a Federation Account. All federally collected revenue (except income tax paid by members of the armed forces, external affairs staff and residents of the Federal Capital Territory) was to be paid into this account and shared among the three tiers of government. The committee recommended the following sharing formula: federal government 57 per cent; state governments 30 per cent; local governments 10 per cent (in addition, state governments were to allocate 10 per cent of their internally generated revenue to their constituent local governments); and special grants account 3 per cent.

Although this sharing formula did not change federal predominance, the committee recommended a return to a more federal structure of revenue allocation that guaranteed greater fiscal responsibility to the constituent units. To this end it recommended the restoration of the constitutional relevance and responsibility of states through the return of their responsibilities taken over by the federal government in the areas of agriculture, housing, primary and secondary education, basic health, youth and sports. For horizontal allocation of revenue the committee suggested the following principles: equality of – and access to – development opportunities, 25 per cent; national minimum standard, 22 per cent; absorptive capacity, 20 per cent; independent revenue and minimum tax effort, 18 per cent; and fiscal efficiency, 15 per cent. For a committee which favoured greater fiscal responsibility and relative autonomy for the states, the de-emphasis on independent revenue generation was something of a contradiction. But this did not matter after all because the committee's recommendations were not accepted by the CA and federal government on the grounds that they were too technical. Nevertheless, aspects of its report, like that of the Dina Commission before it guided revenue allocation in the remaining period of the Obasanjo administration.

There were other notable landmarks of the Obasanjo administration. In May 1976, a nationwide programme called 'Operation Feed the Nation' (OFN) was launched to mobilise the people back to the farms, revive agricultural productivity which had been in rapid decline since independence and especially since the oil boom, and reduce the costly dependence on imported food. The programme, which was a complement to the agricultural development efforts outlined in the third national development plan was one of the earliest responses to the declining economic fortunes of the country. It was a prelude to the austerity measures introduced in the 1977 and 1978 budgets to arrest the escalating balance of payments deficits. OFN was well received, but it was too superficial to address the deep-rooted agricultural and food crisis. For one thing, its main target seemed to be the urban elites and working classes rather than the rural producers, and for another, the programme never really progressed much beyond the impressive launching ceremonies in state capitals. Thus it is not surprising that in 1976-8, when OFN was active, the total estimated area under active cultivation fell from 18.8 million to 11.05 million hectares, while food imports rose from N353.7 million to an astronomical N1 billion (Dudley, 1982: 115).

The regime also reviewed and amended the indigenisation programme following the report of the Industrial Enterprises Panel appointed in November 1975 to assess the programme's implementation (this is discussed below). In 1978 the government issued the controversial land use decree which vested control of land in the state with the main objective of rationalising the country's haphazard land tenure system (the decree was subsequently entrenched in the 1979 Con-stitution). The decree removed the instrument of power and accumulation controlled by traditional leaders, especially in the Southern states, who held land in trust for the community (Francis, 1984).[13] Despite its progressive objectives, which included facilitating government ac-quisition of land for agricultural and other developmental purposes, the decree transferred the rent-seeking opportunities offered by land to state power-holders and gave them an important instrument of control over property relations. It also gave state and local government administrators an instrument for excluding non-indigenes of their states from property ownership, thus defeating one of the very purposes for which it was enacted. It thus had the unintended consequence of strengthening regionalism and statism.

The most serious students crisis up to that point in the country's history also took place in 1978. In November 1976, General Obasanjo had announced the cancellation of tuition fees in all tertiary institutions at the founder's day convocation of the University of Ibadan. An attempt to raise the cost of feeding in the universities, which students saw as inconsistent with the policy of 'affordable' university education, was the immediate cause of the crisis which involved all the twelve universities then existing in the country. Students staged violent demonstrations denouncing government and demanding the resignation of Col. A.A. Ali, the federal commissioner of education (the event is remembered as the 'Ali-must-go' crisis). The government's high-handedness and ill-considered deployment of anti-riot police squads to the universities led to several deaths on the campuses, but the students were unyielding.

---

[13] While in the South land was communally owned, in the North it was vested in the state, though this did not stop traditional leaders there from wielding a strong influence over land allocation and use. The land tenure law of 1962, which was only slightly different from the land and native ordinance of 1910, vested government with the power to hold and administer land for the use and common benefit of natives of Northern Nigeria.

The crisis, in which the students enjoyed widespread public support, got so serious that fears arose over the possibility of its affecting the transition programme or even providing grounds for the overthrow of the regime. The head of state had to cut short a state visit to Eastern Europe and reach a 'truce' with students before the crisis could be resolved. However, the federal government introduced measures to weaken students' union activities, including making membership of student unions voluntary rather than compulsory as previously. For the students, whose national leader Segun Okeowo became a national hero, one important lesson of the crisis was that they had a great role to play in articulating civil society grievances under the military. The rest of that society generally lacked proper and effective organisations and were too closely controlled and repressed to do so. Students subsequently spearheaded revolts against unpopular government policies and actions, and their uprisings often gave the signal for the rest of society to join issues. Gradually strong alliances were built between students, labour, the press, professional associations and various other fledgling civil society organisations. These were the antecedents of the formidable and militant civil society which evolved in the late 1980s.

The rest of 1978 and 1979 were taken up by the final stages of the transition programme. In July military 'administrators' were appointed to replace governors in the states, and as part of the process of military disengagement four military federal commissioners disengaged from 'politics' to return to military duties. On 21 September, the new constitution was signed into law, and the state of emergency which had been in force since May 1967, together with the ban on political activities, was lifted. Within twenty-four hours of the lifting of the ban, the formation of Chief Awolowo's Unity Party of Nigeria (UPN), which had been in the wings since Gowon's botched transition, was announced. Some fifty-five others followed, of which nineteen applied for registration with FEDECO. Ostensibly in accordance with the criteria laid down by the electoral decree, FEDECO registered only five of these parties.

FEDECO then conducted elections into state and federal legislative and executive seats in July-August 1979. The last of these to be held was the presidential election on 11 August and its outcome proved controversial and the subject of legal dispute. Alhaji Shehu Shagari was declared the victor and on 1 October was sworn in as president, simultaneously with the governors in the states. Thus ended thirteen years of military 'interregnum'. The impact of continuous military rule on the political system has been fairly well covered in the literature, and need not detain us here (see Oyediran, 1979;

and Graf, 1988). Suffice it to say that the centralisation of power, which weakened aspects of the country's federal system, was problematic for the civilian regime and was one of the major sources of tension which led to the demise of the Second Republic.

THE ECONOMY IN THE FIRST PHASE OF MILITARY RULE

The crisis of 1966-70, especially the civil war, had serious consequences for the national economy, some already referred to. In particular, it affected the production of crude oil which, from the mid-1960s became a major source of revenue for the federation. 'Oil politics' was indeed at the heart of the civil war, as Biafra's secession was partly encouraged by the promise of wealth from the large oil reserves in its region, and the federal fight to keep the country one was also partly to regain control of the oilfields. Thus the federal war plan revolved around the strategic oilfields located in the minorities' parts of the region that had been carved out as separate states in 1967. The years following the civil war, as we have seen, were devoted to reconstruction of the war-damaged areas. The process was enhanced by the oil boom which marked a turning-point in the post-war economy.

The boom followed a sharp increase in the world market price of light-grade crude oil from US$3.8 per barrel (pb) in October 1973 to US$14.7 pb in January 1974 (by 1981 it reached an all-time high of US$38.77 pb). Total revenue from oil increased correspondingly from N1 billion to N4 billion, and external reserves rose from N180 million to N3.7 billion in 1975. According to the Aboyade committee on revenue allocation, total federal revenue increased from N785 million in 1970/1 to over N6.1 billion in 1976/7. However, dependence on oil and a few other primary export commodities meant that the Nigerian economy was vulnerable to the fluctuations and shocks of the world market. It was partly to mitigate this vulnerability by being able to influence price movements on the world market that Nigeria in 1971 decided to join the organization of Petroleum Exporting Countries (OPEC) which had emerged as a powerful 'third world' cartel (this was after the country had joined Venezuela to play the spoiler role in the 1967 Arab oil embargo). OPEC's policies helped to maintain the high price of crude oil all through the 1970s, although the immediate reason for the oil boom of 1973/4 was the Egyptian-Israeli war of October 1973 and the decision by the Arab countries which dominate OPEC drastically to reduce oil production to force the United States to mediate in the Middle East crisis.

We have already discussed how its increased wealth led the federal

government to start a rapid expansion of the public sector to take
over responsibilities which had previously belonged to the state governments, and to embark on capital-intensive projects. On balance, as
we have seen, while the boom brought an expansion of economic
activity and conspicuous prosperity, its management amounted to a
squandering of riches as the accent was placed on expanding distributive
rather than productive capacity, and on increased dependence on foreign
goods and inputs. The agricultural sector, which retained the greatest
absorptive capacity in the economy, was neglected except for short-lived
and *ad hoc* programmes like the OFN. Between 1975 and 1978
the total area under active cultivation fell from 18.8 million to 11.05
million hectares, while in the same period food imports rose from
US$353.7 million to over N1 billion. The neglect was so serious
that oil palm, rubber and groundnut, for which Nigeria was once
among the world's leading producers, were being imported to offset
local shortfalls. Although the Gowon administration was widely held
responsible for squandering the oil boom, Oluleye (1985: 209ff.) who
was federal commissioner for finance under Mohammed-Obasanjo
points out that the Mohammed-Obasanjo administration was no less
guilty – indeed, as he puts it, the economy could have been saved
if the regime had not persisted in huge indefensible spendings. He
notes that Mohammed in particular had a 'fatalistic' attitude to public
finance, and believes that 'if he had not been plucked early, he
would have successfully run the economy into bankruptcy.' Nevertheless,
the overall performance of the two regimes suggests that the Moha-
mmed/Obasanjo regime had a more disciplined approach to economic
management and was thus able to respond fairly well to the downturn
in the economy in the late 1970s.

The oil sector received especially close attention from successive
military regimes. Under Gowon, there was a review of contract agreements with the oil majors, which gave the country lower rents than
countries like Libya, Saudi Arabia and Venezuela, and the federal
government (through the NNPC) increased its participation to maximise
revenue from oil. This resulted in higher share holdings in oil companies
which, in the case of ELF and Agip, rose from 35 and 33.5 per
cent respectively to 55 per cent, and in more favourable terms for
joint participation, production sharing and risk-service contracts (Panter-
Brick, 1978; Soremekun, 1987: 280-1). This active participation by
the government led it to use the oil sector in later years as a weapon
of foreign policy, as in the nationalisation of Shell-BP over the company's
involvement in South Africa. The central role of oil also led the
federal government to expand its investment in other areas of the
sector. New refineries were built in Warri (1978) and Kaduna (completed

in 1981) to bring the number of refineries to three (the third and oldest was that in Port Harcourt, built in 1965). The Liquified Natural Gas (LNG) project initiated by Shell in 1966 and the early 1970s finally got off the ground in 1976-8, with the formation of the Bonny LNG consortium in which the NNPC had a 69 per cent controlling share in partnership with Phillips, Shell, British Petroleum, Agip and Elf. This project had enormous potential both for increased revenue and diversification of the economy, as Nigeria had the largest deposits of natural gas in Africa, estimated at over 2,400 million cubic metres located with petroleum deposits (less than 20 per cent of the gas was used, with the rest being flared at an estimated loss of over US$4 billion per year). But the LNG initiative collapsed almost as soon as it started, due to the failure to reach agreement with potential European and American distributors.

The federal government also finally managed to make headway in the construction of the iron and steel industry, which had been the subject of inter-regional wrangling and foreign technical partners' *realpolitik* since the late 1950s. In 1979 the construction of the Ajaokuta steel complex, which was designed to produce 5.2 million tonnes of steel annually making it potentially the largest steel mill in Africa, began with Russian technical partners who came to the rescue after several years of fruitless negotiations and partnership with German, American and British firms. In anticipation of the take-off of the project (which remained uncompleted and was in decline by June 1996), the government introduced a middle-level technical manpower training programme under which hundreds of young Nigerians were sent abroad by the government, mainly to East European countries.

With the exception of these attempts at productive investment, the military governments seemed content to let imports flow. For example the manufacturing sector, which seemed to have grown rapidly following the boom, actually benefited from 'tariff manipulations which encouraged the expansion of assembly activities dependent on imported inputs. These activities contributed little to indigenous value added, or to employment, and reduced subsequent industrial growth' (Nafziger, 1992: 184).

But with the overall tendency of almost uncontrolled and ambitious expenditure which increasingly ran ahead of revenue, it was only a matter of time before a shock in the world market would bring the boom to an abrupt end. The Obasanjo regime tried to reverse this tendency through a series of low-profile austerity measures, but because it left the third national development plan intact (it even raised the total expenditure under the plan from N33 billion to N43 billion), pressed ahead with FESTAC and continued with high defence expenditures, these measures proved too feeble. But there was no problem as long as receipts from oil remained high, which they were in the period between 1974 and 1978 when annual receipts averaged N4-5 billion. When the boom burst with the crash in oil prices in 1978, the effects were immediate. Oil production fell from 2.1 million to 1.5 million barrels a day and budget and balance of payments deficits rose sharply – from N259.3 million in 1976 and N656.5 million in 1977.

The Obasanjo administration responded by introducing austerity measures which included import restrictions, foreign exchange controls (foreign exchange tribunals were set up to try offenders), massive cuts in capital and social sector expenditure, and new taxes. The measures also involved the multiplication of bureaucratic controls such as the notorious 'Form M' which was introduced for pre-shipment inspection of certain categories of imports, and the introduction of tax clearance certificates as a requirement for foreign exchange, contracts and other major transactions with government. These of course created a new class of *austerity bourgeoisie*, comprising mostly permanent secretaries and directors in the federal ministries of finance, trade, and industries.

As these failed to arrest the slide,[14] and external reserves were insufficient to meet the costs of implementing the projects in the third national development plan, the government resorted to borrowing US$1 billion dollars from the Euro-American capital market. Oluleye points out that because Nigeria was an oil-producing country, it was precluded by the then EEC from obtaining bilateral loans, and had to settle for the less favourable multilateral ones. Assistance was also sought from Kuwait, Saudi Arabia, Japan and West Germany, with little success. A German consortium, however, managed to raise some loans which were mostly tied to projects like the steel rolling mills in Jos, Osogbo and Katsina, Bauchi Styer Assembly Plant, and projects assisted by the World Bank (Oluleye, 1985). The problem was that the maturity dates of these loans which had floating interest rates were fixed for a time when real interest rates were high and the country's foreign exchange receipts were declining. All of this was done in anticipation of a recovery of oil prices which never came (a momentary recovery in 1979/80 was not enough to reverse the steady economic decline). This is the background to the debt overhang and economic crisis which was the catalyst for the collapse

---

[14] The measures worsened the situation in some ways. For example, smuggling increased phenomenally, although imports fell marginally from N1.2 billion to N950 million in 1979.

of the Second Republic and imperilled the country in the 1980s and 1990s.

Another major theme of the economy during the first phase of military rule was the subordination of the states to the federal government which, contrary to basic federal principles, became the 'master government', the controller of almost all of the country's major resources, and the centre of development on which the states had to depend.

The major factors for this ascendancy included the oil boom which encouraged the federal take-over of responsibilities previously borne by the states, and the centralisation in 1976 of the commodity marketing boards which were a major independent source of regional and, later, state revenue. Other factors were the changes introduced to the structure of revenue allocation which included centralisation of revenue collection, a system of grants-in-aid, federal jurisdiction over major taxes, and a greater share of vertical revenue allocation; and the military organisational principle of centralisation of authority highlighted by Ironsi's unitarist design (it produced the peculiar brand of federalism Elaigwu (1979) has described as 'military federalism').

The national development plans which were coordinated by federal officials provided the major instrumentality for federal take-over of economic development, a process which, as we saw in Chapter 2, began with the 1962-8 Development Plan. The almost complete loss of fiscal autonomy by the states was manifest in the fact that, with the exception of Lagos state and, to some extent, Rivers and Kano states, all states depended on federally-allocated revenue for between 70 and 90 per cent of their revenue needs. This development, and the emphasis on the principle of equality in horizontal allocation, heightened the demands for the creation of more states whose main role came to be seen increasingly as being distribution outlets for federal resources and federal-directed development. The overall effect of all this was an overload of the federal government and consequent decline in efficiency, which was partly why the Aboyade committee called for a de-concentration of powers to the states.

The final aspect of the economy we shall consider was the attempt to 'indigenise' it. The aim was to place 'control' of the economy in the hands of Nigerians, and ensure that they were the main beneficiaries of the country's resources. Indigenisation was one of the main objectives of the second and third national development plans (others included self-reliance and industrialisation). It must be emphasised, as Graf (1988: 56ff) does, that *indigenisation* did not mean *nationalisation* which implies transfer of 'ownership' of the economy from foreigners to nationals (or, as was the case in most African countries, to the state). Rather, it was 'part of an overall programme of elite accumulation within the parameters of the given social order', and involved 'the transformation of the distributive rather than productive sectors of the economy to a different or "higher" level of dependency' (Graf, 1988: 57, 56). As long as foreign capital and technology remained the preferred means of economic development, indigenisation could only mean a process that allowed the Nigerian capitalist class to work out more acceptable terms of 'compradorisation' with its foreign benefactors.

The first phase of the indigenisation programme was introduced by the Gowon regime, which issued the Nigerian Enterprises Promotion Decree in 1972. The decree, came into effect on 1 April 1974 and had two schedules of enterprises. Foreigners were excluded from ownership of, or participation in, the twenty-two types of small-scale and labour-intensive enterprises listed under Schedule I, which included baking of bread and cakes, bottling of alcoholic beverages, assembly of radiograms and television sets, haulage of goods by road, clearing and forwarding, manufacture of singlets, rice milling and tyre retreading. Schedule II, in which foreigners were only allowed no more than 40 per cent of the equity, had thirty-three enterprises which included wholesale distribution, manufacture of cement, bicycles, detergents and soaps, boat building, beer brewing, construction, and printing. In Schedule II, foreign participation was not allowed in enterprises whose paid-up capital was less than N400,000 and/or whose turnover was less than N1 million. Following this, the federal government acquired 40 per cent ownership of the three largest foreign banks. To facilitate access to capital needed by local entrepreneurs to buy shares, the Nigerian Enterprises Promotion Board and the Bank for Commerce and Industry were established. But the programme was sabotaged by foreign investors who acted through their commissioned agents and in collusion with corrupt government officials.

This was one of the major findings of the panel instituted by the Mohammed-Obasanjo regime to investigate the first phase of the indigenisation programme. The panel found that only 314 of about 950 enterprises had fully complied with the provisions of the 1972 decree by 1 July 1975, and that foreign owners were circumventing the decree by appointing Nigerians to front for them, becoming naturalised Nigerians or using other devious means. Following the report of the panel, government revised the indigenisation decree and introduced the second phase of the programme. There were now three schedules of enterprises instead of two, and affected enterprises were given till 31 December 1978 to comply with the provisions of the new decree. To show it meant business, the federal government took over and sold 120 foreign-owned companies for violating Schedule I of the decree.

Under the revised programme, Schedules I and II were enlarged. More than fifty types of enterprise in Schedule I were to continue to be owned 100 per cent by Nigerians. In Schedule II enterprises, the minimum Nigerian equity participation, which included all banks, breweries, department stores/supermarkets, insurance, wholesale distribution and construction, was raised to 60 per cent. The government increased its participation in the three major banks to 60 per cent and pronounced an earlier deadline of 30 September for compliance with the revised rules. Schedule III enterprises, in which Nigerians were to have at least 40 per cent equity participation, were those not listed in Schedules I and II, and were presumably ones (like food processing) in which Nigerians did not have sufficient experience to take over control. The government used this argument to acquire share-holdings in a number of industrial enterprises, including Amalgamated Tin Mines (Nig) Ltd., as a way of checking the practice of fronting.

As part of the revised programme the federal government also undertook to address allegations of ethno-regional and individual dominance of previous indigenisation efforts by ensuring 'a wider and more equitable spread of enterprises ownership'. Most notable of these allegations was that by Northerners and Igbos that Yoruba-Westerners had exploited their predominance in (and control of) the federal bureaucracy and parastatals in the post-civil war period to take over most of the indigenised enterprises. Indeed, the great majority of those who bought shares under the indigenisation programme were concentrated in Lagos, Oyo and Anambra states (70 per cent of the shares were obtained by residents of Lagos) while, by contrast, very few people in the Northern states bought shares – indeed Kano state, whose residents purchased only 1.10 per cent of the shares, had the highest Northern showing (Soyode, 1989). Whatever steps the Obasanjo administration took to redress this and other imbalances had little effect because the same patterns of indigenisation continued – indeed there were allegations that Yoruba predominance increased rather than declined under Obasanjo, himself a Yoruba. The issue of ethno-regional imbalances in government-directed consolidation of elite accumulation was to resurface in the 1980s and 1990s when the federal government implemented a privatisation programme as part of the Structural Adjustment Programme (SAP).

The indigenisation programme nevertheless yielded some dividends. It took retail trading from the Asians and Lebanese, who had formerly dominated the sector, and firmly established it as a sector for Nigerians.

The foreign presence in agriculture was virtually wiped out, as it was in some areas of the financial and service sectors like insurance, media ownership and consultancy. In spite of these, indigenisation, as pointed out earlier, did not mean a transfer of ownership of the economy to Nigerians. According to Ohiorhenuan (1989: 157-8),

.... the focus of [indigenisation] on equity ownership rather than organizational control and the absence of a definite technology policy reinforce the interpretation that, functionally, the indigenization programme merely consolidated and generalized the dependent insertion of the Nigerian economy into the international economy. It seems obvious that the dominance of foreign capital in the Nigerian economy ... cannot be hampered simply ... by channelling it into so-called high technology sectors or by insisting that every foreign investor must involve some Nigerian capital.

The commanding heights of the economy in the distributive, manufacturing (assembly), industrial and oil sectors were still dominated by foreign multinationals. UAC and John Holt and their subsidiaries, 'refurbished' with Nigerian 'control', remained the giants of large-scale retail trade, distribution and soft manufacturing. Even the major banks were still largely controlled by foreign capital, and simply operated as Nigerian subsidiaries of foreign banks. Again, to cite Ohiorhenuan (1989: 158), 'the participation of foreign capital [was] shifted to "technical collaboration". Thus, foreign capital continue[d] to appropriate a substantial part of the surplus produced in Nigeria while having a smaller stake in generating it since its share [was] now regarded as production costs.'

The oil sector, the lynchpin of the economy, was dominated by multinationals – Shell, Agip, Elf, Texaco, Mobil and so on, whose Nigerian operations had government equity participation. Shell, which pioneered oil production from Oloibiri in 1956, together with British Petroleum (BP) its partner till 1979, dominated the oil sector, producing half the total oil output in the 1970s. In 1978 the federal government nationalised BP's 20 per cent share in the oil partnership, partly in retaliation for BP's participation in an oil-swap agreement which led to the 'indirect' shipment of Nigerian oil to South Africa, and partly to pressurise Britain to support the holding of elections in Zimbabwe (then Rhodesia) (Wilmot, 1989). The federal government's equity participation in the oil companies (private Nigerian entrepreneurs were excluded from this sector till the SAP regime of the 1980s and 1990s) was vested in the Nigerian National Petroleum Corporation (NNPC), established in 1971 as the Nigerian National Oil Corporation (NNOC) (this was merged in 1977 with the inspectorate division

of the federal ministry of petroleum resources to become NNPC).
NNPC ran joint venture agreements with all oil companies, though
for most of the 1970s, the agreements governing terms of operation
of the petroleum producing companies were not officially signed (this
was only done in 1984!).

In essence, the Nigerian economy remained the peripheral capitalist
economy it had been at independence. Perhaps the most significant
change in the 1970s was the decline of Britain as Nigeria's major
trading partner. Its export and import shares of Nigerian trade fell
from 70 and 47 per cent respectively at independence to 38 and
32 per cent in 1976. The United States took over as the major
trading partner.

FOREIGN POLICY

Nigerian foreign policy underwent major and sometimes dramatic
transformations during the thirteen years of military rule covered
in this chapter. In general the transformations were part of the efforts
by the military to redeem the country from the failings of the First
Republic. But the changes were not always the result of deliberate
policies. For example, the oil boom of the 1970s, which enabled
the country to pursue more assertive policies and actualise its manifest
destiny, was a matter of circumstance. The same can be said of
the civil war, which marked a turning-point in Nigeria's relations
with Eastern European countries. Be this as it may, successive military
regimes in the period consciously set about asserting Nigeria's position
in the West African sub-region, Africa, and the rest of the world.

By way of an overview, we may summarise the main thrusts
of foreign policy under the three military regimes as a more militant
approach to the liberation of South Africa and other countries under
colonial tutelage, the assertion of Nigeria's role as a black and African
leader, positive neutrality – involving the diversification of relations
to the Eastern countries and a vigorous challenge of Western global
hegemony, and the promotion of regional integration. Compared to
the conservative Balewa regime, the military regimes were more adventurous, pragmatic and populist in their approach, and this meant
less reliance on the legal instrumentalities of international organisations.
The emergence of oil as a major weapon of foreign policy strengthened
this orientation. Another major reason for more adventurous policies,
especially in the post-civil war period, was the relative peace and
unity in the country which modified the effects of the regional cleavages
on foreign policy-making. Otubanjo (1989) has also referred to the
size of the post-civil war army as an important factor. Efforts were

also made to strengthen the structures of foreign policy formulation and management and improve the quality of policies. Thus, in addition to the restructurings at the external affairs ministry, the Nigerian Institute of International Affairs (NIIA) became the think-tank of foreign policy (the National Institute for Policy and Strategic Studies at Kuru also emerged as a major actor in policy formulation). From time to time, foreign policy consultative forums were also set up to review policies. Although these led to a marked improvement in the logic of policies, the policies still suffered from incoherence and discontinuity.

To complete this overview, there were marked differences between each of the three military regimes of the 1960s and 1970s in the tempo of their foreign policy. This had to do partly with the prevailing circumstances and partly with the orientation of the military leaders. Domestic problems did not allow the Ironsi regime to articulate and pursue any serious foreign policy other than to maintain policies inherited from Balewa. According to Ofoegbu (1979: 124), 'The brief six-month period of the first military government illustrated vividly that no state which is extremely disturbed and is unstable at home can be effective in international relations.' Nevertheless, Ironsi stopped the practice of sending regional economic missions overseas, and closed down regional consulates abroad. The political crisis of 1966-70, especially the civil war, made the Gowon regime only a little better than Ironsi at the initial stage, since most external relations hinged on the crisis. However, one of the major gains from the war was closer ties with the Soviet Union, China and other Eastern European countries which came to Nigeria's rescue when Britain and other West European countries refused to sell heavy weapons[15] to the federal government to fight Biafra – this was partly due to the successful propaganda launched by Biafra which presented the war as genocide against the Christian Igbo by the Muslim Northerners. Britain's refusal to play a more supportive role also led the federal government to downplay the relevance of the Commonwealth in its foreign relations. After the war, and thanks to the oil boom, Gowon pursued a vigorous regional and African policy. Finally, the Mohammed/Obasanjo regime took Nigeria's assertiveness to the populist high ground. It pursued the most radical policies of the three regimes, and made the greatest use of the oil weapon in the pursuit of foreign policy objectives.

---

[15] Britain refused to sell heavy field guns, bombs and aircraft to the federal government, but continued to supply light weapons. The federal government then turned to Russia which supplied military hardware from August 1968, and provided technical support to the federal forces.

Let us then examine the nature of foreign policy under the military regimes at three levels: global, African and West African. We shall begin with the African level because almost every policy was anchored on African interests which Nigerian leaders saw the country as leading (this was of course secondary to Nigeria's own national interest where the two clashed). The Africa-centredness of the military regimes was clearly articulated by Ironsi shortly after he came to power:

> 'In the whole sphere of Nigeria's external relations, the government attaches the greatest importance to our African policy. We are aware that because of our population and potentials, the majority of opinion in the civilized world looks up to us to provide responsible leadership in Africa; and we realize that we shall be judged, to a very large extent by the degree of success or failure with which we face up to this challenge which this expectation throws on us. We are convinced that whether in the political, economic or cultural sphere, our destiny lies in our role in the continent of Africa.' (Cited in Gana, 1989: 123)

The liberation of Africa from the last vestiges of colonial and racial domination and the development of the different countries and the continent as a whole were the major pillars of the African policy. For the former, Nigeria's foreign policy was preoccupied with the liberation of South Africa and other Southern African white-ruled territories – Rhodesia (Zimbabwe) and Namibia – as well as of Portuguese-ruled Angola, Mozambique, Guinea-Bissau, São Tomé and Principe, and Cape Verde which were the last colonies on the continent. The international organisations – the UN, the Commonwealth, the OAU, the Non-Aligned Movement – and other international forums remained a major channel for the initiatives on liberation, but bilateral material assistance to liberation movements and other diplomatic channels also grew in importance. Of all the anti-colonial offensives, the liberation of South Africa and the independence of Rhodesia and Angola provoked some of the most radical foreign policy postures in Nigeria's history. On South Africa, Nigeria rapidly moved under Gowon away from dialogue to full support for armed liberation. The support of the South African authorities for Biafra and the active roles of mercenaries from the country in Biafra's army emphasised this shift. The country's overall commitment as well as financial and material support to the liberation movements in South Africa led to its being given the status of an honorary frontline state and the chairmanship of the UN's anti-apartheid committee being reserved for Nigeria's permanent representative in the world body. Nigeria intensified its anti-apartheid campaigns for the imposition of more sanctions on the regime in Pretoria, and its further isolation. The country spearheaded the boycott of international sports meetings, notably Commonwealth and Olympic games, to back these protests. On Rhodesia the Obasanjo administration nationalised the assets of British Petroleum and Barclays Bank in Nigeria in 1978 as a reprisal for the sale of oil to the UDI regime of Ian Smith and this was said to have forced the British government to defer to the demands for an all-party conference which ultimately led to the independence of Zimbabwe.

But it was Nigeria's decision, under the Mohammed/Obasanjo regime, to take on the United States over Angola that was sensational. In the run-up to Angola's independence Nigeria opposed the United States, which supported UNITA and FNLA, by strongly backing the MPLA and mobilising the rest of Africa behind that position. The anti-American crusade, including military and material support to the MPLA and diplomatic shuttles, was estimated to have cost the country over US$20 million. The triumph of the MPLA, which formed the first government of the newly-independent country, was a major defeat for the foreign policy of the United States, especially since Angola was tied in with its strategic Southern Africa interests, and many Nigerians believed the assassination of General Mohammed in the abortive coup led by Col. Dimka to have been linked to US determination to eliminate the threat by Nigeria. The later friendly overtures from the Carter administration, including a state visit in 1978, were in acknowledgement of Nigeria's new 'African superpower' status – which arose not only from the Angolan connection but also from Nigeria's emergence as an oil power.

Nigeria's new-found status as an African leader and champion of anti-imperialism on the continent, especially under the Mohammed/Obasanjo regime, resonated in several other areas of its African policy. This mainly took the form of financial and material support to several countries for a variety of purposes: to assist drought-affected countries like Ethiopia, Chad, Mali and Senegal; to assist newly-independent countries – Cape Verde, São Tomé and Principe, Mozambique, Angola and Zimbabwe; and to Cameroon, Sudan, Zambia, Gambia and other countries for miscellaneous reasons. In addition, technical assistance was offered to Algeria, Botswana, the Gambia, Swaziland and other countries, while scholarships were make available to students from all over the continent. Nigeria was particularly generous to its neighbours, partly to compensate them for their support for the federal government in the civil war and to elicit their support for the country's initiatives on regional integration. It sold oil at concessionary rates to West African countries, although this was also used to 'punish' regimes to which Lagos was opposed, e.g., Rawlings in Ghana in the initial stages of his regime. Other acts of generosity included funding the building of a presidential palace and a petroleum refinery in Lome, Togo; provision of electricity from the Kainji dam to Niger; and the granting of a N2 million interest-free loan to Benin. This was in addition to, among other projects, investing N7.2 million in joint cement and sugar projects and building the N1.8 million Idiroko-Port Novo stretch of the trans-African highway. The bulk of these donations were initiated by the Gowon regime, but one of the consequences of the petro-naira mentality was that financial assistance to African and black countries became an integral part of Nigeria's Africa policy. This was entrenched institutionally by the establishment of the US$80 million Nigeria Trust Fund at the African Development Bank (ADB) from which needy African countries could draw loans on easy terms. Such donations as these, even those which involved investment, were criticised at home as irrational display and squandering of wealth.

At the West African sub-continental level, Nigeria maintained a policy of good neighbourliness and peaceful coexistence. The generous contributions to several countries noted above was a major plank of this policy, as was involvement in the peaceful settlement of disputes between countries and the search for solutions to the protracted Chadian civil war. But by far the most significant landmark of Nigeria's West African policy in this period was the formation of the Economic Community of West African States (ECOWAS) in 1975. Regional integration was aimed amongst others, at consolidating the gains of good neighbourliness and the above-mentioned peaceful coexistence, enhancing the bargaining and competitive capacities of the countries in the sub-region in their dealings with EEC countries and other economic powers, and underlining Nigeria's leadership roles (cf. Edozien and Osagie, 1982). Given the suspicions and envy with which many countries in the sub-region, especially the Francophones which already had formed their own economic communities (the most notable of these was the Communauté Economique de l'Afrique de l'Ouest), regarded Nigeria, the emergence of ECOWAS was scored as a major foreign policy achievement by the Gowon regime. The Mohammed/Obasanjo regime gave more attention to Africa-wide issues, but they also worked to consolidate the gains of ECOWAS.

At the global level, there was, as we have seen, a more positive approach to non-alignment, following the opening of ties with the Soviet Union and other East European countries. There was also an attempt to extend Nigeria's de-linkage from Britain, which had become a competitor in oil protection, by further diversification of trading partnerships. Thus, although it remained the main source of imports and destination of non-oil exports, Britain's share of Nigerian trade declined considerably (the United States became Nigeria's most important trading partner as she bought nearly half of the country's oil export). However, Nigerian-British relations, which had flourished under Gowon despite the problems caused by the civil war, became turbulent under Mohammed/Obasanjo, whose populist and anti-imperialist postures and militant offensives against Rhodesia and the apartheid regime put Nigeria on a collision course with Britain. As we saw earlier, the assets of BP and Barclays Bank were nationalised in 1978 over British violation of sanctions against Rhodesia. Relations went to an all-time low in 1976 when Britain was accused of complicity in the assassination of General Mohammed and refused to extradite General Gowon to face charges over the coup.

The increased de-linkage with Britain was part of Nigeria's emergent radicalism and assertiveness in the world system, whose hallmarks were the efforts to establish its political and economic autonomy, positive non-alignment, and a challenge of US and European hegemony. The attempts to indigenise the domestic economy, stepped up under the Mohammed/Obasanjo regime, were an integral part of the new orientation. Nigeria joined other Third World powers to demand restructuring of the IMF, the World Bank and GATT which perpetuated Western hegemony, and a new world economic order. For these purposes it sought greater collective action by Third World *medium* powers at various forums, including the Non-Aligned Movement and the Group of 77. Nigeria was also instrumental in the formation of the African-Caribbean-Pacific (ACP) group which strengthened the bargaining power of those countries in economic agreements with the EEC. But the major propellant of the country's autonomy-seeking foreign policy initiatives was the oil weapon which was reinforced by membership of OPEC where forces were joined with the powerful Arab states to establish a third force of power play in the international arena. But oil was also the major cause of the decline in the adventurous foreign policy in the late 1970s. The slump in prices, which was attributed to Western conspiracy, and the start of a period of recession forced Nigeria to relink with the capitalist powers on terms dictated by them. This was to be the country's lot in the 1980s and 1990s.

4

THE SECOND REPUBLIC, 1979-1983

CONCEPTUAL NOTES AND BACKGROUND

The Second Republic refers to the second civilian regime in the country, to which the military transferred power on 1 October 1979, and which lasted till 31 December 1983, when it was overthrown by the military. The collapse of the First Republic informed the measures taken to engender democratic stability in the 1975-9 transition programme, but the fact that the Second Republic did not even last as long as the First indicates the inadequacy of the constitutional engineering approach to political stability. This is especially the case where, as in Nigeria, this is given emphasis over more fundamental issues of the social, economic and even political terrain (for a similar argument, see Joseph, 1987). In other words, a 'perfect' constitution may be a necessary factor for democratic stability, but it is not usually enough in itself to create stability.

Much depends on who the operators are and how the constitution is operated, and this is determined by the nature of the political society and by the prevalent social and economic forces. The makers of the 1979 Constitution approached the question of power – the core of politics in the country – from the point of how it should be shared out without seriously addressing the character of the state and why its control is so crucial to the various groups. Similarly, the institutional approach adopted for dealing with regionalism (e.g. the requirement that parties be 'national'), pervasive corruption and 'prebendalism' (the creation of 'corrective' and ombudsman agencies) could not be expected to work well as long as there is a continuation of the underlying social, cultural and economic forces which propel these undesirable tendencies (uneven development, perception of the state as a system of opportunistic accumulation, and the general amorality of the civic public) and make the state's operators generally unable to enforce rules (the so-called soft state). It is in this vein that Adamolekun (1985: 9) attributes the failure of presidential government in the Second Republic to 'serious conflicts and contradictions in the national consensus that was [necessary] to underpin its operation'.

While it is possible to explain the problems of the Republic in these terms, it is another question altogether whether military intervention was the solution. Could not the Republic have been left to continue, in the hope that its maturation process would resolve the problems facing it? This takes us to the supportive perceptions of the roles of the military in politics which help to explain why military intervention was a key feature of Nigerian politics. First, there is the self-appointed 'custodian' role of the military, which was generally accepted by the majority of citizens who, like the military, had a fundamental distrust of, and impatience with, politicians. Thus an element of self-fulfilling prophecy underlay the inevitability of civilian rule failing and the military intervening. Furthermore, the military served as a check on 'bad' civilian rule, implying that civilians could only rule for as long as the military judged them to be doing well.

Secondly, and closely related to this, was the perception of the military as a 'saviour' at times when unpopular and corrupt civilian regimes could not be removed from power through the normal electoral process. In the Second Republic one of the leaders of the National Party of Nigeria (NPN), which by 1983 had become the dominant party, openly boasted that there were only two 'parties' in the country – the NPN and the military. Where dominant parties entrench themselves in power, presumably through manipulation of the electoral process and other strong-arm tactics, aggrieved opposition parties and frustrated critics often 'invite' the military to intervene. This was the case both in the First and Second Republics and in 1993 when the military were seen as alone capable of removing the 'tin gods' from power, and saving the country from the crisis which engulfed it at the time.

Caution is necessary here. We have implied by the term 'military' a corporate, homogeneous institution acting in a collective or hegemonic way. Indeed, soldiers who organise coups usually claim to do so on behalf of the armed forces (exceptions were Dimka who claimed to act on behalf of the revolutionaries, and Orkar who did so on behalf of the Southern and Middle-Belt groups). But this does not detract from the critical questions raised by what are essentially self-appointed and partisan roles:

> Are such self-perceptions and self-definitions generalizable to the military as an institution? Or do they apply to only some critical segments of the military? What is the status of these self-perceptions and self-definitions anyway – are they not subterfuges, *post facto* rationalizations and exculpatory declarations? (Olagunju *et al.* 1993: 48)

There is a threefold answer to these questions. First, at any point in time there are officers and men of the armed forces whose primary concern is their profession and who are not favourably disposed to military governance. Thus, even within the military itself, the question of intervention is a contested one. Secondly, coups and military governments are organised by, and around the interests of, a small number of officers, typically those who are the most politicised or have a high sense of political efficacy. This is clear from the profiles of most officers who have been part of coups and military governments, not only in Nigeria, and the fact that the most ardent among them end up becoming heads of state. Thirdly, some interventions – e.g. the July 1966 counter-coup and the April 1990 Orkar coup – have been propelled by factors emanating from more partisan issues of the larger political society, which have little or nothing to do with the military's corporate interests. What this demonstrates is that the whole notion of 'military' intervention has to be examined more critically if the character and role of military regimes is to be understood. Those who search for the 'logic' of military intervention need to be sensitive to this fact. We shall have more to say on this in subsequent chapters.

So let us return to the demise of the Second Republic, for which the military was responsible. Given the continuous threat of military intervention, one of the pitfalls of the transition to the Republic (and subsequent civilian republics) was the failure to address the fundamentals of military intervention and how to prevent or deal with it. All that was done in the programme for the transition to civilian rule was to 'outlaw' military coups in the draft constitution. That the military leaders at the time deleted this clause from the final constitution showed clearly enough that the Second Republic would last only for as long as the military would let it. Perhaps, then, it is misleading to talk of the 'collapse' or 'failure' of the Second Republic (and indeed the First Republic before its 'termination'), which directs attention to why the military intervened rather than on what went wrong with the Republic(s), may be a better term. It is to underline what went wrong with the Second and First Republics that notions of collapse and failure are used.

There is a vast literature on the Second Republic, with most of the works dealing with the overall life of the Republic, including why it failed (cf. Dudley, 1982; Diamond, 1984; Falola and Ihonvbere, 1985; Adamolekun, 1985; Mohammed & Edoh, 1986; Joseph, 1987; Graf, 1988). There are others which deal with more specific aspects of the Republic like elections (Ollawa, 1981, 1989; Oyediran, 1981, 1983; Joseph, 1981); administration and inter-governmental relations (Ayeni and Soremekun, 1988; Gboyega, 1981; Adamolekun, 1989);

ethnicity (Diamond, 1982, 1983; Ayoade, 1986); federalism (Nwabueze, 1983); and so on. Our analysis of the various aspects of the Republic leans heavily on these works. We begin the chapter by examining the institutional framework of the Republic as defined by the 1979 Constitution, and the major participants in the Republic, the political parties. Next we analyse the 1979 elections and its aftermath. The third section thematically examines the major developments in the Republic, the fourth section the 1983 elections and the overthrow of the Republic, the fifth section the economic situation in the Republic, and the final section Nigeria's foreign policy during the period.

THE CONTEXTUAL FRAMEWORK

The contextual framework for the Republic, whose institutional parameters were embodied in the 1979 Constitution, consisted of the various measures introduced during the four-year recivilianisation programme of the Mohammed/Obasanjo regime to foster democratic stability and prevent the failures and weaknesses of the First Republic being repeated. The major institutional parameters which have usually been analysed in contradistinction to those of the First Republic (cf. Osaghae, 1992), are described below.

EXECUTIVE PRESIDENTIALISM

To avoid the political problems attributed to the parliamentary system of the First Republic, an American-style executive presidential system was adopted. Its main features were as follows.

(*a*) An elected president (and vice president) who headed the executive, and had wide-ranging powers. Some of these powers, e.g. over fiscal appropriation and appointments to top government positions, required the concurrence of the National Assembly. A similar system was provided for in the states, where the governor (and his deputy) headed the executive.

(*b*) A separation of powers between the executive, legislature and judiciary, and a delicate system of checks and balances. This made the legislature more powerful than it had been under the Westminster-type system of the First Republic when it was an extension or appendage of the executive. There was emphasis on legislative checks over the chief executive who, some members of the CDC and CA feared, could become an untameable leviathan. In addition to ratificatory powers over appropriation bills and appointments (e.g. of judges), the legislature had the absolute power to impeach a chief executive who was proved guilty of 'gross misconduct in the performance of the functions of his office' (1979 Constitution, SS. 132, 170). A decision taken to impeach a chief executive could not be challenged in any court.

(c) There was a bicameral legislature at the centre, called the National Assembly (each state had a unicameral chamber, called the House of Assembly). The first chamber of the National Assembly was the House of Representatives (HOR), whose members represented state constituencies on the basis of population, and the Senate, with equal state representation (under the First Republic members of the Senate were appointed by regional governments; now they were elected like members of the HOR). In theory, the two chambers had co-equal powers, but the fact that the Senate had the powers to ratify appointments, that its president was constitutionally the 'number three' state official (in the event of the presidency falling vacant, he ranked next in succession after the vice-president), and the historical and universal conception of the Senate as an 'upper' house, gave it an edge over the HOR. This was a major source of rivalry between the two houses, leading to unnecessary delays and controversies in the passing of bills; this, together with the huge costs involved in operating two co-equal chambers, was the main reason why *The Report of the Political Bureau* (FGN, 1987a) recommended abolition of the Senate and adoption of a unicameral federal legislature.

CONSTITUTIONAL RECOGNITION OF POLITICAL PARTIES

For the first time political parties were given constitutional recognition in the bid to ensure that only national rather than sectional ones would be able to function. The electoral decree and constitution provided that only parties registered by FEDECO could function as such, and outlined the criteria for registration and requirements for continued recognition (1979 Constitution, SS. 201-7). The criteria for registration, which were intended to prevent the proliferation of political parties, included open membership to all Nigerians irrespective of place of origin and ethnic or religious affiliation; a name, emblem or motto devoid of sectional connotations; location of party headquarters in the federal capital; and representation of the country's federal character in the party executive committee. In addition to these, the electoral decree on the basis of which FEDECO registered parties in 1978 required a party to have 'a properly established branch office in each of at least two-thirds of the states in the federation' and to have branches in local government areas which, in the opinion of the electoral commission, would enable it to present its programme effectively to the electorate.

FUNDAMENTAL OBJECTIVES AND DIRECTIVE PRINCIPLES OF STATE POLICY

There was a settlement of the 'fundamental objectives and directive principles of state policy' (1979 Constitution, Chapter II) which, among others, outlined the political, economic, social, educational and foreign policy objectives of the state. The chapter also spelt out the principles which were to guide the conduct of government, and the relations between government and the people. Perhaps the most important of these principles, which was also one of the most notable inventions of the 1979 Constitution, was the federal character principle (Ekeh, 1989b; Ukwu, 1987). Because of the crucial importance of this principle in Nigerian politics since its invention, it deserves more than a passing comment.

THE FEDERAL CHARACTER PRINCIPLE

The CDC and CA had been concerned with how to remove fears of political domination, and assure every group, state and region access to power in the federation. The CDC, partly following General Mohammed's guidelines, came up with the federal character principle. The issue of access to power was hotly debated in the CA, with many Southern delegates, whose main concern was to stop the virtual monopoly of political power by the North, favouring a presidency that would rotate between the zones into which the country was to be divided. In the end, the 'zoning' school failed, and had to settle for the federal character principle.

Simply defined, the federal character principle is a variant of the consociational principle of proportional representation or quota system where the main objective was to ensure that the kaleidoscope of the country's diversity was reflected in composition of government at all levels. The principle was to apply to appointments to ministerial and other top government positions, and the composition of the armed forces, public service, and other agencies of government. It was hoped that this would 'promote national unity', 'command national loyalty' and ensure 'that there shall be no predominance of persons from a few states or from a few ethnic or other sectional groups in ... government or in any of its agencies' (1979 Constitution, S 14[3]).

The federal character principle was widely hailed as an important Nigerian contribution to the search for democratic stability in divided societies (Dent, 1989; Osaghae, 1995; for its application and problems, see Ukwu, 1987; Ekeh and Osaghae, 1989). Nevertheless, it had two serious limitations which, as the application of the principle since 1979 showed, made it an inadequate instrument to ensure democratic stability. First, the use of states that did not correspond to the ethnic and religious divisions was unrepresentative of the country's kaleidoscopic diversity and the necessary balances were not guaranteed. Moreover, because there were more states belonging to ethnic majority groups in the federation, the application of the federal character principle had the unintended consequences of accentuating minority marginalisation and heightening demands for greater political and economic autonomy by the minorities (Osaghae, 1988, 1989; Okpu, 1989). Secondly, federal character was not really a *state power* sharing device. Its underlying assumption was that representation in executive bodies is an acceptable index of power-sharing, which is correct. But state power-sharing requires more than the sometimes token appointment of ministers; it has more to do with who actually holds and controls executive power. This is where the system of rotational presidency proposed by delegates to the CA appeared to be a more realistic model of power sharing. It took the experience of the Second Republic and continued misgivings over 'Northern domination' for makers of the Constitutional Conference meeting in 1995 finally to adopt a system of rotational presidency to operate alongside the federal character principle. The rotational presidency model will be discussed in Chapter 7 in the context of the political transition programme of the Abacha regime.

ENTRENCHMENT OF CORRECTIVE PRINCIPLES

The fifth schedule of the 1979 Constitution contained the code of conduct for public officers which was intended to address the major problems arising from an amoral government sector. Among other things, public servants were admonished not to get themselves into situations where their private interest was likely to conflict with their duties; they were precluded from engaging in private business, from seeking or accepting any gifts or benefits in kind for the discharge of official duties, and from membership of societies incompatible with public service. The president, vice-president, governors, deputy governors, members of the executive and legislature were forbidden to operate foreign bank accounts; and every public officer was required to declare his or her assets shortly after coming into office and at the end of the tenure. To give effect to these provisions, a code of conduct bureau and tribunal to try and punish erring public officers were created.

    These provisions reflected the concern of both the military leaders and the CDC members to reform the social order, but as was argued at the beginning of this and borne out by the experience of the

Second Republic, social engineering produces little result unless accompanied by measures that address the root causes of amorality.

STRUCTURAL CHANGES

Unlike the anomalous three-regional set-up in the First Republic which violated Mill's 'law' of federal stability because of the preponderant size and population of the Northern region and because of the subjected ethnic minorities in the regions, the Second Republic had nineteen fairly well-balanced states with fewer minority problems. But this did not obliterate regional tendencies and historical fears of domination because the registered political parties were virtual reincarnations of the ethno-regional parties of the First Republic. The resurrection of old fears and anxieties underlay the political problems which beset the Republic from the beginning.

Like the 1963 Constitution, that of 1979 laid down a very cumbersome procedure for creating new states (S. 8). This would begin with a request for a new state, supported by at least a two-thirds majority of the representatives of the areas concerned in the National Assembly, state House of Assembly and local government councils. Thereafter the request had to be supported by at least two-thirds of the people in the area concerned in a referendum, by a simple majority of all states in the federation, and finally by a resolution passed by a two-thirds majority in each house of the National Assembly.

Despite this cumbersome procedure, the creation of states was a major issue, since many agitators for new states who were disappointed by the 1976 exercise looked forward to more favourable responses from the politicians. As in the First Republic, the creation of states became an electoral pawn for the political parties. No party manifesto or campaign was complete without a commitment to the creation of new states, each party supporting or initiating demands for states in areas where it was assured of electoral support. This brought further excitement to state agitators, and demands for no less than fifty new states were submitted to the National Assembly. The Assembly's and federal government's responses to these demands further heightened the expectations of agitators for new states. In December 1982 the HOR committee on state creation proposed the creation of twenty-one new states, and in January 1983 its Senate counterpart recommended twenty-six. Earlier, in 1981, a presidential committee on state creation, comprising representatives of the political parties and headed by Vice-President Alex Ekwueme, was instituted to 'streamline' and reconcile conflicting demands in order to reach consensus on the states to be created and 'simplify' the procedure for their creation. Non-cooperation by the 'opposition' parties which saw the initiative as political capital for the NPN wrecked the work of the committee.

A similar fate befell a 1982 bill on creation of new states and boundary adjustment proposed by a joint committee of the National Assembly, which also sought to 'bypass' the stringent constitutional procedure for state creation – it was defeated by 'opposition' legislators. The parties were not alone in the states game. The issue generated considerable debate in the mass media, with many opinion formers arguing that the country's deep economic recession made the creation of more states ill-advised and irrational. However, it was not adverse public opinion or even the worsening economic conditions that dissuaded the parties from creating states, even if some of the less powerful parties pretended to go along with the public; it was rather the mutual distrust among party leaders who were anxious not to give political advantages to opponents.

The second major structural change was the constitutional guarantee of local government as the third tier of government; the constitution's fourth schedule spelt out its roles and functions. Although in important ways local governments were still under the control of state governments – e.g. state governments were required to pass laws to ensure their very existence (S. 7 [1]) – the fact that they had areas of legislative competence, and were entitled to statutory revenue allocation, expanded the scope of inter-governmental relations, especially those characterised by rivalry and conflict. As for the latter, local governments were a major source of conflict between the federal government, which actively supported local government autonomy which it saw as weakening the states, and the states which took local government subjugation as part of the process of reclaiming ground lost under military rule.

THE MAJOR ACTORS: POLITICAL PARTIES

The major actors in the Second Republic were of course the political parties. After the ban on politics was lifted in September 1978, about fifty-five political associations were formed. This high number was an indication of the excitement generated by the lifting of the ban, but some of these associations were bargaining chips intended to obtain better accommodation for their founders within the main parties. Thus of the fifty-five or more associations, thirty-five obtained registration forms and only nineteen applied for registration. Of these FEDECO, presumably following the criteria stipulated in the electoral decree, registered five on 22 December 1978: Great Nigeria Peoples' Party (GNPP); National Party of Nigeria (NPN); Nigerian Peoples Party

(NPP); Peoples Redemption Party (PRP); and Unity Party of Nigeria (UPN). Later, in 1982, the Nigeria Advance Party (NAP) was registered as the sixth party. We will discuss briefly the origins, character and leadership of these parties.

GNPP/NPP

The two parties began as one party, the NPP, and later split into two. The original NNP was formed by Alhaji Waziri Ibrahim from a fusion of three groups active in the CA, namely National Union Council (NUC), Club 19, and Committee For National Unity and Progress (CNUP), representing three discernible interests. One was the interests of Northern and Eastern ethnic minorities whose solidarity Alhaji Waziri, himself a minority Kanuri from Borno state, sought to combine with the support of the Muslim North to realise the presidential ambition which he had nursed since 1976. The NUC represented this segment. Second was the old NCNC, represented by the Western-Yoruba branch who led the CNUP. Third were the Igbos, who at the time were still searching for a political platform – unlike the Yorubas and Hausa/Fulani, who already had consolidated platforms. They aligned with the Bendel-Middle Belt minorities in Club 19.

Under the circumstances it came as no surprise when the party split following the entry of Nnamdi Azikiwe, the acclaimed leader of the Igbos, as the party's presidential candidate. Waziri led his faction to form the GNPP of which he became chairman and presidential candidate. The latter party was built around the Borno-Gongola minorities axis, and had a significant following in the Eastern minorities' states of Cross River and Rivers. It also had some support in Sokoto state where there was some sympathy for Waziri's contention that power should 'rotate' between Sokoto and Borno, the two Northern Muslim 'Capitals' so as to preserve the unity of the region. The Igbo-Western NCNC faction, together with the Middle Belt segment, formed the NPP which had Olu Akinfosile and later Adeniran Ogunsanya (both old Western NCNC chieftains) as chairman and Azikiwe as presidential candidate. In ideology or objectives there was little or no difference between the NPP and GNPP. They articulated liberalist ideas and programmes to function within a mixed economy.

NPN

The origins of the NPN were said to lie in the pro-*Sharia* group in the CA, which gave birth to the National Movement, from which in turn the party emerged. It was from the onset a Hausa/Fulani platform, more or less regrouping old NPC stalwarts. The vehemence of Christian Southern-Middle Belt opposition to the *Sharia* clause convinced these stalwarts that they should close ranks to protect conservative Northern political interests. This explains why a supposed radical like Aminu Kano first joined the National Movement, and left to form his own party (PRP) only because his bid for the presidential ticket was thwarted by the more conservative elements he had fought since the 1950s. The Northern group managed to secure an alliance with a group in the CA of protagonists from the new Eastern states led by Chuba Okadigbo. This easily attracted politicians from many minority groups, especially in the South, because the experience of the First Republic had taught them that a Hausa/Fulani-led party was in the best position to secure control of the federal government and 'reward' them generously (after all, it was the support of the NPC that gave the Mid-West minorities a region).

The NPN's 'nationwide' expansion did not however detract from the fact that it was primarily a party of conservative Northern-Hausa/Fulani-Muslim leaders who were regarded as the "founders" of the party; all the others, in essence Southerners, were 'joiners' (Omoruyi, 1989: 202-3). The bloc pattern of membership in the party led to the adoption of a zoning formula for sharing party offices and later, after it won the presidential election, positions in government. Thus the presidency was zoned to the North (Shehu Shagari), the vice presidency to the East (Alex Ekwueme), the party national chairmanship to the West (Adisa Akinloye), and the Senate presidency to Southern minorities (Joseph Wayas). After specified terms, positions were supposed to be rotated, a point which became hotly contested in the run-up to the 1983 elections when the Yoruba-Western members of the party, led by M.K.O. Abiola, argued that it was their turn for the presidency. Although it did not always work well, the zoning formula, which was applied at all levels of party organisation, made the party attractive to various ethnic blocs, as it at least guaranteed access to 'power' for every bloc. Ideologically the NPN was a conservative party committed to maintaining law and order, human rights, a free market and respect for traditional institutions.

PRP

To a large extent, the PRP was a more Northern-oriented reincarnation of the old NEPU, both being led by the late Aminu Kano. The major difference between the two was that while NEPU represented the attempt by radical Kano-Hausa politicians led by Aminu Kano to challenge the conservative Fulani-led NPC, and they allied with the NCNC and AG for this purpose, PRP had a converted Aminu Kano, who had parted ways with Azikiwe and Awolowo, and whose pro-*Sharia* position put him in the resurgent Northern political bloc. As we saw earlier, he even joined the NPN, and only left when, to his disappointment, the best job he could be offered was national publicity secretary. The PRP was therefore formed to enable him to realise his presidential hopes. Its main base was restricted to Kano and Kaduna states largely because Aminu Kano lacked the material resources to extend the national spread of the party. The party attracted the remnants of the old NEPU, radical/leftist Northern politicians, and their counterparts from the South who could not find accommodation in other parties. Although it has been described as the most ideological and leftist of all the parties in the Second Republic (populist, anti-neocolonialism, anti-multinationals, advocating social revolution and income redistribution), Aminu Kano's new-found inclinations toward protecting Northern interests represented by the NPN created considerable ambivalence, and resulted in conflicts between the 'great leader' and his more radical governors.

UPN

Like the PRP and GNPP, the UPN was built around one man, Chief Obafemi Awolowo, who had worked hard since the Gowon days to build a national party to further his presidential ambition. The Committee of Friends, a regrouping of Awolowo's old AG allies in the West and faithful (UNIP) alliance partners in the Eastern minority states of Cross River and Rivers, and a badly divided old UMBC in the Middle Belt, was the product of the Chief's clandestine movements across the country while the ban on politics was still in force. The committee metamorphosed into the UPN, whose formation was the first to be announced after the ban was lifted. It was primarily a Yoruba-Western party, to give the group a pedestal to compete with the other majority groups for central power.

The UPN, like the AG of old, was reputed to be the most disciplined of all the parties, and continued with the same socialist/welfarist agenda: free education, free health care, full employment and so on. There was also a resurrection of the old disagreement between Awolowo, a staunch advocate of the Yorubas going it alone, and the Yoruba 'accommodation' school represented earlier by Chief Akintola, over whether or not the Yorubas should maintain a 'principled' opposition to Northern political hegemony. This was a major cause of the tensions which led to splits within the party as Adisa Akinloye, national chairman of NPN, also a Yoruba, sought to forge a Yoruba-Hausa/Fulani coalition reminiscent of the old NPC-NNDP alliance.

For one thing, try as he might to mobilise support in the core North, Awolowo failed to make any headway, largely because he was still regarded with deep suspicion by the conservative leaders who believed him to be anti-North. This made it difficult for him to find a vice-presidential candidate from the region, and he ended up the only presidential candidate with a running mate from the same section of the country (Chief Phillip Umeadi, an Igbo). Of course this seriously affected the performance of the party in most parts of the North, as the NPN, especially, capitalised on his inability to find a Northern running mate, which was attributed to 'disdain' for Northerners and Muslims. As we shall see, one of the interesting developments of the Second Republic, was a dramatic realignment of political forces, which by 1983 not only gave Chief Awolowo a Northerner and Muslim as a running mate, but also gave the party entry into the core North for the first time.

NAP

NAP was registered in 1982, after failing the first time round in 1978. It was perhaps the only party without a clearly ethnic or regional location. Although Lagos was its major base and its leader Tunji Braithwaite was a Yoruba, the party was an all-comers affair, and most of its members belonged to the 'new breed' of politicians – in other words, those without a past history of involvement in politics. Nevertheless, the circumstances under which the party was registered by the increasingly partisan FEDECO on the eve of the 1983 elections suggested that it was part of a plan by NPN to split Yoruba voters and weaken support for the UPN in the West. There was also speculation at the time that the party was registered for reasons of effecting a political balance between the North (which had three parties) and the South (which had two). These suggestions are plausible because, as I argue shortly, FEDECO's decision to register parties was guided by reasons other than those contained in the electoral decree.

Although, it was a newbreed party, the NAP was not very different from the other parties which, with the exception of the NPN, were expressions of the political ambitions of individual politicians. It was founded by Braithwaite to advance the political interests of himself and other like-minded people. Ideologically, despite the party's vague commitments to radical policies, it was basically liberal-centrist. NAP represented an experiment in Nigerian politics: could a non-ethnic, non-regional, newbreed party succeed in Nigeria? The 1983 elections, in which the party polled only about 1 per cent in the presidential election, showed that the experiment was a failure. The 'ethnic trap' (Joseph, 1981) remained the core variable in party politics, although the NAP's lack of material resources – an equally important determinant of electoral success in Nigeria – had much to do with its failure.

Given the character of the parties described above, it is obvious that, with the exception of the NPN which commanded a nationally representative following in spite of being a resuscitation of the old NPC, and NAP (which anyway was not registered until 1982), the parties of the Second Republic were – contrary to the spirit of the constitution – not 'national' parties. So how did they come to be registered by FEDECO? One reason would of course be that they satisfied the *formal* requirements for registration; FEDECO would have acted illegally had it gone outside the criteria laid down, even if it had reason to suspect, or in fact knew, that the parties were sectional and not national.

But this does not seem to have been the case. Available evidence suggests that the five parties in question were registered in 1978 because by their origins, leadership and membership they represented the major ethno-regional groups whose interests needed to be 'balanced' to ensure political stability. Hence, to have refused to register any of the parties would have been to invite tension and anxiety due to the group represented being excluded from the political mainstream and from access to power in the federation. For instance, the tension aroused by the mere possibility of Azikiwe's possible disqualification from the presidential race over tax problems (later resolved), among Igbo leaders, including those who were not even in the NPP, was enough evidence of what could have happened if the NPP which Igbos regarded as their own (even if they were not going to vote for it), had failed to be registered.

It was in order to keep such political balances or, as Omoruyi (1989) puts it, to ensure political 'security' that these parties were registered. Omoruyi in fact suggests that the speed with which they were registered (in one day – hardly enough to ascertain their presence in all 499 local government areas of the country, as was legally required) shows that FEDECO had already made up its mind, whether the parties fully satisfied all the requirements or not. The fact also that the registration of the GNPP and PRP was renewed in 1982, when the parties had lost almost any pretence to national spread, reinforces this view. So, for the sake of political 'security', parties which were really no different from those of the First Republic were allowed, and with such actors the Second Republic could not have been expected to be too different from the First.

Table 4.1. 1979 NATIONAL ASSEMBLY ELECTIONS

State	Total no. of Seats		NPN		UPN		NPP		GNPP		PRP	
	S*	HR*	S	HR	S	HR	S	HR	S	HR	S	HR
Anambra	5	29	–	3	–	–	5	26	–	–	–	–
Bauchi	5	20	5	18	–	–	–	1	–	1	–	–
Bendel	5	20	1	6	4	12	–	2	–	–	–	–
Benue	5	19	5	18	–	–	–	1	–	–	–	–
Borno	5	24	1	2	–	–	–	–	4	22	–	–
Cross River	5	28	3	22	–	2	–	–	2	4	–	–
Gongola	5	21	1	5	2	7	–	1	2	8	–	–
Imo	5	30	–	2	–	–	5	28	–	–	–	–
Kaduna	5	33	3	19	–	1	–	2	–	1	2	10
Kano	5	46	–	7	–	–	–	–	–	–	5	39
Kwara	5	14	3	8	2	5	–	–	–	1	–	–
Lagos	5	12	–	–	5	12	–	–	–	–	–	–
Niger	5	10	5	10	–	–	–	–	–	–	–	–
Ogun	5	12	–	–	5	12	–	–	–	–	–	–
Ondo	5	22	–	–	5	22	–	–	–	–	–	–
Oyo	5	42	–	4	5	38	–	–	–	–	–	–
Plateau	5	16	1	3	–	–	4	13	–	–	–	–
Rivers	5	14	3	10	–	–	2	4	–	–	–	–
Sokoto	5	37	5	31	–	–	–	–	–	6	–	–
Total	95	449	36	168	22	111	16	78	8	43	7	49

* S: Senate; HR: House of Representatives.

Table 4.2. 1979 STATE ELECTIONS

State	Seats	GNPP	UPN	Assembly NPN	PRP	NPP	Governor/party
Anambra	87	1	–	13	–	73	Nwobodo/NPP
Bauchi	60	9	–	45	2	4	Ali/NPN
Bendel	60	–	34	22	–	4	Alli/UPN
Benue	57	6	–	48	–	3	Aku/NPN
Borno	72	59	–	11	2	–	Goni/GNPP
Cross River	84	16	7	58	–	3	Isong/NPN
Gongola	63	25	18	15	1	4	Barde/GNPP
Imo	90	2	–	9	–	79	Mbakwe/NPP
Kaduna	99	10	3	64	16	6	Musa/PRP
Kano	138	3	1	11	123	–	Rimi/PRP
Kwara	42	2	15	25	–	–	Atta/NPN
Lagos	36	–	36	–	–	–	Jakande/UPN
Niger	30	2	–	28	–	–	Ibrahim/NPN
Ogun	36	–	36	–	–	–	Onabanjo/UPN
Ondo	66	–	65	1	–	–	Ajasin/UPN
Oyo	126	–	117	9	–	–	Ige/UPN
Plateau	47	3	–	10	–	34	Lar/NPP
Rivers	42	1	–	26	–	15	Okilo/NPN
Sokoto	111	19	–	92	–	–	Kangiwa/NPN
Total	1347	157	333	487	144	226	

Source: Graf, 1988: 88.

Table 4.3. 1979 PRESIDENTIAL ELECTION

State	Total votes cast	% of total votes				
		GNPP	UPN	NPN	PRP	NPP
Anambra	1,209,038	1.67	0.75	13.50	1.20	82.58
Bauchi	998,683	15.44	3.00	62.48	14.34	4.72
Bendel	669,511	1.23	53.23	36.19	6.73	8.60
Benue	538,879	7.89	2.57	76.39	1.35	11.71
Borno	710,968	54.04	3.35	34.71	6.52	1.35
Cross River	661,103	15.14	11.76	64.40	1.01	7.66
Gongola	639,138	34.09	21.67	35.52	4.34	4.35
Imo	1,153,355	3.00	0.64	8.80	0.89	86.67
Kaduna	1,382,712	13.80	6.68	43.12	3.66	4.72
Kano	1,220,763	1.54	1.23	19.94	76.41	0.91
Kwara	354,605	5.71	39.48	53.62	0.67	0.52
Lagos	828,414	0.48	82.30	7.18	0.47	9.57
Niger	383,347	16.50	3.69	74.88	3.99	1.11
Ogun	744,668	0.53	92.11	6.23	0.31	0.32
Ondo	1,369,547	0.26	94.51	4.19	0.18	0.86
Oyo	1,396,547	0.57	85.78	12.75	0.32	0.55
Plateau	548,405	6.82	5.29	34.73	3.98	49.17
Rivers	687,951	2.18	0.33	72.65	0.46	14.35
Sokoto	1,348,697	26.61	2.52	66.58	3.35	0.92
Total	16,846,633	10.02	29.18	33.77	10.28	16.75

Presidential candidates:
GNPP: Waziri Ibrahim
UPN: Obafemi Awolowo
NPN: Shehu Shagari
PRP: Aminu Kano
NPP: Nnamdi Azikiwe

THE 1979 ELECTIONS

Five staggered elections were held between 7 July and 11 August 1979. Following the order in which they were held, these were elections to the Senate, HOR and state HOAs; gubernatorial elections and, finally, the presidential election. The candidates for the elections were screened by FEDECO, and only those approved by it were allowed to contest. About 1,000 prospective candidates were disqualified, mainly on grounds of tax problems, and their parties had to replace them. The case of two presidential candidates – Nnamdi Azikiwe (NPP) and Aminu Kano (PRP), who faced disqualification over tax problems

– was the most sensational, but after protracted legal battles they were allowed to contest. The results of these elections, showing how the parties fared, are presented in Table 4.1, 4.2 and 4.3. On the whole, the results confirmed the sectional character of the political parties. As in the First Republic, each secured control of its ethno-regional (or state) base.

The UPN finally realised the Yoruba-Western hegemonic control which its predecessor the AG had found difficult to attain. It won the elections in all the Yoruba-speaking states of the West, narrowly losing Kwara, a Yoruba-dominated state in the 'North', as well as Bendel state, which had previously been part of the Western region. Its victory in Bendel was attributed to the appeal of its welfarist programmes, especially its free education and free health promises. In essence, the UPN controlled the 'LOOBO' states – Lagos, Ogun, Ondo, Bendel and Oyo. It also scored significant victories in states with historical ties to the AG: Cross River and Gongola.

The NPP confirmed itself as a true reincarnation of the NCNc by securing control of the Igbo-speaking states of Anambra and Imo, and reaping the benefit of its alliance with powerful Middle-Belt politicians to win in Plateau state and secure some legislative seats in Benue, Kaduna and Gongola states. It also did well in Rivers state, thanks to the high number of Igbos in that state. The PRP, clinched Kano state as had been expected, and had a tenuous hold on Kaduna state where it benefited from divisions within the more formidable NPN to secure the gubernatorial position, but not control of the House of Assembly. This proved one of the most challenging situations of the Republic, which ended with the impeachment of Governor Balarabe Musa. The GNPP won in Borno and Gongola states, and scored significant victories in the Eastern minority state of Cross River and a few conservative Northern states – an indication of how well Waziri Ibrahim's calculations would have paid off if the Igbos had not hijacked his original NPP.

The NPN was, in relative terms, an exception to this sectional pattern of support. Although it was fully anchored in the core Northern (Hausa/Fulani) states, it emerged as the most nationally accepted party for reasons already referred to. It controlled seven states: Bauchi, Benue, Cross River, Kwara, Rivers and Sokoto. Most significantly, it won HOA seats in all states with the exception of Lagos and Ogun states which were strictly controlled by one party (the UPN). It is important to emphasise the role of the support of minorities in the party's overall national success: this always provided the key to controlling the federal government. With each party concentrating on its (majority) ethnic homebase, the party that had the greatest support from the dispersed minorities was the one most likely to control the centre. Indeed, since colonial times the struggle to get minority support has been the major strategy of ethnic majority-based parties wishing to become national. What got the minorities, especially Southern minorities, on the side of the NPN was the calculation that, from past trends, a Hausa/Fulani-based party was the most 'advantaged' and likely to control the federal government (this was one of the myths of Nigerian politics that was broken by the annulled 12 June 1993 presidential election). In national spread the NPN was followed by the GNPP, which also leaned heavily on its original image of a minority party.

The elections proceeded quite smoothly. This was a welcome departure from the warring politics of the First Republic, except where the most important one of all, the presidential election, was concerned. The controversy generated by the outcome of the election, which badly rocked the foundations of the Republic, arose from how to interpret or determine what constituted two-thirds of nineteen states, which was one of the requirements for victory in the election. The electoral decree provided that in order to be declared winner in a presidential election a candidate, in addition to obtaining a simple majority of the total cast at the election, also had to obtain no less than a quarter of the votes cast in each of at least two-thirds of all the (nineteen) states in the federation.

Alhaji Shehu Shagari, the NPN presidential candidate, satisfied the first requirement of a simple majority, polling 5,688,857 votes compared to 4,916,651 polled by Chief Awolowo, his closest rival. But he failed to win a quarter of the votes in thirteen states, which was widely assumed to be two-thirds of nineteen (in ascertaining that parties had national spread as required by law, FEDECO itself gave this interpretation). Shagari won a quarter of the votes in twelve states, and about 19.4 per cent in the thirteenth (Kano). Yet the chief returning officer for the election, F.L.O. Menkiti, declared Shagari winner on the grounds that

> ... in the absence of any legal explanation or guidance in the electoral decree, [FEDECO] has no alternative than to give the phrase 'at least two-thirds of all the states of the federation' in section 34A sub-section 1(c) (ii) of the electoral decree the ordinary meaning which applies to it. In the circumstances, the candidate who scores at least one-quarter of the votes in twelve states and one-quarter of two-thirds, that is, at least one-sixth of the votes cast in the thirteenth state satisfied the requirement of the sub-section. Accordingly, Alhaji Shehu Shagari is hereby declared elected President of the federal Republic of Nigeria. (cited in Dudley, 1982: 169)

This became the cause of a protracted legal tussle, especially since the same interpretation of two-thirds of nineteen had earlier been given by Richard Akinjide, NPN's legal adviser and later federal attorney-general and minister of justice. Chief Awolowo challenged the declaration at the election tribunal, hoping to get a run-off election between the two leading contestants in the event of the presidential election not providing a clear winner, as the constitution provided. In taking this step the Chief was encouraged by the initial opposition of the other parties, notably the NPP and PRP, to the declaration of Shagari as winner. In fact, there was a temporary alliance between the UPN and NPP, whose high-point was a press conference at which the NPP leader announced his party's support for Awolowo's action. But at the very time when the conference was being held, the NPP was also engaged in negotiations with the NPN, which eventually resulted in an accord between the two.

The electoral tribunal upheld the decision of FEDECO saying it was 'absurd' to read anything more than the ordinary meaning into the 'plain words' of the sub-section. According to the tribunal it did not require 'the opinion of an expert in mathematics or a computerist to work out what two-thirds of nineteen means. It is enough to say that any student in a primary school, tutored in the subject of 'fraction' in simple arithmetic, will have no difficulty in getting twelve [and] two-thirds if asked to find two-thirds of nineteen.' Chief Awolowo then appealed to the Supreme Court. In an unprecedented ruling, which was not to be regarded as a legal precedent, five judges out of seven, including the Chief Justice, upheld the ruling of the tribunal, declaring that Alhaji Shagari's election was 'substantially' in accordance with the provisions of the electoral decree.

Thus Shagari became 'president by mathematics' (Bolaji, 1980; also Ojigbo, 1983), although it was widely believed that the party's victory was possible because it was the favoured party of the departing military regime. Turner and Baker (1984) suggest that the NPN was favoured because it was the most likely to continue the capitalist agricultural agendas of leading members of the regime. The party was also said to have had the backing of the powerful 'Kaduna mafia' which controlled the military at the time – this is important because it helps to explain the so-called disappointment of the mafia with the performance of the Shagari administration, the defection of a section of it to the UPN, and its return to power with the Buhari military government (cf. Othman, 1989). Chief Awolowo, the UPN and their supporters continued to reject the validity of Shagari's election, and this heightened the fragility of the Republic. For a long time afterwards, the UPN-controlled LOOBO states refused to display the president's photographs in public buildings, and opposed the federal government on most issues, especially those to do with what was seen as federal intrusion into areas of state competence. This was the background to the emergence of the 'progressive governors' forum (comprising UPN, NPP, GNPP and PRP governors) which became the mainstay of extraparliamentary opposition in the Second Republic.

Given the groundswell of opposition mobilised by the UPN against it, the NPN rightly concluded that it needed a working majority in the National Assembly to get ratification for presidential bills and appointments and to run the government effectively. Although, as Table 4.1 shows, it won the highest number of seats in both Senate and HOR, the NPN did not have the majority needed to ensure the passage of executive bills (this amounted to parliamentary reasoning in a presidential setting – one of the abiding legacies of the First Republic). The NPN found a ready ally in the NPP, whose Igbo leaders were desperate to be reintegrated into the *mainstream* of national politics, i.e. to have access to political patronage and benefit (from which alliance with the UPN would have excluded them).

This was how the NPN-NPP accord – reminiscent of the NPC-NCNC coalition in the First Republic – was born. The NPP was given eight ministerial appointments (most notably Ishaya Audu, Azikiwe's vice-presidential running mate, was appointed foreign affairs minister), the post of HOR speaker, and Senate deputy president, and other plum board appointments, in addition to a promise to resolve outstanding issues from the civil war like abandoned properties, and relative underdevelopment of Igbo states. In return, NPN received legislative support in getting presidential appointments and bills ratified. However, the accord was prematurely broken in 1981 partly because of pressure from non-Igbo elements (and Igbos opposed to Ekwueme, the vice-president) in the NPP who felt excluded from the benefits accruing to the party (Omoruyi, 1989). The NPN for its part had used the accord to consolidate itself in power, and was not averse to breaking it because it had built a solid patronage network in addition to a 'working accord' with the PRP that assured it of majority legislative support.

One significant aspect of the NPN-NPP accord was that it showed, once again, the difficulty Igbo and Yoruba leaders found in working together or uniting. In choosing to work with the NPN rather the UPN, the Igbos were simply replaying the events of 1959 when they chose coalition with the NPC for similar reasons to those which led them to the accord in 1979. But just as in the First Republic, when the Yoruba accommodation school led by Akintola sought to supplant Igbos in the competition for an interest-begotten alliance with Northern politicians, the Akinloye-led Yoruba bloc in the NPN was believed to have played a major part in the break-up of the accord, presumably to enable Yorubas to maximise their own share of patronage. This pushed the NPP more over to the side of the opposition, and its governors joined the progressive governors forum, although Azikiwe 'still harboured the feeling that some day a new arrangement would be worked out with the NPN' (Omoruyi, 1989: 205).

DEVELOPMENTS IN THE INTER-ELECTION YEARS

Since it is practically impossible to cover all the important areas of the life of the Second Republic, this section selectively examines those which are especially relevant for understanding the problems of the Republic and its demise.

RELIGIOUS AND POLITICAL CONFLICTS ; AUTHORITARIAN TENDENCIES

The controversy generated by the *Sharia* issue in the late 1970s finally stirred the hornets' nest of religious conflict in the country (cf. Kukah, 1993; Enwerem, 1995). Quite early in the Second Republic's life, in December 1980, Kano witnessed the first in the wave of fundamentalist Muslim uprisings in many parts of the North which were to characterise the 1980s and 1990s. The Maitatsine riots, as these violent uprisings came to be popularly known, were instigated by members of the sect of that name led by Muhammadu Marwa, an Islamic scholar who had migrated to Kano from Northern Cameroon in 1945 (Tamuno, 1991).

The factor underlying the religious strife in Northern Nigeria are deeply etched in the nature of Islamic conquests, the 'counter-penetration' of Christianity, the propagation of Islam as the official religion by various state governments and, before them, the regional government, and the close links between religion, political culture and behaviour (cf. Dudley, 1968; Whitaker, 1970; Paden, 1973, 1986; Crampton, 1975; Adamu, 1978; Ayandele, 1967; Tseayo, 1975; Clarke and Linden, 1984; Ekoko & Amadi, 1989; Northern Regional Government, 1953). Within this larger context, the Maitatsine riots which spread to Yola, Kaduna and Maiduguri in 1982, basically had to do with the personality cult around Marwa himself, who denounced Islamic practice based on the Quran and the teachings of prophet Mohammed, and convinced his followers that his version of Islam was the only genuine one (cf. Elaigwu, 1993). His anti-state activities and forced method of recruiting followers, which had a long history in Kano and had led to banishments from the city in the past, constantly put the sect on a collision course with the authorities and the Emir. The immediate cause of the 1980 uprising was the attempt by the Rimi administration in Kano state to dislodge the sect which was believed to have smuggled a lot of weapons into the country from abroad and was therefore considered a danger. Marwa then mobilised his followers all over the North to resist attempts by 'infidels' to suppress both himself and the sect.

In the riots which followed and which were put down by military action, more than 5,000 lives were lost, including those of soldiers, police and Marwa himself, and property worth millions of naira was destroyed. Other reasons that have been advanced for the riots, which spread to other parts of the North, include the marginalisation of the urban poor, thus making them easy recruits (Usman, 1987; Umar, 1989; Albert, 1994;); the meddling of politicians, who encouraged and mobilised support for the riots to further their goal of unseating the PRP government (the NPN was accused in this regard, and matters were not helped by the presidential amnesty granted to over 1,000 rioters); and foreign sponsorship, which seemed to be confirmed by photographs of Gadaffi of Libya and Ayatollah Khomeini of Iran found on members of the sect, and the fact that many of its members were not Nigerians – they were Chadians, Malians, Nigériens, Burkinabes and Cameroonians (for elaborations of the various factors and aspects of the Maitatsine riots, see the Reports of the different panels set up by the Kano state government [Kano State, 1981] and the federal government [FGN, 1981]). Whichever of these reasons had the greater validity, Kano state and the federal government disagreed over how to deal with the problem, and this led to the setting up of two rival panels of enquiry, which only served to politicise the problem further and make its resolution more difficult. Thus the banning of the sect by the federal government in November 1982 was of little consequence. It took the military regimes of Buhari and Babangida to deal with the Maitatsine problem decisively.

The Maitatsine riots were closely followed by more pointed conflicts between Muslims and Christians in many parts of the North. Perhaps the most notable case was the October 1982 clash in Kano resulting from attempts by Muslim fundamentalists to stop reconstruction work on a church in Fagge quarters which they claimed was too close to a mosque. The anger of the Muslims was subsequently unleashed, as in previous occasions, on *sabon gari* (strangers' quarters) where the vast majority of Christian Southerners and Middle-Belters resided. Churches were burnt, several people were killed, and hotels and other business premises belonging to Southerners were destroyed. The clashes spread to Zaria and Kaduna in neighbouring Kaduna state, and these too were attributed by some commentators to NPN-related manipulations to unseat the PRP from Kaduna and Kano states. While this could well have been so, there was no doubt that the clashes were manifestations of the increased Christian-Muslim polarisation since the *Sharia* episode. Like ethnicity, religion was fast becoming a political resource to be manipulated in furtherance of the objectives of politicians and political parties.

Meanwhile there were other political conflicts of various magnitude taking place. In 1982 the discovery of a coup plot which had allegedly been financed by Alhaji Zana Bukar Mandara and supported by Libya was announced. Quite unlike other coups in the country, the ringleaders and main actors arrested were civilians who were subsequently tried by civil courts rather than military tribunals, and sentenced to long jail terms. Another alleged coup plot, involving a member of the National Youth Service Corps, Ojaoro Igbuku Otu, was also 'discovered' by over-zealous security men in 1983, but the young graduate was found not guilty by the federal high court. There was also a rash of workers' strikes, student riots and other forms of civil disturbance largely in reaction to economic recession and the austerity measures imposed. In many states workers – especially teachers – were owed huge arrears of salaries, and even when they were paid their purchasing power had become drastically reduced by inflation. While all this was happening and workers and the masses were being called upon to make sacrifices, the politicians and legislators carried on in affluence and blatant corruption.

Partly in consequence of the increased political turbulence, the NPN-controlled federal government developed an appetite for authoritarianism which led it to transform the police force into a paramilitary outfit. (It was believed that this was done to counterbalance the army, and it is remarkable that one of the first acts of the military regime which overthrew the Second Republic was to dispossess the police of its military hardware.) The total strength of the police increased astronomically from about 10,000 in 1979 to over 100,000 in 1983. Also, total expenditure on arms and ammunition including armoured tanks, patrol vans and aircraft rose sharply from N3 million in 1979 to over N36 million in 1982 (Oyediran, 1989). Specially trained commandos manned the special mobile field squadrons which were located in every state. The full force of the militarised police force was unleashed on the peasants of Bakalori in Sokoto state.

When they staged an uprising over their displacement from the land on which a new dam was built, it was crushed and hundreds of them were killed. Students of tertiary institutions also felt its force any time they demonstrated. Fully armed police contingents constantly broke up political party meetings, rallies and campaigns, ostensibly because the police had not issued the required licences for the events to take place. Not only did such actions lead state governors to contest control of the force, but a few of them (cf. Oyo and Anambra) established pseudo-police forces. Anambra state became embroiled in a violent struggle for supremacy between two 'private police forces': the 'Ikemba Front', a parliamentary force organised by Odumegwu Ojukwu, the returnee former Biafra leader who joined the NPN and enjoyed police protection for the activities of the Front, and the state road safety force.

These activities of the police, combined with those of the secret service (National Security Organisation [NSO]) – caused some journalists to call the country a 'police state'. Indeed, the press had its share of state repression. For alleging that President Shagari offered bribes of 50,000 naira and Mercedes-Benz cars to opposition legislators in the National Assembly, the premises of the *Nigerian Tribune*, a mouthpiece of the UPN, were sealed off by a contingent of armed police and its editors were detained. Other opposition papers which belonging to state governments controlled by UPN, NPP and others – the *Daily Sketch, Nigerian Observer, Standard* etc. – were given similar treatment from time to time. The deportation of Alhaji Darman Shugaba, the GNPP majority leader of the Borno state House of Assembly, on the grounds that he was a foreigner and a security risk was another symptom of the burgeoning state authoritarianism. The deportation which had political undertones, being related to NPN strategies to take over control of Borno state, was successfully challenged in court by the progressive governors' forum, and became a reference point for anti-NPN elements.

INTER-GOVERNMENTAL RELATIONS (IGR)

After thirteen years of 'military federalism' whose main characteristics were the over-centralisation of power and the corresponding loss of state autonomy, it was only to be expected that with the return of constitutional and democratic government the states would struggle to reassert their position in the federation. This struggle was the main theme of IGR, which consisted mostly of conflict and rivalry, in the Second Republic (Osaghae, 1994). The multiparty system, which made it possible for different parties to control the centre and the states, provided the enabling environment for this.

To understand the nature of IGR, it is necessary to be take account of two structural details. One was the configuration of party controls. The NPN controlled the federal government and seven states (Bauchi, Benue, Cross River, Kwara, Niger, Rivers and Sokoto), as well as the legislature in Kaduna state. The UPN had control over the LOOBO states; the NPP over Anambra, Imo, and Plateau states; GNPP, Borno and Gongola states; and PRP, Kano and Kaduna states. The other was that although the constitution provided for a three-tier (federal, state and local) IGR system, local governments were subjugated and tightly controlled by state governments which feared their possible use by the federal government to undermine their authority under the guise of upholding their autonomy. Thus one of the first acts of many state governors on coming to power was to dissolve democratically–elected local councils and replace them with caretaker committees comprising party faithfuls (this despite a declaration by the chief judge of Bendel state, Justice Ovie Whiskey, that governor Ambrose Alli's dissolution of elected local councils was unconstitutional). In 1982/3 many state governments split local government areas and created new ones in their domains, partly to extend control over them and partly to mobilise the support of the electorate in the general elections which were around the corner. Thus the IGR grid had state and federal governments as the main *dramatis personae*.

Compared to the First Republic, where horizontal IGR involving inter-regional relations was highly conflictual and the source of major political problems in the federation, state-state relations in the Second Republic did not produce serious problems. They were largely shaped by the historical legacy of regionalism and patterns of party control, hence discrimination against non-indigenes by state governments in the provision of social goods was commonplace. This was most pronounced in the Northern states, where Southerners continued to be denied social goods, and LOOBO states where efforts were made to exclude non-indigenes from enjoying the UPN's welfarist programmes, notably free education and free health care. Regional ties and loyalties continued to be strong among ethnic-majority-dominated states, especially in the East and West which, as in the First Republic, were one-party-dominant, and this led many minorities' states to persist in regional dissenting politics. But on the whole, and despite the acrimonious effects of party differences which in many cases pitched the NPN against states controlled by the other parties, horizontal IGR was not very problematic relative to vertical IGR which involved federal-state relations.

Federal-state relations in the Second Republic have been described variously as characterised by rivalry, confrontation and conflict, and destabilising. Some writers have even gone so far as to characterise aspects of these relations, such as calls by the Governors of Bendel and Kano states on the citizens of their states to refuse to welcome President Shagari during official visits to the states, as 'unfederal' and 'confederal' (Nwabueze, 1982). The conflictual relations mainly involved the NPN, which controlled the federal government, and the states controlled by the other parties which were championed by the UPN governors who, following the disputed outcome of the 1979 presidential election, were the NPN's bitterest opponents. Before highlighting some of the most notable cases of federal-state conflict, it is necessary first to account for the conflictual relations.

There were two major reasons for this. The first, which was highlighted earlier, was the struggle by the states to reassert their status and powers which had been almost completely eroded under military rule. This was all the more important because, unlike the First Republic Constitution which tilted the balance of power slightly in favour of the regions, the 1979 Constitution favoured the centre, ostensibly to consolidate the centrist/integrationist processes of thirteen years of military rule. But when the federal government attempted to operate along the lines of previous military regimes, it met with opposition from the states. The second reason was the weakness of opposition in the National Assembly, as the NPN made maximum of the patronage and rent-seeking resources at its disposal to forge working alliances with the other parties and mobilise support for federal bills and actions from legislators of supposed opposition parties (Osaghae, 1995b). The mantle of opposition then fell on the governors of these parties whose opposition was somewhat institutionalised and turned into a formidable force by the regular meetings of the so-called 'progressive governors' which was started by the UPN, PRP and GNPP governors who were later joined by NPP governors.

The states based their confrontation with the federal government mainly on the grounds that certain federal actions violated their constitutional rights and legislative competence. Thus, the Oyo state government prevented the federal government from executing its housing programme in the state, and even went so far as physically demolishing housing units under construction because (1) the state government had not allocated land to the federal government for this purpose, and (2) housing was a state matter. The Ondo state government embarked on oil exploration which clearly fell under federal jurisdiction. The Anambra state government disrupted road construction by the federal government in the state, arguing that the road in question was state, not federal. The LOOBO states also reintroduced pools betting and gambling, which had been banned by the federal government since Obasanjo. Underneath the apparent reasons of state rights were those of inter-party rivalry, and the struggle to win the support of the electors. Thus such actions as the demolition of low-cost houses and roads were highly counter-productive.

Revenue allocation was, as usual, a major source of federal-state conflict. Issues of constitutionality and demands for greater state shares of revenue to enable them to discharge their constitutional responsibilities were advanced in the opposition to the Revenue Allocation Bill of 1981 by many state governments, including the NPN-controlled Cross River state whose governor argued that the allocation formula in the bill was at variance with the huge responsibilities of the states. The bill had allocated 58.5 per cent of federally collected revenue to the federal government, 31.5 per cent to the states, and 10 per cent to local government. What irked the governors was not only that their share fell below the 40 per cent which they demanded (some demanded 50 per cent) and which was recommended by the HOR, but that the Senate increased the federal share from 53 per cent in the original bill submitted by the President to 58.5 per cent, and reduced state shares from 34.5 to 31.5 per cent. Although the Senate amendment was subsequently passed by a joint committee of the Senate and HOR, many governors argued that the Senate action and manipulation in the joint committee was unconstitutional and amounted to the imposition of the views of a few members of the National Assembly upon the body politic. The progressive governors championed opposition to the bill and, through Supreme Court actions instituted initially by Governor Jim Nwobodo of Anambra state and later Governor Ambrose Alli of Bendel, successfully nullified the Act.

Another matter which generated serious tension and conflict in state-federal relations was control of the police. Public order was a concurrent matter, but federal control of the police force nullified state powers on the matter. In theory, state governors had powers to direct police commissioners on maintenance of order, but some commissioners insisted on obtaining 'clearance' from Lagos before complying with governors' directives. The matter was complicated by the Public Order Act of 1979 which empowered state police commissioners rather than governors to licence public meetings and processions, thereby subordinating the governors in a matter of crucial importance to campaigns and political mobilisation.

The governors saw this as an attempt by the NPN to intimidate and harass them for the purpose of securing electoral advantages, and subsequently went to court to challenge the act. Instances such as the refusal of the Ogun state police commissioner to licence the UPN delegates' conference in March 1981, the withdrawal of police escorts and security from the governor of Anambra state who alleged that there was a plan to assassinate him, and restrictions on political meetings convened by the governors of Kaduna and Kano states were cited by the 'progressive' governors in support of their contention that the police had been politicised. Increased loss of faith in the neutrality of the police force led states like Anambra to establish para-police and para-military agencies like the road traffic corps whose functions overlapped with those of the police. Although the responses of some governors bordered on the extreme, the high-handedness of the federal authorities, and their failure to consult them on issues of security in their domains in the cooperative spirit required to discharge concurrent responsibilities were at the root of the problems over control of the police.[1]

Lack of consultation and high-handedness were also major factors in the controversy generated by the appointment of Presidential Liaision Officers (PLOs) whose ostensible role was coordination of presidential and federal activities in the states. The PLO was more than a liaison between the President and state government:

> He [was] intended to represent and embody the presidency in the state, to provide for it the physical presence needed to establish a personal closeness and intimacy between the President and the People, *which would put him at par with the Governor, and thus enable him (the President) to compete more effectively and advantageously for support in the state.* (Nwabueze, 1982: 34, emphasis added)

With roles like these, notwithstanding the facilitative roles PLOs could play in furthering federal-state cooperation, they were rejected by many state governors, including those belonging to the NPN, who saw them as agents of the federal government sent to undermine their authority and/or rivals (PLOs carried on in some states as though they were alternative governors). It did not help matters that many of those appointed PLO were defeated gubernatorial candidates or aspiring candidates – indeed rivalry between governors and PLOs was so intense in states like Anambra, Bendel, and Rivers that the PLOs had to be re-posted outside their states of origin.

To a large extent the conflictual nature of vertical IGR was part and parcel of the intense competition among political parties. Thus, although the non-NPN-controlled states often acted confrontationally

---

[1] The 1963 Constitution made consultation with regional premiers a legal requirement for appointing police commissioners, which at least helped to reduce tension and conflicts.

on constitutional grounds over matters of jurisdictional competence, and in most cases did well to go to court, the overriding considerations were political and mostly to do with securing political advantages and winning public support. In this the federal government was no less guilty. In addition to the cases of the police and PLOs already referred to, the allocation of television and radio channels and licences, was also used to punish states controlled by opposition parties. In the celebrated case of Lagos state television, federal authorities went so far as to jam the station even after the channel had been allocated.

DEVELOPMENTS IN THE STATES

Discussions of political dynamics in Nigeria generally tend to focus on the country as a whole, and in practice this means to focus on the central government. However, it is an approach than fails to account adequately for the dynamics of the country's federal system. It might be suitable for military federalism in which the states have restricted lives of their own, but not for a democratically-run federal system in which states operate within certain parameters of autonomy, as in the Second Republic. Thus we should look briefly at the states, as well as their status in the dynamics of IGR considered earlier.

Unlike the situation at the federal level where the NPN had formidable legislative opposition, most states – like the regions in the First Republic – were virtually one-party. Lagos, Ogun, Ondo, and Oyo, were all UPN; Anambra, Imo and Plateau were NPP; Niger, Bauchi and Sokoto, NPN; and Kano, PRP. Bendel, Kwara, Gongola and Cross River were multiparty, although the parties which controlled the executive had majorities in the Houses of Assembly. The exception to all this, which proved to be one of the greatest tests to the politicians' capacity for consensual politics, was the situation in Kaduna state where the PRP governor, Balarabe Musa, was faced with an NPN-dominated opposition assembly. For reasons which had to do with the 'recalcitrance' of Musa to toe the pro-NPN paths of Aminu Kano and other PRP leaders, preferring instead to pitch camp with the anti-NPN 'progressive' governors, his tenure as governor witnessed the most serious ex-ecutive-legislative conflict in the Second Republic. The House of Assembly refused to ratify the governor's nominees for commissionership and other executive positions, and accused him of unconstitutional unilateral actions which required legislative assent, like the abrogation of traditional councils and cattle and community tax. The conflict reached its climax with the impeachment of the governor on 22 June 1981. This politically motivated act was a clear abuse of legislative prerogative, since as no case of gross misconduct, as required by law, was proved against Musa.

Although most of the states were one-party, many governors had strong opposition from legislators, including those who belonged to the same party. The legislators were determined to assert their powers to check and balance governors, who mostly acted like the authoritarian military governors before them. To this extent the legislatures were effective in scrutinising political appointments, passing budgets and so on, though at the initial stages most of them were rubber-stamp bodies, ignorant of what their main functions were (Oyediran, 1980). But there were several instances of abuse of legislative powers, especially the power of impeachment which at one stage became an instrument of blackmail for securing largesse from chief executives and speakers of the assemblies. By 1983 the governors of Bendel, Rivers, and Cross River states were under threat of impeachment, the speaker of the Ondo state house had been impeached, and the speakers of the Lagos and Sokoto assemblies had been suspended. Such abuses of the power of impeachment led the Political Bureau which drew up the blueprint for transition to the Republic to temper the absoluteness of the power which, under the 1979 Constitution, could not be reversed by the courts.

INTER- AND INTRA-PARTY FACTIONALISM

This was a major theme of party politics in the inter-election years. Parties split into factions, and there were realignments of coalitions and alliances, and massive movements of politicians from one party to the other. Not surprisingly, the PRP, GNPP, NPP, and UPN, in that order, were more adversely affected as the NPN employed its federal might and patronage to attract those who had decamped from these parties and precipitate splits within them. The PRP and GNPP were the worst hit. The PRP split into two – the Imoudu and Aminu Kano factions – over the participation of Governors Rimi (Kano) and Musa (Kaduna) in the regular meetings of the twelve 'progressive' governors in defiance of the orders of Aminu Kano who, together with S.G. Ikoku and a few other leaders, favoured accommodation with the NPN.

Matters came to a head when the two factions turned to FEDECO to determine which was the 'authentic' PRP. The Kano faction, which was virtually restricted to Kano state, got approved although thirty-eight of the party's forty-seven HOR members, five of the seven senators and the two governors belonged to the Imoudu faction. The impeachment of Governor Balarabe Musa by the NPN-controlled state House of

Assembly in 1981 was in part a consequence of the intra-party feud and of the 'cooperation' which the Kano faction had entered into with the NPN in the state. After the death of Aminu Kano in 1983, Ikoku resigned from the party to join the NPN, and was rewarded with a position as presidential adviser on National Assembly affairs. Alhaji Hassan Yussuf and Barkin Zuwo, who took over leadership of the party thereafter, pledged themselves to a policy of non-confrontation with the federal government. The rump of the party found accommodation in the 'progressive' opposition to the NPN camp, and attempted to register a new party formed in alliance with the NPP – the Progressive Peoples' Party (PPP). The party was not approved by FEDECO.

The GNPP split into three factions. The first was the Senator Mahmud Waziri faction comprising GNPP senators and HOR members expelled from the party for supporting the NPN in the National Assembly. This faction was virtually co-opted into the NPN, and the Assembly men remained GNPP only in name. The second was the Yoruba-Igbo axis of the party led by Kola Balogun, Nduka Eze and Ben Nzeribe, which later joined the NPN. And the third was the Waziri Ibrahim faction which managed to secure the loyalty of the governors of Gongola and Borno because of Waziri's favourable attitude towards the 'progressive' opposition front championed by the UPN and NPP. By the time Ibrahim realised that he and the party were only being used by the UPN and NPP to gain ground in the North and that these parties were actually precipitating splits within his party and pulled out of the loose alliance, what was left of the GNPP was barely in a position to muster half the support it had got in 1979.

The NPP's problems began from the time the party broke away from its accord with the NPN. Top leaders like Matthew Mbu, the national vice-chairman, and Professor Ishaya Audu, Azikiwe's presidential running-mate, refused to quit their positions in government, and in effect crossed the floor to the NPN. In the National Assembly Senator Anah and others continued to support the NPN in defiance of the party, and led rebellious factions. But the divisions within the party in its Igbo-speaking states base were more serious. Pressure on Vice-President Alex Ekwueme, an Igbo, to extend the NPN presence in the East was a serious threat to the NPP's stronghold and underlay the vehement opposition of the governor of Anambra state to the spate of federal developmental activities in the state, including road building. Nevertheless, the party lost many of its supporters to the NPN, which generously deployed federal resources and patronage to Easterners and exploited to the full intra-state divisions within the NPP such as at between Anambra south and north. The return in 1982 of the former rebel leader Odumegwu Ojukwu from exile in Côte d'Ivoire and of Michael Okpara, First Republic premier of the Eastern region, and their subsequent membership of the NPN (widely believed to be part of the deal for the amnesty granted to Ojukwu), created more problems for the NPP in the Igbo-speaking states, as many more party members decamped to the NPN. The consequence of all this, according to Oyediran (1989: 167), was that the party 'was in a much weaker position in the two Igbo states in 1983 than before and immediately after the elections of 1979'.

Although the UPN with its highly centralised organisation at the federal and state levels was reputed to be the most disciplined of all the parties, it was not spared the splits which afflicted the others. These had at their heart the age-long question of whether Yorubas should remain in uncompromising opposition to the conservative Northern-led federal government. While Awolowo and his loyalists, including the governors, were all for uncompromising opposition, the Yoruba front in the NPN led by Adisa Akinloye, national chairman of the party, and Richard Akinjide, federal minister of justice and attorney-general, drew enough flak to sway many Yorubas to the side of 'accommodation'. Other major sources of intra-party crisis were the highly controversial and sometimes inconclusive primaries held to elect party candidates for gubernatorial and legislative elections and serious divisions within state branches. These led to massive defections from the UPN to the NPN by dissatisfied top-notchers and their followers. The most notable of these were those by Sunday Afolabi and Busari Adelakun, the 'strongman' of Ibadan politics, in Oyo state, and of Omoboriowo, deputy governor of Ondo state; in the NPN Omoboriowo won the gubernatorial ticket. But in general the UPN remained the vanguard of the opposition front.

Opposition to the NPN and the determination to unseat it, which brought together the UPN, NPP and rumps of the GNPP and PRP in an opposition alliance, served as a counterveiling force to the NPN's hegemonic project of weakening and possibly eventually co-opting other parties. The NPN's strategy was more or less successful in the National Assembly where, with the exception of some UPN and NPP HOR members and senators, most non-NPN representatives were 'bought over' by patronage. This left the regular meetings of the twelve UPN, NPP, PRP and GNPP 'progressive' governors as the bastion of opposition. They challenged many of the actions and policies of the NPN-controlled federal government, including the Revenue Allocation Act, appointment of PLOs, and the attempt to deport Alhaji

Shugaba, the GNPP speaker of the Borno state House of Assembly on the grounds that he was an alien. The regular meeting also provided the means of forging strategic alliances as the 1983 elections drew closer. The Progressive Parties Alliance (PPA) formed at a 'summit' of the progressives in Maiduguri in March 1982 was the main alliance that emerged, but like the UPGA alliance it was bedevilled from the outset by deep-rooted mistrust between leaders of the UPN and NPP which made them unable to agree on a common presidential candidate, which would have allowed the parties in the alliance to field their own candidates. Failure to agree on this crucial issue, which was the key to giving the NPN a good fight, was however compensated for by the inroads into the North which the alliance afforded especially to the UPN.

In fact, Awolowo was said to have received the backing of a major faction of the 'Kaduna mafia' – the Committee of Concerned Citizens – which had fallen out with the NPN, and the defection of several heavyweights from the NPN in its enclaves like Sokoto and Bauchi seemed to lend credence to this. A significant indicator of Awolowo/UPN's brightened prospects was the fact that he was able to get a Northern-Muslim presidential running mate (Alhaji Kura from Bauchi state), and this was why, ultimately the UPN was unmoved by the decision to have more than one presidential candidate, believing it had garnered sufficient Northern (and Eastern) support from the alliance to go it alone. The NPP for its part got an even better deal from the alliance in terms of extending its support-base in the North; it was preferred by the rumps of the PRP and GNPP which, desperate for a party platform on which to contest the 1983 elections, actually fused with it to form a new party, the PPP. However, the new party was denied registration by FEDECO (much to the relief of the UPN!), even after the NPP applied to have its name changed to that of the new party. Rimi and other PRP and GNPP members then contested the 1983 elections as members of the NPP.

As already pointed out, once Waziri Ibrahim saw that the main interest of both the UPN and NPP was to use the PPA as a pedestal for extending their national spread at the expense of his own party, he withdrew from the alliance. Thus a golden opportunity was lost to forge a truly national progressive front which had the potential to overthrow the conservative Northern-led alliance which had ruled the country since independence. Members of the 'progressive' parties even failed to agree on passing a bill in the National Assembly allowing for parties and factions of parties to merge. Nevertheless, the PPA and PPP were useful beginnings, and they were in a sense resurrected and consolidated in the aborted transition to the Third

Republic. The victory of Alhaji M.K.O. Abiola in the presidential election (annulled by the military) was an indication of what could have happened if the progressives had managed to reach agreement in 1982/3.

The NPN, the main beneficiary of the crises in the other parties, got its own share of intra-party crisis. At the federal level, the nomination of a presidential candidate badly rocked and divided the party. Leading Yoruba members, notably M.K.O. Abiola, argued that following the party's zoning formula it was the turn of the South, specifically the South-West, to produce the presidential candidate. Adherents of this position – Akin Deko, Fani Kayode and Adeyinka Adebayo – then formed the 'Yoruba Solidarity Front' to oppose the re-election of Adisa Akinloye as national chairman of the party because he was a strong supporter of Shagari's renomination (Akinloye did this in the hope that in 1987 Shagari would back his presidential candidacy). As it turned out, Shagari got the presidential ticket and Akinloye was returned as chairman, and these factors partly account for the resignation of Abiola from the party.

However, it was in the states that the NPN faced serious crises. These revolved mainly around the nomination of gubernatorial candidates, and were exacerbated by the entry of factors from other parties. This was most clearly the case in UPN-controlled states like Ogun, Ondo and Lagos in which defecting UPN heavyweights sought gubernatorial candidatures. In Bendel state the entry of Samuel Ogbemudia, formerly military governor under Gowon, into the NPN and his subsequent nomination as the party's gubernatorial candidate created rifts in the party, although increasing opposition to the Alli UPN government in the state swayed many supporters of the party to the side of the more popular Ogbemudia. In Sokoto state an early division in 1982 led Shehu Bayero, speaker of the NPN-controlled House of Assembly to defect to the UPN. The party lost more supporters to the UPN and NPP after the incumbent Governor Garba Nadama was renominated as a candidate for re-election. A similar situation ensued in Kwara state where Olusola Saraki's unsuccessful attempt to stop the nomination of the incumbent governor Adamu Atta led to a shift of support to the UPN by Saraki's followers.

In Benue state, divisions also followed gubernatorial primaries which saw Issac Shaahu and other heavyweights defecting to the UPN after losing the ticket to the incumbent governor, Aper Aku. In Niger state the NPN faced a grave problem with ethnic dimensions. Here the Nupes and Igalas in the party reacted against alleged Hausa/Fulani domination of the state and many of them moved to the NPP, which then became a serious rival to the NPN in the state. In Cross River state, intra-party divisions were between the 'Lagos group' led by the Senate president Joseph Wayas, which wanted Senator Donald Etiebet to be the gubernatorial candidate in the state, and the 'Home Front' led by the incumbent governor Clement Isong. Etiebet won the ticket, and although Isong did not join the bandwagon by decamping from the NPN, the misgivings produced by his defeat seriously affected the party's strength in the state. Already J.U. Esuene, formerly military governor under Gowon and a popular politician, had emerged as the UPN's gubernatorial candidate. His entry increased the UPN's strength and opposition to NPN dominance in the state.

This spate of party factionalisations and realignments was obviously the result of efforts by the parties and politicians to maximise their advantages as the 1983 elections drew closer. For politicians, the prospect of material advantage, patronage and political appointments was usually the overriding consideration. It could also be said that the short period between the formation of the parties in 1978 and the 1979 elections did not allow for stable alignments, and that the reshuffling of politicians and their camps provided the opportunity for this. One point that stands out clearly is that although the parties retained their sectional strongholds, the realignments, though largely expedient and instrumentalist, enabled them to extend their pan-Nigerian character.

THE 1983 ELECTIONS

Given the realignments of party forces – which on the one hand gave opposition parties, specifically the UPN and NPP, hopes of faring better than in 1979, and on the other reinforced the increasingly zero-sum competition for power – the 1983 elections were expected to be hotly contested. They therefore belonged to William Riker's category of 'critical' elections. For the UPN and NPN, especially, the stakes were quite high: while the UPN saw the prospects of finally defeating the conservative forces, the NPN was determined to extend its hegemony and, if possible, transform the country into a one-party-dominant state; indeed, its leaders had openly boasted that there were only two parties in the country: the NPN and the army.

Preparations for the elections and their setting looked certain to make their outcomes controversial. To begin with, the arrangements generated serious controversies. The opposition parties questioned the appointment of electoral commissioners, many of whom were alleged to be NPN members or sympathisers. Even the appointment of Justice Ovie Whiskey as chairman of FEDECO was challenged – unsuccessfully

– in court. How could elections be freely and fairly conducted by officials whose neutrality and integrity were in doubt? To reduce the scope for malpractice, the UPN and NPP proposed that votes be counted *in situ* at the polling stations. The proposal was approved by the National Assembly, despite opposition from NPN and FEDECO.

Secondly, the voters' register showed astronomical increases of voters in states controlled by the NPN and those in which it expected to win, and this aroused suspicions and apprehension among the 'opposition' parties which saw the apparent inflation of figures in NPN-controlled states as calculated to facilitate rigging by the NPN. States like Kaduna and Rivers not only recorded stupendous increases: in the seven NPN-controlled states a total of 5.2 million, and in the UPN- and NPP-controlled states 2.4 million and 1.75 more respectively. There was no doubt that the voters' register had been fraudulently inflated, as the total of 65.3 million voters was only possible if the country's population had increased from an estimated 80.56 million in 1976 to about 109 million in 1983, which was plainly incredible (see Oyediran, 1989). The attitudes of the parties clearly showed that they relied more on rigging and other malpractices than on the support of the electorate to secure victory.

Thirdly, FEDECO's reversal of the order of elections in 1979 by scheduling the presidential election first was opposed by the UPN and other opposition parties, which argued that the new order, which could well be repeated in subsequent elections, was designed to favour the NPN (the only party that welcomed the reverse order). Newspapers pointed to the dangers inherent in the new order of elections, and appealed for a change by FEDECO. As (an editorial in) *The Guardian* put it,

> ... if FEDECO changes the order of the elections and holds the presidential election first ... the bandwagon effect would turn the elections into a winner-takes-all affair, which could then turn Nigeria into a one-party state. (13 March 1983)

Similarly, the *Sunday Tribune*, a pro-UPN paper argued:

> ... no one should underrate the importance of the presidency – in a system that is essentially winner-takes- all – or misjudge the premium the electorate attaches to that office. Reason therefore dictates that the presidential election which is the climax of the whole exercise be preceded by the other four elections preferably in order of importance. [...] Given the 1979 experience which showed a slightly higher voter turn-out at the presidential than the other four elections, to reverse the order ... may be to risk dampening the voter's enthusiasm and interest after the first election. (13 March, 1983)

None of these arguments or the reservations expressed by the UPN and others could make FEDECO change its mind.

In addition to all this, the 'opposition' parties expressed problems with the roles of the police and other security agencies, as well as the federal government-controlled national media – Radio Nigeria, the Nigerian Television Authority and the newspapers *Daily Times* and *New Nigerian* – which were accused of being pro-NPN. The campaigns for the elections were volatile, with the parties trading allegations of intimidation and harassment by thugs, private armies, police and security forces. The opposition parties in particular alleged that the NPN was using its federal might, especially control of the police, for partisan advantage, for example by refusing to grant 'opposition' parties licences to hold meetings and campaigns. The tension that accompanied the campaigns and run-up to the elections was so great that there were calls that the military and even a neutral, outside body like the United Nations should take over the conduct of the election to ensure that they were free and fair.

The presidential election took place on 6 August and was followed by the gubernatorial, senatorial, HOR and states HOA elections, in that order, between 13 August and 3 September. The results of these elections are presented in Tables 4.4, 4.5 and 4.6. Contrary to all predictions and expectations, the NPN emerged the dominant party in all the elections. It won a landslide victory in the presidential election, with Shehu Shagari beating Obafemi Awolowo, his closest rival, with more than 4 million votes, and securing the mandatory quarter of the total votes cast in seventeen of the nineteen states (Lagos and Ogun, which remained solidly UPN, were the only exceptions).

In the gubernatorial elections, the NPN initially won in thirteen states but when the electoral tribunal reversed the result in Ondo states in favour of the UPN, this was reduced to twelve: Sokoto, Niger, Benue, Bauchi, Rivers and Cross River, all of which had been controlled by the party since 1979; Borno and Gongola, which it captured from the GNPP; Kaduna, its stronghold which had been lost to the PRP by default in 1979; Bendel and Oyo, which were wrested from the UPN; and Anambra, which the NPP lost as the result of a protracted legal struggle. In effect, the NPN doubled the gubernatorial strength it had in 1979, only losing Kwara state to the UPN ostensibly due to the irreconcilable split between its Saraki and Atta factions in the state.

Table 4.4. 1983 NATIONAL ASSEMBLY ELECTIONS*

State	Total no. of seats S	HR	NPN S	HR	UPN S	HR	NPP S	HR	GNPP S	HR	PRP S	HR
Anambra	5	29	1	15	–	–	4	14	–	–	–	–
Bauchi	5	20	5	20	–	–	–	–	–	–	–	–
Bendel	5	20	5	18	–	2	–	–	–	–	–	–
Benue	5	19	5	15	–	–	–	4	–	–	–	–
Borno	5	24	5	24	–	–	–	–	–	–	–	–
Cross River	5	28	5	26	–	2	–	–	–	–	–	–
Gongola	5	21	5	21	–	–	–	–	–	–	–	–
Imo	5	30	1	10	–	–	4	20	–	–	–	–
Kaduna	5	33	5	33	–	–	–	–	–	–	–	–
Kano	5	46	–	3	–	–	–	2	–	–	5	41
Kwara	5†	14	1	9	2	5	–	–	1	–	–	–
Lagos	5	12	–	–	5	12	–	–	–	–	–	–
Niger	5	10	4	8	–	–	1	2	–	–	–	–
Ogun	5	12	–	–	5	12	–	–	–	–	–	–
Ondo	5	42			Elections put off							
Oyo	5	22			Elections put off							
Plateau	5	16	–	–	–	–	3	6	–	–	–	–
Rivers	5	14	5	14	–	–	–	–	–	–	–	–
Sokoto	5	37	5	37	–	–	–	–	–	–	–	–
FCT	1	1	1	1	–	–	–	–	–	–	–	–
Total	96	450	55	264	12	33	12	48	1	–	5	41

S: Senate; HR: House of Representatives.
* The sixth party, the NAP, did not win any seat.
† Election postponed in Assa/Ilorin senatorial district.

Table 4.5. 1983 STATE GUBERNATORIAL ELECTIONS*

State	Governor/party
Anambra	Onoh/NPN
Bauchi	Ali/NPN
Bendel	Ogbemudia/NPN
Benue	Aku/NPN
Borno	Jarma/NPN
Cross River	Etiebet/NPN
Gongola	Tukur/NPN
Imo	Mbakwe/NPN
Kaduna	Kaita/NPN
Kano	Zuwo/PRP
Kwara	Adebayo/UPN
Lagos	Jakande/UPN
Niger	Ibrahim/NPN
Ogun	Onabanjo/NPN
Ondo	Ajasin/UPN†
Oyo	Olunloyo/NPN
Plateau	Lar/NPP
Rivers	Okilo/NPN
Sokoto	Nadama/NPN
FCT	
Total	

* The NAP did not win any state seat.
† Omoboriowo of the NPN was declared the winner earlier.

Table 4.6. 1983 PRESIDENTIAL ELECTION

State	Total votes cast	NPN	UPN	NPP	GNPP	PRP	NAP
				% of total votes			
Anambra	1,158,283	33.36	2.06	57.79	3.12	1.39	2.38
Bauchi	1,782,122	84.57	5.55	3.66	2.09	3.05	1.07
Bendel	1,099,851	41.17	51.45	4.35	1.05	0.67	0.79
Benue	652,795	58.83	12.21	23.31	3.05	0.98	1.62
Borno	718,043	48.60	16.73	3.76	24.96	3.76	2.19
Cross River	1,295,710	54.00	39.43	3.61	1.29	0.54	0.85
Gongola	735,648	38.44	21.85	20.13	3.47	11.04	5.07
Imo	1,588,975	25.07	1.43	66.99	3.29	1.16	2.06
Kaduna	2,137,398	59.28	10.57	10.58	3.08	14.02	1.75
Kano	1,193,050	32.19	4.06	22.98	2.95	36.63	1.19
Kwara	608,422	49.25	45.22	2.66	1.26	0.61	1.00
Lagos	1,640,381	7.59	83.39	7.28	0.72	0.04	0.05
Niger	430,731	63.17	3.66	25.23	3.01	2.03	1.90
Ogun	1,261,061	3.47	95.00	0.04	0.55	0.35	0.23
Ondo	1,829,343	20.03	77.25	1.11	0.63	0.39	0.58
Oyo	2,351,000	37.55	59.39	1.48	0.57	0.39	0.42
Plateau	652,302	44.86	43.05	5.86	2.85	1.77	1.61
Rivers	1,357,715	67.88	18.55	11.15	0.95	0.34	1.11
Sokoto	2,837,786	91.83	2.66	2.23	1.65	0.85	0.78
FCT	135,351	94.10	0.81	3.07	0.81	0.47	0.72
Total	25,454,166	47.33	30.98	13.88	2.51	4.08	1.21

Presidential candidates:
NPN: Shehu Shagari
UPN: Obafemi Awolowo
NPP: Nnamdi Azikiwe
GNPP: Waziri Ibrahim
PRP: Ibrahim Yussuf
NAP: Tunji Braithwaite

An account of the 1983 gubernatorial election results would not be complete without a few words on the drama that ensued in Ondo state. Here Akin Omoboriowo, the avowed Awoist and former deputy governor who defected to become gubernatorial candidate of the NPN, was at first declared the winner. In a state with an electorate that was unwavering in its practically monolithic support for the UPN in all other elections, both in 1979 and 1983, this was a most unlikely result, and there was a widespread conviction that the NPN's victory had been rigged. This was the basis for spontaneous rioting which greeted FEDECO's declaration of Omoboriowo as winner of the election.

Hundreds of lives were lost and properties destroyed in the riots in which NPN stalwarts and FEDECO offices were the main targets (cf. Apter, 1987). Omoboriowo fled to Lagos where he hibernated as governor-elect-in-exile until his election was overturned by the electoral tribunal.

A similar situation occurred in Oyo state, another UPN stronghold taken over by the NPN. Violent riots erupted after Omololu Olunloyo, the NPN candidate, was declared the winner of the gubernatorial election, but unlike the largely monolithic situation in Ondo, Oyo state was already badly polarised between the Ibadan, Ijesha and other groups, and this prevented the UPN from mustering the kind of support it enjoyed in Ondo. Besides, A.M.A. Akinloye, NPN's national chairman, who eyed the party's presidential ticket in 1987, was determined to ensure that this home state was won at all cost.

In the national and state assembly elections the NPN scored stupendous victories in most states, amounting in aggregate to a two-thirds majority of the National Assembly seats. In the state HOA elections, except for Lagos and Ogun states which remained absolutely UPN, the party won seats in all states, with overwhelming majorities in most. On the other hand, the UPN and NPP surprisingly fared worse than in 1979, despite their increased national strengths through the PPA. The UPN lost gubernatorial control of Bendel and Oyo states to the NPN, and only managed to add Kwara state to its stable. Although the party managed to better its performance in a few Northern states, its major victories were restricted to its now denuded Yoruba enclave. The NPP lost control of Anambra state to the NPN, but managed to retain control of Imo and Plateau states, though with much smaller majorities than in 1979. Like the UPN, its showing in the North also improved, notably in Kano and Niger states. The other parties were almost eclipsed. Not unexpectedly, the NAP failed to win any seat in all the elections, and the GNPP won only a solitary senatorial seat in Kwara state. The PRP kept a tenuous control of Kano state.

As indicated earlier, the landslide victories of the NPN were shocking, although the outcomes were not altogether unexpected. But in the eyes of the opposition parties, especially UPN and NPP, what took place was not so much an election as a preplanned and stagemanaged 'allocation' process by which the NPN, in collusion with FEDECO and the security forces, installed itself in power. In other words, FEDECO, under instruction from the NPN, simply allotted seats and states to the parties as it wanted. The parties rejected the results of all the elections but, unlike in 1979, their leaders appeared too daunted to go to court to challenge the result of the presidential election.[2] They seemed content with the mixture of bewilderment, opposition, and loss of confidence in the entire political system which greeted the outcome of the elections in several parts of the country, as well as the various court actions instituted by losers in gubernatorial and legislative elections. The elder statesman and NPP leader, Nnamdi Azikiwe, did however issue a statement titled 'History Will Vindicate the Just' in which he left the riggers to God's judgement:

> 'It is an irony of fate that these [NPN] politicians have become so intoxicated with the lust for power that they are now in league with unpatriotic lucifers in human form to destabilize Nigeria as a democracy...I am supremely confident that Almighty God will frustrate their knavery and ultimately expose their machinations and consign them to the scrap heap of forgotten tyrants. History will continue to vindicate the just and God shall punish the wicked.'
> (*Newswatch*, 20 May 1985: 14)

The 1983 elections were widely believed to have been massively rigged by all the parties: 'There [was] sufficient evidence of brazen and cynical rigging of the votes, to suggest that ... [all parties] approached the elections without much faith in either themselves or in the electorate' (*The Guardian* editorial, 11 September 1983). But it was the party with control over the electoral and security apparatus, and the resources to out-rig the other parties – namely the NPN – that won the elections (the so-called 'incumbency factor', a euphemism for rigging, also ensured the return to power of the party-in-power in the states).

This was the conclusion of the judicial commission of inquiry into the FEDECO's affairs and its conduct of the 1983 elections, whose report (FGN [Babalakin Report], 1991) provides the strongest evidence that the election was won and lost by means of rigging. It contains a list of the major forms of rigging: inflation of the voters' register through compilation of fictitious names (said to be most pronounced in Cross River, Lagos, Oyo and Rivers states); use of an unofficial voters' register; illegal printing of voters' cards; illegal possession of ballot boxes; stuffing of ballot boxes with illegal ballot papers; falsification of counting and results (e.g. Kasa Ngala polling station in Borno state where 55 people voted but 1,551 votes were recorded); declaration of results where no elections took place; unauthorised announcements/publications of results; and so on. The commission indicted the police, security and FEDECO personnel for their roles in facilitating the rigging, and recommended that some

---

[2] However, the GNPP leader, Waziri Ibrahim, did challenge the re-election of President Shagari in court, but to no avail.

FEDECO officials should not be allowed to hold public office requiring political neutrality in future (FGN, 1991).

While rigging was the most plausible explanation for the electoral outcomes, especially the wide margins of the NPN's victories, ethno-regional patterns and, in particular, the minorities' dissenting and instrumentalist calculations could still be discerned in the electorate's behaviour in different parts of the country. Besides, as we saw earlier, support for the NPP in the East had declined because of a combination of forces, not least the strengthening of the NPN through the federal development projects brought by Vice-President Ekwueme who was eager to establish a political constituency, and the fact that Ojukwu and Okpara, two eminent Igbo leaders who had returned from exile, were members of the party. Similarly, in the UPN-controlled states, with the exception of Ogun and to some extent Lagos and Ondo, the NPN had good chances anyway of winning elections. These factors, while not invalidating the effects of rigging, do mean that it was not the sole explanation for the electoral outcomes.

The election results were hotly disputed. In some cases, notably gubernatorial elections in Imo and Oyo states, state governments broadcast their own versions of the results through state government radio and television media even before FEDECO was ready to announce the official results. As Governor Sam Mbakwe of Imo state argued, this was to pre-empt FEDECO's plan to award the state to the NPN. But even FEDECO itself officially altered the declared results in many instances due to recounts, protests from candidates and instructions by the law courts (Oyediran, 1989: 174). The publication of contradictory results was largely responsible for the disputes and riots which followed the release of FEDECO's results in some states, with every party claiming that its own version was the authentic one. The disputes meant that in many cases the electoral outcome could only be decided by the courts. The extent of disputed results was enormous: almost every assembly and gubernatorial election was the subject of legal proceedings at the electoral tribunals and high courts, whose verdicts reversed results declared by FEDECO, sometimes on technical grounds but in many cases on grounds of rigging and other electoral malpractices, thus eroding what little credibility was still attached to the elections. The fact that many successful candidates won in courts rather than through the ballot box was reason enough to describe the elections as a farce.

The larger implication of the failure of the 1983 elections is that it confirmed still further the inability of civilian politicians to conduct free and fair elections on their own. The only relatively free, fair and uncontroversial elections in the country were those conducted by the colonial regime and the military – supposedly 'neutral' bodies. In both the First and Second Republics, the politicians were unable to conduct elections with outcomes acceptable to all parties, and it was the violent disputes over the election results that provided the ultimate justification for military intervention. This is why some commentators proposed that a neutral body (some said the military) or an outside body like the UN should take charge of the conduct of elections in the country for the sake of democratic stability (for analyses of Nigeria's election problems see Adekanye, 1990; and Oyediran, 1990). Joseph (1987: 169) has aptly summarised the whole question of elections and political stability in Nigeria:

> Until Nigerians find a way to create institutions which, like the electoral bureaucracy of India and other multicultural, multiparty democracies, can remain part of the state or policy itself, and not become instruments susceptible to being captured by factions of civil society which win (temporary) control of the state, any hope for a constitutional democracy is certain to be regularly frustrated.

The problem of credible elections under civilian regimes emanated from (1) the ethno-regional character of competing parties which heightened the zero-sum, do-or-die nature of elections and led parties to invest in tactics that by-pass the ballot box; (2) the way in which the electoral commission was composed, which did not insulate it from partisanship; (3) the misuse of state-owned media by incumbent parties to the disadvantage of all other parties; and (4) the partisan use of the police and other security agencies. These problems, some of which were highlighted by the Justice Babalakin Commission set up in August 1985 to inquire into the affairs of FEDECO (FGN, 1991; also see Kurfi, 1983), had to be addressed if civilian regimes in the country were not to go on failing and providing grounds for military intervention.

The country was in a state of virtual anarchy in the aftermath of the 1983 elections. There were calls for the cancellation of the elections, and for the military to intervene. Some newspapers in particular made veiled invitations. The pro-UPN *Nigerian Tribune*, for example, said that the NPN was assuming office on borrowed time (editorial, 1 October 1983), and daily published in its conspicuous sideline column the words of late American president J.F. Kennedy: 'Those who make peaceful change impossible make violent change inevitable.' The Kano-based *Triumph* (21 August 1983) in an editorial titled 'Violent Change Inevitable' reminded the NPN of the consequences of the rigged elections in the First Republic and said that Nigerians did not want a repeat of what happened then – military intervention

– 'but if that is precisely what the NPN is driving us towards, by any means we are ready.'

One notable fall-out from the elections with clear implications for political stability in the country was the advocacy of confederalism by Southern, especially Yoruba politicians, who saw a pulling apart of units of the federation as the only way out of perpetual domination of the country by the conservative forces led by Hausa/Fulani politicians. Confederation was first advocated by Olu Aboderin, once proprietor of *The Punch*, in December 1982, and after the 1983 elections this gathered momentum. It was championed by Bisi Onabanjo, then UPN governor of Ogun state, who referred to a 'cabal of native imperialism': through massive rigging, falsification of results and paramilitary police forces which he said constituted armies of occupation, this had taken over control of most Northern states and effected a 'conquest' of Southern states. Although Onabanjo's outburst was promptly disowned by the UPN, partly because the federal-controlled Nigerian Television Authority interpreted it as signalling the beginning of an UPN-led Yoruba secession. It heralded a new phase of Southern-based challenge to the political domination of conservative Northern élites, this time spearheaded by Yorubas. The challenge continued and gathered momentum long after General Buhari sacked the Second Republic: the lopsided representation of Northern officers in the military regime seemed to confirm suspicions that it was an offshoot of the same conservative forces. The major advocates of confederation included retired military officers like Brigadier Adekunle and Lt-General Alani Akinrinade. Even the former head of state General Obasanjo became an advocate of more equitable sharing of power and resources and criticised the Northern hegemonic policies of the new regime. The Buhari regime considered the confederation debate dangerous enough to warrant banning it in July 1985.

The confederation debate (analysed in Osaghae, 1990) was symptomatic of the inadequacies or failures of power-sharing structures which guaranteed various groups access to federal power. The Mohammed-Obasanjo regime and makers of the 1979 Constitution had hoped to establish the structural basis for consensus politics by insisting on national political parties, the federal character principle, and a non-majoritarian presidential system of government. But the experience of the Second Republic showed that these could not be guaranteed and, even if this had been possible, were not sufficient measures to eliminate zero-sum political contest and assuage fears of domination. The critical problem was how to conduct free, fair and acceptable elections, and not turn losers into advocates for military intervention or disintegration of the country. Other germane issues of power-sharing are dealt with in subsequent chapters.

COLLAPSE OF THE REPUBLIC

On the night of 31 December 1983, the military struck once again to overthrow the young Republic. The chaos that followed the 1983 elections provided only the last straw for this, if justification had to be found. More powerful underlying reasons were the massive corruption, economic mismanagement and authoritarian tendencies that characterised the Republic. Panels instituted to probe governors and other officials after its overthrow found evidence of widespread abuse and embezzlement of public funds, for which they were sentenced to various jail terms and/or asked to refund their misappropriations to the state. Some of the more powerful politicians, who were alleged to be the most corrupt, fled abroad.

The corruption was largely due to the patronage basis of political relations and support. This had been adopted by most of the parties, but especially the NPN which was a party of business people, contractors and *nouveaux riches* held together, as Graf says, by links of patronage and mutual advantage. As such, the parties were

> ... under continuous pressure to 'deliver' to these party stalwarts. In a situation of constant growth and surplus, this strategy had worked effectively. But in times of a shrinking national cake, the party's pay-off capacity could only be maintained at the expense of the other sectors of society. As the gap between the party elite and the generality of society thus increased and grew more visible, overall system legitimacy was undermined to a degree that would have been inconceivable had the party officials been seen to be sharing in the 'national sacrifice.' (Graf, 1988: 94-5)

While politicians corruptly enriched themselves, workers were being retrenched in large numbers and were owed huge salary arrears, and the masses were called upon to make sacrifices by accepting the deprivation of their social and material rights. Many were forced to withdraw their children from school, reduced to searching for food in dustbins and refuse depots, and exposed to preventable disease and death.

Even in the depth of the economic recession, the political class continued its reckless spending, corruption and scandalous patronage-building. After the 1983 elections, no less than forty federal ministers of different ranks were appointed to a bloated cabinet which the president and NPN needed to spread their patronage to the large number of politicians to whom they owed their victory at the polls (a similar situation arose in 1965, although that was because of the large number of parties that had to be represented in the 'national government'). Federal and state public services were inflated with sinecure appointments, which increased rapidly in the run-up to the 1983 elections and after, while legislators and top government officials made endless overseas trips (which attracted generous allowances) as members of over-sized government delegations, legislative study groups and the like, or simply on pleasure trips at government expense.

Adamolekun (1985: 75) also identifies the politicians' preoccupation with winning elections and, by implication, being a beneficiary of some of the huge amounts wasted (the total cost of the 1983 elections – FEDECO, rigging and all – was estimated at over N2 billion) as a major source of corruption and resource wastage. Then there was the rush to complete Abuja, the new federal capital, in five years rather than the ten years originally proposed. 'Abuja contracts' were a major source of corruption. These were the housing, construction and other sundry contracts handed out to party members, who then executed sub-standard projects in the new capital. A similar abuse were the kickbacks taken on contracts awarded to multinational firms. The authoritarian tendency of the regime was strengthened by the militarisation of the police force and by the 'discipline' required to implement the austerity measures introduced in 1982, and this further alienated the masses of the people from government and eroded the claim to legitimacy of the Republic's political order. The Shagari administration made an effort to redress the anomalous situation, and 'rid' the system of corruption. Its 'ethical revolution', which was meant to achieve this, was launched with a great fanfare but, in the midst of the pervasive corruption of the political class it was too hypocritical to be of any serious consequence.

THE ECONOMY

Of all the failings of the Second Republic, the one on which commentators are agreed, and which the military gave for a fresh intervention, was the gross mismanagement of the economy, especially by the NPN-controlled federal government. The indicators of this mismanagement were all too clear. From an average annual growth rate of 6-7 per cent between 1975 and 1980, GDP fell by 8.5 per cent in real terms between 1981 and 1983, while consumer prices increased by over 20 per cent. Agricultural production, especially of cash crops, declined from 4.0 per cent in 1979 to 3.4 in 1981 and 2.7 per cent in 1982, although domestic food output rose by 7 per cent at the end of 1983 (due largely to good harvests in those years). Foreign currency reserves declined from N5.462 billion in 1980 to N798.5 million which was barely enough to pay for one month's imports in 1983, while total external debt rose from about US$9 billion in 1980 to about US$18 billion in 1983. Thus from an acclaimed 'underborrowed' status (as Nigeria was designated on the Eurodollar market) the country climbed from being the thirty-first highest borrower in the market in 1981 to thirteenth in 1982 (Okolie, 1995). The economic downturn discouraged direct foreign investment and encouraged capital flight, which in many cases took the form of fraudulent practices of overinvoicing import inventories and underpricing exports by foreign businessmen and corrupt Nigerian officials and businessmen. Total capital flight between 1979 and 1983 was estimated at US$14 billion. A vivid picture of the Shagari administration's mismanagement is presented by Okolie (1995: 202) thus: 'Despite the country earning N56 billion (N44 billion from oil alone), the highest amount ever recorded for such a period in Nigeria's history ... the Shagari government left a total external debt of N17.7 billion at the end of 1983.'

The domestic economy was also in deep recession. Workers, especially primary school teachers in the states, were owed huge arrears of salaries, in some cases for upwards of ten months. With unofficial inflation rates of between 30 and 50 per cent, purchasing power declined massively, as the costs of consumer goods and services, including food, housing, transportation, education and health care, went beyond the reach of most ordinary people. The situation was most devastating for the urban poor who also lost their jobs as various enterprises retrenched workers in order to keep afloat, but those in rural areas also suffered greatly. By contrast, politicians, the business élite and top civil servants were enjoying something of a boom, thanks to the multiplication of rent-seeking and corruption opportunities through the several controls introduced under the austerity regime, and thanks to smuggling, which by December 1983 accounted for almost 20 per cent of total imports. The manufacturing and industrial sectors, which depended on imported raw materials, were operating far below their capacities, and many were forced to shut down. The federal and state governments also recorded huge budget deficits all through the period, with state governments netting a combined debt of N13.3 billion.

The most popular explanation for the economic recession that beset the Second Republic, and the one the Shagari administration continually offered, was the oil glut which resulted in a fall in the spot price of crude oil. Nigeria's response to the glut, which was dictated by its membership of OPEC, was to drastically reduce its crude oil production from 2.06 million barrels per day (bpd) in 1980 to 1.3 million bpd in 1982.[3] By so doing, OPEC hoped to maintain a price of US$34 per barrel (pb). Reduction in production of course meant reduction in Nigeria's revenue from oil, which fell from N12.9 million in 1980 to N11.2 million in 1981, N10.5 million in 1982, and N7.8 million in 1983. As the situation worsened, Nigeria was forced to reduce the spot price of its Bonny Light brand to US$30 and later US$28 pb, after Britain and Norway, which produced a similar brand, reduced their own prices. But even this did not improve the situation as the oil market remained sluggish.

Granted that the glut and global economic recession seriously affected the Nigerian economy, the Shagari administration and indeed all state governments were largely to blame for failing to respond early to the economic downturn which was apparent by early 1980 and, when they did respond, for failing to show the high degree of discipline required for effective management of recession. Like all other governments since Gowon, they failed to appreciate fully the dangers of relying exclusively on oil. In particular, the initial steep rise in the oil price from US$19 pb in April 1979 to US$38 early in 1981 whetted the appetite for reckless spending on ambitious projects and building patronages. Although the federal government launched a Green Revolution programme to mobilize increased agricultural production and even signed a two-year contract with Brazil to export rubber in 1982, the petro-naira mentality of the good life through oil wealth continued to make agriculture, the main revenue earner at independence, a neglected sector. A timely warning on the bad state of the economy and the need to arrest the drift by Chief Awolowo, leader of the UPN, was dismissed as intended to score a cheap political point, as the federal government denied that the country's economy was in bad shape (but even the states controlled by the Chief's party did not heed his call – they did little to reduce their equally huge spending). With such a mindset, some of the responses to the economic crisis were *ad hoc* and uncoordinated, and included the search for scapegoats, which led to the expulsion of over 2 million illegal aliens, most of whom were nationals of Ghana and Niger, early in 1983.

The federal and state governments, hoping for a quick recovery of oil prices, continued with profligate expenditure ostensibly to make good electoral promises and increase their popularity. The federal

---

[3] Not even a bait by President Jimmy Carter for Nigeria to redouble its oil production to maximise its profits from the problems in the Gulf in 1980 during President Shagari's visit to the White House could tempt Nigeria away from its commitment to OPEC.

government committed over N2 billion to a housing project which was fraudulently executed by party members-turned-emergency contractors, while it competed with state governments to award generous bursaries to students in tertiary institutions. For purely political reasons, it embarked on building a federal university, college of education and polytechnic in every state, in addition to establishing federal radio and television stations in all the states. State governments decided to compete with the federal government in these spheres and most of them, especially in the South, established state universities and radio/television networks. Huge sums were also sunk into militarising the police force and strengthening the military, building the new federal capital at Abuja with very little to show for it, and iron and steel projects at Aladja and Ajaokuta. The hurry to build Abuja at a time of economic depression was one of the more notable instances of misallocation of resources in the Second Republic. The NPN government appeared more interested in using the inflated Abuja contracts to lubricate its patronage system, with the result that there was no effective monitoring and supervision of the projects in the new capital. By the time the Republic was dismissed by the military in 1983, all that could be shown to the huge contracts and advance payments were signposts at construction sites and sub-standard buildings.

Imports of all manners of goods, including food and used vehicles, went on almost unrestricted. The government appeared more interested in winning political support and extending its patronage than in getting the economy back on course. Thus it raised the national minimum wage from N70 in 1979 to N125 in 1981 while taking no serious steps to increase the real value of the naira, and set up the presidential task force on rice to make the commodity – which had been fraudulently bought by party stalwarts from the Nigerian National Supply Company (NNSC) and later hoarded and resold for a large profit – available at a cheaper rate in the country. The task force became a notorious establishment of corruption.

That the Shagari administration failed to salvage the economy was due not so much to lack of effort as it was to a fundamental lack of will and discipline in the governments of the Republic, and the desperate corruption of party members and government officials. The government made efforts to resuscitate the agricultural sector and diversify the economy. The Green Revolution Programme, for example, was launched to mobilize self-reliant food and agricultural production. It required multinational corporations to invest part of their profits in agricultural development; the river basin authorities were reinvigorated with generous funds to assist the programme; and generous funds were pumped into World Bank assisted Agricultural

Development Programmes (ADPs). The government also launched the 'ethical revolution' to address the aspects of the crisis which had to do with corruption and moral decay. But these efforts were to no avail.

However, the most significant and concerted policy responses of the Second Republic regime to the economic crisis lay in the deflationary austerity measures embodied in the Economic Stabilisation (Temporary Provisions) Act of 1982, which ran against the current of prevalent neo-classical economic thought. In the neo-liberal or new political economy perspective of the Bretton Woods institutions and other members of the donor community who advocated structural adjustment, the austerity therapy introduced by the federal government – which emphasised the role of the state, and failed to devalue the currency, remove subsidies on goods and services, especially petroleum products, privatise, and so on – was outdated and inappropriate (for the theoretical underpinnings of the new orthodoxy, see Olukoshi and Nwoke, 1994).

The need for some form of structural adjustment of the economy was recognised, but the state operators were not willing to vacate the driving seat of the economy and 'sell out' the country, as it were, to external creditors. These were the major reasons for the failure of negotiations with the IMF, to which the federal government turned as a last resort after failing to secure private loans totalling US\$2 billion to clear trade arrears on the Euro-dollar market. Although it was able to secure over N1 billion from its reserves with the IMF, this was well short of what the country needed. The extent of external assistance needed and the desperate moves to secure new loans, which provided the classic setting for the IMF to move into the country, can be gleaned from Olukoshi's insights (1995: 141):

> ... in April 1983, the government submitted an application to the [IMF] for an Extended Fund Facility (EFF) loan of about 2.5 billion US dollars. Another application was sent to the World Bank for a structural loan of between 300 and 500 million US dollars. Also, three financial advisers – Messrs S.G. Warburg and Co., Lehman Kuhn, and Lazard Frères – were appointed by the government to assist it with its efforts to reach agreement with 30 Western banks on the refinancing of nearly 2 billion US dollars in trade arrears.

Later negotiations with the IMF were stalemated, with the Fund insisting on a full-scale structural adjustment programme, devaluation, removal of subsidies, privatisation, trade liberalisation and all, and the federal government willing to accept reduction in capital expenditure and rationalisation of parastatals but nothing more, and certainly not devaluation. Western creditors, including the US Eximbank and the British

Export Credit Guarantee Department (ECGD), subsequently agreed with the IMF a condition for granting any further credit facilities (Olukoshi, 1995: 142). Despite the enormous pressure this well-known international capitalist conspiracy put on the Shagari administration, no headway was made in negotiations with the IMF until the military overthrew the Republic. But it was clear that, as a *rentier* state, Nigeria was economically at the end of its tether. The struggle to turn the situation around, which became worse in later years is an underlying theme of the rest of this book.

In the Second Republic, the hope for economic recovery was pinned on implementation of the Economic Stabilisation (Temporary Provisions) Act of April 1982. The Act embodied short- and medium-term austerity measures (in the hope that the oil glut was only temporary) which aimed at monetary controls, import restrictions and public expenditure reduction. Stringent import, foreign exchange and price controls were introduced (and old ones strengthened), tariffs were raised and more goods were made subject to import duties, new capital projects were suspended, overall public investment expenditure was cut by about 40 per cent, interest rates were increased by an average of 2 per cent, and so on. Appropriate as some of these measures were, they came a shade too late. Moreover, rather than deal with the problems, these measures, some of which dated back to Obasanjo's austerity measures, multiplied rent-seeking and patronage opportunities, and encouraged smuggling and corrupt practices: in this the famous import licence regime, 'Form M' for foreign exchange control, and bans placed on imported beer, cigarettes, food, and other commodities, were particularly notable.

FOREIGN POLICY

The following is typical assessment of foreign policy under the Second Republic:

> The ... regime of Shehu Shagari inherited a foreign policy which was very popular with the people as well as being the object of respect in the international system. But while adapting its principles, goals and rhetoric, the regime quickly showed that it neither had the zeal nor the competence to keep up the pace it inherited.[...] The result was that Nigeria's foreign policy remained at the level of routine observance of existing relations and obligations.[...] The four years of the regime were, therefore, a period of recess for Nigeria's foreign policy. (Otubanjo, 1989: 6)

Assessments like this underplay the differences in the foreign policy setting between a military government, which has its right of way and is not accountable to the people even when its policies are populist, and a democratic government whose autonomy of action is seriously constrained by a complex network of legislative controls, intra- and inter-party differences, accountability to the electorate and so on. In the case of the Shagari regime, the crisis of legitimacy that attended his attainment of power, and the economic recession which imperilled the Second Republic and caused Nigeria to risk losing the little amount of autonomy it had managed to wrestle from the capitalist majors in previous years, also had serious consequences for foreign policy. Be that as it may, foreign policy in the Second Republic was, like that of the First Republic, conservative, cautious, pro-Western and sometimes unpopular, which Okolo (1989) attributes to the fact that President Shagari was a political pupil of the Balewa government. Shagari nevertheless showed a few flashes of non-conservatism, as in the strong opposition to the bloody *coup d'état* that brought Master-Sergeant Doe to power in Liberia and the subsequent attempts to isolate the regime, and the opposition to Reagan's policy of engagement in Southern Africa. But as Otubanjo observes, it was mostly routine, meaning that Africa remained the cornerstone of foreign policy. As in previous chapters, we shall analyse the different spheres of the Shagari government's foreign policy.

At the African continental level, decolonisation and the eradication of racism remained the main focus, and the OAU, the UN, the Commonwealth and other international forums were the major channels for articulating demands for sanctions and isolation of the Pretoria regime and mobilising the support of other countries. Support for the liberation movements in Southern Africa was maintained, although in 1980 the decline in the economy led the federal government to stop the yearly allocation of nearly N5 million to aid these movements (the government however gave a grant of US$10 million to the newly-installed Zimbabwean government to enable it acquire the *Zimbabwe Herald* from its white South African owners). The regime pursued the anti-apartheid struggle in other spheres, albeit more consciously than many Nigerians would have expected, especially in its dealings with the United States and other Western powers. Following the preferences of the liberation movements themselves and pressures from home, the regime found itself having to take some hardline positions against the United States on Southern Africa. Thus, Nigeria opposed its so-called 'constructive engagement' policy which linked the independence of Namibia to the withdrawal of Cuban forces from Angola. In other spheres of African relations, there were no major departures from the past, although there was considerable interest in the affairs of the OAU (however, Nigeria was criticised for failing to rally support for the OAU summit in Tripoli in 1982). This interest was manifested in Nigeria's frontline role in the Lagos Plan of Action which set out the blueprint for an African economic community and advocated collective self-reliance and inward-looking policies as the key to African development.

At the sub-regional level, commitments to ECOWAS were maintained, although the federal government was forced, as part of the desperate measures to arrest the precipitous decline in the economy and check the rising spate of religious riots in which several foreigners were involved, to adopt more realistic approaches to its policy of good neighbourliness and its role as a regional benefactor. It was for this reason that it embarked on a massive deportation of illegal aliens originally from Ghana and other neighbouring countries who had flooded Nigeria in the wake of the economic decline in their own countries. There was also a drastic reduction in aid to countries in the sub-region, although concessions continued to be made on oil sales. One area where the Shagari administration drew serious criticisms, especially from the military, was in its tame response to border disputes with Chad and Cameroon and the incursions into Nigerian territory by soldiers of these countries. Shagari's preference for 'peaceful resolution', which top army officers saw as detrimental to Nigeria's status, was partly responsible for his overthrow, as we see in the next chapter.

At the global level, Nigeria was preoccupied with negotiations with the IMF and other Western creditors. As we saw earlier, the negotiations were stalled over the refusal of the Shagari government to accept the bitter pills of devaluation and removal of subsidies. Nigeria also remained committed to OPEC despite strong agitation for pulling out because of the limitations it placed on production quotas. The final notable theme of global relations worth noting was the increased US presence in the country, marked by the visit of Vice-President George Bush to Nigeria in 1982. This had to do with Nigeria being the supplier of a large proportion of America's oil needs, US assistance to Shagari's Green Revolution programme, and Nigeria's operation of an US-type presidential system. Britain nevertheless remained a traditional ally, although its influence in Nigeria had considerably waned.

5

THE RETURN OF THE MILITARY:
THE BUHARI REGIME, 1983-1985

The return of the military, following the overthrow of the Second Republic, brought in its wake an era of authoritarianism such as had not previously been known in Nigeria's post-independence history. This was closely connected with the desperate efforts to revive the ailing economy which involved the curtailing of liberties, and the subsequent uprising of the civil society to defend them. As the economic situation worsened, popular resistance and the intensity of authoritarian rule increased. The addition of what turned out to be crisis-laden democratic transition programmes to these in the later part of the second phase of military rule beginning with the Babangida regime not surprisingly provoked political instability of a kind that kept the existence of the country as one entity on the brink throughout the period. Perhaps, then, the plan of the Buhari regime to revive the economy first before embarking on a democratic transition was the most rational and less problematic sequence, but the irrepressible demands for democratisation, increasing intolerance of military rule, and pressures from Western creditors, the United States, European Community countries and other members of the international community, not to mention the economy's continued decline, left no room for the luxury of such an ideal sequence. The Buhari regime paid the price for refusing to accept the limitations, and the later regimes which did accept them met with extreme difficulty in managing the crisis generated by the largely contradictory forces and pressures.

However, it would be a mistake to assume that even though they were more authoritarian, the regimes in the second phase of military rule differed fundamentally in character from those of the 1960s and '70s. While it is partially true, as Olagunju *et al.* (1993) assert, that military regimes have often deferred to the dictates of the liberal-federal traditions in the country, there has been a tendency to underestimate the authoritarian character of previous military regimes and to mistake the pretensions to democracy of military leaders for liberalism. Military governments are, without exception, authoritarian and undemocratic, and operate within a framework of what Nwabueze

(1994: 4) aptly terms 'lawless autocracy, that is to say, a government not limited by law'.

We only need to recall the draconian nature of decrees issued by the first military government of Aguiyi-Ironsi to see the point. Basically they all operated within the framework stipulated by the Constitutional (Suspension and Modification) Decree no. 1 of 1966 (amended to suit the circumstances of different regimes) whose ouster clause established the omnipotence of decrees by forbidding their challenge in the courts. Following the celebrated Lakanmi case where the Supreme Court had the courage to declare null and void decree no. 45 under which Mr Lakanmi's assets had been confiscated, the Federal Military Government (Supremacy and Enforcement of Powers) Decree no. 28 was issued to put the omnipotence of decrees beyond all doubt (for an interesting debate on the rule of law under the military, see Shyllon and Obasanjo, 1980). Previous military regimes also enacted the Robbery and Fire Arms (Special Provisions) Decree of 1970, amended in 1977; the Counterfeit Currency (Special Provisions) Decree of 1974; and the Petroleum and Distribution (Anti-Sabotage) Decree no. 35 of 1975 whose provisions made it a forerunner to the Miscellaneous Decree no. 20 of 1984, all of which stipulated the death penalty for offenders. Decree 2, under which critics and opponents of government were detained without trial in the 1980s and 1990s, had a forerunner in Decree no. 24 of 1967 which, ostensibly to back the declaration of a state of emergency, empowered the inspector-general of police or the chief of army staff to arrest and detain anybody without trial (Tai Solarin, Wole Soyinka and other critics were detained under this decree).

It is arguable that the authoritarianism of the military regimes of the 1980s and '90s, though more intense and flagrant, was not unlike that of their predecessors, and that it was the culmination of earlier creeping authoritarianism, and of the perception of the military as 'custodians', which invoked notions of a higher morality and a superior vision of how to organise society. These notions were often presented as the antithesis of the 'indiscipline' and conflict-ridden relations of civilian political formations, and were supported by the preference for 'strong' governments in a milieu of public amorality such as prevailed in Nigeria; the point is that, as between one military regime and another, authoritarianism can only differ in degree rather than in kind. In other words, to the extent that all military regimes are authoritarian, the degree of the authoritarianism applied by a regime will, among other factors, depend on its perception of how serious was the crisis that warranted a military solution. This way, the heightened authoritarianism of the 1980s and

'90s can be attributed, as has been mentioned earlier, to the desperate economic crisis that plagued the country, the anarchy that came to characterise political and social relations, and the potent threats to the country's survival as a single entity.

One reason for the hostility towards the military regimes of the 1980s and '90s both inside and outside the country was that, unlike previous military regimes which operated within a 'world time' (a loose translation of *zeitgeist*) that was tolerant of modernising and corrective military rule in developing countries, military rule had by the 1980s become an anachronism and out of tune with the world time whose defining characteristics, as defined by the United States and other majors of the post-Cold War era, were democracy and democratisation (for the concept of world time as it refers to a summary characterisation of particular epochs, see Eberhard, 1973). The changing milieu meant that, even with the best of intentions on the part of non-democratic military regimes which could have been forgiven or understood in the past, the human rights abuses and arbitrariness endemic to such regimes were now heinous crimes in the view not only of the country's citizens, but even more by an international community led by the Western capitals of liberalism. As the military in Nigeria refused to respond to the dictations of the new international political order, the country was gradually relegated to the club of the world's isolated states.

The purpose of this long introduction has been to put the military regimes of the 1980s and '90s in their proper perspective, and to indicate that even though they differed in terms of specific policies and orientations, they were essentially variants of the same type joined, as they were, by the imperatives of economic recovery and democratic transition in a hostile milieu. This chapter is concerned with the first of them, the Buhari regime, which served as a pathfinder in the new dispensation.

THE COUP OF 31 DECEMBER 1983

The possibility of a coup had been the subject of speculation as early in the life of the Second Republic as 1981 when senior officers in the army were said to have expressed dissatisfaction with the performance of the civilian administrators. However, it was clear to the plotters that a coup at that time was not likely to enjoy popular support, because the civilian regime's 'cup of iniquity' was not yet full. They had to wait for a more opportune time to strike – after politicians had bungled elections and shown their incapacity in the face of economic crisis. It is even said that the coup that finally took place in December was rescheduled twice after the 1983 elections (see *West Africa*, 30 January 1984); if this is correct, it can only mean that the reasons for it were far deeper than the altruistic ones advanced in the dawn broadcast by the then Brigadier Sani Abacha announcing the coup, and subsequent addresses by General Buhari and other key figures of the regime.

Indeed, it is believed that the coup was staged to pre-empt another one planned by junior officers which would have swept most generals out of the army – rumours of junior officers' coups persisted in 1984, and according to one account an attempt was actually made by a group of junior officers, forty-two of whom were secretly executed in September 1984 (*The Observer*, London, 18 Nov. 1984). A point which suggests that opportunism was present is that although the new regime advanced economic mismanagement and decline as the main reasons for overthrowing the civilian regime, they nonetheless continued with the short-term austerity-based blueprint formulated by the Shagari administration. Othman (1989: 136) talks of the soldiers own 'lack of distinct economic strategy, and the pilfering of Shagari's own policy document'. More specifically, Adamolekun (1985: 84-5) points out that not only was the new government's decision to rephase development projects a continuation of a policy already started by Shagari, but the task of rephasing the projects was entrusted to the same person who performed the function under the discredited civilian regime.

But opportunism is only one of the explanations for the coup. There were others, ranging from military organisational and corporate image-related factors, and sectarian interests, to custodian-type, supposedly altruistic and nationalistic factors. Othman (1984, 1989) has put these factors into perspective. Under the category of organisational and corporate image factors, he highlights the disappointment of top officers with the decrease in defence expenditure under Shagari, in marked contrast to the huge defence budgets under Mohammed/Obasanjo: the lowest percentage of annual budget allocated to defence under the latter regime (9.1 per cent in 1977) was more than the largest allocation under Shagari (8.6 per cent in 1980). Although the decrease could have been seen as a consequence of the economic recession which followed the crash in oil prices (which was tolerable for as long as defence expenditure was devoted largely to meeting welfare and personnel needs, as Shagari did), the scandal involved in the £300 million contract with British Aerospace for the supply of eighteen Jaguar jets, from which NPN stalwarts were said to have received 'kickbacks' of £22 million, made light of any austerity argument. Moreover, the corresponding huge increases in capital expenditure on internal security, the lion's share of which went to the police, bred inter-organisational hostility and opposition by the military, to whom any attempt to build the police as an 'alternative' military force, especially at the expense of the army and other arms of the military, was absolutely unacceptable.

Another corporate image-related factor was the perceived humiliation the army suffered in Chad and Cameroon through the cautious and indecisive foreign policy approach of the Shagari administration. The unceremonious withdrawal of the Nigeria-led peacekeeping mission in Chad, and the seeming inability of the Nigerian authorities to respond as a regional power to attacks over border disputes by Cameroonian and Chadian soldiers, which resulted in the deaths of some Nigerian soldiers, were seen as a slur on the reputation of the Nigerian army; it took the Cameroon authorities more than two months to respond to Shagari's demand for unqualified apology and compensation for the killing of five Nigerian soldiers by that country's gendarmes. Rather than deal decisively with Chad when its soldiers attacked Nigerian territory, the then minister for external affairs, Ishaya Audu, was prepared to forgive the 'affront' as the handiwork of guerrilla forces opposed to the Chadian leader Hissene Habre, whom Nigeria supported. Such lame responses did not go down well with some senior officers, one of whom in late 1983 defied orders from the presidency in Lagos to launch an image and confidence-restoring attack on Chadian forces who were holding Nigerian soldiers hostage. Such actions were the products of the military custodian complex which had been entrenched by prolonged military rule in the 1970s, and made civilian control of the military a farce.

In terms of sectarian interests, some accounts interpret the coup as having been staged to restore to power the Kaduna mafia which had led the transition to civilian rule in 1979 (cf. Turner and Baker, 1984; Graf, 1988; Othman, 1989). This interpretation was based on the domination of Hausa/Fulani and Northern Muslim officers in the regime which, as we saw in the last chapter, resurrected the confederation debate.[1] Several other actions of the junta reinforced its pro-North

---

[1] Of the twenty members of the Supreme Military Council, only eight were Southerners; and the head of state and the *de facto* deputy, the chief of staff at supreme headquarters, were, contrary to the unwritten code of regional and religious balance in the country, both Northerners and Muslims (although General Tunde Idiagbon, the powerful chief of staff, was a Yoruba from Kwara state). Moreover, like Ironsi who surrounded himself with Igbo core advisers, Buhari's 'inner cabinet' comprised Northerners, notably Mamman Daura who was said to be highly influential on economic matters; Mahmud Tukur, minister of commerce and industry who controlled the key accumulation instrument of import licence; Lema Jubrillu, major exponent of the counter-trade policy; and Rafindadi, the powerful head of the NSO (cf. Graf, 1988: 172).

complexion. These included the attempt to introduce *Sharia* law at
the federal level by fiat, which was stymied by the failure of the
governors of the ten Northern states to agree on how this should
be done (*Newswatch*, 24 February 1986: 12-13), and the pattern of
retrenchments in the top echelons of the federal public service (in
the name of purging the service of incompetent and redundant people
and trimming it to size as part of economic restructuring) which
affected more Southerners than Northerners.

The underlying reasons outlined above were of course different
from the more altruistic and nationalistic reasons advanced for the
military's return – which is not necessarily to discount the weight
of the latter factors or to dismiss them as mere rationalisations. The
welcome that greeted the coup all over the country was evidence
enough of the disenchantment with the civilian politicians of the
Second Republic, especially since they had proved incapable of reversing
the country's deep economic recession and the desire for the change
in the direction promised by the new military government. According
to a public opinion poll conducted by *The Punch* (4 January 1984),
97.7 per cent of respondents in Lagos, Ogun and Oyo states (which
were UPN strongholds) and 79.1 per cent in Bendel, Borno, Cross
River, Niger and Rivers states welcomed the overthrow. The Nigeria
Labour Congress, the central labour organisation, also expressed support
for the new military administration. According to Adamolekun (1985:
73), the widely support for the regime sprang from the hope that
it would offer better securing of lives and property and restore declining
standards of living. The seriousness of purpose with which Buhari
and Idiagbon, the key actors in the government, pursued the regime's
recovery agenda (which unfortunately was the justification for repression), can also be cited as evidence that the intervention was well
intentioned.

But, above all, the declared reasons for military take-over are
useful and deserve to be taken seriously because, like party manifestos
and campaign promises, they provide an empirical basis for assessing
the performance of the regime. So what reasons were advanced for
the take-over? There were standard allusions to the 'national duty'
of the military as the promoter and protector of the national interest'.[2]
As Buhari put it in his maiden broadcast to the country as head
of state, 'We have dutifully intervened to save the nation from imminent

---

[2] In the coup broadcast the then Brigadier Abacha said: 'I and my colleagues in the
armed forces have in the discharge of our national role as the promoters and protectors
of our national interest decided to effect a change in the leadership of the federal republic
of Nigeria, to form a military government.'

collapse'. Mismanagement of the economy and the consequent decline in living standards were cited as the central reasons for taking over:

'Our economy has been hopelessly mismanaged. We have become a debtor and beggarly nation. There is inadequacy of food at reasonable prices for our people.[...] Health services are in shambles as our hospitals are reduced to mere consulting clinics, without drugs, water and equipment. Our educational system is deteriorating at an alarming rate. Unemployment figures ... have reached embarrassing and unacceptable proportions. In some states, workers are being owed salary arrears of eight to twelve months and, in others, there are threats of salary cuts. Yet our leaders revel in squandermania, corruption and indiscipline [and] continue to proliferate public appointments in complete disregard of our stark economic realities.' (Excerpts from radio broadcast announcing the coup by Brigadier Sani Abacha, 31 December 1983)

Economic mismanagement, as in January 1966, was attributed to the corrupt practices' of politicians which the government promised to reverse as part of the presumed superior moral order of the military: 'This government will not tolerate kickbacks, inflation of contracts and overinvoicing of imports ... nor will it condone forgery, fraud, embezzlement, misuse and abuse of office, and illegal dealings in foreign exchange and smuggling' (Ibid.).

Reasons of electoral malpractices and democratic instability which followed the 1983 elections were also advanced, but these were secondary to the economic consideration. This is contrary to the suggestion by Olagunju *et al.* (1993) that democratic restoration was central to the intervention. Generals Buhari and Idiagbon consistently emphasised that the question of a return to civilian democratic rule could only be considered after the health of the economy had been restored.

The regime was so obsessed with economic recovery that every action it took (or failed to take), including denying people their rights and governing with an iron hand, was justified by it. The desperate situation, as leaders of the regime continually emphasised, required desperate solutions. As General Buhari told interviewers from the London *Financial Times*:

'What we are trying to put across is to make Nigerians understand how much we are in trouble economically. If we can get that message across, then Nigerians will be prepared to work hard and allow the government to pull the country out of the economic mess. After that, they can, if they like, resume their haggling and squabbles. But for now, we have no time to quarrel, no time to waste, only time to work hard.' (cited in Olagunju *et al.*, 1993: 67)

This approach, appropriate as it might have seemed, was inconsistent with the complex demands of a highly politicised society like Nigeria, a point well made by Olagunju *et al.* Although the reasons it advanced for taking over were widely acclaimed by the public, the regime was mistaken in assuming that its essentially authoritarian approach to salvaging the economy would assure it of continued public support in the absence of compensatory balances in other spheres (how, for example, could respect for people's rights be divorced from a project which aimed at raising their living standard?). What made the regime's case even worse was that, in the critical short run, it not only had little to show for the suffering it imposed on the people, but adamantly refused to temper its approach marked by self-righteousness and in-tolerance of alternative views. We return to this later in the chapter, but will now examine how the regime sought to handle the herculean task it set for itself.

'PULLING THE COUNTRY OUT OF THE ECONOMIC MESS'

The various efforts by the Buhari regime to revamp the economy are well summarised in the objectives of the ten-point programme it outlined in a world press conference shortly after taking power. These were

(i) maintenance of national unity and stability; (ii) charting better and more purposeful sense of direction; (iii) prudent management of resources and economic diversification to reduce reliance on oil; (iv) food and industrial raw material self sufficiency within a targeted period; (v) encouragement of labour-intensive projects to boost job creation; (vi) rephasing of capital-intensive development projects, especially those with huge foreign exchange input; (vii) eradication of corruption; (viii) maintenance of law and order as well as ensuring security of lives and property; (ix) entrenchment of public account-ability and proper work ethics; and (x) arresting the activities of hoarders, smugglers and other economic and social 'saboteurs.' (cited in Olagunju *et al.*, 1993: 66)

The economic recovery project – the fulcrum of the Buhari regime – will be analysed under three headings: (1) attempts to salvage what it could from the 'ruins' of the Second Republic and punish the main culprits; (2) the creation of what was deemed to be an enabling environment for economic recovery; and (3) the external economic and political dimensions of these efforts.

SALVAGING FROM THE RUINS OF THE SECOND REPUBLIC

By adopting and more or less continuing Shagari's blueprint for economic recovery, which centred around short- and medium-term austerity policies, the Buhari regime seemed to suggest that the problem with the administration of the Second Republic was not lack of appropriate strategy but absence of the will, discipline and ethics of public service to implement it.[3] The task of salvaging the ruins of the Second Republic hinged on correcting these and other ills, in the hope that the economy would then be put back on track. The major policy instrument for economic recovery was the economic stabilisation provisions order of 1984 which, as already indicated, differed little from the 1982 Economic Stabilisation Act. Four new decrees were issued to strengthen the temporary stabilisation measures in the areas of import prohibition, export prohibition, customs duties and excise duties.

The regime in typical military fashion promptly proscribed political parties and placed a ban on political activities. It then proceeded with administrative rationalisation, which involved drastic reductions in the size of government at federal and state levels. To make good its claim to being an offshoot of the Mohammed/Obasanjo regime (retired Generals Obasanjo, Danjuma, and Yar'Adua endorsed the regime as soon it came to power), it reintroduced the same organs established by the regime – a nineteen-member (including four civilians) Supreme Military Council which was to be the omnipotent decision-making body; Federal Executive Council which comprised seven military and eleven civilian ministers; and the National Council of States composed by state military governors and through which the affairs of the states were coordinated and supervised. In terms of fiscal relations, the 1982 Revenue Allocation Act was retained. This gave 55 per cent of federally collected revenue to the federal government, 32.5 per cent to the states, 10 per cent to local governments, 1.5 per cent to the development of mineral-producing areas, and 1 per cent to the ecological fund. Next was a scaling-down of the size of government: the number of federal ministers was reduced from over forty to eighteen, the number of ministries in the states was pegged at nine, and the new local government units created by state governments in the Second

---

[3] In addition to these, the head of state identified a disregard for advice by appropriate government agencies as a major reason for the failure of management (see *Daily Times*, 2 January 1984).

Republic, which took the number of units to over 1,000, were abolished, and the pre-Second Republic structure of 301 units was restored.

In pursuit of the regime's corrective and salvaging mission, panels were appointed to probe major agencies and parastatals like the Federal Capital Development Authority (FCDA – the agency which handled the bulk of the famous Abuja contracts) and the NNPC where an estimated N2.8 billion was said to be missing; the NNPC case had a sensational element because General Buhari himself had once headed it, but nothing was found against him by the panel. Elaborate reviews of major contracts, oil and import licences were also undertaken to reduce the improprieties that surrounded their authorisations in the Second Republic. To check smuggling which was correctly identified as being responsible for the failure of import and export restrictions, borders with neighbouring countries were closed for several weeks after the regime took over. It took entreaties from the heads of state of these countries, whose economies depended heavily on (mostly informal) movements of goods from Nigeria, for the borders to be re-opened. The offences of oil smuggling and illegal bunkering were made subject to the death penalty.

The politicians and other major actors who were held responsible for the economic decline were detained and tried in what became the most massive political trials in the country's post-independence history. These involved hundreds of Second Republic political office-holders at the federal and state levels, including the president, vice-president, governors, deputy governors, (federal) ministers, (state) commissioners, and advisers and special assistants to the president and governors, as well as people who were not part of government but had corrupt dealings with officials. By a strange reversal of normal legal procedure, those on trial were presumed guilty and the onus was on them to prove their innocence. The head of state defended the 'logic' of this reversal: 'There will be no wasteful probes of public officials who misapplied or stole government property.[...] Rather, those who misused or misappropriated public funds will be locked up till they clear themselves' (*Nigerian Tribune*, 6 January 1984). The trials were conducted by special military tribunals established under the Recovery of Public Property (Special Military Tribunals) Decree of 1984. The regime also made unsuccessful attempts to recover money stolen by corrupt politicians and deposited in foreign banks. Estimated at billions of dollars, the sums involved were believed to be more than enough to settle the country's external debts. The attempts were frustrated by the unwillingness of Western governments to cooperate with the regime. For example, the British government responded to requests by the government to recover stolen wealth in British banks by threatening to publish the names and account details of all Nigerians with bank accounts in the United Kingdom which would certainly have destroyed the credibility of military officers, many of whom were believed to operate foreign accounts. Perhaps the most sensational episode arising from these efforts to bring corrupt politicians to book was the botched attempt to repartiate Umaru Dikko forcibly from London where he had fled after the coup. He was placed in a crate that was to be flown to Lagos by Nigeria Airways on 5 July 1984 as 'federal government property'. Although the federal military government promptly denied involvement in the abduction, there was ample evidence linking the Nigerian high commission in London to the abduction. Dikko had been chairman of the notorious presidential task force on rice, through which several millions of naira were believed to have been misappropriated; in addition, he was chairman of the re-election of Shagari campaign team and one of the most powerful politicians in the Second Republic, and as such was perhaps the 'most wanted' man in the eyes of the Buhari junta (some accounts, including statements by Dikko himself, suggest that this was a result of his having fallen out with powerful Northern interests represented by the Kaduna mafia). The Dikko affair (as the crate abduction episode came to be known) strained Nigerian-British relations, and they steadily deteriorated as Nigeria temporarily detained a British airliner, both governments withdrew diplomats from each other's capitals, and Britain rejected Nigeria's application in January 1985 for Dikko to be extradited. Relations between the two countries did not return to normal until after Buhari's overthrow.

The trials of politicians by special military tribunals in Lagos, Kaduna, Ibadan, Jos and Enugu meanwhile went ahead despite opposition by the Nigerian Bar Association (NBA), which called on its members to boycott the tribunals. Persons found guilty were, on conviction, jailed for twenty-one or twenty-five years or for life, depending on the extent of the corruption involved. The severe punishments were defended by the head of state in the following words: 'Given the utter failure of exhortations and mild punishment in the past, ... the scale of the problem called for extraordinary punishment' (*The Guardian*, 1 August 1984). With a few exceptions like governors Lateef Jakande (Lagos), Adekunle Ajasin (Ondo), Muhammed Goni (Borno), Balarabe Musa (Kaduna), Clement Isong (Cross River) and Tatari Alli (Bauchi) and later President Shagari and Vice-President Ekwueme, most political office-holders, especially governors, were sentenced to long jail terms, having been convicted on multiple charges. The commonest charge against governors was abuse of 'security votes' – which, though approved by state Houses of Assembly as part of budgetary estimates, were under the absolute control of governors and were never accounted for. Another common charge was corrupt enrichment of a political party (rather than of an individual governor). We can consider a few examples. Ex-governor Adamu Attah of Kwara was sentenced to twenty-one years' imprisonment on six counts, to run concurrently; one charge was that he could not account for a security vote of over 16 million, 2 million of which he withdrew after losing the 1983 gubernatorial election; Solomon Lar of Plateau got eighty-eight years on four counts, one of which was unlawful withdrawal of a N27.3 million security fund from the state account; Olabisi Onabanjo of Ogun got twenty-two years for enriching his party, the UPN, with a N2.8 million 'kickback' from a contract awarded to Bouygues Nigeria Ltd and Shote Dawodu Consultants, as did Abubakar Rimi of Kano for enriching PRP with N593,000; and Bola Ige of Oyo got twenty-one years (later reduced to ten) for enriching the UPN. Ex-governors Barkin Zuwo of Kano and Ambrose Alli of Bendel received sentences running to hundreds of years which, in the case of Zuwo, was reduced to ten years. All those convicted were also ordered to pay back to the government all the sums they had corruptly accumulated or spent. This led to the recovery of huge amounts, ostensibly corruptly acquired. By October 1984 it was an-nounced that the various tribunals on recovery of public property and special investigation panels had recouped a total in excess of N112 million and £688,000 from politicians, over N348 million from FEDECO, and about N48.5 million from the National Assembly.

There was no doubt that, as Graf (1988: 151) puts it, 'The regular announcements not merely of crimes committed by the ruling class of the Second Republic but also and especially ... of the sheer scope and scale of state plunder ... enhanced the Buhari government's "cor-rective" legitimacy...'[4] The essence of the trials as a strategy of economic recovery was soon lost in controversies and in public scepticism over the real motives of the trials among which the need to discredit the politicians and thereby strengthen the military's claim to rule was pre-eminent.[5] Especially controversial matters that came to imperil

---

[4] It was announced that huge sums were recovered from the homes of governors and other top federal and state officials: N3.4 million from Barkin Zuwo, N1 million from Mbakwe, N204,000 from Aper Aku, N80,000 and unspecified foreign currency from Shehu Musa, N42,000 from Ekwueme, N50,000 from Yunusa Kaltungo, and N136,000 from Sale Jambo. Ten politicians were also said to have spent N3.5 billion buying private jets between 1979 and 1983 Thirteen companies owned by Alhaji Isiaku Rabiu, a NPN stalwart, were said to have made a profit of N140 million from political patronage. Umaru Dikko was alleged to have deposited 250 million pounds in a British bank.

[5] There were said to be disagreements within the SMC – Othman (1989: 138) points to disagreements between the 'Buhari faction' and the 'Babangida camp' in the Supreme

the exercise included the head of state's power to determine who should and should not be tried; the secrecy in which the trials were conducted; the known fact that basic rules of evidence were undermined despite the presence of high court judges on the tribunals; the dis-criminatory patterns of confirmations or revisions of sentences which were reduced in a number of cases by the SMC; and the apparent double standards that attended some of the trials and government's decisions on them. For example, a former commissioner in Lagos state was ordered to be retired after being absolved of corrupt enrichment by the special tribunal; although the ex-governor Lar of Plateau state was sentenced to a long term of imprisonment, the case of corruption against him had not been established, while ex-governor Goni of Borno state, whose case was similar, was discharged and acquitted. But the most controversial aspect of the trials was the palpable regional and ethnic discriminations in the review of verdicts of the tribunals by the SMC, especially the fact that Southern and non-NPN politicians received more severe punishments than their Northern and NPN counter-parts. Why, for example, were the jail sentences of former Northern governors (cf. Barkin Zuwo, Garba Nadama, Abubakar Rimi) reduced from twenty-one years and over to between one and five years, while those for Southern politicians were either confirmed (cf. Ambrose Alli and Sam Mbakwe) or reduced only by token amounts? Also, why were former President Shagari and Vice-President Ekwueme, the presumed chief culprits for the ruin of the Second Republic, not tried? And, worse still, why was Shagari, a Northerner, held under 'house arrest' and Ekwueme, a Southerner, detained in prison?

Alongside these essentially political measures were the more pointed efforts directed at achieving economic recovery, which were mostly part of the continuing deflationary austerity regime. According to Olukoshi (1995a: 142-3; 1995b: 167-71), there were three main sources of the austerity policies: the 1982 Stabilisation Act, the report of the National Economic Council expert committee submitted to Shagari shortly before he was overthrown, and elements of the IMF recom-mendations which were perceived as being capable of restoring the health of the economy. The various measures, which were embodied in the 1984 and 1985 budgets, included reductions in sectoral allocations except debt servicing and agriculture,[6] foreign exchange controls (notably

---

Military Council over how to deal with political detainees, some of whom were never tried. The public also increasingly questioned some of the judgements of the tribunals and the government's decisions based on them.

[6] Even the defence budget – a 'sacred cow' – was cut. As Othman (1989: 139) points out, the total annual defence allocations in 1984 (N928.2 million) and 1985 (N975 million) were all below the lowest of Shagari's expenditure of N1,090 million for 1983.

reduction in the basic travel allowance and in the allocation for procurement of raw materials by as much as 40 per cent in the drive for self-sufficiency); reductions in the numbers of Muslim and Christian pilgrimages and the banning of children from them; introduction of new taxes and levies (sales and poll taxes, education levies, and so on); reductions in salaries and wages and freezing of appointments and promotions in the public service; introduction of user fees in hospitals, and increases in tuition and boarding fees in secondary schools, and in the charges for electricity and water consumption. In pursuit of economic diversification, efforts were made to rejuvenate the agricultural sector by adapting policies initiated under Shagari's Green Revolution Programme, but credit and import restrictions affected the importation of inputs, especially fertilisers and machinery.

Import restrictions and reduction in the foreign exchange allocation for the procurement of raw materials also affected local industries, which depended heavily on foreign raw materials and technology. This led to further falls in capacity utilisation, in some cases by as much as 70 per cent (only banks and breweries made any significant recovery in the period), and inevitably to shutdowns and further retrenchment of workers (over 3 million private sector workers were estimated to have been made redundant between 1981 and 1985). A similar fate befell the public service. With a drastic reduction of capital spending to about 50 per cent of the 1983 figures, public service rationalisation (including foreign missions) was carried out through the dismissal of many thousands of workers, estimated by *West Africa* (4 February 1985: 215) to be between 150,000 and 200,000.

The banking and monetary sector also fell under the regime's scrutiny. An international racket which became known as the Johnson Matthey Bank (JMB) affair was blown open. This involved Nigerian officials, Asian merchants and British banks, which swindled the country of several million pounds through overinvoicing and the foreign inspection certificates on imported items, and abuse of banking procedures. Subsequently, payments for letters of credit issued under the Second Republic were stopped, and bills of lading, invoices and certificates of delivery in Nigeria were requested for all overseas claims (Graf, 1988: 151-2). But the master-stroke was the decision to change the country's currency notes in April-May 1984. This was done to curb the illegal printing of the outside the country and short-change those who held billions of the naira currency abroad, especially in Britain where the naira was legal tender on the streets (a proposal to do this during the Second Republic failed because of political differences and vested interests). To ensure the effectiveness of this measure, the country's borders were once again closed for some weeks, although a major scandal arose over fifty-three suitcases, believed to contain old naira notes, brought into the country under official cover by the Emir of Gwandu and Ambassador D.A. Waziri. Incidents like this (and General Idiagbon taking his young son on pilgrimage to Mecca in violation of the new rule banning children from pilgrimages) attenuated the regime's claim to the moral high ground on which it staked its legitimacy.

Then there were efforts related to the 'salvaging' objective, and others of a more *ad hoc* and unfocused nature, some of which also aimed at extending the regime's legitimacy. State governments were ordered to pay the backlog of salaries owed to public servants within the first four months of the regime, and with the trimming of public service and cuts in salaries, payment of the latter became more regular, although in some states it was still sluggish. Soldiers carried out sporadic raids on warehouses and stores in Lagos and state capitals, to check hoarding of goods which partly accounted for the scarcity and high prices of essential commodities. To arrest escalating prices further, 'essential commodities' like rice, toiletries, sugar and salt were rationed and sold directly to the public at controlled prices through government ministries and departments, cooperative societies and organized groups (rackets in essential commodities became a goldmine for officials and contractors of the Nigerian National Supply Company [NNSC] and the various state government bulk purchasing agencies). Some state governments also made largely unsuccessful attempts to control rents and the high cost of services in urban areas.

New sources of revenue generation which weighed further on the already milked masses were also introduced, especially by state governments. In addition to special levies and salary cuts (so-called 'compulsory savings'), states like Ogun and Ondo introduced taxes on 'street' and public parties. Other related *ad hoc* 'salvaging' measures included a return to the low-profile policy of the Mohammed/Obasanjo era and restrictions on the use of government vehicles to office hours; the outlawing of 'frivolous' industrial action, including strikes and lockouts; and the expulsion of over 700,000 illegal immigrants, many of them Ghanaians, in May 1985. On balance, the impact of these measures was a far cry from what was needed to salvage the ruins of the Second Republic or turn the economy around. Graf (1988: 152) has attributed this to the regime's failure to formulate a coherent recovery programme: 'For all its more or less well conceived measures and pronouncements, the Buhari regime did not manage to formulate a consistent strategy, much less a coherent programme. Its basic approach might be termed indignant (albeit measured) activism.' There was also an obstinate streak of nationalism which prevented the regime from adopting a more comprehensive programme of structural adjustment which the IMF had been pushing on it since the Second Republic (this is discussed below). Not wanting Nigeria to be a beggar, the regime was desperate to pay off its external debt within the shortest time possible and avoid accepting orders from powerful foreign interests.

Lack of coherence was not the only thing wrong with the regime's efforts to cope with the ruins of the Second Republic. The efforts were marred by displays of insincerity and double standards on the part of the military rulers. We have already referred to the instances of these in the trials of politicians and the change of naira notes. A far more serious indictment was that at a time when the rest of the country was being forced to accept hardships and make sacrifices, the regime felt no qualms about continuing with ambitious defence projects inherited from past regimes and initiating new ones, despite cuts in defence budgets:

> General Buhari...proceeded with all previously planned major defence expenditure projects: notably the upgrading of the Nigerian Defence Academy to a university status, the building of an air force and naval academy, the establishment of the 30 million naira armoured personnel carrier plant in Bauchi, and a number of military reequipment and modernization programmes. Indeed local military production [was] strengthened under his government. The hitherto somnolent Defence Industries Corporation began to produce military explosives and arms;...an army bank was planned; and several retired or serving military commanders received prominent appointments at home or as diplomatic representatives abroad. (Othman, 1989: 138)

In addition to these, a change in army uniforms at an estimated cost of N9.75 million was planned, and there were promotions of military officers, including the head of state and other leading members of the regime, and over 500 junior officers. Most of these actions were insensitive to the needs and conditions of the increasingly desperate and restive public. If national interests could be sacrificed for selfish corporate and personal interests, many citizens wondered aloud, in what way were military rulers different from the politicians whom they had in turn accused of insensitivity to the sufferings of others?

AN 'ENABLING ENVIRONMENT' FOR ECONOMIC RECOVERY

Consistent with the assumption that the desperate economic situation called for desperate solutions, the Buhari regime proceeded to promulgate tough decrees which laid the foundations for the increased authoritarianism of military governance in the 1980s and 1990s. The basic premise of authoritarian rule – similar to other military regimes – was the Constitution (Suspension and Modification) Decree no. 1 of 1984 which proscribed all political parties and suspended sections of the 1979 Constitution (the suspended sections, it should be noted, did not include the provisions on human rights). A complementary decree – the Federal Military Government (Supremacy and Enforcement of Powers) Decree no. 13 of 1984 – established the supremacy of military decrees which could not be challenged by any court of law (the so-called 'ouster clauses'). Several stringent decrees then followed, notable among them being the Recovery of Public Property (Special Military Tribunals) Decree, already discussed; Exchange (Anti-Sabotage) Decree, prescribing jail terms for traffickers of old naira notes; Counterfeit Currency (Special Provisions) Decree; and Banking (Freezing of Accounts) Decree no. 3 of 1984, which authorised the head of state to freeze the bank accounts of persons *suspected* of having been involved in corrupt practices and to investigate their finances.

There was also the Special Tribunal (Miscellaneous Offences) Decree no. 20 of 1984 under which persons convicted of 'serious' or criminal offences such as drug trafficking or use, tampering with oil pipelines and electric and telephone cables, and the unlawful import and export of mineral oil and ore were to be executed by firing squad; those convicted of 'less serious' or civil offences like cheating in examinations, wilful destruction of public property and smuggling of prohibited items were liable to penalties of up to twenty-one years in jail. To show that it meant business, and despite strong pleas from the public not to do so, the regime ordered the public execution of three young men convicted of drug trafficking (the sentence was carried out in Lagos on 10 April 1984), and another set of convicts, including some women, were on death row by the time it was overthrown.

Closely related to the Miscellaneous Offences Decree was the Robbery and Firearms Decree – in existence since the time of the civil war but suspended in the Second Republic – whereby persons convicted of armed robbery also faced death by firing squad; between January and August 1984, there were ninety-three executions in various parts of the country. A particularly monstrous decree, which remained the major instrument of state repression in the later regimes of Babangida and Abacha, was the State Security (Detention of Persons) Decree of 1984 which authorised the chief of staff at supreme headquarters to detain for up to three months (renewable), without trial, anyone deemed to be a risk to state security or to have contributed to the country's economic crisis. This decree enabled the Buhari and subsequent regimes to detain critics and opponents without trial in police and security cells. The wide-ranging powers given to the National Security Organization (NSO) to hunt for, detain and deal with enemies of the regime, even within the armed forces, combined with this decree to unleash a reign of terror: 'Arbitrary arrest, torture and indeterminate detention were widely practised, and this systemic brutality which Nigeria had hitherto largely been spared under military rule – entailed breaking suspects skulls during interrogation...' (Graf, 1988: 166).

The press was not spared. As the main channel for articulating critical and dissenting views, it had till then been substantially free compared to other countries in Africa, but now the notorious Public Officers (Protection Against False Accusations) Decree no. 4 of 1984 authorised the arrest, detention and trial of journalists and the closure of any medium making 'any false statement' or rumour embarrassing to public officers or calculated to subject them to ridicule or disrepute. Under the decree, the *Guardian* journalists, Tunde Thompson and Nduka Irabor (the latter became chief press secretary to Vice President Aikhomu in the Babangida years), were convicted and jailed for a year each, and Guardian Newspapers Ltd., publisher of the newspaper, was fined N50,000. The editor of *National Concord*, Duro Onabule (later chief press secretary to Babangida) was detained for two weeks. The decree muzzled the press, especially the usually vibrant newspapers, whose columnists temporarily 'went to Afghanistan', an expression coined by the journalist Sonala Olumhense to describe the less offensive reporting and analysis of foreign events, and resorting to cartoons and satirical writings, to escape the wrath of the military government. The emerging reign of terror became complete with the replacement of law courts by military tribunals to try offences under these decrees. The tribunals were further strengthened by the Military Courts (Special Powers) Decree of 1984 and the Judgement and Tribunals (Enforcement) Decree no. 8 of 1985. The latter stipulated: 'With effect from 31 December 1983, judgements of all tribunals set up under the various decrees shall be final and conclusive in respect of all pronouncements, orders, sentences, fines and forfeiture of assets.'

The regime's tyrannical behaviour and the economic hardships stirred civil society out of its lethargy and into vigorous opposition. The Nigerian Bar Association (NBA) was at the forefront of opposing rule by absolute decrees and the trial of suspects by tribunals – it actually made an effort to prevent these tribunals from functioning by directing its members to boycott them, but without success. Members of the Nigerian Medical Association (NMA) and National Association of Resident Doctors (NARD) went on strike in September 1984 to protest at the poor state of health care delivery in the country and later joined the anti-authoritarianism movement when Beko Ransome Kuti and its other leaders were harassed, arrested and detained, and the associations were proscribed. The National Association of Nigerian Students (NANS), the umbrella association of students of institutions of higher learning, was also proscribed after persistent demonstrations by students in tertiary institutions all over the country in protest at the government's withdrawal of subsidy for students' meals in tertiary institutions, worsening economic conditions, the rising cost of social goods, and the detention of critics of government. As well as proscribing NANS, the military government also threatened to close down permanently any institution where students' protests resulted in a breakdown of law and order. Various labour unions also staged strikes demanding better conditions of service and improved living standards. The NLC opposed the massive retrenchment of workers and the failure by the government to repay deductions made under compulsory savings from workers' salaries. The government's response to the groundswell of opposition was to expand its repressive apparatus. Students' demonstrations were violently brought down by armed police and soldiers who maimed and killed scores of students, while leaders of various associations were detained under Decree 2, or else forced to go underground. The regime had declared war on society to create an 'enabling environment' for economic recovery.

Perhaps the only group to which the regime was favourably disposed was traditional rulers. Doubtless because their support was indispensable for mass support, especially among the largely traditional rural dwellers who could be relied upon to counterbalance urban-based opposition. The head of state admonished newly-appointed governors to 'make every effort to maintain a good relationship with traditional rulers in your state. Whether you are an indigene or not, you will find that it is in your best interest to study the recognized system of traditional rulership' (*The Guardian*, 7 January 1984). The predominance in the regime of conservative Northern officers who deferred to traditional authority influenced this attitude.

Adamolekun (1985: 81-2) finds a contradiction in the romance of the regime with traditional rulers: how could the regime align itself with a class that was in league with the discredited politicians of the Second Republic and was therefore part of the mismanagement of that era? A similar point was made by Oyovbaire (1989: 392ff) from a different perspective. He saw the cultivation of a working relationship with traditional rulers as 'most reactionary' because as champions of pristine groups, traditional rulers were the antithesis of national unity, and secondly, the close alliance with them was responsible for the return of the feudal order, manifested by the reimposition of *baraji* and *jangali* taxes which had long been abolished in the Northern states. The alliance was no doubt reactionary, but the seeming contradiction of a 'progressive', radical and nationalist regime aligning itself with such a conservative institution is easily explained by the regime's obvious need of the traditional 'father' in order to survive. This did not prevent the regime from descending heavily on them when it felt its interests (easily construed as the national interest) threatened or its authority challenged. Thus, in August 1984, the Emir of Kano and the Ooni of Ife, two of the country's most powerful traditional rulers, had their movements restricted to their domains as punishment for making an 'unauthorised' trip to Jerusalem and entering into talks with the Israeli authorities, with which the country had no diplomatic relations at the time.

By far the most elaborate and celebrated attempt to build an enabling environment for economic recovery was the 'discipline' project, which the regime pursued with characteristic authoritarian zeal. At the heart of this project was the 'War Against Indiscipline' (WAI), with objectives that were not very different from those of the 'ethical revolution' launched by Shagari. However, it differed from the ethical revolution in conception and execution, having been launched by the military as a veritable war on a 'lawless', 'indisciplined', 'corrupt' and 'unpatriotic' society. As stated by General Tunde Idiagbon, the chief of staff at supreme headquarters, the objective of WAI was 'to instill in the minds of our people the noble ideals of national consciousness, mobilize their minds, and gear them up to a sense of nationhood, patriotism and, above all, discipline' (*The Guardian*, 21 March 1984). The 'war' was 'fought' in three phases: the 'queue culture' phase in which people were taught the virtues of patience and taking turns at bus stops, post offices, banks and other public places; the work ethics phase; and the patriotism and nationalism phase. The war also extended to environmental sanitation and beautification. In pursuance of these latter objectives, specific days of the week were allocated for clean-up exercises, and so-called illegal structures – mainly street kiosks and trading places set up by the urban poor – were bulldozed by contingents of armed soldiers. Non-commissioned officers in the army were also deployed to secondary schools to 'enforce' discipline. Although WAI enjoyed wide acclaim as members of the public readily accepted its goals, the way it was carried out cost the programme popular support. Meanwhile, the repressive character of the regime became more pronounced in other spheres.

THE EXTERNAL DIMENSIONS OF THE RECOVERY EFFORTS

By the time the Second Republic was overthrown, as we saw in the last chapter, Nigeria was virtually at the mercy of international creditors led by the IMF, and on the verge of being forced to accept the unpalatable IMF therapy of structural adjustment. Although it resumed negotiations with the IMF, the Buhari regime was most unwilling to accept its conditions and SAP package. It hoped that by demonstrating fiscal discipline, ability to manage a deflationary austerity regime, prompt payment of debt-servicing charges and commitment to honouring other debt obligations, it would impress the creditors. The short-term objective was to transform the country from its status as a 'debtor and beggar' to one where it could negotiate with creditors from a position of strength.

The regime soon found that it needed more than merely discipline and nationalism to deal with the external dimensions of the economic crisis. Oil continued its slide in the world market, and there were strong pressures by middlemen (dating back to the Second Republic) for the country to pull out of OPEC, which continued to insist on ceilings to member-states' production quotas. Although Nigeria consistently exceeded its quota, the government reaffirmed the country's commitment to OPEC, and successfully negotiated an increase of 250,000 bpd with it in 1984. However, commitment to OPEC limited the options open to the regime, and partly forced it to adopt the counter-trade policy which began in December 1984. This modern form of trade-by-barter 'represented a final *ad hoc* attempt by the Buhari government to escape from its economic immobilism by obtaining the technology, spare parts and other raw materials essential to domestic economic recovery while circumventing the need for an IMF loan and not too blatantly violating OPEC rules' (Graf, 1988: 172). In different deals with a total value estimated at over US$2 billion, Nigeria's oil was bartered for goods from Austria, Brazil, Canada, France, Italy, Romania and the Soviet Union.

Given the country's dire straits, counter trade was expedient, but the costs far outweighed the benefits. For one thing, under the largely unfavourable terms of the trade, the country paid more for imported items and virtually auctioned off its oil (for example, the price at which Brazilian sugar was imported was known to be inflated, while oil bartered to France was discounted by at least 10 per cent). The Aboyade panel instituted by the Babangida government to probe counter-trade deals reported many cases of sharp practice and other irregularities – overinvoicing, suspicious haste in signing deals, absence of inspection and price controls, and so on. But by far the most serious problem with the policy was that it undermined oil prices and threatened

Nigeria's membership of OPEC. The major oil partners and buyers also insisted on enjoying counter-trade discounts, and refusal by the regime to do so led to a temporary refusal to lift oil, leading to a sharp fall in production from 1.6 million bpd in June to 800,000 bpd in August 1985. Thus on balance, counter trade, rather than bringing relief, only served to heighten the desperate economic situation.

The Buhari administration found itself with no viable alternative to negotiating with the IMF, especially as its trade creditors in the Paris club tied any further negotiations on debt rescheduling and refinancing of trade arrears to the country reaching agreement with that body. 'The rejection of this cross conditionality', according to Olukoshi (1995: 144) led 'to the cutting off of lines of credit ... and an intensification of the financial boycott of the country which began under Shagari.' Failure to secure an alternative loan of N1.6 million from Saudi Arabia finally put paid to any serious alternatives to the IMF option. Negotiations with the IMF were deadlocked over the regime's non-acceptance of three of the conditions it set: devaluation of the naira by at at least 30 per cent; removal of subsidies on petroleum products; and trade liberalisation.[7]

Except for these three areas, agreement was reached on other 'conditionalities' and the regime, to demonstrate its capability for reform, was already implementing most of them: rationalisation of the public service involving massive retrenchments: drastic reduction in public sector expenditure including introduction of user fees in the health sector; and a wage freeze. However, the regime was most reluctant to privatise, preferring instead to commercialize state-owned enterprises (nonetheless, by the time of its overthrow, it had announced its intention to privatise government-owned hotels and agricultural enterprises). Underlying the rejection of the three conditions was a fear of popular revolt of the kind which greeted the introduction of the SAP therapy to other countries in Africa – the people were already overstretched. Another factor was the populist nationalism of Generals Buhari and Idiagbon, continually manifested in the regime's emphasis on self-reliant development, a philosophy that ran counter to that of trade liberalisation. A vigorous campaign was launched to promote local sourcing of raw materials by manufacturers and thereby conserve foreign exchange and reduce the country's dependence on the industrialised countries.

Perhaps this would have saved the regime and bettered the economy

---

[7] On trade liberalisation, the regime was willing to accept in principle the abolition of the advance deposit scheme on imports. This was one of the two conditions specified by the IMF, but the second condition namely elimination of import restrictions, was not accepted because of balance of payment deficits.

if it had not alienated the very people whose interests it professed
to be defending; but a more likely scenario is that the regime would
have been forced, with all alternative doors closed, to accept the
conditions and adopt a comprehensive programme of structural adjustment. The further hardships which this would have entailed, and
the authoritarian manner in which it would probably have been implemented, would certainly have served to alienate the regime further
and hasten its overthrow.[8]

A BALANCE SHEET

At the start of this chapter we adduced a number of underlying
reasons for military coups: personal ambition, the furtherance of sectarian
interests by military means, and corporate-cum-organisational interests.
These certainly underlay the coup which brought General Buhari
and the equally powerful General Idiagbon to power. But in spite
of this, few Nigerians doubted the two generals' 'patriotism' and
commitment to restoring the country's economic health and correcting
the ills of society. Indeed, long after the regime was overthrown,
it was remembered with nostalgia as perhaps the only one that would
have been capable of halting the country's decline.

But the regime had little to show beyond populist nationalism
for the reign of terror and tough austerity measures it unleashed
on the country, ostensibly as a necessary part of its salvaging mission.
In the area of economic recovery on which it based its mission
and justified its actions, and which therefore provided a good empirical
measure for its performance, most commentators do not rate it very
high. For example:

> The Buhari regime was neither able to overcome the economic crisis
> it inherited, nor manage it adequately, thus producing a systemic
> legitimacy crisis. Practically every sector and elite faction was there-
> fore disaffected. True Buhari had managed at least to *contain* the
> economic crisis, but the basic dilemma, which his authoritarianism
> could not address, at least not without further fragmenting the various
> elite factions, was how to effect economic change without forfeiting
> elite and mass backing. (Graf, 1988: 169)

---

[8] Hindsight suggests that the regime had a much better opportunity to make a good job
of the SAP than did the Babangida and Abacha regimes in later years. But this is only
a counterfactual argument whose validity lies in the fact that the Buhari regime did not
implement the SAP – after all, some would say, it did not even make a good job of the
austerity programme it religiously pursued.

Adamolekun (1985: 87, 85) also argues that the regime failed to embark on a 're-orientation' of the nation's economy, and that its policies achieved no 'real improvement'.

The regime also had problems over its image as a cabal of conservative Northern interests. There was a preponderance of Northerners in the Supreme Military Council, and as beneficiaries of appointments to top positions and the distribution of other forms of patronage (contracts, fertiliser distribution etc.), and Northern politicians were given preferential treatment in the trials and punishment of officials of the Second Republic. The pattern of retrenchments in the top echelons of the public service also seemed to suggest a deliberate attempt to replace Southerners by Northerners. As we saw in the last chapter, this resurrected the confederation debate which began in the Second Republic in response to what was perceived to be 'unstoppable' Northern domination by some Southern politicians.

The agitations became even more pronounced under Buhari, and it was significant that retired military officers from the South-West – notably Brigadier Benjamin Adekunle, the legendary 'Black Scorpion' of the civil war, and Lt-General Alani Akinrinade, joint chief of defence staff in the Second Republic – joined the ranks of the confederalists (cf. Osaghae, 1990b). The most serious indictment of the regime along this line was that by General Obasanjo, former head of state, who not only criticised the regime's Northernisation policy but denied it its legitimisation instrument of being an offshoot of his (Mohammed/Obasanjo) regime (Obasanjo, 1985). The regime was sufficiently alarmed by this agitation to ban all forms of political debate in the country. According to Othman (1989: 138), 'In themselves, all these divisive issues undermined the credibility and stability of the regime. More fatally, they intensified the strains within the ruling junta.' These strains and the division which they produced between the Buhari-Idiagbon and Babangida factions underlay the overthrow of the regime by the Babangida faction.

FOREIGN POLICY

Despite its preoccupation with economic recovery, the Buhari government managed to articulate an aggressive foreign policy posture in line with its claim to be an offshoot of the Mohammed/Obasanjo regime. However, the realities of the economic situation made its posture less adventurous than that of the previous military regime. The other major difference between the two regimes with implications for foreign policy was that in contrast to the Mohammed/Obasanjo regime, the Buhari regime was unpopular with the vast majority of the people. Thus, even though some of its policies were well received at home, it could not match the wide acclaim that had added to the vibrancy of foreign policy in the previous regime. Support for its policies was muted.

Given the regime's short life, which was not sufficient to make any lasting changes in Nigeria's foreign policy, we need only highlighted its most significant initiatives. It kept Africa as the centrepiece of foreign policy, and attempted to redress the slackness of the Shagari administration. As usual, South Africa and Namibia were at the top of the agenda, and the American policy of constructive engagement was opposed even more vigorously than before. Monetary and other contributions to the liberation movements through the OAU liberation committee were restored, and the foreign minister, Ibrahim Gambari, undertook a tour of the frontline states to reassert Nigeria's commitment to the liberation struggles. Policy on South Africa received a great boost with the appointment of Joseph Garba, the exuberant external affairs minister under General Mohammed, as the country's permanent representative to the UN and therefore to the chairmanship of the anti-apartheid committee. In addition, the federal government also decided to recognise Polisario as the legitimate government of the Saharawi Arab Democratic Republic.

Within the West African sub-region, the realistic policies initiated by the Shagari administration were maintained. This led to the expulsion of more illegal aliens, and the closing of borders to check smuggling and sabotage the change of naira notes. The regime also dealt decisively with the threats from Chad and Cameroon by stationing military contingents along the borders with those countries. At the global level, the regime found itself unable to pursue the assertive policy of Mohamme/Obasanjo, largely on account of the debt trap. Although bold statements were made about the need for a new world economic order, these lacked substance. The continued decline of oil prices and the inability of OPEC to do much to change the situation, and the counter-trade and other alternative economic arrangements into which Nigeria was forced could not bring about the much desired autonomy of action.

6

THE BABANGIDA YEARS AND AFTER, 1985-1993

The Babangida years could be described in terms of Charles Dickens' *A Tale of Two Cities* as 'the best of times and the worst of times'. They were the years in which the potential for economic recovery was very bright, and a return to prosperity seemed likely. The country's 'past glory' appeared restorable, with its improved standing in the international community, thanks to final agreement with Western creditors and General Babangida's high international profile. The World Bank and the IMF in fact regarded Nigeria as one of the few 'success stories' of SAP, and some commentators even spoke of the possibility of an 'economic miracle'. There was also the democratic transition programme which reinforced the regime's credibility in the international community, as it was in consonance with the world time.

In the domestic scene there were also giant steps forward: ambitious attempts were made to address chronic political, social and economic problems. The regime managed to organise a fairly successful census in 1991; it created new states and local government councils, and made strenuous efforts to bring about genuine local government autonomy; and it set up state agencies to address unemployment, rural neglect and infrastructural development, and to provide the poor with access to credit facilities. If Buhari had been obsessed with economic recovery, Babangida's obsession was the creation of a 'new socio-political order': an 'ideal state' around which his highly experimental transition programme and other reformist projects would revolve. This preoccupation was presumably informed by the failures of the Second Republic, which would arguably have performed better if the social setting had been re-oriented. But it plunged the country into the 'abysmal tunnel' of an endless search for the ideal state, as Obafemi Awolowo had predicted long before, and in the end threatened the very foundations of the state itself (Joseph, 1996). Among the aspects of the new social order project were the institution of a Political Bureau whose report provided the blueprint for the regime's transition programme and whose members later formed the core of intellectuals who devised and implemented the transition's sundry experiments; the creation of a Directorate of Social Mobilization (DSM); attempts to create a so-called 'newbreed' of politicians – which turned out to be a new comprador elite; and the imposition of a two-party system by fiat.

But the Babangida years were also some of the country's worst years, with unprecedented levels of bureaucratic corruption, repression and political turbulence. New dimensions of political instability such as letter-bombs, assasinations and aircraft hijackings were added to the list. These years were punctuated by perennial strikes, demonstrations, riots and protests by students, labour unions, and pro-democracy and other civil society organisations. Behind this uprising of civil society were SAP—the Structural Adjustment Programme which brought untold hardship and misery to the vast majority of the people, especially the urban poor and other vulnerable groups, and the complicated democratic transition programme which seemed headed for a perpetuation of military rule.

This chapter examines, under thematic headings, the Babangida regime, the longest headed by a military ruler after Gowon, and its immediate aftermath which, as part of the effort to reduce the damage caused by the annulment of the June 1993 presidential election, led to the institution of an interim government. We begin with a preliminary overview of the Babangida government.

THE 'REDEEMER' COMETH?

As with other military interventions, attempts have been made to 'explain' the overthrow of the Buhari regime in the palace coup of 27 August 1985.[1] First were the reasons advanced by the new regime in the coup broadcast and subsequent statements by its key members – Buhari's failure to salvage the country's economic decline and restore social services which instead deteriorated, lack of progress in negotiations with the IMF (this was obviously calculated to win the support and confidence of Western creditors), the regime's lack of consultation with the rest of the military and society combined with the angrily self-righteous approach of Buhari and Idiagbon, its authoritarianism and poor human rights record, and its failure to articulate a programme of a return to civil rule. Such a line of argument appealed to the public and was designed to win their support.

On the basis of these reasons, Graf (1988: 169) asserts that the

---

[1] It was a palace coup because the removal of Buhari and Idiagbon, who were subsequently retired from the army and put in detention (or house arrest as the Babangida regime called it) for forty months, was the major objective of the coup. Except for the retirement of about forty other officers belonging to the Buhari-Idiagbon camp, structural changes and shuffles of key commanders and holders of political office, which brought officers of the Bida and Langtang 'mafias' into the core, the junta remained virtually intact.

coup, like that which brought General Mohammed to power in 1975, represented 'a reconsolidation of the military's corporate interests and factions'. For Olagunju, Oyovbaire and Jinadu, the trio who formed the Babangida regime's intellectual core, the coup 'was executed in order to bring back on the political agenda the restorative democratic content of the 31 December [1983] coup' (Olagunju *et al.*, 1993: 59; also see essays in Uya, 1992). However, the eventual outcome of the so-called restorative democratic agenda does not support this view, and suggests that other factors for the overthrow of the Buhari regime should be examined.

This brings us to the latent reasons which, as we tried to argue in the last chapter, provide a clearer perspective on the character of the ensuing regimes. These have been discussed in terms of the factionalisation of the Buhari regime over the trials of politicians, the IMF loan and other critical issues, opposition to 'Northern domination', and the pre-emption of another coup by junior officers (cf. Graf, 1988; Othman, 1989). It is important to note that General Babangida had been involved in most coups in the country and a member of the SMC since the Mohammed/Obasanjo regime (the same was true of General Abacha, who was nicknamed '*Khalifa*' (king in waiting). If these prior involvements are taken as a process of 'training' and 'preparation', then it becomes a little easier to explain Babangida's unique mastery of the art of manipulative military governance which made him a powerful ruler, and kept him in power despite opposition from civil society. For example, his choice of the title of president rather than head of state was a product of what he saw as the limitations of the powers exercised by a head of state who was only a 'first among equals' rather than a 'chief executive'.

But these remained hidden factors which do not in any case obliterate the fact that the overthrow of the repressive Buhari regime was welcomed by most of the public, as was made clear by newspaper reports and editorials at the time of the coup. Once again, timing was the critical factor that sold the coup to the people. In their eyes Babangida presented the image of a 'redeemer'. Not only had he overthrown a dictatorship which appeared impregnable, but he also reached out to the people through support-seeking actions avowedly hinged on justice, human rights observance, and reconciliation. These mostly involved retractions of policies and actions of the Buhari regime, especially in the area of human rights and consultative decision-making. Among other things, he instituted a committee (headed by Commodore Ebitu Ukiwe, the CGS) to review cases of human rights violation under Buhari; ordered a review of the trials and sentences of politicians and other public officers, which led to reductions in jail terms and the release of most of them; repealed the press gagging Decree no. 4, and the death penalty for drug trafficking offences; released scores of political detainees, including the two journalists jailed under Decree 4; threw open the detention cells and torture chambers of the NSO and exposed the atrocities committed by security operatives; and de-proscribed NANS, NMA, and NARD.

These were followed by a restructuring and reconstitution of key organs of government. These included the change in the names of the Supreme Military Council (SMC) to Armed Force Ruling Council (AFRC), and of the chief of staff at supreme headquarters, the *de facto* 'No. 2', to chief of general staff (CGS) (unlike his titular predecessor, the CGS had no control over the armed forces), the expansion of the Federal Executive Council, and application of the federal character principle in the composition of key organs of government to redress the North-South imbalances created by the Buhari regime.[2] One of the new structures which served as the regime's think-tank and played a key role in the formulation of policy was the Presidential Advisory Committee (PAC), directly responsible to the president.[3] This was only one of the manifestations of the key roles academics played as Babangida's ideologues, advisers and programme managers. The president's speeches were mostly written by these academics, whose influence was reflected in their high intellectual quality. The academics played a crucial role in both authoring and propagating the political transition programme, which became an opportunity for some of them to put their theories into practice. The academics, especially those who served on the Political Bureau, were partly responsible for the 'experimental' and 'learning' nature of the transition, which the president kept emphasising – as well as the confusion which beset the process, as we shall soon see.

[2] In addition to federal character considerations, the composition of the cabinet was also designed to garner the support of critical segments of civil society. This was obvious from some of the 'strategic' appointments made: among others Bola Ajibola, chairman of the Nigerian Bar Association which led the struggle to enthrone human rights and the rule of law under Buhari, was appointed attorney-general and minister of justice; Tony Momoh, veteran journalist and crusader for press freedom, was made information minister; and Olikoye Ransome-Kuti, a respected professor of medicine, was appointed minister of health. He was the elder brother of the radical Kuti brothers – Beko, leader of NMA, and Fela, renowned leader of the musical arm of the anti-establishment, anti-military infrapolitical movement.

[3] The committee was headed by Professor Ojetunji Aboyade, and had mostly academics (Professors Isawa Elaigwu, Ikenna Nzimiro, Iz Osayimwense and others) as members. Although its specific functions were never known, it was believed to have been responsible for formulating and monitoring most of the economic and political policies, especially those of SAP and the political transition programme.

But by far the most crucial aspect of the regime's restructuring was the added strength given to the position of 'president and commander-in-chief', which made General Babangida arguably the most powerful of the country's military rulers. In contrast to the earlier SMCs, the 'supremacy' of the AFRC was circumscribed by the fact that, as president rather than head of state, Babangida was the ultimate authority. Nwabueze (1994) reveals that most decrees enacted by the regime were issued directly by the president, and never went through the AFRC (later National Defence and Security Council, NDSC). The president also had powers to determine the membership of the AFRC.

There was also a redefinition of the role of commander-in-chief of the armed forces, which normally goes with the position of head of state but as such was always taken to be titular. The control of the 'no. 2' over the armed forces was abolished, and the president became 'chief executive' of the military. In this new role he had greater control over the appointments, promotions, postings and retirements of military officers, including service chiefs – Decree no. 17 of August 1985 transferred from the SMC to the president the power to appoint the CGS, chief of defence staff, service chiefs (army, navy, air force, and inspector-general of police), minister of defence, and director-general of the State Security Service (SSS – the new name for the NSO). It was with such powers that he established an elite unit – the national guard – when opposition to his regime was at its height. The guard, which was designed to be a 'quick strike force', operated outside the regular military establishment, and its command was directly under Babangida. Its creation was opposed by most senior army officers, who saw it as a rival establishment enjoying lavish funding and arms supplies at a time when the rest of the military was subject to reduced expenditure, but they were powerless to do anything about it.

In addition to these wide-ranging powers, the president was also minister of defence (till 1990, when Abacha was appointed to the post) and chairman of the Police Service Commission, the National Council of States, and the Council of Ministers. The Central Bank, the State Security Service (SSS) and the budget department were among the bodies, placed under the direct supervision of the presidency (Ihonvbere, 1991: 611).[4] The full extent of Babangida's powers is best captured by Nwabueze (1994: 4):

[4] The president manipulated his control of the budget department to punish 'erring' states, local governments, ministries and universities which harboured opposition elements (whose statutory allocations from the Federation Account or stabilisation fund were sometimes reduced or delayed, and to reward loyal institutions and their heads. At one stage,

IBB [the name by which Babangida was popularly known] as president was the repository of the full plentitude of the military government's absolute power, which he exercised as a personal ruler unrestrained by any law whatsoever.[...] He was to all intents and purposes the sole legislature of the federal military government.

The dire consequences of these changes for the body politic were shielded for a long time by the regime's populism and avowed human rights posture. To consolidate its populism, the regime at the initial stage adopted a participatory and public-sensitive approach to decision-making on crucial issues of national significance. This took the form of prefacing the adoption or introduction of critical policies with open debate and public choice, described by Legum (1987: B125) as 'plebiscite by newspaper', thereby giving the impression that the regime, unlike Buhari and Idiagbon, was guided by and responsive to public opinion. This way, the regime successfully imposed SAP through the back door, leaving the people to enjoy the illusion that the government was implementing a 'home-grown' and self-chosen SAP rather than one forced on the country by the 'imperialist' IMF/World Bank. The nationwide debate sponsored by the regime in September 1985 on whether the country should take the US$2.5 billion IMF loan and its condition, or reject the loan but adopt the conditions, was predictably resolved in favour of the latter.[5] By so doing, the nationalist pride of not being a beggar-like or dependent country, and the feeling of resistance and independence, were kept intact while the protests that would have greeted an externally imposed SAP were defected – after all, the hardship of SAP was a self-inflicted 'sacrifice': no price was too great to pay for economic recovery.

Babangida himself put these in perspective in his address on the outcome of the debate:

'After due consideration of all the opinions expressed by Nigerians ... government has come to the conclusion that for now, the path of honour ... lies in discontinuing the negotiations with the IMF for a support loan. We have therefore decided to face the challenge of restructuring our economy, not through an IMF loan, but a determination of *our own people* to make all the sacrifices necessary to put the economy on the path of sustained growth; doing so at *our own pace* and on *our own volition*.[...] We must by *ourselves* and on *our own terms*, do all those

---

the disbursement and allocation of federal revenue and resources seemed to depend more on personal relations with the president than on statutory procedure.

[5] The strongest opposition to the loan was predictably from the labour unions and local manufacturers, while greatest support was from big corporations like the UAC.

things which will help restructure our economy, no matter what pains are involved during the adjustment period.' (quoted in Olagunju *et al.*, 1993: 83, emphasis added)

This clever move helped to resolve the highly contentious issue of 'ownership' of SAP which affected its implementation in most other countries, and was applauded by the international community for its ingenuity (on the later 'abandonment' of ownership of SAP by civil society, see Faruqee, 1994). The policy making-by-debate approach was also adopted for working out the transition to civil rule programme, although in several ways the eventual programme was a marked departure from what the people 'voted' for.

However, the redeemer, 'human rights' and civil society-friendly image soon gave way to the full force of military authoritarianism, enhanced by a more powerful president. The repressive imperative of SAP implementation (cf. Gibbon *et al.*, 1992, especially article by Beckman; Mkandawire, 1995) reinforced and catalysed the authoritarian bent. But the regime also had a survival imperative, and this became more urgent with the increased hostility of civil society, whose demands included the termination of military rule and opposition from within the military itself.

The exigency of the survival imperative came soon enough. In December 1985 the government announced that it had uncovered a coup plot involving General Mamman Vatsa, former class-mate and close ally of General Babangida, and minister for the Federal Capital Territory, and several other officers and men (eight of the fourteen officers named as core planners were from Benue state). The plotters were said to be dissatisfied with the regime's rejection of the IMF loan, its liberal human rights posture, appointments of middle-level and junior officers to public office, and cuts in officers' salaries. Surely the plotters would have had extreme difficulty in selling such reasons to the public, and in all likelihood they were not the real reasons for the coup anyway. There was indeed widespread scepticism over the truth of the coup story, and many felt it was a ploy by the regime to get rid of its opponents. Despite appeals for clemency from various bodies, especially the Association of Nigerian Authors (ANA), of which General Vatsa (himself a writer and poet) had been national chairman, ten officers convicted by a tribunal headed by General Charles Ndiomu were executed on 5 March 1986, only a few hours after their sentences were confirmed by the AFRC.[6]

---

[6] Those executed included General Vatsa, Squadron Leader Martin Luther, Lt.-Col. Chris Oche, Lt.-Col. Musa Bitiyong, Lt.-Col. Mike Iyorshe, Maj. Daniel Bamidele, Wing-Commander Ben Ekele, Wing-Com. Adamu Sakaba, Squ.-Ldr. Asen Ahura, and Navy

One significant feature was that for the first time air force officers were deeply involved in a coup – something which had usually been a prerogative of the army. Most of them were pilots in the presidential fleet (Squadron Leaders Martin Luther and Asen Ahura, and Wing Commander Ben Ekele) and government attributed their involvement to the plan of the coup plotters to bomb Dodan Barracks, the seat of government at the time, and other strategic locations in Lagos from the air. It is believed that the subsequent neglect and under-development of the air force, which by August 1993 barely had five servicable jets in its fleet (the Jaguars and other fighters had been auctioned off), was in retaliation for the role of these officers in the coup.

The coup plotters were executed as a signal to the civil society that the regime was, after all, a military regime. Babangida had let it be known in one of his public addresses that his regime's human rights posture was not to be taken for granted: 'We do not intend to rule by force. At the same time, we should not be expected to submit to unreasonable demands. Fundamental rights and civil liberties will be respected. But their exercise must not degenerate into irrational expressions that border on subversion' (cited in Alagbe, 1986: 138). And in April 1986 he warned politicians and other activists not to mistake the regime's civil rights posture for weakness, and said he would not 'permit any Nigerian, no matter his social status, to flout the laws of our land and our sense of public morality'. These threats became fact in April 1986 when armed contingents of policemen and soldiers descended in a vicious manner on students at Ahmadu Bello University (ABU) demonstrating in remembrance of their predecessors killed in the famous 'Ali-must-go' riots of 1978. At least twenty students were killed on this occasion and, as students in other universities rose up in solidarity, so brutality by the army and police spread round the country. Nine universities were immediately closed, NANS was proscribed once again, and a ban was clamped on demonstrations. The NLC was prevented from staging a solidarity rally, and its leaders were detained for 'subversion'.

The regime next turned on the press. By the end of 1987, *Newswatch* (whose editor, Dele Giwa, was killed by a letter bomb), *The Guardian*, *Punch*, *Lagos News*, *Champion*, *Vanguard* and *Concord* had all experienced closure and detention of their journalists. Next to receive attention were the civil liberties organisations: their leaders were regularly detained, and leaders of the Civil Liberties Organization (CLO, Olisa

---

Commander Andrew Ogwiji. Brigadier Malami Nassarawa was retired, as were scores of other officers like Squ.-Ldr. Salaudeen Latinwo, former governor of Kwara state, who was questioned in connection with the coup.

Agbakoba), Civil Rights Project (CRP, Clement Nwankwo) and other human rights activists (Femi Falana, Gani Fawehinmi, Alao Aka Bashorun) had their passports confiscated at various times to prevent them from travelling outside the country. This was the beginning of the suppression and elimination the regime meted out to 'extremists' – the euphemism it used for its critics and opponents. For this purpose it was well armed: except for the cosmetic repeal of Decree no. 4, almost all the decrees enacted by the Buhari regime were intact or became even more stringent – for example, the period of arrest and detention without trial by the CGS or IG of police was extended from three to six months (for a discussion of laws with ouster clauses under the Babangida regime and a critical analysis of its human rights record, see Momoh, 1995). With the short-lived honeymoon over, the stage was set for a tyranny which arguably surpassed that of Buhari. We next turn to the SAP regime which, as already indicated, was a major catalyst and reinforcer of the regime's increased authoritarianism.

STRUCTURAL ADJUSTMENT

There is a large body of literature on structural adjustment in Nigeria, its implementation, and social, political and economic consequences (cf. Agbaje, 1992; Olukoshi, 1995a, 1995b; articles in Olukoshi, ed., 1991, 1993; Sanusi, 1988; Fashoyin, 1993; Mustapha, 1992; Osaghae, 1993, 1995c; Isamah, 1994, 1995; Albert, 1995; Adejumobi, 1995). Many analysts rightly ascribe the 'inevitability' of economic adjustment to the contexts of colonial disarticulation, reliance on single export commodities and the global economic recession which followed the oil shocks of the 1970s (cf. Toyo, 1984; Abba *et al.*, 1985; Usman and Bangura, 1984; Usman, 1986; Onimode, 1988; Forrest, 1993; and Nnoli, 1981, 1993). Because the historical and conceptual background of SAP is well covered in the literature, and much of it has already been dealt with in previous chapters, it need not detain us here. We need only say that by the time Babangida took over in August 1985, the adoption of SAP was inevitable and only a matter of time. Indeed, the deadlock of negotiations with the IMF was one of the main reasons given for the overthrow of Buhari.

Although the outcome of the national debate on the IMF loan was a useful reassurance that most Nigerian citizens were prepared to face and bear the hardships of SAP, especially in a home-grown and short-lived form, pressure from international capitalist consortia gave the government little choice in the matter. Babangida himself was a known apostle of the free market and structural adjustment, and his appointment of Idika Kalu, a well-known SAP advocate, as finance minister clearly reflected his preferences. Thus even before the outcome of the national debate was known, he declared a fifteen-month period of economic emergency as a prelude to SAP. But external creditors needed more than personal convictions and demonstrations of the capability to exercise the high degree of repression (called 'discipline') needed to undertake reform. There were the outstanding issues of debt re-scheduling and IMF clearance, and for the creditors these seemed more important. Ultimately the adoption of SAP was the result of pressures from the creditors. Nigeria had defaulted on the repayment of a debt principal of US$1,500 million resulting from promissory notes issued for pre-1984 short-term trade debts, and when it refused to take the IMF loan (presumably following the wishes expressed by citizens in the debate) which members of the Paris and London Clubs made a condition for debt rescheduling, it appeared to be in deep trouble.

Nigeria had to accept IMF's 'enhanced surveillance' of the adjustment programme, and obtain a medium-term 'sound' and 'credit worthy' assessment from the World Bank for the creditors to agree to reschedule debts (Olukoshi [1995b: 174] points out that SAP without an IMF loan meant that the country would have to rely on the World Bank, which subsequently played the key surveillance roles). SAP therefore opened the door to debt rescheduling and new lines of credit. In November 1986 commercial bank creditors agreed to reschedule US$1,500 million medium-term debts, and US$2,000 million in letters of credit arrears on provision of a new commercial loan of US$320 million. This was followed in December by the Paris Club's agreement to a ten-year rescheduling of medium- and long-term loans accumulated before the end of 1983, whose total was estimated at over US$7500 million. Other reschedulings and fresh commercial loans were successfully negotiated in the following years.

SAP was introduced incrementally. The first phase was a trial state of national economic emergency, which was declared for fifteen months to run from 1 October 1985. This declaration enabled Babangida to assume full powers of control over the economy. During the period of emergency, a compulsory savings scheme under which the salaries of public servants, including members of the armed forces, were cut by between 2 and 20 per cent, was introduced (in addition, some states like Imo reduced transport and rent allowances by half). A special fund – National Economic Recovery Fund – into which the 'savings' were to be paid was established in the Central Bank. Further preparatory steps to SAP were taken in the 1986 budget and the first half of the year. These included an 80 per cent cut in subsidies on petroleum products; a 30 per cent surcharge on imports; 5-15 per cent tax on after-tax profits declared by companies; a 19 per cent cut on defence expenditure; the introduction of incentives for exporters; the scrapping of commodity boards, including the Nigerian National Supply Company; and a privatisation/commercialisation programme under which the provision of services by most parastatals was to be de-subsidised (this was done through a 50 per cent reduction on non-statutory grants to parastatals), and government shares in hundreds of federal and state government enterprises were to be sold. Bans were placed on the importation of wheat, rice, maize and vegetable oil to encourage local production, though after the introduction of SAP the number of prohibited import items was cut from seventy-four to sixteen. The ban on wheat importation which Andrae and Beckman (1986; also Osaghae, 1987) identified as a major source of Nigeria's dependence, generated enormous controversy and opposition from powerful wheat merchants and master-bakers, as well as their American benefactors.

One notable feature of the countdown to SAP was the introduction of more taxes and levies by the federal and state governments in the drive to generate more funds. These included sales tax, registration of business premises fees, and education levies, ranging from the special levy for funding free primary education introduced by the federal government to sundry levies by state governments and school authorities. Various state governments also launched special development appeal funds which the then governor of Plateau state, Col. Mohammed Alli, defended as the only means left for looking inwards for development in times of hardship (*West Africa*, 28 April 1986: 901). The bulk of the several millions of naira realised from the appeal funds was believed to have ended up in the pockets of state government officials and were never accounted for. Local government councils and poor communities squeezed themselves to contribute to the funds, having been mobilised (actually blackmailed) by governors who made contribution a condition for government patronage in the distribution of amenities.

Finally, in July 1986, SAP was formally introduced. In deference to the sensitivities of Nigerians who – as the so-called national debate had clearly shown – were unlikely to accept any long-term programme of hardships, it was announced that the programme would only last until June 1988. But it lasted far beyond that and, except for a 'suspension' by the Abacha regime in 1994, lasting one year only, it remained the main theme of the country's economy till the end of the 1980s and through the 1990s. According to Synge (1993: 44), SAP

....was designed to deal with underlying imbalances in the Nigerian economy and thereby establish a basis for stable growth and development. It had two mutually reinforcing components: macroeconomic stabilization aimed at controlling inflationary tendencies and achieving a viable balance of payments and, secondly, the elimination of imbalances in the structure of production and expenditure to ensure the efficient allocation of resources in the economy.

Synge (pp. 44-5) has further summarised eight 'primary elements' of SAP as follows:

1. The strengthening of demand management 'through monetary and fiscal policies designed to ensure growth of aggregate demand was compatible with a low and stable inflation rate and a sustainable balance of payments position'. Fiscal deficit reduction and diversification to generate more revenue from non-oil sources were key instruments here.
2. Stimulation of domestic production through deregulation and interplay of market forces.
3. Devaluation of the naira which aimed at curbing imports, encouraging non-oil exports, inflow of foreign capital, including capital held abroad by Nigerians.
4. Rationalization and restructuring of customs tariffs which involved abolition of import licence and reduction of protection of local industries 'to create a more competitive and efficient industrial sector'.
5. Improved trade and payments systems which, amongst others, allowed exporters to retain their foreign exchange earnings.
6. Reduction of complex administrative controls through scrapping of commodity boards which ended the price control system, and the deregulation of the banking system, especially exchange rates.
7. Adoption of appropriate pricing policies which basically had to do with the removal of subsidies on petroleum products and provision of services like water, electricity, telephones, public transportation, as well as on social goods like health care and education (removal of subsidy or 'appropriate pricing' simply meant bringing the costs of public goods and services to 'international levels').
8. Rationalization of public sector enterprises which basically entailed privatisation and commercialisation.

For a country with a welfarist-oriented state-regulated economy, in which the state operated as 'Father Christmas', these and other elements of SAP (such as rationalisation of the public service, leading to retrenchment of more workers) were definitely bitter pills for the people to swallow. SAP had an economistic bias, which meant that its success was calculated by the ability of a country to service its external debt repayment and attract foreign investment, a positive balance of payments, and vague indices of economic growth (often made up for by currency devaluation), rather than improved quality of life, a bias usually described in terms of 'adjustment without a human face'. Thus the entire package become something of a war on ordinary people. This is not to say that SAP did not have its beneficiaries (the banks, foreign exchange merchants, local agents of foreign companies, and so on, as scholars who distinguish between 'winners' and 'losers' of SAP point out, but these were only a tiny minority).

A comprehensive assessment of the implementation and consequences of SAP under Babangida cannot be undertaken here; these are well covered in the literature to which reference has already been made. We can best attempt a selective assessment, but of sufficient scope to permit a reasonable and fair conclusion. To begin with, SAP required strong fiscal discipline which the regime basically lacked. Increased revenue because of depreciation of the naira encouraged reckless spending on a scale far larger than that of the Gowon years. Nothing demonstrates this better than the huge budget deficits it recorded from year to year. For example, the deficits in the federal budget rose from N14.3 billion in 1989 to N21.7 billion in 1990, and N35.3 billion in 1991 (the states fared better, recording deficits of N1.5 billion, N1.2 billion and N2.6 billion in the three years). Some of the deficits were settled by 'ways and means' bills, which meant printing more naira without productive back-up, a practice which increased the amount of 'useless' money in circulation in astronomical proportions, and so heightened inflation and the depreciation of the naira. Recourse to ways and means partly reflected the weak controls exercised by the Central Bank, which was under the direct control of the presidency. The deficits were largely accounted for by profligate spending on support-buying 'donations' to sundry bodies,[7] by huge extra-budgetary expenditure mostly incurred under the transition to civil rule programme (discussed below), and by the numerous agencies established either to handle various SAP related or enhancing projects or to extend the regime's corporatist designs. The Babangida years would be remembered for the proliferation of extra-departmental agencies and institutions at a time when government and public sector expenditure were supposed to be shrinking.

---

[7] These included N10 million to the Performing Musicians' Association of Nigeria; N10 million to the Olympic fund in 1992; N30 million to Awo Foundation; N50 million to the National Ecumenical Centre in Abuja; N87 million to the NLC mass transit project; and so on.

These agencies and institutions included the National Directorate of Employment (NDE), created to generate non-public sector 'self-employment', and to promote the development of small-scale enterprises; the Directorate of Food, Roads and Rural Infrastructure (DFRRI) to handle rural development, one of the pillars for the creation of an enabling environment for SAP; the Federal Urban Mass Transit Programme, to ensure the provision of cheap transport with the removal of subsidies; the 'Better Life Programme', begun as a pet project of the president's wife to improve the quality of life for rural women but taken over by government because of its enormous legitimation – mobilisation and patronage – building potential; and the people's and community (and later mortgage) banks to ensure access to credit for the poor and to encourage savings. There were also the Directorate of Social Mobilization, the Centre for Democratic Studies, and the National Council for Inter-Governmental Relations, which were more relevant to the democratic transition programme. Some of these agencies were undoubtedly well-intentioned and even necessary, and a few had a positive impact on giving SAP a human face at least at the beginning (NDE, DFRRI, urban mass transit), but they became channels of corporatism, generating superflous patronage, legitimation-building, rent-seeking and bureaucratic corruption (cf. Osaghae *et al.*, 1994). Huge expenditure also went into ambitious and capital-intensive projects like the completion of the new federal capital at Abuja, which became the seat of government at the end of 1990; the aluminium smelting plant in Ikot Abasi on which over N4.5 billion was spent, and which a World Bank report described as the most expensive of its kind in the world; hosting high-profile international events like the OAU and ECOWAS summits; and the peace-keeping mission to Liberia.

The privatisation and commercialisation of government enterprises proceeded fairly well. Decree no. 25 of 1988 assigned this responsibility to the Technical Committee on Privatization and Commercialization (TCPC; from 1995, the committee became known as the Bureau for Public Enterprises, BPE). State enterprises were classified into four categories. Those in the first category – hotels and agro-allied companies – were to be fully privatised. Oil companies, steel rolling mills, banks, and fertiliser companies, which formed the bulk of enterprises in the second category, were to be part privatised (the decision on banks was not stable – in 1992 some were put up for full privatisation, only for the government to reacquire controlling shares in the three of the major ones – UBA, Union Bank and First Bank in 1995). Enterprises in the third category which included the National Electric Power Authority, Nigerian Railways Corporation, and federal television and radio stations, were to be commercialised with partial removal of subsidies. Finally, enterprises in the fourth category – NNPC, Nigerian Telecommunications Limited (NITEL), the Nigerian Ports Authority (NPA), the Nigerian Coal Corporation etc. – were to be fully commercialised.

By 1993 most of the targets had been met. The TCPC announced that about N3.3 billion had been realised from the sales of government shares in fifty-five firms at the end of 1992 (the Abacha regime regarded the low returns from these sales as evidence that the parastatals had failed). But the allocations and sales of government shares became politicised, as they resurrected the question of ethnic and regional access to, and control of, the economy, first raised with the indigenisation programme of the 1970s. The guidelines on privatisation did include equity considerations and the need to balance 'interregional, interpersonal and interstate distribution of shares', but these could not prevent the controversy generated by the low responses in most Northern states even after state governments arranged special loans for citizens to buy shares, and the sales of 'Southern-Yoruba' companies like Cocoa Industries Ltd. (cf. Ate, 1991; Agbese, 1992; Yahaya, 1993; Osaghae, 1995). Other steps besides privatisation were taken to strengthen local private capital, one of the most notable of these being the granting of oil prospecting licences to eighteen indigenous oil companies (mostly owned by close business associates of the military leaders). However, the capital and technology required by the industry were beyond the reach of these companies, and most were forced to 'mortgage' their concessions to foreign companies when the federal government threatened to revoke their licences.

The balance-sheet of economic recovery – the main objective of SAP – was far from impressive, contrary to the World Bank verdict that Nigeria was one of the showcases of successful adjustment. The growth-rate of the economy, which was said to have recovered from negative before 1986 to an average of 5 per cent after SAP, has been challenged. According to Fadahunsi (1993: 43), although at 1984 constant factor cost the economy recorded a growth-rate of 1.8 per cent in 1987, 4.16 per cent in 1988 and 3.92 per cent in 1989, 'when account is taken of the population growth-rates averaging about 3 per cent per annum and annual inflation rates of between 40 and 50 per cent, growth rates since the introduction of SAP and the massive devaluation of the naira will be found to be actually negative in real terms.' Other chronic problems of the economy remained. Despite the incentives offered, including the introduction of tax-free holidays, generous concessions for industries using local raw materials and/or export-oriented, and the establishment of the Calabar Export

Processing Zone in 1991,[8] foreign investment remained sluggish and was mostly directed towards the oil sector.

According to *West Africa* (3-9 December 1990), European investors not only complained that the liberalisation had not gone far enough, but there was actually a decline in overall European investment. The report gives the example of new British investment which fell sharply (even with devaluation of the naira) from N435 million in 1987 to N184 million in 1988, although Britain maintained its record of 60 per cent of total foreign private capital input in Nigeria. In some other sectors, notably pharmaceuticals, there was disinvestment by foreign interests, attributable to the country's fragile political situation. The relaxation of restrictions on foreign equity participation in, and ownership of, enterprises under the new industrial policy of 1989 only succeeded in ensuring the return and expansion of Asian and Lebanese businesses, especially in the retail and textile sectors. At the same time, it also facilitated capital flight by foreign firms whose money had long been 'tied down' in Nigeria.

The industrial and manufacturing sectors remained in the doldrums. Capacity utilisation continued to be low, averaging 30-40 per cent, and many more firms were forced to close down, as the devaluation of the naira raised costs of production, especially the importation of raw materials, and depressed demand. Although the local sourcing of raw materials increased slightly, and the footwear, printing materials and pharmaceutical manufacturers recorded impressive performance, disinvestment plagued the industrial and manufacturing sectors – the 1992 Central Bank Annual Report noted that economic agents had abandoned more productive endeavours for quicker gains in commercial and speculative activities. A persistently low oil price (it dropped in 1986 to an all-time low of less than $10 pb) and the decline in foreign exchange receipts worsened the situation.

Diversification of the economy and, in particular, the stimulation of agricultural and food output recorded only marginal improvements. Oil remained the dominant export commodity, accounting for an average 94 per cent of all exports under SAP. Central Bank Annual Reports indicated that the performance of the non-oil sector weakened after a vigorous beginning when SAP was introduced, and attributed this to inconsistencies in policy implementation and an unfavourable world market. Total agricultural output increased by an average of 5.3 per cent in 1986-91, compared to the 1.0 per cent growth in 1980-5.

[8] To attract foreign investors, the EPZ introduced tax exemptions, removed restrictions on imports and the repatriation of profits, freed goods from pre-shipment inspection, aimed for the provision of an efficient infrastructure, and permitted 100 per cent foreign ownership of enterprises.

The scrapping of commodity boards and deregulation of prices boosted the production of cocoa especially – there was talk of a 'cocoa boom', which was later discovered to have been artificially created by over-invoicing and other sharp practices by Asian and other foreign 'exporters' who cashed in on the situation to transfer large sums of money abroad. Agricultural export also increased (from an annual average of 393,000 tonnes in 1981-5 to 441,000 in 1987-90), but Synge [1993: 48] has attributed the so-called gains of the agricultural sector to the devaluation of the naira. In any case, the major beneficiaries of the gains were not the rural dwellers, as the authors of SAP hoped (Fadahunsi [1993: 48] reports an erosion of the purchasing power of rural dwellers due to inflation, high costs of agricultural inputs and non-farm goods and services), but the agricultural capitalists and exporters. Imports of consumer goods, especially secondhand vehicles, continued to increase, with the result that only marginal improvements were recorded in the balance of payments (from deficits in 1986 and 1988, surpluses were recorded in 1987 and 1989-91). External debt servicing rose from $12 billion in 1987 to $27.7 billion in 1990 and $29.3 billion in 1991, while other debt management strategies, including the debt conversion programme, recorded mixed results (cf. Adejumobi 1995: 172-3).

Finally it was in the overall impact on the standard of living and quality of life that the implementation of SAP had devastating consequences. The 1991 World Bank Report ranked Nigeria as the thirteenth poorest country in the world, while the United Nations Development Programme concluded from a human deprivation index survey in 1990 that it had one of the worst records for human deprivation of any country in the third world. *Per capita* income, which does not show the whole picture, vividly reflected declining standards; from an estimated $778 in 1985 it fell to $175 in 1988 and $105 in 1989. The decrease could be attributed to the devaluation of the naira, but the effect of SAP was all too obvious. Except for the tiny category of 'winners' – foreign exchange speculators, banks which emerged in large numbers to reap huge profits from forex speculation and high interest rates (over 100 new commercial and merchant banks, most of which had become distressed by the early 1990s, were established in the SAP period), multinational and other foreign firms which benefitted from devaluation and repatriated huge surpluses, importers of secondhand goods, government officials who maximised rent-seeking opportunities as corruption became a major mechanism for coping with the hardships – the vast majority of the ordinary people were 'losers' through SAP. This was especially true of the urban dwellers, whom SAP had declared 'parasites' for being producers of non-tradeables, but the rural dwellers who produced so-called tradeables fared no better.

The removal of so-called subsidies, especially on petroleum products, and massive devaluations of the naira raised the cost of living beyond the reach of many average families. Through the operations of the foreign exchange market and parallel market activities, the naira plummeted from N1=$1 in 1985 to N4.21 in April 1988, N7.48 in 1989 and finally, after the currency was 'floated' to place it at par with unofficial rates in 1992, to N22 in December 1993 (by which time it was N40-50 = $1 in the 'black' or parallel market). Unemployment remained at an all-time high, with continued retrenchments in the public sector and endangered industrial and manufacturing sectors. Inflation, which actually stood at an average of 70 per cent despite official estimates of 20-30 per cent, denuded purchasing power and salary increases. The escalating costs of food, rent, transport, electricity, health care, education and other social goods and services completed the picture of misery. Although the government introduced various 'palliatives' like higher salaries and allowances after the wage freeze was lifted in 1988, the relaxation of controls on the import of secondhand vehicles and spare parts, and so on, these were of little consequence.

Most urban dwellers then devised various strategies for coping. These included moonlighting and the creation of rent-seeking avenues by civil servants, withdrawal of children from school, a drastic reduction in food consumption, increased patronage of herbalists and 'traditional' or spiritual healing rather than hospitals and clinics, increased religiosity and the cultivation of fatalistic complexes which served to reduce the spirit of protest, crime,[9] prostitution, drug use and so on. A 'brain drain' gathered momentum. Along with these responses there was an upsurge in civil society contestation, resistance and opposition, implying an abandonment of SAP and massive withdrawal of support from the Babangida regime. The regime raised the stakes of opposition by declaring that there was no alternative to SAP and mustering its military force to muzzle attempts to articulate alternatives. As the regime became more intolerant and insensitive to public demands, strikes demonstrations and riots resulted. Students of tertiary institutions and members of labour unions were in the forefront of the famous

---

[9] There was an explosion of violent crime, especially armed robbery. Dare-devil gangs terrorised urban dwellers, and the government seemed unable to cope with the situation. Many convicted robbers justified their acts by the SAP and the wide gap between rich and poor. A particularly sensational case was that of 'Anini', leader of a gang of robbers in the then Bendel state, who became a national folk hero for defying the authorities (see Marenin, 1987; also see Adisa, 1994 for the rise of 'Area Boys' or street gangs who unleashed terror in Lagos).

SAP riots which were staged to protest at increases in the price of petroleum products and at higher living costs generally. The price of a litre of petrol went up from 39.5kobo(k.) to 42k. in 1988, to 60k. in 1989 and to 70k. in 1990 (100k.=N1). An attempt to raise the price to N7.50 in August 1993 with the pretext of introducing a new grade of petrol was shelved after threats of more violent demonstrations, but it was finally increased by the interim national government which replaced Babangida to N3.25 after an initial increase to N5.00.

The problems of the petroleum sector were complicated by the perennial fuel shortages. These were most acute in Northern parts of the country where petrol stations were closed for several months at a stretch. The judicial commission of enquiry headed by Mr Justice Alfa Belgore attributed the shortages to large-scale smuggling of fuel to neighbouring countries;[10] breakdowns in the four refineries (all mysteriously gutted by fire at various times) which were in arrears of servicing and were producing at low capacity; and the activities of ethnic minority agitators in the Niger Delta which disrupted exploration and refining activities. These problems were adduced to strengthen the case for so-called appropriate pricing of fuel and other petroleum products. The price hikes for petroleum products led to higher prices in all other sectors, but there were no commensurate hikes in salaries (the main reason for the uncontrollable rise and pervasiveness of bureaucratic corruption). From the time SAP was introduced in 1986, therefore, no year passed without some violent riot, strike or demonstration. Tertiary institutions, whose students were in the vanguard of these protests, were continually closed down due to student riots and, later, demands by lecturers for better conditions of service. These uprisings provided the basis for later demands for political reforms – partly because the government tied SAP to its political transition programme, as we discuss below. For example, the nation-wide demonstrations ordered by NANS, the national student organisation, in all institutions of higher learning in May 1992 (over twenty people were killed by police and military anti-riot squads in the demonstrations) were in protest at 'excruciating' economic conditions, and to demand the termination of SAP, the resignation of Babangida, and the convening of a sovereign national conference to resolve the 'national question'.

It could be argued, as some commentators have done, that the underlying economic recession, rather than SAP in itself, should be blamed for these numerous woes. Campbell (1989) cautions against

[10] This was very lucrative, as a litre of petrol cost 70 kobo in Nigeria as against N14 in neighbouring countries – at one stage Cameroon was said to have shut its refinery because of cheap petrol smuggled from Nigeria.

making SAP the new 'scapegoat'. It can even be argued that a more 'disciplined' implementation of SAP in Nigeria would have yielded better results. For example, many believe that the windfall which the country gained from the high oil price during the Gulf war might have gone a long way towards repaying external debts and putting the economy back on track. These points of view have merit, but the economic crisis in the country also had deep roots. In any case, there can be no doubt that Nigeria needed structural adjustment, at least to reduce its dependence on oil and imports, ensure efficiency in monetary and fiscal policies, and get out of its debt overhang. Nevertheless, largely because it was designed to respond to external rather than internal demands, SAP aggravated the crisis through measures like devaluation and removal of subsidies on social goods and services. The steep increases in the prices of petroleum products in particular aggravated the crisis. The Nigeria Labour Congress (NLC) alluded to the profit motive in policies like this, which it said the government had placed 'over and above the health and wellbeing of the Nigerian people' (*Newswatch*, 24 July 1989). The resulting hardships for the vast majority of the people wiped out its actual and potential benefits, and once it (and its owner-regime) lost their support, the chances of these benefits being realised were remote.

THE LABYRINTH OF A POLITICAL TRANSITION

The 'democratic restorative' project was central to the Babangida regime. Olagunju *et al.* (1993) regard it as the most important reason for the overthrow of Buhari, and the author of most of the regime's policies, including those of economic adjustment. The economic reform-democratisation nexus was in consonance with the new conventional wisdom prescribed by the Bretton Woods institutions and imposed by Western governments and donor agencies, in which economic and political liberalisation were to be undertaken simultaneously on the assumption that (liberal) democracy was not possible without the entrenchment of market forces (an update of the old modernisation wisdom that democratic viability requires economic development). The Babangida regime did not however need political conditionality to embark on a transition programme, partly because of the entrenched democratic culture in Nigeria and partly because a return to democracy was one of the stated reasons for overthrowing Buhari.

However, the transition programme confirmed two popular hypotheses: first, that democratic transition is less likely to succeed if undertaken at the same time as structural adjustment with its contradictory authoritarian imperative (the corollary of this, which repeated failures of transitions in Nigeria support, is that military regimes, by their authoritarian nature, are bad midwives of democratic transition). The second and fairly obvious hypothesis is that democratic transition can be used to legitimise and prolong or perpetuate the life-span of transiting military regimes. Only further research can show if, in Nigeria's case, the two hypotheses are related – that, for example, the Babangida regime deliberately pursued a programme of structural adjustment to prevent a successful transition to democracy – meanwhile it must be assumed that the two were unrelated. But while the disabling consequences of SAP for democratic transition could not have been foreseen, it is doubtful whether the same can be said for the design of the transition programme – the vacillations on the hand-over date, confusion over who could contest elections, and the eventual annulment of the presidential election. The disjointed transition may thus be regarded as part of a Machiavellian tactic to cling on to power (although this disjointedness partly derived from the experimental blueprint recommended for the transition by the Political Bureau, as we shall see shortly). This popular perception of the transition programme derived from the image of Babangida as a manipulative leader[11] and seriously weakened the credibility of the programme, especially in the difficult final stages.

General Babangida announced his commitment to return the country to civilian democratic rule quite early in the life of his regime. Even before the details of the transition timetable had been worked out, he committed the regime to a hand-over date: 1 October 1990. Olagunju *et al.* (1993: chapter 4) have identified three main sources of Babangida's transition programme. The first was a 1984 memorandum by the National Institute of Policy and Strategic Studies (of which he himself was an alumnus), proposing a long-drawn-out transition programme to enable the necessary institutional and political cultural framework for democratic stability to be established. Second was a confidential memorandum which recommended, among other things, the establishment of a political bureau in the president's office to coordinate the transition programme, the lining of political and economic reform, and a 'sequential development' of the transition timetable. Finally, there was the report of a committee of eight federal permanent

---

[11] This reputation earned him the nickname 'Maradona', first used by the ex-governor Bisi Onabanjo, after the famous Argentine footballer, for his dribbling skills. The following is an insider's account of Babangida as a person: 'For the whole period of my tenure, I experienced nothing of his reputed Machiavellianism; nothing of the Maradona-like skill in dribbling people to achieve his ends; nothing of the smooth manipulator of men and events; nothing of the crafty, unreliable, overweening autocrat interfering in, and directing, all affairs of state from his office or bedroom. He might well be crafty. How else really could he have survived in that office for eight long years?' (Nwabueze, 1994: 9)

secretaries (including John Odigie Oyegun and Emeka Ezeife, who later became governors in the short-lived diarchical transition, Alhaji Alhaji and Mrs F.Y. Emmanuel). The recommendations from the first two sources are strikingly similar to the political transition pro-gramme eventually adopted. A fourth source that Olagunju *et al.* understandably omit was the group of academics who served as the regime's think-tank.

The transition institutions, programmes and timetable derived largely from the *Report of the Political Bureau*. This seventeen-member body headed by Samuel Cookey[12] was set up in January 1986 with the principal objectives of organising a national debate on the political problems of the country, distilling from the contributions and the Bureau's review of Nigeria's political history a viable political future and guidelines for the attainment of consensus objectives, and identifying a basic philosophy of government. The national political debate lasted from February to September 1986, and took the form of memoranda by individuals, groups and organisations, commissioned debates on assigned topics by associations of professionals labour, women and students, and contributions to newspapers, electronic media and public hearings organised by the bureau in all state capitals. Altogether 27,324 contributions were received by the Bureau, and these ostensibly guided the formulation of its blueprint for the political transition programme. The major recommendations of the Bureau were contained in the *Report* referred to earlier. Space does not permit us to consider more than the most important and novel of the *Report*'s recommendations for the political transition, but it must be emphasised that it is an important document touching on almost every aspect of Nigeria's socio-political and economic formulations and problems.

The recommendations on political transition hinged on the creation of a new socio-political order which, according to the Bureau, required a reversal of the existing unacceptable system and a 'well-thought out' and 'ordered' transition programme (FGN, 1987a: 220-1). In contrast to the 'hurried' transition to the Second Republic, this was to be done through a process of social engineering based on a new ideology and political culture, new institutions and social mobilisation (for an interesting comparison of the two transitions see Koehn, 1989). Given the all-encompassing dimensions of the new social order to be created, the *Report* touched on most sectors of national life. Its mostly radical and populist recommendations included the adoption of a socialist ideology; the nationalisation of the oil industry; dis-

---

[12] Of the seventeen members, ten were academics. Two, Ola Balogun and Edwin Madunagu, resigned from the Bureau.

continuation of privatisation and some other macroeconomic policies; a ban on the participation of 'old brigade' politicians from the new dispensation; constitutional entrenchment of the referendum as an instrument to ratify new constitution and subsequent major amendments, and a system of 'recall' by which electorates could withdraw the mandate given to elected representatives; a non-renewable tenure of five years for the president and state governors; abolition of the senate, to be replaced by a unicameral legislature at the federal level; the creation of six new states; establishment of a permanent national revenue and fiscal commission and review of the existing revenue allocation ensuring local governments at least 20 per cent of the Federation Account; the strengthening of local government as an autonomous tier of government and the anchor of the new 'grassroots-based' political system in which the flow of power would be bottom-up rather than top-down; a programme of social mobilisation and political education; and a two-party system.

The government white paper on the *Report*, based on the deliberations of a nine-member panel headed by General Paul Omu which had been set up to review it, rejected almost all the 'radical' recommendations – socialism, nationalisation, and termination of privatisation – as well as a unicameral legislature and restriction on the tenure of president and governors (FGN, 1987b). The two-party system, programme of social mobilisation (the political education component was dropped) and most of the other recommendations were accepted with slight modifications. Of the institutional novelties which emerged from the *Report*, perhaps the most fundamental was the two-party system. The question of an appropriate party system had been central to the search for viable democracy in post-independence Nigeria for the obvious reason that the nature and character of political parties have serious consequences for the stability of civilian rule. The experience of the First Republic clearly showed the inherent dangers of ethno-regional parties under a majoritarian system (cf. Diamond, 1988).

The decision to adopt a presidential system and introduce guidelines for ensuring that political parties were national was part of the measures taken to ensure that a suitable system was put in place in the Second Republic. In deciding on the most appropriate party system, the Constitution Drafting Committee (CDC) rejected the two-party system on the following grounds:

> This is a system we cannot possibly legislate for. In societies with a two-party system, such a system has been the product of an historical growth. It may be that Nigeria, over time, will develop a two-party system but we cannot legislate for it. (FGN, vol. II, 1976: 178)

As we showed in Chapter 3, constitutional guidelines were insufficient to bring about national political parties. This fact, the two party tendencies evident in the broad coalitions formed by the parties in the First and Second Republics, and the need for what Oyediran and Agbaje (1992: 218) call 'an imaginative programme of cleavage management', informed the Bureau's decision to do what the CDC hesitated to do, by settling for a two-party system.

To prevent the two parties from becoming expressions of the mutually reinforcing political dichotomies in the country (North/Muslim-South/Christian), as many critics feared, the Bureau's *Report* reasserted part of the regimentation code for parties in the 1979 Constitution, to which it added the requirements that the two parties accept the national philosophy of government and that the differences between them should be 'the priorities and strategies of implementation of the national objectives' (FGN, 1987a: 126). In addition, the *Report* recommended that the two parties should be substantially funded by the state, which in effect meant they were to operate like government 'parastatals'. The inadequacies and short-sightedness of the two-party system by fiat (since, as the Bureau proposed, the law establishing the two-party system was to be enacted by a decree and confirmed by the constitution) have been well articulated in the literature, and need not detain us here (cf. Oyediran and Agbaje, 1992; Uwazurike, 1990; Akinola, 1989, 1990; and Adeniran, 1991 for a more favourable view). It suffices to point out that by recommending substantial state funding and failing to articulate any serious ideological divide between the two proposed parties – it said only that the two parties should differ on the priorities and strategies of implementing national objectives – the Bureau laid the basis for the regime's eventual decision – as Akinola (1990) puts it – to 'manufacture' two parties.

The other transition aspect of the Bureau's *Report* was the question of timing. Here the major consideration was how to overcome the 'poverty and inadequacy of previous programmes of transition'. To do this, the *Report* said,

.... what we need is not a hand-over programme of the 1979 experience, but a broadly-spaced transition in which democratic governance can proceed with political learning, institutional adjustment and a re-orientation of the political culture, at sequential levels of politics and governance, beginning with the local government and ending at the federal level. (FGN, 1987: 221)

This was the origin of the 'learning', 'experimental', 'sequential' and 'methodical' epithets which became the rationalisations for the confusing twists and turns, and forward and backward movements, that came to characterise the transition. For example, a portion of Babangida's broadcast in November 1992 annulling the presidential primaries conducted by the parties was like a direct quotation from the Bureau *Report*: 'The logic of the transition programme has an in-built learning process that makes room for making critical assessment of the immediate event and instituting corrective measures where necessary, for the greater good of the nation.' Although it accepted the 1990 terminal date for military rule 'imposed' on it by the regime, the *Report* was not clear on whether by that date the transition learning would have been completed. It only could hope that if the learning began in 1987, 'it should achieve reasonable maturity by 1990'. With the further insistence that 'the final determination of the progression from one stage to the other ... should depend on the conviction of the executors that reasonable minimum progress has been made and that proceeding to the next stage would not jeopardize the entire programme', the *Report* gave the regime complete freedom to maneouvre and manipulate the transition as it pleased. Thus, in cancelling the presidential primaries of 1992, the president said he would not allow 'time consciousness' to prevent him from achieving the goal of putting a new political order in place. To a large extent, then, the Political Bureau should take responsibility for the failure of the Babangida regime's transition programme, especially since its members went on to play key roles in the implementation of the programme.

It was such ambivalence that led four members of the Bureau to issue a minority report in which they proposed a terminal date of 1992 – which, following the recommendation of the Omu panel, the government decided to adopt. Another area in which the Bureau's *report* was disappointing was that of military intervention in politics. Not only was the *report* ambivalent; it actually reiterated the 'entrenched' custodian roles of the military in the country's political life. Thus it identified the role of the military as 'the defence of the nation

Table 6.1. TIMETABLE FOR TRANSITION TO CIVILIAN RULE, 1987-93

SCHEDULE 1
Programme for 1987

3rd Quarter
— Establishment of Directorate of Social Mobilization
— Establishment of National Electoral Commission
— Establishment of Constitution Drafting Committee
4th Quarter
— Elections into local governments on a non-party basis

SCHEDULE 2
Programme for 1988

1st Quarter
— Establishment of National Population Commission
— Establishment of Code of Conduct Bureau
— Establishment of Code of Conduct Tribunal
— Establishment of Constituent Assembly
— Establishment of National Revenue Mobilization Commission
2nd Quarter
— Termination of Structural Adjustment Programme (SAP)
3rd & 4th Quarters
— Consolidation of gains of SAP

SCHEDULE 3
Programme for 1989

1st Quarter
— Promulgation of new constitution
— Release of new fiscal arrangements
2nd Quarter
— Lift of ban on politics
3rd Quarter
— Registration of two political parties
4th Quarter
— Election into local governments on party basis

SCHEDULE 4
Programme for 1990

1st & 2nd Quarters
— State assembly and gubernatorial elections
3rd Quarter
— Inauguration of state legislatures
4th Quarter
— Inauguration of state governors

SCHEDULE 5
Programme for 1991

1st, 2nd & 3rd Quarters
— Census
4th Quarter
— Local government elections

SCHEDULE 6
Programme for 1992

1st & 2nd Quarters
— Elections into Federal Legislature and Inauguration of National Assembly
3rd & 4th Quarters
— Presidential election
— Inauguration of new president and final disengagement of the military

and the constitution', and recommended that the military should participate in key national commissions, including those on electoral and population questions, and that an Armed Forces Consultative Committee be established (which Babangida later did) to hold dialogue on national and professional issues of interest to the military. Although the *Report* observed that military intervention and rule had had negative consequences, these recommendations could well have had the opposite effect of encouraging the military to hold on to power or intervene at will as the country's custodians.

Despite its ambivalence on some issues where clarity was called for, the Bureau managed to come up with items, for a transition programme, including the establishment of national commissions and other institutions, the creation of new states, a census, a new constitution, the registration of two political parties, and staggered elections from local right up to federal level. This was the basis for the Transition to Civil Rule (Political Programme) Decree no. 19 of 1987 (Table 6.1). Several, seemingly endless, amendments were made to the time sequence and specific institutions of the transition programme (how else could it have been an experimental and learning process?); this precipitated serious crisis and uncertainty, and led to doubts about the sincerity of the regime's promise to hand over power and about whether, even if it did, the creation of a stable and democratic political system would result (cf. Joseph, 1990: 18). As Obasanjo put it in an interview:

'In the name of political engineering, the country has been converted to a political laboratory for trying all kinds of silly experiments and gimmicks. Principle has been abandoned for expediency. All kinds of *booby traps* were instituted into the transition process. The result is the crisis we now face.' (*Tell*, 30 November 1992: 12)'

The most notable of the 'amendments' – which badly rocked the credibility of the transition – were the confusing banning and unbanning of certain categories of politicians, the decision to impose two 'test-tube' parties (Adeniran, 1991) that were so regimented that they functioned no better than government parastatals, and the vacillations over elections and the hand-over date. We shall briefly examine each of these.

WHO WAS QUALIFIED TO BE A POLITICIAN?

The frequent banning and unbanning of certain categories of politicians and uncertainty over who exactly could participate in the politics of the transition were a major source of the confusion that marked the entire transition. It began in June 1986 with a blanket ban on 'all past politicians' from seeking or holding any public office for ten years from the date when the ban on politics was lifted. The Political Bureau supported this ban as part of the necessary measures for creating a new political morality, but recommended that it be narrowed to those who had held political offices between August 1975 and August 1985. Then followed the Participation in Politics and Election Prohibition Decree no. 25 of 1987, which banned for life former office-holders who had been found guilty of corruption and embezzlement of public funds, and disqualified for the period of transition those who might not have been indicted but who, in the government's view should have their political rights curtailed. Those banned and disqualified were also barred from sponsoring, forming or belonging to any political association or party. A few of the politicians who came into this category, notably Balarabe Musa and Arthur Nzeribe, were arrested for forming political associations and engaging in political activities (Musa was actually tried and convicted by a special tribunal).

Decree no. 9 of 1989 increased the number of those disqualified to include chairmen and members of transition agencies – the National Electoral Commission (NEC), the Directorate of Social Mobilization (DSM) and the National Population Commission (NPC). In December 1991, Decree no. 25 was again amended to lift the ban on former public office-holders who had not been convicted of wrong doing by any tribunal or court, followed by another amendment in 1992 which allowed former chairmen and members of transition agencies to participate in transition politics. Then, in 1992, after the cancellation of the presidential primaries conducted by the two parties, all the twenty-three presidential aspirants who took part in the primaries were again banned, only to be unbanned after the annulment of the 1993 presidential election.

Apart from issues of justice and human rights raised by the bans, the frequent reversals showed the confusion that riddled the transition programme. Two plausible explanations can be advanced for the manipulative nature of the bannings and unbannings. The first is that it was part of the search for ideal politicians to operate an ideal democracy – the president was said to have won many politicians over with the argument that they were the right people to operate the ideal democracy he dreamed of. The second, not unrelated to the first, is that it was part of a grand design by the military to build a comprador political class – the famous 'new breed' – which could then form the support-base for prolonged military rule. Unpredictable politicians, as well as those whose loyalties could not be taken for granted, were at the receiving end of the bans and were even tried for contravening the decrees, while decrees were sometimes amended just to bring loyalists on board. Indeed, it was popularly believed at the time that many politicians, especially those who contested gubernatorial and senatorial elections, had been 'drafted' and 'sponsored' by the regime. But even if the president did not intend to remain in power, he certainly intended to hand over power only to those acceptable to his regime. As he said in an address in Kuru in 1987, 'we have not chosen, and have not sought to choose, those who will succeed us. We have only decided on those who would not.'

This is the only way one can make sense of the arbitrariness involved in deciding those who could be politicians or contest elections in the transition period. Decree no. 48 empowered the NEC to 'clear' candidates for elections and disqualify those demands unsuitable to contest *without explanations* (as with every other decree, the NEC's decision could not be challenged in any court). This enabled 'enemies' of the regime and those whom the regime had decided could not succeed it to be disqualified even after the bans on their participation had been lifted. Thus, among others, twelve gubernatorial candidates (nine SDP and three NRC), and several state and National Assembly and presidential aspirants were disqualified. The criteria used by NEC were never precisely known, but there was no doubt that they were arbitrary. In two interesting cases, Joe Nwodo and Hyde Onuaguluchi were disqualified from contesting the gubernatorial elections in Enugu state in 1991, but cleared to contest the presidential election. It was also obvious that the final decision on disqualification lay with the government rather than the NEC. For example, Ebenezer Babatope, Sam Mbakwe and some other senatorial candidates who had been cleared by the NEC were disqualified by the government. Intervention by the latter even went so far as to reverse electoral outcomes and order fresh party primaries for National Assembly candidates in constituencies where apparently favoured candidates lost.

THE 'TEST-TUBE' PARTIES

The response to the lifting of the ban on political activities in May 1989 was the emergence of several political associations which had to compete to be one or the other of the two parties to be registered by NEC. Many of these had been formed in the Constituent Assembly and Constitution Review Committee convened to produce the 1989 Constitution, and were merely waiting for the ban to be lifted. Within one week no less than twenty-three associations emerged, and in two months the number rose to eighty-eight (see Oyediran and Agbaje,

1991 for a list of forty-nine of these associations).[13] As in 1978, most of these associations were bargaining platforms for the more powerful coalitions which emerged later. Thus, of the large number only thirteen applied for registration. These were the All Nigeria People's Party (ANPP); Ideal People's Party (IPP); Liberal Convention (LC); National Unity Party (NUP); Nigeria Labour Party (NLP); Nigerian National Congress (NNC); Nigerian People's Welfare Party (NPWP); Patriotic Nigerian Party (PNP); People's Front of Nigeria (PFN); People's Patriotic Party (PPP); People's Solidarity Party (PSP); Republican Party of Nigeria (RPN); and United Nigeria Democratic Party (UNDP).

The criteria for registration stipulated by the NEC's Guidelines on Party Formation and the attached explanatory notes were much stricter than those of the Second Republic. Unlike the latter, the electoral commission was to confirm the nationalness of the parties in all local government areas of the country physically: for this purpose, each party applying for registration had to supply not only the number of registered members but also their names, passport photographs and residential addresses to facilitate physical confirmation. The parties were given less than two months to do all this and more – establish an office in all state capitals (twenty-one at the time) and local government headquarters and pay a registration fee of N50,000! (the Guidelines were issued on 4 May, and the cut-off date for meeting the requirements was 15 July). The parties rightly complained that it was impossible for them to meet these conditions within such a short space of time.

In addition to the physical requirements, each party also had to meet other national, intellectual and ideological requirements: its membership had to be open to all Nigerians excluding banned politicians, its national headquarters had to be in the federal capital, and its organisation at all levels had to reflect the country's federal character. The party's manifesto, which was to be graded by the NEC like

---

[13] Notable among these associations were the New Progressives Party led by Awolowo's daughter, Tokunboh Dosunmu; the Ideal Party of Nigeria led by Sani Mohammed Shaban; the People's Front of Nigeria led by Ango Abdullahi; the People's Liberation Party led by Balarabe Musa, who was subsequently tried and convicted for contravening the ban on old politicians; the Liberal New Movement led by Abba Dabo; the People's Party of Nigeria led by P.O. Ighofose; the People's Solidarity Party led by Mohammed Arzika; the Nigeria National Congress led by Emmanuel Iwuanyanwu; the People's Alliance Party led by Odili Ibuakah; the New Democratic Alliance led by Aliyu Ahmed; the All People's Party led by Dilibe Onyeama; Nigerian People's Welfare Party led by G.B.A. Akinyede; the Black But Beautiful Party of Nigeria led by Sunday Oyegoke; the Nigerian Labour Party formed by the Nigeria Labour Congress; and the National Union Party led by Fola Akinrinsola.

an examination script, had to be consistent with the Fundamental Objectives and Directive Principles of State Policy in the constitution, and had to address no less than twenty-six stipulated issues of national significance.[14] These difficult conditions, according to Adele Jinadu, a former NEC commissioner, were derived from a 'mass or grassroots-based party' theory which involved 'a highly decentralized party system in which party hierarchies are diffuse and power deconcentrated among various levels...' (Jinadu, 1955: 82; also, Olagunju *et al.*, 1993: 211ff). Whatever the merits of the underlying theory, the conditions for a party to qualify were such that none of the associations could reasonably have met them except by fraudulent means like padding their membership.

Therefore, it was not surprising that the parties did not do well in NEC's assessment. The assessment schema by which the parties scored was as follows: number and national spread of membership, 50 per cent; number and national spread of administrative organisation, 30 per cent; and articulation of issues in the manifesto, 20 per cent. The scores for the top six, based on the various criteria in the Guidelines, were PSP 43.9 per cent, NNC 42.6 per cent, PFP 41.2 per cent, LC 34.1 per cent, NLP 17.9 per cent, and RP 17 per cent. This was the summary of the report which the NEC submitted to the AFRC, which had the final say on which parties to register – Jinadu (1995: 83) points out that, contrary to popular belief at the time, the NEC did not recommend any party to the council for recognition.

All the parties were said to be poorly organised, to have been funded from questionable sources, to have strong links with banned politicians and past parties, to have falsified claims of membership, and to be factionalist and personalistic (FGN [NEC], 1989). Oyediran and Agbaje (1991: 226) note that most of the associations actually tended to reflect influences from the past: the NNC, with its Northern base, had links going back to the NPC and NPN while the PSP was a return of the AG/UPN-centred 'progressive' coalition. They blame this on the short period given to party formation, for which a fallback on existing configurations provided an easy solution. For reasons best explained by the fact that 'nature does nothing in a leap', it was unrealistic to expect to have parties without links to past political formations. Even the 'brand new' parties which the government later manufactured found their anchor in these formations with time. However, the government did not give up on its unrealistic

---

[14] The issues included the roles of labour, women, youth, traditional rulers, the role of the armed forces in national politics, ethnicity, revenue allocation, statism, nationality and citizenship, corruption, census, mass media, strategy for development, and external relations.

determination to create a 'new breed' political system run by 'new breed' politicians. For example this attained farcical properties when, on 9 December 1991 – the eve of the gubernatorial elections – scores of old politicians who were still banned were locked up to prevent them from influencing the outcome of the elections (only to be unbanned a few days later because the transition had progressed to a point where the old politicians could no longer influence the new breed!).

Notwithstanding the poor assessments of the associations, the government's decision to proscribe the thirteen political associations which applied for registration, ostensibly on the basis of the NEC's report, and subsequent announcement of the formation of two new parties, came as a shock to many. The new parties were the National Republican Convention (NRC) and Social Democratic Party (SDP). However, it is known that even before NEC submitted its report some academics had been asked to write manifestos for two 'ideal' parties: one 'liberal' and the other 'social-democratic'. This could be taken to mean that it had been decided to manufacture two parties, irrespective of the performances of the political associations; in other words, no matter how well they had performed, none of the associations would have been registered. If this was the case, why were the politicians and the NEC (whose expenses from the exercise were estimated at N2 billion [Ihonvbere 1991] allowed to waste their resources on this futile exercise (to be repeated many times in the course of the transition)? The answer is hard to find, but the confusion created by the 'experiments' of the ideal-driven transition suggests itself.

It is possible that the futility of the registration exercise was realised only after the character of the associations became known and that the government was sure that none of them was likely to meet its vision of a new social order. In other words, the manufacturing of two new parties was more likely a fallback option, just in case none of the associations failed to meet the mark. In any case, although the thirteen associations were dissolved, their 'good' qualities were incorporated into the new parties. As Jinadu (1995: 83-4) emphasises, the associations did not fail in every respect. Their major problem, he says, 'was not with their articulation of constitutional objectives and political goals but with their thin structures on the ground and their spurious membership claims, both of which suggested that they were not grassroots based.'

Since the government wanted grassroots-based parties, as the weighting of NEC's scoring schema showed, the test-tube parties simply amounted to providing new bodies to house the ideas already articulated by the politicians themselves, and calling them by different names. As Babangida himself said, the dissolution of the associations may have 'rebuffed the legitimate political aspirations of all the political associations that vied for registration', but this did not deny the eligible members of these associations participation in the new arrangement. The fact (as the NEC claimed) that the constitutions and manifestos of the thirteen associations were synthesised and differentiated to produce those of the two new parties seems to support the refurbishing thesis.[15] But it also raises the question whether the AFRC could not have achieved the same end simply by compelling the political associations to coalesce into two parties on their own (which in a way is what they did, but with the difference that the associations did not then have the opportunity to bargain the terms of coalitions, which is the hallmark of party formation). According to Olagunju *et al.* (p. 215), the failure to take this option (it was indeed one of the seven options considered by the AFRC[16]) meant that perhaps 'a wrong detour [was] taken in the transition'. The factionalisations and other serious problems which rocked the artificial parties and the entire transition process as time went on showed the rightness of this conclusion.

Then there is the possible 'hidden agenda' factor: that the dissolution of the thirteen associations was part of a design to perpetuate the military regime in power. However, the whole idea of a state-funded two party system and of the potential it was supposed to have for fostering democratic stability was not the regime's in the first place; and the devastating report of NEC made it difficult for the AFRC to recognise any of them. Olagunju (1992: 58-9) says that it would have been 'politically irresponsible' to do so). Therefore, all that can be said is that the two-party system may have fitted well into the hidden agenda, but this is not likely to have been its original intention; it was rather part of the process of political engineering to bring about the ideal state. As the president himself said in the 7 October broadcast, 'We have consistently warned against the temptation to exploit ethnic and religious sentiments for political ends. When we said new social order "new breed" politicians, we meant business.' Here it should be noted that this process did not end with the creation of the parties. The politicians themselves had to undergo 'reorientation'

---

[15] According to Olagunju *et al.*, 1993: 216), 'The analysis showed broad ideological divisions along two lines, thereby suggesting that the 13 political associations could be grouped into two broad categories, "a little-to-the-right" (liberal capitalist) and "a little-to-the-left" (social democratic) of the political spectrum'.

[16] The seven options were: that all political associations should be subject to electoral competition and elimination, voluntary merger among the associations, a repeat exercise, ideologically-based parties, labour-based parties, serial order/descending order of performance, and a grassroots party system. AFRC settled for the last (Adeniran, 1991: 35).

under the mass mobilisation organisation MAMSER and 'training' in the art and science of the new political order at the Centre for Democratic Studies (CDS) – Olagunju *et al.* (1993: 215) point out that the origins and development of the CDS were related to the new party formation process (for the 'ironies' of these reforms, see Reno, 1993).

Indeed, from the objectives of the new 'grassroots party system' outlined by the president in his national address on the formation of the new parties, it is clear that the new parties were meant to usher in a new social order in a way none of the dissolved associations was capable of doing. The objectives were to:

(*a*) provide a grassroot basis for the emergence of political parties;
(*b*) establish a grassroot or mass platform for the emergence of new leadership;
(*c*) give equal rights and opportunities to all Nigerians to participate in the political process irrespective of their wealth, religion, geopolitical background and professional endeavours;
(*d*) de-emphasise the role of money in politics;
(*e*) reduce, to a minimum level, the element of violence in the electoral process;
(*f*) preclude the emergence of political alliances along the same lines as in the First and Second Republics and give Nigerians a new political structure within which to operate;
(*g*) ensure the emergence of a new, more dedicated and more genuine leadership cadre, which will not be a mere proxy for old political warlords;
(*h*) chart a new pattern of political recruitment and participation which will enhance the country's stability;
(*i*) establish strong institutional structures which will not only sustain future governments, but be strong enough to stand the test of time;
(*j*) establish a political system that will be operated according to the spirit and letter of the constitution. (cited in Adeniran, 1991: 36)

This is how the two 'state' parties were born. The NEC supposedly wrote the constitutions and manifestos. The transition committee headed by Air Vice Marshal Ibrahim Alfa, together with other relevant government agencies like the NEC and DSM, devised party symbols, erected party buildings in all state capitals and local government headquarters, provided party vehicles, and supervised the recruitment of members and the election of executive officers at all levels, while the federal government substantially funded the parties all the way through, including

their primaries and conventions. Funding was reduced after the gubernatorial elections of 1991, when it was thought that the parties were
strong enough to stand on their own (however, to prevent 'money-
bags' from taking them over, donations by individual members were
limited to N100,000).[17] The organisational structures of the two parties
were the same: they were grassroots-based, which meant 'originating
the base of party membership and leadership recruitment at the ward
level, which is also the smallest unit of the country's political
organization'. The selection of candidates for elective public office
in both parties was through a system of primaries, which encouraged
factionalist tendencies within them.

The success of the entire transition programme hinged largely
on the extent to which the experimental two-party system worked.
Some of the main problems with its working have been well treated
by Oyediran and Agbaje (1991), Olagunju *et al.* (1993), Lewis (1994)
and Jinadu (1995), among others. The problems included the inter-
factional and personal wranglings which arose within the parties,
recourse to old political divisions, the hijacking of the parties by
so-called 'money-bags' who sometimes created parallel party structures,
the fluidity of membership and failure to evolve stable alliances and
concrete identities (this was mainly attributable to the recurrent banning
and unbanning of politicians), rather strict control by the NEC, and
undue government interference. The latter reached its peak at the
end of 1992 when the controversial presidential primaries in the parties
were cancelled, the executive committees of the parties at all levels
were dissolved, and caretaker committees were appointed in their
place, the parties then had to embark on a new membership registration
exercise. There could be no doubt that the two parties did not yield
the political results desired by the government. But from the civil
society point of view, the greatest problem with the parties was
their artificiality and absolute lack of autonomy, which made their
manipulation by government easy. They failed woefully when it mattered
most: on the annulment of the presidential election of June 1993,
they broke into factions and could not dissociate themselves from
the government, since they risked being dissolved again if they refused
to do so. It is arguable that self-forming and autonomous parties
with strong identities and defined stakes would have posed a more
formidable opposition. But the parties showed that it was possible
to mitigate the effects of the country's dominant ethno-regional cleavages
although there were strong demands for a return to multipartyism

---

[17] It was an open secret that rich presidential aspirants in the parties were spending
heavily to build support. *Tell* (1 July 1996: 16) estimated Arthur Nzeribe's expenses on
organising the Eastern states arm of the SDP, called CARIA, at about N112 million.

as the transition's failure was blamed on the 'artificial' parties. The result of the 12 June presidential election in which Abiola performed well in most parts of the federation could at least be regarded as a major gain for the manufactured party system.

AN ENDLESS TRANSITION?

The frequent changes in the transition timetable further undermined the transition's credibility. The date originally proposed for completion of the transition was 1 October 1990 – subsequently moved to 1 October 1992, then to 2 January 1993, and finally to 27 August 1993. The confusion and anxiety that these changes created were heightened when, in November 1992, Babangida announced that he needed the NEC's advice to determine the hand-over date! At this stage the Nigerian Political Science Association issued a statement in which it called for Babangida's resignation and for the convening of a national conference by the National Assembly to save the transition. Greater consternation followed changes in other important elements of the transition. Following the decision to establish government parties, the transition timetable was amended by Decree no. 26 of 1989, which slotted the process of party formation – registration of members, congresses at ward, local, state and federal levels – into the first three quarters of 1990. The local government elections slated for the last quarter of 1989 were postponed by a year, as were the state legislative and gubernatorial elections slated for the last quarter of 1990.

The dates for the presidential and National Assembly elections were also changed. The latter were brought forward from November to July 1992, apparently to reassure people that the transition 'was still on course' despite the frequent changes; and the presidential election was rescheduled from 5 December 1992 to 12 June 1993 after the presidential primaries of the two parties were cancelled and all the candidates who took part in them were disqualified. How credible could the transition be when time after time the president kept reiterating commitments to particular dates, only to renege on them 'for good reasons'? For example, he had said that the revision of the transition timetable following the new system of party formation would not affect the 1992 exit date:

> 'Government is aware of the implication of this method of party formation on the timing ... of our political transition programme. I assure you that while there will be changes in the timing of events, our outer limit of 1992 remains unchanged.[...] It is uncharitable to insinuate that this military government does not want to go. We are already going.' (broadcast to the nation, 7 October, 1989)

The cynicism that greeted subsequent declarations of the same kind is aptly summarised by retired General Danjuma's verdict on the rescheduled presidential election of June 1993: 'The two presidential candidates are applying for a post that is not vacant, and that will not be vacant in August' (interview in *Tell*, 18 January 1993).

Tinkering with the dates of elections was not the only thing that caused suspicions of a 'hidden agenda'. There was also the dramatic changes in personnel in key transition institutions. We have already mentioned the dissolution of the executive committees of the parties at all levels in December 1992, only six months before the end of the transition. The NEC, DSM, and NPC were also affected: Eme Awa was removed as NEC chairman in 1988 and replaced by Humphrey Nwosu, who in turn was replaced by Okon Uya after the annulment of the 1993 election. In the case of the DSM and NPC, the chairmen – Jerry Gana and Shehu Musa respectively – resigned amid great controversy to take part in presidential primaries. Then there were the frequent changes of, and experimentations with, electoral systems. Presumably to reduce electoral malpractices and make the outcome of elections more acceptable, especially to losers, the NEC devised ingenious but confusing ballot systems – 'open' 'secret-open' and 'modified open'.

No election seemed complete without some experiment. By far the most complicated of NEC's ingenious formulations was 'Option A4', devised for presidential primaries after those of 1992 were cancelled. The contest for presidential tickets began from the ward level (there were 6,927 wards), and progressed right up to the national conventions at which state delegates had to elect one candidate from the thirty state presidential candidates. This system produced the highest number of presidential candidates ever in the country – 286 candidates applied, of which 215 were given 'provisional' clearance to contest.[18] The idea was to give every individual politician and state an equal opportunity, but the huge expense involved in the several levels of primaries and the large number of contestants were read as 'booby traps'. It was not surprising that one of the reasons the government advanced for annulling the 1993 presidential election was that the two candidates had practically 'bought' the presidential tickets at the national conventions.

---

[18] The list of candidates read like a 'Who's Who' of élites in the country. Some of the more prominent candidates included: for the NRC retired General Yakubu Gowon, Bashir Tofa, Ango Abdullahi, Ahmed Joda and Ali Munguno; for the SDP Adebayo Adedeji, Bolaji Akinyemi, Babagana Kingibe and M.K.O. Abiola.

BACK TO THE TRANSITION: THE REMAINDER

As was pointed out at the beginning of this chapter, the Babangida years saw some of the boldest initiatives and attempts at institutional reform in Nigeria's history. In this section we briefly touch on aspects of the transition agenda which involved some of the reforms.

A NEW CONSTITUTION

As with every other transition programme in the country, the writing of a new constitution was central to the transition programme of the Babangida regime. The process of producing the 1989 Constitution actually started with the Political Bureau, and many of its recommendations went into the new constitution. Indeed, the *Report* of the Political Bureau and the 1979 Constitution were the main working documents of the Constitution Review Committee (CRC) and Constituent Assembly (CA), and the Bureau's recommendations formed the core of the 'no-go' areas which the president forbade the Constituent Assembly from altering (though not from improving upon). These areas, which Babangida referred to as 'the agreed ingredients of Nigeria's political order', included federalism, a two-party system, presidentialism, non-adoption of state religion, the banning or disqualification of certain categories of politicians from participating in politics, and certain basic laws such as the Land Use and National Youth Service Corps Decrees. The president also prescribed the search for 'a visionary realist' and transformation as parameters for the crafting of the new constitution.

The draft of the new constitution, which was basically a slight modification of the 1979 Constitution, was produced by the CRC. The committee had forty-six appointed members, mostly lawyers and academics, and was headed by Mr Justice Buba Ardo. It was inaugurated in September 1987 and given six months to complete its assignment. The draft constitution was then deliberated upon by the CA, which produced the final constitution submitted to the AFRC for ratification. The CA was chaired by Mr Justice A.N. Aniagolu, and had 567 members, 450 of whom were elected to represent 'federal constituencies',[19] and 117, mainly members of the CRC, nominated by the federal government. As in 1977/8, the most explosive issue in the CA was that of the extension of *Sharia* law to the federal level.

[19] The breakdown of the state representations was: Akwa Ibom 20; Anambra 29; Bauchi 20; Bendel 20; Benue 19; Borno 24; Cross River 8; Gongola 21; Imo 30; Kaduna 13; Kano 46; Katsina 20; Kwara 14; Lagos 12; Niger 10; Ogun 12; Ondo 22; Oyo 42; Plateau 16; Rivers 14; Sokoto 37; and Federal Capital Territory 1.

What made the issue even more contentious this time was the intense politicisation of the Muslim-Christian cleavage following on Nigeria's membership of the Organization of Islamic Countries (OIC) and the upsurge of fundamentalist Muslim riots in the North of the country, which Christians interpreted as part of an attempt to transform the country into an Islamic state (for an insight into how the *Sharia* issue rocked the CA, see Aniagolu, 1993: 93-147). It took the intervention of the CGS in November 1988 and the inclusion of *Sharia* in the list of no-go areas for the deadlock in the Assembly to be resolved (the provisions of the 1979 Constitution, except that a non-Muslim would no longer be tried by a *Sharia* court, were finally retained). Other issues that generated 'angry debate' were revenue allocation, the language question, creation of states, the continued application of the federal character principle in the composition of public agencies, the length of tenure of the president, state governor and local government chairmen, the executive powers of the president where deployment of the armed forces outside the country was concerned and the question of traditional rulers (Aniagolu, 1993: 158-92).

The new constitution contained certain innovations and improvements on some provisions of the 1979 document. These included the clause which forbade the National Assembly from removing the governor of a state or his deputy under the guise of maintaining public order and security; the entrenchment of a minimum educational qualification of school certificate for candidates seeking election to state and federal legislatures; reduction of the number of senate seats per state to three; prohibition of persons seeking elective office from membership of secret societies; prohibition of changing party allegiance; and the principle of recall (an innovation which made it possible for constituents to effect the withdrawal of their representative from the legislature on the grounds of unsatisfactory performance). In ratifying the new constitution which was submitted to it in April 1988, the AFRC rejected, amended or expunged certain sections including, significantly, the one (clause 1(4) of the final draft) declaring any unconstitutional take-over of government to be a crime. This was expunged.[20]

The constitution was to take effect on 1 October 1992, but with the changes in the hand-over date this was moved, first to January and later August 1993. The constitution-makers, especially members

---

[20] Other notable amendments were the lowering of minimum ages for elective office, retention of the renewable tenure of four years for president/governor, and senate confirmation rather than consultation for appointment of ministers. The clauses providing for (among other things) the establishment of an armed forces service commission to ensure compliance with the federal character principle, and for an autonomous judicial service commission to reduce executive interference, were expunged.

of the CA, were however criticised for failing to include transitional provisions to govern the difficult final phase of the transition in the draft constitution. Olagunju *et al.* (1993: 187-8) believe that such provisions, which were actually recommended by one of the committees of the Assembly, would have helped to resolve some of the tensions and conflicts inherent in the system of 'limited diarchy', which at the end of 1992 had an executive military government and a democratically elected National Assembly at the federal level as well as full-fledged civilian governments at the state and local levels. Conflicts between local government chairmen in Anambra and Cross River states, which led to the removal of the chairman in Anambra state, and the tension between the National Assembly and the military government indeed raised questions of the extent to which military and democratic structures could coexist and which should take precedence in the event of conflict. Such considerations are certainly important, but in the context of military rule, where power flows from the barrel of the gun, they are academic: for example, would the president have deferred to higher sovereign authority exercised by the National Assembly or a state governor if the transition provisions had said that he would? The answer is clear from the transition decrees relating to the exercise of the powers of the National Assembly and of the state and local civilian governments, and their relations with the federal military government. The regime issued these at the same time as it promulgated the new constitution, and it was plain that the military were the source of all laws and the ultimate authority.

STRUCTURAL REFORMS

Here we briefly consider two aspects of structural reforms: those concerned with the creation of new states and local government areas, the strengthening of local governments and changes in inter-governmental relations on the one hand, and on the other the politico-administrative changes introduced in the final phase of the regime ostensibly to facilitate a smooth transition.

Under the Babangida administration the federal structure underwent important changes in terms of constituent units and inter-governmental relations. The former involved the creation of new local government areas and states. In May 1989 the number of local government areas in the country was increased from 301 to 453, and in August 1991 to 589. As for states, two new ones – Akwa Ibom and Katsina – were created in 1987, partly following the recommendation of the

Political Bureau.[21] In creating the two new states, each of which received a take-off grant of about N33 million, Babangida announced that no further demands for new states would be tolerated, but in August 1991 the regime back-pedalled and created nine new states to bring the number to thirty (see Table 6.2). Although it advanced the standard justifications – the need for a balanced federation, bringing government nearer to the people, even-handed development etc. – and the reason that transition was a 'social experiment', the 1991 exercise was largely intended to galvanise support for the regime, whose strength was ebbing, and to compensate its close allies.[22]

This is not to discount the importance of the intense agitations for new states, especially by the Igbos, but at the time that they were created, the states issue was not high on the national political agenda. The fact that some of the states were created to compensate or reward allies, or for reasons that went beyond the traditional justifications, could be seen clearly in the anomalies in composition of some of the new states (and local governments), despite the long history of demands for the creation of many of them. For example, the shape of the new Delta state was different from what its agitators wanted – not only did this new state have the former Bendel East, which had consistently demanded an Anioma state, joined to it, but its capital was Asaba in Bendel East, the home town of the president's wife. From Kano, Jigawa was created rather than Hadejia state, for which agitation had been more pronounced. A similar thing happened in Sokoto state with the creation of Kebbi rather than Zamfara state. The situation of some new local government areas was even more perplexing. In Edo state the old Iyekuselu District Council was rescusitated as a local government area, but its capital was taken from Ekiadolor to the outlying Okada to please a millionaire friend of the regime. In one or two other cases, non-existent towns were named as local government headquarters. Some of these anomalies led to riots, especially in Kano and Sokoto states which added to the chaos of the transition.

---

[21] The Bureau recommended the creation of six new states – Akwa Ibom, Delta, Katsina, Kogi, Sardauna and Wawa – to reduce the instability and political and social tensions bred by demands for them. However, Suberu (1995: 63; also 1991) points out that some influential members opposed the creation of more than the two states finally created. The Bureau report highlighted the case of the Igbos who alleged injustice in the 'distribution' of states.

[22] Suberu (1995: 64-5) however identifies three sources of the pressure which forced the government to change its mind on states creation: the CA, whose members strongly advocated the creation of at least four new states; the abortive coup of 1990 which had marginalisation of Middle-Belt and Southern minorities as a major issue; and the vigorous Igbo campaigns for ethnic justice in states distribution.

Table 6.2. 1991 CREATION OF STATES

19-state structure	30-state structure
Anambra	Anambra
	Enugu
Bauchi	Bauchi
Bendel	Delta
	Edo
Benue	Benue
	Kogi[*]
Borno	Borno
	Yobe
Cross River	Cross River
	Akwa Ibom[†]
Gongola	Adamawa
	Taraba
Imo	Imo
	Abia
Kaduna	Kaduna
	Katsina[†]
Kano	Kano
	Jigawa
Kwara	Kwara[‡]
	Kogi[*]
Lagos	Lagos
Ogun	Ogun
Ondo	Ondo
Oyo	Oyo
	Osun
Plateau	Plateau
Rivers	Rivers
Sokoto	Sokoto
	Kebbi

[*] Kogi state was carved out of both Benue and Kwara states.
[†] These states were created earlier in 1987.
[‡] Borgu province of Kwara state was joined to Niger-state.

Although the creation of more states and local government councils partly served the purpose for which the regime intended it, namely enhancement of its support, the exercises also received serious criticism. Many commentators felt the creation of more states to be inconsistent with economic belt-tightening since establishing new state structures was costly – the federal government advanced N30 million each to the states, and undertook to provide administrative buildings and other physical infrastructure. Others lamented that the creation of too many states reduced the viability of the country's federal system, while yet others saw the conflicts that ensued from asset-sharing and realignment of public servants between split states, and other problems created by the exercises as part of the plans to scuttle the transition programme (for an analysis of the inter-governmental dimensions of these problems, see Osaghae 1994) – after all, did the British colonisers not threaten to postpone the date of the country's independence if the new states that were demanded at the time were created?

The regime embarked on structural and administrative reforms in other spheres as part of its political and economic reforms and the preoccupation with creating a new socio-political order. The most far-reaching of these were the local government reforms, which sought to make that level of government more viable, and the civil service reforms introduced in 1988 to enhance professionalism and efficiency, among other objects. The reforms had mixed results, and added to the confusion and uncertainty of the transition process by their highly experimental and unstable nature. The consequences of these reforms, whose potential for resolving some of the chronic problems of development administration was overshadowed by the crisis of confidence which rocked the larger political and economic reforms, have been analysed in the literature (cf. Gboyega, 1987, 1991; Oyediran, 1988; Osaghae, 1989c; Yahaya, 1989, for local government reforms; and Phillips, 1988; Gboyega, 1995; and Oshionebo, 1995, for civil service reforms).

The final structural changes of note involved the creation in January 1993 of two new bodies – the National Defence and Security Council (NDSC) and the Transitional Council (TC) – to replace the AFRC and the Federal Executive Council respectively. These changes, which were said to be necessary to ensure a smooth transition, gave the impression that the military government was in the final stages of disengagement, but in reality they were cosmetic. The TC was headed by Ernest Shonekan, former chief executive of UAC, and comprised high-calibre technocrats, professionals and business people. Yet it was excluded from the law-making process and participation in decision-making (even the 1993 budget, which the council was asked to implement, was not produced by it), and its powers were never clearly defined (Nwabueze, 1994: 22). In effect the military remained firmly in charge, despite Shonekan's membership of the NDSC. The events that led up to and immediately followed the annulment of the 12 June presidential election, on which Nwabueze reveals that the TC was not consulted, showed this clearly.

CENSUS

One of the major successes of the Babangida years was the conduct of the census of 1991. As is well known, the census is one of the most politically explosive issues in Nigerian politics and, as suggested in Chapter 3, the failure of the 1973 exercise informed Gowon's decision to renege on his promise to hand over power to civilians. Notwithstanding the Gowon experience, many Nigerians still believed that only a 'neutral' body like the military could conduct a census successfully. This, combined with the elaborate technical and administrative efforts of the National Population Commission (NPC), the enlightenment campaigns mounted by the Social Mobilization Directorate and federal and state ministries of information, and the involvement of independent monitors and United Nations observers, all contributed to making the exercise more successful than previous ones.

Enumeration took place on 27-29 November, which were declared work-free days. But the publication of the provisional results presented in Table 6.2 still generated controversy over a number of issues. There was much questioning of the total population figure of 88.5 million, which was far less than the estimated 112 million (UN), 113.8 million (World Bank), and 122 million (US Bureau of Census) based on the 1963 figures and an annual growth rate of 3 per cent (the widely accepted estimate in Nigeria was 100 million). The NPC's explanations that the growth-rate had actually been 2.1 per cent or that the 1963 figures were inflated, did not convince many cynics. But the bulk of the problems with the figures were as usual about the political implications, although the complaints and disagreements were less than in 1962/3 and 1973.

Political leaders in many Southern states did not so much dispute the fact of Northern preponderance as they did the under-counting of their populations. For example, the Oyo state House of Assembly rejected the figures, which showed that the population of the old Oyo state (now Oyo and Osun) had increased by only 400,000 since 1963, a figure which could not have been accepted for the city of Ibadan alone. Abia and Imo states, which were carved out of the old Imo state, also disputed that their population had risen by only 1 million since 1963. These complaints and disputes were referred to the census tribunals that had been created for this purpose, and guided the verificatory tests the population commission had to carry out before the final results were published. In spite of these problems, the 1991 census can be regarded as a success when compared to previous exercises. This, however, is not to say that the political sensitivity of the census was ended, since even publication of the

232   *Crippled Giant: Nigeria since Independence*

final results of the 1991 exercise was delayed for a long time, partly for political reasons (by August 1996, five years after enumeration, they were still not published). As long as population figures continue to be used for revenue allocation, creation of new states and local governments, siting of government establishments and so on, the census will continue to be a sensitive political issue.

Table 6.3. 1991 CENSUS PROVISIONAL FIGURES

State	Male	Female	Total
Abia	1,108,357	1,189,621	2,297,987
Adamawa	1,084,824	1,039,225	2,124,049
Akwa Ibom	1,162,430	1,197,306	2,359,736
Anambra	1,374,801	1,393,102	2,767,903
Bauchi	2,202,962	2,091,451	4,294,413
Benue	1,385,402	1,393,102	2,780,398
Borno	1,327,311	1,269,278	2,596,589
Cross River	945,270	920,334	1,865,604
Delta	1,273,208	1,296,973	2,570,181
Edo	1,082,718	1,077,130	2,159,848
Enugu	1,482,245	1,679,050	3,161,295
Imo	1,178,031	1,307,468	2,485,499
Jigawa	1,419,726	1,410,203	2,829,929
Kaduna	2,059,382	1,909,870	3,969,252
Kano	2,858,724	2,773,316	5,632,040
Katsina	1,944,218	1,934,126	3,878,344
Kebbi	1,024,334	1,037,892	2,062,226
Kogi	1,055,964	1,043,082	2,099,046
Kwara	790,921	775,548	1,566,469
Lagos	2,999,528	2,686,253	5,685,781
Niger	1,290,720	1,191,647	2,482,367
Ogun	1,144,907	1,193,663	2,338,570
Ondo	1,958,928	1,925,557	3,884,485
Osun	1,079,424	1,123,592	2,203,016
Oyo	1,745,720	1,743,069	2,488,789
Plateau	1,645,730	1,637,974	3,283,704
Rivers	2,079,583	1,904,274	3,983,857
Sokoto	2,158,111	2,234,280	4,392,391
Taraba	754,754	725,836	1,480,590
Yobe	719,763	691,718	1,411,481
FCT	206,535	172,136	378,671
Total	44,544,531	43,969,970	88,514,501

ELECTIONS

The elections which took place under the transition fell into two categories. In the first were the intra-party elections to elect members of party executives at all levels, from the ward right up to the federal level, and the primaries to select candidates for elective local, state and federal elections. These were conducted by the parties themselves through their electoral commissions, though from time to time, NEC had to intervene. The second category consisted of the inter-party elections for legislative and executive seats at the local, state and federal levels, which were conducted by the NEC. Although the outcomes of elections in the first category had implications for those in the second and affected the performance of parties contesting them, space does not permit us to examine them. Our focus is on the inter-party elections, which give insights into the intra-party ones.

In consonance with the 'grassroots theory' of the evolving political system and the sequentiality of the transition which involved the consolidation of democracy at one level before proceeding to the next, the arrangement of elections was pyramidal, with the presidential election at the apex. Two local government elections were held: the first, on a non-party basis, in 1987 to 'test the waters' and revive democratic instincts, and the second in 1990 to consolidate the grassroots anchor of the new parties. In the 1990 elections, the SDP won 3,765 council seats and 315 chairs, and the NRC 3,360 seats and 274 chairs. The results showed that the SDP was slightly more powerful and that the two parties were 'national', although solid patterns of old bloc voting could be discerned in the support for the SDP in the South-West, including Edo and Delta states (the NRC performed poorly throughout Edo, the home state of its national chairman Tom Ikimi), and for NRC in the Eastern states and core Hausa/Fulani parts of the North.

These patterns were reinforced in the state legislative and gubernatorial and National Assembly elections which followed in 1992, as shown in Tables 6.4 and 6.5. In the state legislative elections, the SDP won a total of 650 seats all over the country and secured control of sixteen assemblies, while the NRC won a total of 545 seats and took control of twelve assemblies (the two parties won an equal number of seats in Enugu and Taraba states, (see Table 6.4). In the gubernatorial elections, the NRC won in sixteen states to the SDP's fourteen states. This was against the trend from previous elections, and was largely due to factional strife in Lagos, Cross River and Katsina states among others, which cost the SDP victory in states where it had consolidated support. But the SDP reasserted its strength

Table 6.4. 1992 STATE ELECTIONS

State	No. of Assembly seats NRC	SDP	Governor/party
Abia	25	9	Onu/NRC
Adamawa	18	14	Michika/NRC
Akwa Ibom	35	16	Isemin/NRC
Anambra	14	18	Ezeife/SDP
Bauchi	39	7	Mohammed/NRC
Benue	14	22	Adasu/SDP
Borno	15	27	Lawal/SDP
Cross River	13	15	Ebri/NRC
Delta	14	22	Ibru/SDP
Edo	10	17	Oyegun/SDP
Enugu	19	19	Nwodo/NRC
Imo	27	16	Enwerem/NRC
Jigawa	10	32	Birnin-Kudu/SDP
Kaduna	20	16	Lere/NRC
Kano	35	32	Gaya/NRC
Katsina	18	30	Barda/NRC
Kebbi	29	19	Musa/NRC
Kogi	10	22	Audu/NRC
Kwara	2	22	Lafiagi/SDP
Lagos	4	26	Otedola/NRC
Niger	26	12	Inuwa/NRC
Ogun	1	29	Osoba/SDP
Ondo	6	45	Olumilua/SDP
Osun	2	42	Adeleke/SDP
Oyo	13	37	Ishola/SDP
Plateau	11	35	Tapgun/SDP
Rivers	29	19	George/NRC
Sokoto	55	3	Abdulkarim/NRC
Taraba	12	12	Nyame/SDP
Yobe	8	18	Ibrahim/SDP

in the National Assembly elections, winning a total of 52 senate and 312 house of representatives seats to the NRC's 38 and 275 respectively.

These elections were not without hitches. These ranged from disqualifications of candidates by the NEC and the federal government to disputed results. The gubernatorial elections recorded the most serious problems, beginning with the primaries. Sixteen candidates were disqualified and primary results were cancelled in nine states

Table 6.5. 1992 NATIONAL ASSEMBLY ELECTIONS

| | No. of seats won | | | |
| | NRC | | SDP | |
State	S	HR	S	HR
Abia	2	12	1	5
Adamawa	3	14	–	2
Akwa Ibom	3	18	–	5
Anambra	–	4	3	12
Bauchi	3	22	–	1
Benue	–	1	3	17
Borno	1	3	2	17
Cross River	2	10	1	4
Delta	–	3	3	16
Edo	–	2	3	12
Enugu	2	13	1	6
Imo	3	18	–	3
Jigawa	1	3	2	18
Kaduna	2	7	1	11
Kano	1	16	2	18
Katsina	1	20	2	6
Kebbi	3	16	–	–
Kogi	2	9	1	7
Kwara	–	–	3	12
Lagos	–	1	3	14
Niger	3	18	–	1
Ogun	–	–	3	15
Ondo	–	4	3	22
Osun	–	1	3	22
Oyo	–	3	3	22
Plateau	–	3	3	20
Rivers	3	18	–	6
Sokoto	3	29	–	–
Taraba	–	3	3	9
Yobe	–	1	3	11
FCT	–	3	1	1
Total	37	275	53	315

on the grounds of electoral malpractices and claims that most of the disqualified candidates were 'fronts' and protégés of banned politicians. But the problems did not stop even after the elections, because several losers contested the outcomes in electoral tribunals and courts of law. Two such cases were dramatic. In February 1992, the election of John Odigie Oyegun as governor of Edo state was nullified by the electoral tribunal following an action instituted by Lucky Igbinedion, the defeated NRC candidate. The tribunal based its ruling on the action on evidence of electoral malpractice, including the allegation that the Oba of Benin and one of his chiefs (Isekhure) had openly mobilised support for Oyegun on the election day. Between 4 February when the tribunal gave its ruling and 18 March when the court of appeal upheld Oyegun's election, Edo state was in limbo (see Isekhure, 1992). A similar situation occured in Imo state where the election of Governor Evans Enwerem was nullified six months after he was sworn in, but on bizarre grounds: namely that the SDP candidate Enwerem had defeated to become governor was not qualified to contest the election and that, consequently, his own election was null and void. Like Oyegun, Enwerem got a favourable court of appeal judgement and stayed in office.

But the election which proved most difficult and finally led to the abortion of the transition was the presidential election, the final event on the transition agenda. There had been mounting suspicion over Babangida's true intentions, and this was heightened by the emergence of organisations calling for an extension of his regime, and a growing groundswell of opposition. Thus the presidential election was to be the final test of the tortuous transition. The interest generated by it was understandably high, but it seemed headed for a fiasco from the outset. First was the high number of aspiring candidates: twelve for the SDP and eleven for the NRC.[23] This was partly a reflection of the seemingly irreconciliable factions within the parties, most of them built around the presidential ambitions of leaders of the dissolved political associations of 1989. Next was the confusion over the form the primaries were to take, which was finally resolved by deciding to stagger the elections on the basis of three zones of ten states each.

Then came the eventful primaries, of which the results were rejected outright by the losers in both parties. In the SDP, ten defeated candidates alleged that the primaries were manipulated by the national chairman, Babagana Kingibe, and party state governors to impose Shehu Yar'Adua who won with wide margins in most states. They withdrew from the primaries and called on the federal government to dissolve the party's National Executive Committee, appoint a sole administrator

---

[23] The SDP candidates were Olu Falae, P.D. Cole, Datti Ahmed, Arthur Nzeribe, Shehu Yar'Adua, Lateef Jakande, Layi Balogun, Olusola Saraki, Mahmud Waziri, Jerry Gana, Bisi Durojaiye and Abel Ubeku. For the NRC were Bamanga Tukur, Adamu Ciroma, Umaru Shinkafi, Emmanuel Iwuanyanwu, Lema Jubrillu, Shehu Musa, Melford Okilo, Saleh Jambo, Dan Musa, Alfred Aduloju and Inuwa Wada.

to run the party, and cancel the 'massively rigged' elections. There was a similar occurrence in the NRC where Umaru Shinkafi and Bamanga Tukur led other aggrieved candidates in the allegation that the national executive was working to impose Adamu Ciroma on the party. There were other problems with the primaries. Newspapers and magazines alleged malpractices, especially vote-buying, by several candidates, who were also said to have spent several hundred million naira to establish state offices, purchase vehicles, and in 'donations' to ward, local and state branches of parties (cf. *Tell*, 5 October 1992). Alongside these were threats by the Christian Association of Nigeria (CAN) in its Northern zone to boycott the presidential election if the candidates presented by the two parties were Muslims, as would have been the case if the primaries had not been annulled. Finally, and perhaps most significant of all, a communiqué was issued by a meeting of governors from the two parties in Lagos in October 1992 urging the regime not to hand over power in a situation of anarchy. A delegation consisting of Governors Segun Osoba (Ogun), Mohammed Lafiaji (Kwara) and Evans Enwerem was sent to make a presentation in person of the position of the governors to the AFRC meeting where the decision to cancel the primaries was taken.

Because of the foregoing it came as no surprise when the federal government decided in October 1992 to cancel the primaries and disqualify all the twenty-three presidential aspirants, even at the risk of losing such credibility as the transition still retained. Although many still read a 'hidden agenda' into the cancellation of the primaries, it cannot be denied that the politicians themselves deserved the greatest share of the blame for the botched primaries. In short, the conduct of the primaries was simply a replay of the inability of politicians to conduct elections on their own – which in Nigeria usually provided the grounds for military intervention. As the president said on cancelling the primaries:

> 'History will bear us out that the present political impasse...is caused by the inability of the two political parties to conduct successfully their internal selection process for producing presidential candidates.[...] All the presidential aspirants were extremely destructive of one another to the extent that they were unable to engage in politics of moderation, accommodation and consensus-building.'

Even the normally critical *Tell* magazine praised the government's 'Solomonic' wisdom:

> ...the news that most of the 23 aspirants...were guilty of one electoral offence or the other was largely expected because before then, a thousand and one opinions existed in political circles as to how

government should handle the embarrasing impasse which the primaries degenerated into. Immediately, a seemingly relieved nation came alive with reactions that were largely a commendation of the Solomonic wisdom of the AFRC and its rescue of the jolted transition programme. (*Tell*, 2 November, 1992: 11)

However, the government's subsequent decision to dissolve the party executives and order a 'reconstruction' of the parties, membership and all, by caretaker committees, was not welcomed and rekindled suspicions. But there was still the rescheduled presidential election of 12 June, which in the event was to prove critical; indeed the build-up to it ensured that it would be. The primaries involved the use of 'Option A4', which produced a total of 215 candidates who received 'provisional' clearance to contest (it was strongly rumoured that many of them were sponsored by the regime). The primaries at the ward level took place on 6 February, at local level on 20 February, and at state level on 6 March; finally national conventions were held in Port Harcourt (NRC) and Jos (SDP). From the conventions M.K.O. Abiola, a businessman and Yoruba-Muslim from Ogun state, emerged as the SDP standard-bearer, and Bashir Tofa, also a businessman, and a Kanuri-Muslim from Kano state (originally from Borno) won the NRC ticket. The two later respectively chose Babagana Kingibe and Sylvester Ugoh as their vice-presidential running-mates. Some problems were raised about the imbalances in the presidential tickets – two Muslim presidential candidates and the SDP's two-Muslim ticket – but they were not serious (Abiola's choice of Kingibe was hailed as a 'master stroke', although it cost him some support in the Eastern states).

As the election drew closer, there was a sharp increase in the activities of pro-regime associations demanding an extension of the regime's stay in office. At the centre of these activities was the Association for Better Nigeria (ABN) led by a former SDP presidential aspirant, Arthur Nzeribe. The 'Babangida-must-stay' campaign was articulated through rallies in various parts of the country, pamphleteering, and newspaper and magazine advertisements. Shortly before the election the ABN put up posters in Abuja asking for four more years 'of peace, unity and stability' for Babangida, and increased the tempo of its press adverts signed by 'Dr Keith Atkins' or 'Dr Farouk Ahmed', who were generally believed to be fictitious characters. Also in May, a group calling itself the Committee of Elder Statesmen, led by S.G. Ikoku, Tanko Yakassai, and Musa Rimi, proposed the adoption of a French model of presidentialism and a new beginning to the entire transition programme.

Agents of these organisations also tried hard to prevent the presidential election from going forward. In Benin one Prince Ejutse Arawore swore to a 19-point affidavit seeking the disqualification of Abiola for, among other reasons, failing when he was chief executive of ITT to execute contracts awarded to it with a total value of over N1.779 billion. Alhaji A. Coomasie also sought the disqualification of Tofa on the grounds of corruption in Kaduna. Then, two days before the election, the ABN got an Abuja high court ruling by Justice Bassey Ita Ikpeme (delivered at the most unusual time of 9.00 p.m.) restraining the NEC from conducting the election. The US embassy in Lagos immediately issued a statement warning against attempts to scuttle the election. The federal government responded to this 'undue interference' by ordering the immediate deportation of electoral observers from the United States. Nevertheless, the NEC went ahead with the election, citing section 19 (1) of Decree no. 13 of 1993, which nullified any interference in the date scheduled for the election by any court.

Against all the odds, the election took place on 12 June, and was widely hailed as one of the best-conducted elections ever held in the country. This view is well conveyed in the following account by Peter Lewis, one of the foreign observers of the election:

> To everyone's surprise, the election of 12 June was possibly the fairest...in Nigeria's post-independence history. The combined influences of apathy, apprehension and confusion kept many away from the polls – voter turnout was at only 35 per cent. Widespread administrative and logistical problems also prevented a number of voters from registering their ballots (including Bashir Tofa who held an invalid voter registration card), but there was little evidence of systematic fraud or vote rigging ... Polling was generally conducted in a peaceful and orderly manner, and there were no reports of serious violence or casualties. (Lewis, 1994: 326)

Results released by the NEC four days after the election showed Abiola clearly in the lead in twelve of sixteen states (including Kano, Tofa's adopted state) – final though unofficial results available to the press and presented in Table 6.6 showed that Abiola decisively won the election. But, once again, the ABN got an order by the Abuja high court restraining the NEC from releasing the results. Then, on 23 June, a government statement, which was reported by several newspapers to have been issued unsigned and not on official paper, and first broadcast on Kaduna radio, annulled the election, suspended the NEC, and ordered an immediate stop to all legal proceedings concerning the election. In a later national broadcast on 26 June, Babangida tried hard to rationalise the annulment. We shall assess the reasons he advanced and other points of analysis later when we focus specifically on 12 June and its aftermath.

Table 6.6. 1993 PRESIDENTIAL ELECTION

State	Total votes cast	NRC Votes	%	SDP Votes	%
Abida*	256,500	151,227	58.96	105,273	41.04
Adamawa†	334,490	178,865	53.47	155,625	46.53
Akwa Ibom*	414,129	199,342	48.14	214,787	51.86
Anambra*	371,282	159,258	42.89	212,024	57.11
Bauchi†	847,274	513,077	60.56	334,197	39.40
Benue†	406,132	189,302	43.00	216,830	57.00
Borno*	282,180	128,684	45.60	153,496	54.40
Cross River†	342,755	153,452	47.08	189,303	52.02
Delta†	472,278	145,001	30.70	327,277	69.30
Edo*	308,979	103,572	33.52	205,407	66.48
Enugu†	427,190	233,281	54.44	193,969	45.56
Imo†	349,902	193,202	55.22	156,700	44.78
Jigaqwa†	228,388	89,836	39.00	138,552	61.00
Kaduna*	726,573	336,860	46.36	389,713	54.64
Kano*	324,428	154,809	47.72	169,619	52.28
Katsina†	442,176	271,000	61.30	171,169	38.70
Kebbi†	286,974	209,872	73.10	77,102	26.90
Kogi*	488,492	265,732	54.40	222,760	45.60
Kwara*	352,479	80,209	22.76	270,270	77.24
Lagos*	1,033,397	149,432	14.46	883,965	85.54
Niger*	357,787	221,437	61.90	136,350	38.10
Ogun*	484,971	59,246	12.22	425,725	87.78
Ondo†	964,018	160,994	15.70	803,024	84.30
Osun†	437,334	72,068	15.50	365,266	84.50
Oyo†	641,799	105,788	16.48	536,011	83.52
Plateau*	676,959	259,394	38.32	417,565	61.68
Rivers†	026,824	646,952	63.10	379,872	36.90
Sokoto†	469,986	372,260	79.21	97,726	20.79
Taraba	228,393	138,557	60.67	89,836	39.33
Yobe†	176,054	65,133	36.99	110,921	63.01
FCT*	38,281	18,313	47.84	19,968	52.16
Total	13,976,967	5,848,247	41.66	8,128,720	58.34

* Results released by NEC.
† *African Concord*, 28 June 1993: 22.

The annulment of the election and the state of anarchy in which it plunged the country abruptly terminated the tortuous transition. Together with economic and structural reforms, it was one of the most expensive enterprises in Nigeria's post-independence history; its exact costs may never be known, and Olagunju *et al.* (1994: 234-5) doubt if it would be possible to calculate them without distorting the total picture and exaggerating the monetary costs of the transition – how, for example, should the normal costs of running government or the costs of SAP be separated from those of the transition which were intricately interwoven with them? Nevertheless, attempts have been made to calculate the monetary costs of the transition (Olagunju *et al.* also examine the non-monetary social costs of adjustment and less tangible costs in terms of the regime's loss of legitimacy). Omorogiuwa (1987) estimated that with a hand-over date of 1 October 1992 the total cost of the transition – made up of allocations to MAMSER, the NEC, constitution-making, the census, the creation of states, the revenue commission, increased revenue to local governments, and so on – would be about N12.5 billion. In 1991, before the number of states was increased to thirty and local government areas to 589, *Tell* (1 July 1991) estimated that, up till that point, the total cost of the transition was N15 billion, of which a large portion went into manufacturing the two parties and establishing the NEC and other transition agencies.

Olagunju *et al.* also provide privileged totals of actual allocations to five transition agencies – the NEC, the Population Commission, the Centre for Democratic Studies (CDS), the Directorate of Food, Roads and Rural Infrastructure (DFRRI) and the Directorate of Social Mobilization (DSM) – between 1986 and 1992 (the estimates for population commission were for only two years), and these total over N5.9 billion. By the time one adds the costs of the final phase of the transition beginning with the creation of new states and including the conduct of the various elections, the huge expenses on patronage and support inducement, and the expenses of the politicians themselves, the total cost of the transition in monetary terms would run into hundreds of billions of naira. All this is apart from the huge losses to the public and private sectors, universities and other educational institutions resulting from the incessant strikes, demonstrations and riots; the massive flight of capital due to the political turbulence, and disinvestment by foreign capital; and the vast social costs in – among other things – unemployment, broken families, preventable deaths, poverty, increased criminal violence and the erosion of human safety and security.

This was the cost the country had to pay for political transition (and economic/structural reform) when its economy was already in deep recession. The reasons for the failure of the transition are fairly obvious. First, it is not at all certain that it was not meant to fail – in other words, that its twists and turns were not deliberately designed to prolong the life of the regime. But assuming a sincere intention actually to hand over power to civilians, then two further reasons can be given. One is that because of the several amendments to the transition programme and shifts in dates, the programme became 'overcrowded', which did not allow for the preparations required by the hectic last phase of the transition (cf. Olagunju *et al.*, 1994). It can also be argued that the groundswell of opposition from civil society drew the attention of the regime away from the transition programme to devising survival and legitimacy-engendering strategies. The other reason, which is also a commentary on the entire transition programme, is that the 'new political order' whose realisation seemed to be the condition for handing over was an unrealistic project, especially since its parameters seemed to be known only to members of the regime. Either the project of building a new breed of politicians without links to the past, eliminating conflicts in politics (what is politics if it is not about conflict?), wiping out corruption and so on was an exercise in deception intended to ensure that the transition would never succeed, or it was simply a needless experiment in political engineering such as Karl Popper and others have long argued is an inadequate strategy of social revolution (cf. Osaghae, 1991).

THE STIRRING OF CIVIL SOCIETY AND POLITICAL CONFLICTS

The Babangida period has to remembered as one of the most turbulent in Nigeria's post-independence history. This turbulence involved a complex of civil strife and political violence which engulfed the country both during the period of his rule and after. These took the forms of demonstrations, riots, strikes, coups and inter-group conflicts, most but not all consequences of state action and/or directed against the state. The stirring of civil society by the combined and contradictory forces of structural adjustment and democratic transition underlay the political turbulence as various groups struggled to survive economic hardship and diminishing resources, to assert their rights and resist the authoritarian regime, and to install democratic government in the country. These struggles enabled fledgling civil society coalitions to blossom thereby strengthening civil society's efficacy, but at the same time they also deepened centrifugal forces. Civil society was an arena of contending forces rather than a settled terrain, which helps to explain the divisions that seemed to hinder its efficacy.

These divisions were not necessarily a drawback or an indication of the 'absence' of a 'genuine' civil society, but part of the process of its growth and the resolution of the civil society dimensions of the 'national question'.

Political conflicts in the Babangida years would be analysed in two categories: those directed against (and in support of) the regime and those which, even though they were related to the regime, had more to do with conflicts among groups.

STATE-DIRECTED CONFLICTS

Beginning with the first category, we saw earlier in this chapter that the regime's romance with civil society elements did not last long. The basic authoritarianism of military government was a key factor, but the adoption and implementation of SAP as well as the 'dribbling runs' of the transition programme were strong exacerbating factors. The chief opposition groups here were students, especially of institutions of higher learning, acting through NANS and their various unions; labour organisations mostly acting through the umbrella association, the NLC; the press, especially the independent newspapers and magazines which increased greatly in number despite SAP and government repression;[24] the various pro-democracy and civil liberties organisations, which the government constantly accused of having foreign sponsorship; the professional associations, some of which fell to government's corporatist designs; and women's organisations, most notably Women In Nigeria (WIN) and market women's associations like that led by Habibat Mogaji in Lagos.

The opposition of these various segments took the form of demonstrations, riots, strikes, critical and opposition press reporting (including the emergence of underground and light or gossipy – known as 'soft-sell' – magazines), and the propagation of rumours and other forms of what Scott (1985, 1990) calls 'infrapolitical' resistance movements.[25] It was based on the constitutive interests of the organisations – higher salaries and better conditions of service for labour unions and workers, better campus conditions and lower fees for students, lower rents

---

[24] Most of these were based in Lagos – hence the popular reference to the 'Lagos' or 'Western' press – and were accused by Northerners (and some Igbos) of pursuing Yoruba-West interests.

[25] According to Scott, infrapolitical resistance movements involve symbolic, ritualistic, attitudinal and other more hidden forms of popular resistance. These were manifest in critical songs, and stage plays, graffiti, cartoons, pamphleteering, and so on (also see Fatton, jr., 1995, for the increasing importance of this form of protest among the urban poor and rural dwellers in the 'rise' of civil society in Africa).

for market stalls for market women, and so on. However, the emergence of human rights and pro-democracy organisations specifically to demand political reforms, the levelling consequences of SAP, the example set by political struggles in other parts of the world, and support from members of the international community led to expedient and transient coalitions being formed. The federal and state governments worked hard to prevent stable coalitions through outright repression, promotion of rival groups, and divide-and-rule tactics,[26] monetary inducements to union leaders and other means, but the loose coalitions proved capable of concerted action on a number of occasions, especially when opposing increases in petrol prices and the annulment of the 12 June presidential election. Apart from the voluntary associations, the National Assembly (and some state assemblies) which convened in 1992 also became important bases of opposition. The National Assembly in particular became more ardent in opposition after Decree no. 53 of 1993, which established the NDSC and thus made it an irrelevant institution.

In general, the government's response to these activities was repression, but where this did not quieten the opposition or the acts of opposition (such as actual or threatened mass strikes) posed a threat to governance and the economy, it resorted to palliatives: increased allowances and salaries, an urban mass transit system, lower import duties on spare parts and other selected items, and so on.[27] But the mainstay of the federal (and state) governments consisted of such actions as the closure of newspapers and magazines,[28] detention of journalists, students leaders, labour leaders and civil rights activists for indefinite periods (among the last-named group Beko Ransome Kuti, Gani Fawehinmi, Baba Omojola and Femi Falana were constantly in and out of detention); proscription of unions and professional associations (NANS, ASUU, NLC) closing down of universities and other institutions of higher learning for indefinite periods; and violent police and military action to quell demonstrations, resulting in the deaths of hundreds of demonstrators all over the country. The Civil

---

[26] One strategy the regime employed successfully was to set different categories of workers in the same establishment against one another – academic against nonacademic staff in universities, doctors against nurses in the health sector, professionals against non-professionals in the civil service, and so on.

[27] The palliatives approach was weakened on a number of occasions by the inability of state governments to foot the bill for increases in salaries and arrears. This was the case in 1993 when many states were unable to pay 45 per cent increases.

[28] In May 1993, the Newspaper and Magazine Proscription Decree no. 35 gave the government unchallengeable power to proscribe newspapers. This was followed by Decree no. 43 which created the Newspapers Registration Board whose approval had to be secured before a newspaper or magazine could be produced.

Liberties Organization (CLO) annual report for 1990 accused the police of 230 extra-judicial killings, and reported that several thousands of people were being held in detention and that sixty-nine people were executed (in connection with the April 1990 coup).

To the category of opposition also belonged the uprising of the oil-producing minorities to demand adequate compensation for environmental degradation and other hazards of exploration and production activities, a greater share of the federation's revenue which they claimed went largely to members of the majority groups, and greater political autonomy within the federation. These demands were articulated by the various movements and organisations formed by radical elites and youths of these groups to mobilise the rural masses. These included the Movement for the Survival of Ogoni People (MOSOP); the Movement for the Survival of Izon Ethnic Minority in the Niger Delta (MOSIEND); and the Movement for Reparation to Ogbia (MORETO). The groups also rose against oil companies, which they accused of not compensating them sufficiently for the huge profits they obtained from oil production. The uprisings had serious effects on the oil companies and production. According to the *African Guardian* (17 August 1992: 36), Shell's oil production activities in the Niger Delta were held up no less than twenty-two times between January and August 1991 alone.[29] Its total oil production fell from 1 million to 960,000 bpd between 1990 and 1993 largely because of these disruptions. The *African Guardian* (25 July 1994) gave a more vivid picture of Shell's losses from community uprisings and sabotage of oil installations: its Eastern division lost 1,269 man-days and N250.4 million in 1993; the Western division lost US1.4 million in 1992 and US$900,000 in 1993; and of a total 2,645 spillages for 1992, 1,837 were due to sabotage. However, hold-ups caused by oil-producing communities were not new, but they intensified in the prevailing economic depression. Between 1976 and 1988, for example, there were 344 hold-ups, of which 211 resulted in extensive damage to oil pipelines. But hold-ups were not the only reason for the crisis which engulfed the oil industry and resulted in a sharp decline in oil production. The failure of the NNPC to meet its equity obligations to the oil majors was another major reason.

---

[29] The case of the Uzere community in Delta state, which was typical of other oil communities, may be cited. In July 1992 youths of the community seized Shell installations producing 56,000 bpd from Uzere to back their demands for compensation for environmental degradation, employment of Uzere indigenes in Shell and scholarships for those in school, and development aid to build classroom blocks and tar roads. Production only resumed after a truce brokered by the Delta state government which advanced a grant of N28 million to tar the roads in the community and build a 50-bed hospital.

The most famous of the minority movements in the 1990s was the MOSOP, organised by Ken Saro-Wiwa. Beginning with the launching of the Ogoni Bill of Rights submitted to the federal government in 1990, MOSOP took the struggle against the state and Shell to various international forums, and thus attracted world attention to the plight of the Ogonis and other minorities in the country affected by oil production. At home, ordinary Ogonis were mobilised to make demands for economic and political justice through non-violent means, including the boycott of the 1993 presidential election. Links were also forged with other segments of civil society, especially the press and civil liberty organisations. The reaction of government to the Ogoni uprising, which threatened such an important source of the country's revenue, was to crack down heavily on the people, a response Saro-Wiwa described as genocide. According to a Civil Liberties Organization Report on Terror in Ogoni (CLO, 1994), forty Ogonis, many of whom had been raped and brutalised, were in detention without trial, eighteen houses were burnt by soldiers, various sums of money and livestock were extorted from Ogoni villages, twenty Ogonis had been shot dead and more than that number maimed due to gunfire and forty-three villages were under military occupation. Ogoniland became a battlefront with the deployment of soldiers to suppress the uprising (for accounts of the Ogoni uprising, see Naanen, 1995; and Osaghae, 1995d).

The uprising of the Niger Delta and oil-producing minorities did, however, force the government and oil companies to accede to some of their demands, having apparently realised that repression by armed force made oil exploration and production more precarious. The portion of the federation account allocated to deal with ecological and other problems in oil-producing areas was increased from 1.5 to 3 per cent. When this proved insufficient to stem the tide of agitation, the Oil Mineral Producing Areas Development Commission (OMPADEC) was established in 1992 to initiate and execute infrastructural and other development projects in the oil-producing communities of Rivers, Delta, Ondo, Edo, Imo, and Akwa Ibom states.

An instance of opposition under the Babangida regime which combined elements of centrifugal civil society uprising with those of typical military interventions was the unsuccessful coup led by Major Gideon Orkar on 22 April 1990 (for an analysis of this coup and the ways in which it differed from previous coups, see Ihonvbere, 1991). It was unprecedented in conception and execution, being the first organised in the name of only sections of the country. Other more familiar altruistic reasons were alluded to – corruption of the Babangida regime, economic mismanagement, dictatorial tendencies and so on – but the declared sectional character of the coup was new. Orkar declared in his coup broadcast: 'This is not just another coup, but well conceived, planned and executed for the marginalized, oppressed and enslaved people of the Middle Belt and the South, with a view to freeing ourselves and our children yet unborn from eternal slavery and colonisation by a clique of this country.'

Orkar and his collaborators, who were predominantly from the minorities Delta state, were responding to the chronic question of 'Northern domination' and its operational correlate, 'Hausa/Fulani domination'. In the Second Republic and under Buhari, as we saw earlier, opponents of 'endless' domination advocated confederation, but the organisers of the 1990 coup sought a more drastic solution which could have plunged the country into another civil war if it had succeeded: they announced the excision of Sokoto, Borno, Katsina, Bauchi, and Kano states, the supposed bastion of domination, from the federation. This was not the only unique aspect of the coup: there was also a large number of retired non-commissioned officers and some businessmen involved or implicated. One of the latter, Great Ogboru, a wealthy young businessman from Delta state, was alleged to be the coup's main financier.

The coup marked a significant stage in the struggle by the country's ethnic minorities especially, to resolve the 'national question', and was therefore part of the responses from civil society to the political and economic changes – indeed, in a different perspective, Olagunju *et al.* (1993) regard the military as an integral part of civil society. Minority spokespersons, especially those of the groups in the oil-producing areas, believed that the national question could only be resolved with justice through the creation of largely autonomous ethnic states, and a restructuring of the revenue allocation system to reverse the unacceptable situation where those whose areas provided the bulk of national revenue but were politically marginalised and the least developed. Thus the coup broadcast lamented that although the Northern cabal 'contribute[d] very little economically to the well being of Nigeria, they have over the years served and presided over the supposedly national wealth derived in the main from the Middle Belt and Southern parts of the country, while the people from these parts ... have been completely deprived from benefiting from the resources given to them by God.' However, the coup, described by the government as the 'bloodiest' in the country's history, was unsuccessful. Some of the suspected plotters (including Great Ogboru, Colonel Tony Nyiam, and Major Mukoro) fled abroad,[30] but more than 100 officers and

---

[30] In the effort to get the 'fugitives', the government resorted to arresting family members

civilians were tried by a military tribunal headed by General Ike Nwachukwu and about sixty-seven officers were executed. Two of the coup's consequences should be highlighted. First, the regime afterwards became more alert to federal representation in appointments and in the distribution of federal resources – the establishment of OMPADEC was a product of this increased sensitivity. Secondly, the coup accelerated the movement of the seat of power from Dodan Barracks in Lagos to the more fortified Aso Rock in Abuja. The president was somewhat insulated there from the pressures of opposition groups in Lagos, which may partly explain his increased intransigence and his determination to stay on in office. The 1990 coup was therefore a turning-point for the Babangida regime.

Juxtaposed with the activities of opposition groups were those of the groups which supported the regime. These belonged to two distinct groups. First were the neo-corporatist and co-opted structures, notably the various armed forces wives' associations (Nigeria Army Officers Wives Association, Police Officers Wives Association, etc.), the 'Better Life' associations, government-sponsored rival students and other associations, traditional rulers, and the federal and state government-owned media: newspapers (notably the *Daily Times* and the *New Nigerian*), and radio and television channels (notably Radio Nigeria and Nigeria Television Authority). The second and more active group comprised associations like the Association for Better Nigeria (ABN) which openly canvassed for the prolongation of Babangida's regime and the perpetuation of military rule. Apart from the ABN, there were the 'Committee of Patriots' which gave its address as Dodan Barracks, the seat of government till 1990; 'Third Eye' whose specialty was paid advertisements in newspapers, and which later became metamorphosed into a newspaper chain; and various faceless groups; but the most notorious was the ABN whose members Nzeribe claimed included retired supreme court judges, generals and politicians. These groups were believed to operate with the knowledge of the federal government, which nevertheless went through the motions of distancing itself from them. For example, it went to the extent of declaring the ABN illegal, and even obtained a court injunction restraining the association from parading itself as an association campaigning for Babangida, but it took no steps to stop its 'illegal' activities. As opposition intensified after the annulment of the presidential election, the activities of these groups were reinforced by stage-managed

---

in place of suspects who had fled: brothers and sisters of Ogboru and Mukoro and even Mukoro's domestic workers were detained. This practice continued for a long time thereafter.

rallies all over the country and the support of traditional rulers and comprador politicians.

INTER-GROUP CONFLICTS

There were also religious, ethnic, and regional conflicts which, though manifestly of an inter-group character, were for the most part directly or indirectly the consequence of state actions and policies. At a more general level, they were propelled by diminishing returns and the contradictions of SAP and democratic transition. This was certainly true of the proliferating ethno-regional associations which were now a major feature of the political landscape. The more notable included Egbe Ilosiwaju Yoruba, the Northern Elders Forum, the Eastern Forum, the Middle Belt Forum, CARIA, MOSOP, EMIROAF, the Association of Minority States, the Committee of Oil-Producing Areas, and so on. These associations had many 'old brigade' politicians as members, and pursued particularist interests which, especially in the case of the regional and ethnic majority groups, centred around capturing power at various levels in the aborted Third Republic. They functioned as the third force in party politics by attempting to influence the candidate selection processes in the parties and electoral behaviour generally. For example, the Egbe Ilosiwaju tried (unsuccessfully) to prune down the unwieldy number of Yoruba presidential candidates (eight SDP and two NRC) in the 1992 primaries. Although these associations were officially banned in May 1992 for 'destabilising' activities, they continued to function clandestinely and re-emerged strongly to champion the ethno-regional disputes which followed the annulment of the 12 June presidential election.

This form of inter-group conflicts was different from, though not entirely unrelated to, the more serious and generally violent conflicts which ensued among various groups in the country. These included Muslim-Christian conflicts which exploded throughout the country, but manifested themselves chiefly in the religious uprisings and riots in the North and in more localised ethnic or so-called communal conflicts. Although religious conflicts have roots going back to the foundation of the Nigerian state under colonial rule, and the pragmatic involvement of the state in religious activities, religion became an explosive political issue from the time the *Sharia* issue divided the Constituent Assembly in 1977/8. The Maitatsine riots and other Muslim fundamentalist uprisings of the 1980s, and allegations of Muslim dominance in the Buhari regime were evidence of growing religious tension and politicisation.

Under Babangida religion became politicised to an unprecedented degree. It all started with his decision in 1986 to register Nigeria as a full member of the Organization of Islamic Countries (OIC)[31] (in which the country had all along maintained an observer status). The regime had stirred a hornet's nest. Christians, through the Christian Association of Nigeria (CAN) and other bodies, alleged that there was a grand design to transform the country into a Muslim state, and from that point onwards most actions, policies and appointments of governments at every level were seen through the lens of religion. The lens also extended to dress, food, and the balance of religious propagation in educational institutions; allocation of air time on radio and television; a fair balance between Muslim and Christian public holidays; and the religious composition of the armed forces.

It is against this background that the religious riots which broke out in many parts of the North in the late 1980s and early 1990s have to be considered. The major riots and Muslim-Christian clashes were those of Ilorin in 1986; Kafanchan, Kaduna, Katsina, Funtua, Kano and Zaria in 1987; and Bauchi in 1991. Of these the Bauchi riots, in which an estimated 1,000 people were killed and many more injured (the official figures were 312 dead and 582 injured), and property – mainly churches and the residences of non-indigenes – was destroyed, was the most serious, and could only be brought under control by full-scale military action. The riot was sparked off by Shiite Muslim extremists, as was that in Katsina state, where it degenerated into a contest between the state military governor Colonel John Madaki and the Shiite leader Yakubu Yahaya. The latter not only accused the governor, who was Christian, of being a CAN (Christian Association of Nigeria) agent, but stated that his group did not recognise the un-Islamic governments at the local, state and federal levels. All the riots had virtually the same targets: non-indigenes and Christians. Some also involved more latent ethnic conflicts between dominant Hausa-Muslim communities and ethnic minority-Christian/animist groups. For example, as well as the more obvious religious factors, conflicts between the Tsayawa ethnic group of Tafawa Balewa local government and the Hausa Bauchi were central to the Bauchi riots. Indeed, in the aftermath of the riots the Tsayawa sought to be merged with Plateau state to put an end to Hausa domination; in the alternative, they demanded a separate autonomous chiefdom which would not be subject to the Emir of Bauchi.

The Zangon Kataf crisis, involving conflicts between the Kataf

[31] News of the membership was not officially announced, and was picked up from Radio France International. The issue of membership became more controversial when the CGS, Commodore Ebitu Ukiwe, a Christian, said it was never discussed at the AFRC.

and the Hausa, was also similar to the so-called religious riots. It was the culmination of a long history of struggle by the Kataf to be freed from the domination of the Muslim-Hausa/Fulani, represented in this case by the Emir of Zaria. The immediate cause of the violence in May 1992 was disagreement between the Hausa and Kataf over where the Zangon traditional market should be cited. In the ensuing battle in which over 1,000 were believed to have died, mosques and churches were the prime targets, and Muslim and Christian 'reinforcements' were mobilised from adjoining states. (The crisis spread to other parts of southern Zaria, where the minorities in Kaduna state are concentrated.) The trials and sentencing to death (later commuted to short jail sentences) of Zangon leaders like General Zamani Lekwot by the civil disturbances tribunal headed by Mr Justice Okadigbo became the centre of a national controversy which had intense religious coloration. In 1996 the Zangon Kataf were granted an autonomous chiefdom which relieved them of the Emir of Zaria's control.

Most of the other 'communal' conflicts in the North – like those involving the Kuteb, Jukun and Chamba in Takum local government area of Taraba state, the Tiv and Jukun in Benue state, and others – were much more localised, and mostly had to do with the right and access to land and chieftaincy disputes. The same was true of inter-group conflicts in some Southern states, notably Rivers, Cross River and Delta, although some of them, like those involving the Ogoni and Okrika, were believed to have been engineered by state agents to scuttle more serious anti-government uprisings.

The foregoing illustrates the responses of civil society to reforms and other changes in the Babangida years. As we showed at the beginning of the section, civil society was more complex and contested than analysts who see its role only in terms of the 'struggle for democracy' assume. There is no doubt that civil society has been in the forefront of the democratic struggle in the country since colonial times, and that the Babangida years were no exception, but that struggle also had at its core the unresolved and highly contested issues related to the national question. It was the inability of the various groups to resolve or agree on some of these issues, more than anything else, that enabled the military get away with the annulment of the 1993 presidential election. It is to this that we now turn.

12 JUNE AND ITS AFTERMATH

The annulment of the presidential election on 12 June was by far the greatest catalyst of Nigeria's descent into anarchy. On the international scene it set off the country's steady march towards becoming a so-called pariah state, as the United States and other Western countries championed its isolation and the imposition of limited sanctions. The domestic situation was even more devastating. The strikes, riots and demonstrations that greeted the annulment and continued long afterwards brought about a virtual standstill. The already fragile economy was seriously affected, and the resurgence of strong ethno-regional forces rocked the country's very foundations, with the strong possibility of a civil war or disintegration. Surely the price Nigeria paid for the annulment was much higher than anything the Babangida regime could ever have anticipated. But why was the election annulled? What were the responses to the annulment, and how did the government manage the crisis which brought the convoluted transition programme to an end? In this, how did the Interim National Government (ING) fare?

WHY WAS THE ELECTION ANNULLED?

Let us first examine the reasons given by General Babangida in his 26 June national broadcast on the annulment and other statements by him and Vice-President Aikhomu. The following were the main reasons for the annulment:
1. Like the primaries which were annulled earlier, the election failed to meet the NDSC's 'basic requirements' for free and fair elections, chief among which was the absence of electoral malpractices and a prohibition on the use of money to secure victories. The AFRC had evidence of money being paid by both presidential candidates, Abiola and Tofa, at the conventions and elections proper – the amount was put at N2.1 billion – and of malpractices involving party agents, the NEC and some of the electorate.
2. There was a 'documented and confirmed conflict of interest between the government and both presidential aspirants which would compromise their positions and responsibilities were they to become president.'
3. The NEC was not fully prepared for the election; yet it 'deceived' the NDSC – whose members favoured it being postponed for one week following the court injunction secured by ABN – into going ahead with it.
4. The presumed winner of the presidential election (M.K.O. Abiola) encouraged a campaign of divide and rule among the various ethnic groups.
5. The politicisation of the judiciary and the need to save it from loss of credibility.
6. According to Aikhomu, Abiola was unacceptable to most sections of the military, particularly its top brass.
    Taken literally, none of these reasons is convincing. To begin

with the first point, it is strange that the NDSC verdict and that
of the various observers and monitors who declared the election free
and fair could differ so widely. But assuming that the NDSC had
the benefit of 'inside' information not available to the monitors and
observers, and that its information went back to the primaries, why
were Abiola and Tofa cleared to contest the election in the first
place? In his broadcast Babangida said that this was partly because
the NDSC was committed to the hand-over date, but in the next
breath he blamed the NEC, which 'still went ahead to clear the candidates'.
How could a regime which had consistently maintained that it would
not allow considerations of time to prevent it from building a new
political order abandon that principle when it mattered most? Besides,
it was clear from all previous elections that the ultimate responsibility
for clearing candidates lay with the military rulers – as we saw earlier,
candidates still got disqualified even after being cleared by the NEC.
Probably this explains why the NEC gave all the presidential aspirants
who contested the presidential primaries in 1993 only provisional
clearance. The second point was not elaborated upon, but it seems
to be related to Aikhomu's claim that the federal government owed
Abiola 'billions of naira'. Again why was he not disqualified on
this ground? As for the third reason, we rely on the insight of Professor
Omo Omoruyi, Director General of the Centre for Democratic Studies
and one of the key executors of the transition. In an interview with
Tell (29 August 1994: 22) he said:

> '...after the Justice Ikpeme ruling, three of us were invited to the
> villa...Professor Humphrey Nwosu, Olu Adeniji, and myself. We met
> with the top brass of the military and the president. Remember that at
> that time, the American government had warned Nigeria of the possible
> actions it will take if the election did not hold.[...] I remember Adeniji
> asked the president... "What do we do tomorrow [12 June]?" The
> president answered, "Professor Nwosu, the election must go on. We
> will defy the court."'

There is not much to add to this, other than to say that there was
no evidence that the NEC was unprepared for the election – indeed,
despite the manipulation of the institution by the regime, Lewis (1994:
332) still credited Nwosu with a 'modicum of profiency'. The low
voter turnout which the government and the *New Nigerian* continually
harped upon was not out of character with the trend of electoral
behaviour in Nigeria, and could not therefore have been a good
index of the NEC's preparations (the apathy resulting from the twists
and turns in the transition was dissuasion enough). The fourth point
about a 'divide and rule' campaign is basically a contradiction; if

Abiola was promoting division, how did he manage to win in most states of the federation? The fifth point had some merit, but how could a regime that had helped to destroy the judiciary, replacing normal courts with special tribunals, multiplying ouster clauses and defying court rulings overnight, become a champion of judicial integrity? If, as is believed, the ABN enjoyed government support, and judicial processes were manipulated to scuttle the final phase of the transition, could the regime itself be absolved from the desecration of the judiciary? On the final point that Abiola was not acceptable to most sections of the military, why did the military not then simply devise another means other than an open election to choose its successors, especially considering that, from the very beginning, as Babangida himself said, they knew those who would not succeed the regime?

The reasons for the annulment have therefore to be sought elsewhere. This search should begin from the point that both President Babangida and Vice-President Aikhomu implicitly declared that Abiola had indeed won the election. This is important because the Abacha regime later gave the fact that the election was inconclusive as the major reason for its failure to revisit the election or hand over power to Abiola, as some pro-democracy elements demanded. The second point to be stressed is that the annulment of the election was effected by only a few members of the government. Although references were made to the NDSC in the president's 26 June broadcast, it is known that the annulment was not a 'collective' decision, that most members of the council knew of it only afterwards, and that it split the NDSC and the top echelon of the military. The Transitional Council which was supposed to oversee the final phase of the transition was not consulted on the matter at all (Nwabueze, 1994: 33).

Against this background, three plausible reasons which summarise popular and informed views can be advanced for the annulment. The first and most important is that Babangida was unwilling to hand over power. Direct evidence for this includes his tacit support for the ABN and other similar groups championing the Babangida-must-stay campaign, working to scuttle the electoral process, and organising so-called 'solidarity' rallies in Abuja and various other places after the annulment, and the desperate efforts to win his military colleagues, traditional leaders, party leaders and other influential politicians and members of the National Assembly over to his side. In fact, many commentators saw the annulment as the culmination of Babangida's 'hidden agenda' which underlay the 'booby traps' and confusion of the transition programme.

The second reason is that the annulment was an indication of the unwillingness of the conservative North to keep its hands off the control of political power; in other words, that the Babangida regime acted on behalf of a cabal. A different but related reason is that the annulment was Babangida's own way of seeking rehabilitation within the powerful Northern power bloc (including the Kaduna mafia) which viewed his programme of economic and political reforms as injurious to Northern interests. The general acceptance, even justification, of the annulment by leading Northern politicians, elites and mass media, and the emergence of what became an ostensible 'Northern' position which most of the conservative politicians advanced – that the annulment was another military coup and that Shagari, whose term as president was terminated by the military, had first to reclaim his democratic mandate before Abiola could do so[32] – would seem to support this view.

But the view takes little account of the tremendous support that Abiola received in the North. Also, radical Northern politicians and elites (including those in the military) opposed the annulment and joined the 12 June movement, and even those politicians who came to support the conservative Northern position were latter-day converts who had at first opposed the annulment (a good example is Adamu Ciroma). This ethno-regionalist interpretation of the annulment was advanced by many Southern, especially Yoruba-Western politicians, and one of its immediate consequences was to give the struggle (to actualise 12 June) an ethnic and sectional character. The facts that the Yorubas formed the core of the movement, that the uprisings subsequent to the annulment were concentrated in Lagos, Ibadan, Abeokuta and other Western towns, and that the so-called Lagos press spearheaded the actualisation campaign had the unwanted effect of giving the struggle an ethno-regional slant.

The third and final reason for the annulment is related to the personal problems of Abiola with the top echelons of the military. Abiola had a long association with the military and military officers dating back to the Mohammed/Obasanjo regime, during which, as ITT director, he secured major telecommunications contracts. He subsequently became a major contractor for military supplies, especially signals equipment. He was also close to several officers and in particular to General Babangida, whose personal 'clearance' he claimed to have sought before entering the presidential race. These associations were the source of some of the reasons adduced for the annulment – that he was not acceptable to many officers (whom it is said he had

---

[32] A variant of this view went even further back in time to January 1966. In November 1993 one Usman Sami Sani filed a suit in the Kaduna high court challenging, among other things, the 'legality' of previous coups and laws made by military regimes.

planned to force into retirement if he became president) and that the country owed him huge sums of money.

Of the three reasons the first – that General Babangida was unwilling to relinquish power – is the most basic. The two other (and other reasons that may be advanced) were secondary or even coincidental to this, but this does not make them less plausible. The (Abiola) personality factor is very important, but it seems likely that the election would still have been cancelled even if Bashir Tofa had won. This also shows that the so-called 'Northern' factor was really no better than a convenient reason whose emergence and persistence was due largely to the perceived ethno-regional slant of the advocacy for 12 June. It should also be noted that several notable Igbo and Eastern leaders responded in similar ways for precisely the same reasons.

AFTERMATH OF THE ANNULMENT

As was to be expected, the annulment of the presidential election was greeted by serious resistance both within and outside the country. Domestically, spontaneous demonstrations and riots were staged all over the country, though these were more serious in Lagos and other Southern capitals than elsewhere. Most of the acts of resistance and civil disobedience were championed and coordinated by the Campaign for Democracy (CD), a coalition of several pro-democracy organisations, including NANS, WIN and ASUU, which mobilised people between July and August 1993 to demonstrate or simply stay at home. The NLC briefly joined the struggle by declaring a national strike from the end of August, but this failed because of the ethno-regional divisions which also emerged within labour unions and the vacillations of the unions' national leaders. In Lagos, which was historically the hub of popular resistance, persistent rioting paralysed all activities, and only abated after a shoot-rioters-at-sight order went out to police and military anti-riot squads. It was estimated that over 100 demonstrators and rioters were killed throughout the country by these squads. The newspapers and magazines were very active in rallying support for the restoration of 12 June, as a result of which there were several closures – *Abuja Newsday*, the Concord group of newspapers owned by Abiola, *The Punch, Daily Sketch, Nigerian Observer*, and the Ogun State Broadcasting Corporation.

Opposition to the annulment also saw the rise of unconventional forms of resistance and protest. Underground political movements and newspapers appeared in different parts of the country. One of these groups – Movement for the Advancement of Democracy (MAD) – hijacked a Nigeria Airways plane in Niger Republic at the height of opposition to the annulment. These underground organisations were apparently behind the spate of bombings and other isolated terrorist activities which were characteristics of the political struggles to terminate military rule after the Babangida regime. Persistent violent eruptions led to threats by the president to declare a state of emergency in parts of the country where law and order had broken down. But alongside these opposition reactions there were open displays of support for the regime, involving the so-called solidarity rallies and visits to Aso rock in Abuja and to the offices of state governors. Most of the rallies, which were believed to have been stage-managed by agents of the federal and state governments, took place in Abuja and in Kaduna and some other Northern cities. The concentration of the rallies in the North, which was evidently calculated to divide the politicians and civil society groups along ethnic and regional lines, contributed to the hardening of regional and ethnic positions. The solidarity visits on the other hand involved traditional rulers, delegations of some state houses of assembly (notably Bauchi, Kaduna and Katsina), local government functionaries, and women's youth and other organisations, some of which were formed just for this purpose.

However, the greater burden of responding to the annulment fell on the law courts on the one hand, and on political parties and members of the political class on the other. Both failed woefully to live up to the challenge of the crisis. The law courts in particular exacerbated the tension and chaos which followed the annulment, because of the conflicting judgements they handed down. This assumed a dangerous regional and politicised dimension, because while high courts in Lagos, Benin city and Port Harcourt, all in the South, ordered the NEC to release the outstanding results of the presidential election and declared the annulment illegal, those in Abuja and Kaduna in the North upheld the election. This dangerous trend of 'Southern' versus 'Northern' judgements – which continued under the Abacha regime, as we shall see in the next chapter – not only worsened the political crisis but threatened to destroy the integrity of the judiciary, especially given the suspect orders of the Abuja high court on suits by the ABN. It was not surprising that General Babangida cited the need to safeguard the integrity of the judiciary as one of the reasons for annulling the election, although this had little to do with the substance of the election itself and was not strictly relevant considering the ouster clauses in the enabling decree for the election.

The political parties most directly affected by the annulment were even more disappointing. Their inability to reach any consensus or confront what was essentially a military assault was largely due to the activities of the comprador political class which the regime had built up as part of the transition – and to the easy manipulation of the artificial parties. More than anything else, the tame response of the politicians revealed the inadequacies of the parties. Because they were perceived with no concrete identities as government agencies, most politicians merely related to the parties as extensions of the conduit-pipe for government largesse. The stage was then left to the various ethno-regional associations to formulate positions taken in the crisis which ensued. This underlay the emergence of ethnic blocs within the parties. While the NRC understandably played the role of an 'opposition' party, the threats by leaders of the Eastern and Northern factions of the party to 'bring down the country' if the annulment of the election was reversed were expressions of positions taken outside the party – the Eastern position which was articulated by Governors Onu (Abia), Isemin (Akwa Ibom), Nwodo (Enugu), Ebri (Cross River), Enwerem (Imo), and George (Rivers) was believed to have been influenced by a 'deal' struck with Northern politicians to 'concede' the presidency to the East in the next election. By contrast, the Yoruba-Western faction within the NRC was strongly opposed to the annulment.

The situation in the SDP, the supposed victorious party, was not very different. The initial cohesion in the party which, among other things, saw the attorneys-general of fourteen SDP-controlled states come together to challenge the annulment in the supreme court (they were unsuccessful), soon gave way to strong divisions which left the Yoruba-West and rumps of the Eastern and Middle-Belt factions of the party as the only voices for restoration of 12 June. Even the national executive of the party abandoned the party's 'mandate' in the negotiations with the regime and later the interim government, leaving a few SDP governors – Segun Osoba (Ogun), Chukwuemeka Ezeife (Anambra), Isiaka Adeleke (Osun), Kolapo Isola (Oyo) and Bamidele Olumilua (Ondo) – and legislators – Senators Iyorcha Ayu (later impeached as senate president), Bola Tinubu and others – to continue applying pressure for the actualisation of the mandate. The one segment of the political class that attempted to mount a coherent resistance to the annulment was the National Assembly in whose two chambers the SDP had majorities (as well as in some state Houses of Assembly, notably those in the West of the country). The crisis seemed to have finally provided an opportunity for members of the national assembly to demonstrate their relevance in the political process. But this was not to be because a section of the senate – the gang of fifty-seven senators, who were pro-Babangida and believed to have been sponsored by opponents of Abiola in the SDP – engineered the impeachment of the adamant president of the senate Iyorcha Ayu, installed Ameh Ebute in his place, and successfully neutralised opposition to the annulment from the senate (cf. *African Guradian*, 16 May 1994: 12). But this was not before members of the senate had voted against the continuance in power of General Babangida. A similar thing happened in the House of Representatives.

The divisions within the political class, hardening of ethno- regional positions, riots, strikes and demonstrations all plunged the country into deep political crisis comparable to that of 1965/6, which resulted in civil war. Various segments of the Yoruba-Western elite, including traditional leaders, were adamant in their demand for the restoration of the cancelled election, while some called for a break-up of the federation or the secession of the West. Some Eastern and Northern political leaders, including governors, on the other hand, threatened to foment serious trouble if the cancelled election was restored.

The propaganda machinery mounted by Uche Chukwumerije, the former Biafra director of propaganda and federal minister at the time, ostensibly to remind Nigerians of the agonies of war and the need for an amicable settlement of the crisis, unfortunately served to raise peoples' fears and anxieties. Pictures of the Nigerian civil war and of those in Bosnia, Liberia and other places were constantly shown on national television; the 'drums of war' sounded on radio and in government newspapers; and rumours of war started panic mass migrations across the country – in Lagos, it was more than rumours: posters appeared reasserting Biafra and asking people to prepare for war. Southerners, especially Yorubas many of whom felt they had replaced Igbos as the object of attack in the North, moved from there *en masse*; Easterners in Lagos were criticised and sometimes attacked for failing to strongly support the 12 June movement, and returned home to the East; Westerners moved home from the East, and Northerners evacuated Lagos and other parts of the West in large numbers. The country seemed headed for another civil war, but the mixed and pragmatic positions taken by the politicians, and the readiness of the politicians to negotiate with the military, even if this meant abandoning a golden opportunity to resolve the military question decisively, saved the situation.

Abiola's political history and his poor responses to the evolving crisis were partly responsible for the divisions within the political class in general and the SDP in particular. Conservative Northern politicians remembered his strong opposition to the renomination of Shagari as the NPN's presidential candidate which led him to resign from the party in 1982 (there were rumours that he supported the overthrow of Shagari by the military). His close association with the military and particularly Babangida also cost him the support or sympathy of many politicians (some saw an element of poetic justice in the annulment). Then there was the fact that Abiola was a newcomer to the SDP, having only joined it during the fresh membership registration exercise of January 1993. Although one of the cardinal objectives of the manufactured parties was to eliminate the notion of 'joiners' and 'founders', which had in the past strengthened the sectional characters of parties, a situation where a newcomer to the party could manoeuvre his way to the top was unacceptable to some powerful members of the party who had somehow made themselves the 'elders' of the party.

What made the case worse for Abiola was the allegation that he had influenced the decision to annul the presidential primaries of 1992 in order to pave the way for himself, and it was known that to get the presidential ticket he had stepped on the toes of many within the party, the most notable of the latter being Shehu Yar'Adua who had virtually secured the party's presidential ticket in 1992. Yar'Adua and Abiola had in the past had disagreements over joint shipping and banking businesses, and Abiola refused to appoint Abubakar Atiku, Yar'Adua's protégé, as running mate as many expected (cf. *Tell*, 1 February 1993: 13). Abiola also had problems with Arthur Nzeribe, who took part in the 1992 primaries and seemed to have used the ABN's scuttling of the election to settle a personal score. Abiola's victory could have enabled these and other problems to be papered over, but his own responses to the annulment increasingly isolated him from his party and significant segments of the political class. He preferred to deal only with supportive factions of the party, leaving out so-called opponents, and this led him to rely more and more on the Western-Borno axis of the party and parallel non-party structures – in fact, at one stage he was accused of abandoning the party and pursuing the actualisation of his 'mandate' through parallel structures. But of Abiola's actions the most far-reaching was his decision to flee abroad on 3 August for the sake of his personal security, and to remain outside the country till 24 September, long after Babangida had relinquished power. Although he had taken the bold step of declaring himself president on 1 July and continued to insist on the 'mandate' Nigerians had given him, his absence and activities abroad, especially his call on Western countries to impose sanctions on Nigeria, and his claim that the election was cancelled because he was a Yoruba-Westerner, cost him further support and made it easier for the regime to move further away from the restoration of 12 June.

The options open to the regime were rather limited, given the groundswell of opposition to continued military rule which could not be suppressed by the terrorism of a military state which the country had become, and the divisions within the military itself, of which the frequent meetings of the NDSC and its consultations with different segments of the military were a major indication. In his broadcast of 26 June the president had announced plans for a fresh presidential election after July, and before the hand-over date of 27 August to which the regime remained committed. Whether this was a sincere proposal or not, the prevailing circumstances made it unrealistic. Consultations with politicians, party leaders and traditional rulers among others failed to yield any viable solution and only served to alienate some Yoruba traditional rulers (notably the Ooni of Ife) who were accused of supporting the regime and 'selling out' the Yorubas.

THE INTERIM NATIONAL GOVERNMENT

The solution finally found was the formation of an Interim National Government (ING) following the recommendations of the tripartite committee headed by Vice-President Augustus Aikhomu.[33] On 27 August 1993 Babangida finally 'stepped aside' under pressure from the top echelon of the military, bringing to an end the long and tortuous reign of 'the prince of the Niger' (Amuta, 1992). However, before his dramatic exit he announced the retirement of the service chiefs (General Abacha was the only one who remained, and he continued as defence minister), and appointed his protégés to key positions. The interim government, headed by Ernest Shonekan, formerly head of the Transition Council, then took over. Its composition was decided by the departing regime, which made it more or less a continuation of the regime in the popular perception. This was not the only anomaly of the interim arrangement: a more fundamental one was the provision for the most senior minister to take over the headship of the government in the event of the incumbent's resignation or death. This was a highly suspect provision which Nwabueze (1994: 60), who helped to draft the constitution of the ING, points out was 'curious but pregnant; it had not been included in the original

[33] The committee, comprising ten appointees of government of whom three were civilians and representatives of the two political parties, had been set up to consider possible ways out of the political impasse. It recommended the creation of two interim bodies – the ING, which was to have military and civilian members and an interim federal executive council which was to be all-civilian except for the minister of defence – and the appointment of a civilian president and vice-president to head the interim government, to last till December 1994. Within that period the committee recommended a new presidential election to complete the transition programme. The recommendation of the Aikhomu committee was amended to produce the ING, which was to last till 31 March 1994.

draft. It seemed to have been designed to ensure a smooth return to military rule after an interim cooling-off period; later events showed this to be the case.

From the very beginning the ING faced serious opposition and other problems of legitimacy. Its first and most pressing problem was that of identity or image: as we have said, it was perceived as a continuation of Babangida's regime. The presence of General Abacha in the government, and the 'executive' powers he wielded over the military as *de facto* commander-in-chief of the armed forces, suggested that the old order was all but intact and that Shonekan's authority was strictly circumscribed. Indeed, Abacha moved quickly to assert his control. Among other moves, he retired or redeployed the famous 'Babangida boys' (supporters of Babangida) in the military. There was also a problem with Shonekan himself: being Yoruba and specifically Egba like Abiola, his appointment was obviously aimed at weakening the Yoruba-based 12 June movement. It did succeed, along with changes in the political equation (e.g. the prospects for a fresh presidential election and Shonekan's deft deployment of patronage) in breaking the solidarity of the Yorubas to some extent.

However, Shonekan was generally regarded by the most ardent advocates of the restoration of 12 June as a 'sell-out'. This increased their determination to oppose the new regime. Indeed, SDP governors of the Western states refused to recognise the ING and shunned meetings called by Shonekan. He was also viewed with suspicion by some sections of the conservative Northern politicians, who by now had hardened their anti-12 June position. Being Yoruba, he was suspected of being sympathetic to 12 June. The notable exceptions were Yar'Adua, Adamu Ciroma and other members of the Northern Consultative Forum, who fully supported the ING saying it was the 'only way forward under the circumstances', although the real reason for this support was the ING's promise of a new presidential election which Yar' Adua and Ciroma were eager to contest. The other major problem the ING faced was whether it was legal. The view popularised by pro-democracy activists and lawyers was that Decree no. 61 which created the ING was a nullity, since Decree no. 59 which repealed the Constitution (Suspension and Modification) Decree no. 1 of 1984 terminated the life of the Babangida regime from 26 August 1993. It was argued that because Decree no. 61 was signed on 27 August after the Babangida regime had ceased to have any validity, the ING was a nullity, and existed in a 'legal vacuum'. Nwabueze (1994) has responded to the legal issues raised by these arguments, and concludes that the popular interpretation was wrong. In particular, he draws attention to Decree no. 62 of 1993 which postponed the starting date of the 1989 Constitution (the anti-ING school argued that it came into effect by implication after 26 August 1993). But his arguments give insufficient weight to the points raised about the anomalies in date, specifically the fact that these decrees were gazetted on 23 August but actually enacted on the following days. As Femi Falana put it:

> 'How on earth can a gazette published on August 23 contain laws made on August 24, 25 and 26... If a book is published today, it cannot report happenings of three days time. This is symptomatic of the fraud that has characterized the ING.' (Interview in *African Guardian*, 25 October 1993: 14)

Despite the very hostile environment – continued strikes, demonstrations, lack of legitimacy and fears of war – Shonekan tried to salvage whatever he could out of the situation, and halt the drift to complete anarchy. He hinged these efforts on the mission and essence of the ING, as he enunciated in his maiden broadcast to the country:

> 'The rationale for the ING [was] the imperative to move forward as a united and indivisible nation. The nation could not afford to be bogged down much longer in the election quagmire. A solution ha[d] to be found since we all know...the long-term benefit of staying together as one nation...'

This was the 'directive principle' of Shonekan's initiatives. To gain support he made some populist and reconciliatory moves while continuing, like Babangida before him, to rely heavily on the deployment of patronages and 'settlement'.[34] Some pro-democracy activists were released from detention, and assurances were given that state terrorism would end. The plan to pull out Nigerian soldiers from Liberia by 31 March 1994, which Shonekan announced in his maiden national broadcast, was also calculated to gain the support of the public which was very critical of the Liberian peacekeeping mission. But on this the army took the wind out of his sails by annulling the order – an action which showed clearly that final authority on critical issues rested with the military, and thus further complicated the ING's legitimacy crisis and its image as a figurehead government. The ING also embarked on an anti-corruption, house-cleaning crusade. The boards of the NNPC and its subsidiaries, whose impropriety and bad management were said to be a major source of the country's economic problems, were dissolved, and Edmund Dakoru, the NNPC's

---

[34] 'Settlement' became a popular catch-word in the final days of the Babangida regime. It referred to monetary inducement to silence opposition.

managing director, and other top officials of the corporation were put on trial. To demonstrate its corrective posture further, the ING sent an anti-corruption bill to the National Assembly.

But 12 June remained the central issue, and the ethno-regional positions remained unchanged. A panel headed by Mr Justice Mamman Nasir was appointed to look into the annulled election, but Shonekan's clarification that this did not mean the annulment would be reversed was not enough assurance for anti-12 June elements, who were suspicious of his moves. Wada Nas, then Katsina state NRC chairman, argued that 'once we revisit 12 June that will be the end of the country, and secured an Abuja high court ruling that restrained the panel from doing its work (*African Guardian*, 25 October 1993). However, the mainstay of the ING's efforts to resolve the crisis consisted of the consultations and negotiations between Shonekan and various political associations and leaders, including Abiola himself, who was still in self-exile abroad. In the face of seemingly irreconcilable ethno-regional positions, these yielded few dividends. Conservative Northern leaders, acting through the committee for reconciliation and national unity formed by a meeting of the Northern Consulative Forum in November, reiterated their support for the ING and the continued existence of a united Nigeria, as did the Igbo-Eastern faction of the NRC led by Ojukwu, and other NRC leaders. The SDP remained badly divided, but members of its National Executive Committee supported the ING.

Fresh local government and presidential elections were scheduled for February 1994, but the chances for successfully holding elections under the prevailing circumstances were remote.[35] Indeed, the SDP governors resolved in September to prevent the NEC from conducting a fresh presidential election, and in November three members of the party – Tade Ipadeola, I. Udoh and P.C. Agwu – secured an order from a Lagos high court restraining the SDP from initiating candidate selection procedures for the elections. Shonekan's promise to consider unbanning Abiola so that he could contest the proposed election did not change the situation. The efforts to resolve the crisis were also extended to the international arena. Missions were sent to various capitals abroad to 'explain' the situation in Nigeria, persuade Western countries to lift the limited sanctions already imposed, and bring back foreign investors. Shonekan even attended the Commonwealth summit in Barbados to assure the international community that things were returning to normal.

---

[35] Funds were nevertheless allocated to the NEC (N150 million) and the parties (N100 million each), and the prospects of fresh elections generated some political activity. Still, it was unlikely that elections could be held.

But the task of arresting the drift towards disintegration and anarchy proved far beyond the capacity of an ING whose legitimacy was questioned and seemed ultimately powerless. Two events finally accelerated the government's collapse. First was the decision to increase the petrol price from 70k. a litre first to N5 and later to N3.25. The increase was justified in terms of 'appropriate pricing', reducing the huge budget deficit (one of N28.6 billion was built into the 1993 budget), bringing down inflation, and meeting the rising costs of oil production and servicing of refineries, all of which made 'economic' sense. But to an already hard-pressed and hungry population none of this made sense. Instead the increase put the society on the boil once again, led to the withdrawal of what little support the ING had, and for unrelenting supporters of 12 June provided the much-needed reinvigoration. The NLC led the flood of opposition by presenting the government with a seventy-two-hour ultimatum to rescind the increase, after which workers in all sectors went on strike. This was accompanied by rioting in Lagos and other cities in the South demanding the dissolution of the ING. Although most workers in the Northern states refused to join the strike, the new round of chaos badly rocked the interim government. Meanwhile Abiola had returned to the country, and his tough stance on actualising his 'mandate' gave added impetus to the struggle.

Then came the second event which sounded the death-knell of the ING. This was the judgement delivered on 10 November 1993 by Mrs Justice Dolapo Akinsanya of the Lagos high court on the suit filed by Chief Abiola and his vice-presidential candidate Babagana Kingibe challenging the annulment of the 12 June election, and seeking the nullification of the ING. Justice Akinsanya ruled that the ING's empowering decree (no. 61) was illegal since at the time when Babangida signed it, he no longer had the legislative authority to do so. She accordingly declared the ING null and void, and directed that steps be taken to restore the annulled presidential election and give effect to the 1989 constitution as the only valid law by which the country could be governed after 26 August. The ING appealed against the ruling on the grounds that the Lagos high court had erred in treating Decree 61 as an ordinary statute rather than a supreme law; and that consequently the ING was a legal government. But this appeal was not to be because in the midst of the confusion and increased anxiety, the military quietly eased out Shonekan and the ING in yet another coup. This marked the end of the Babangida years. Space does not permit any further assessment of the ING. It suffices to say that the circumstances under which it was born and its apparent subordination to military masters made it, from the very start, very unlikely to succeed. A government of national unity headed by Abiola would arguably have been more successful.

THE INTERNATIONAL CONTEXT

As is well known, the United States and other Western powers played crucial roles in the wave of democratisation which swept across Africa in the 1980s and 1990s. Although in most African countries internal pressures for democratic change had a long history, the nature and final outcome of the struggles were greatly influenced by what came to be known as the 'international community factor'. The transition in Nigeria attracted considerable attention because of the country's 'superpower' status in sub-saharan Africa. Although Babangida's bold economic reforms were applauded by the World Bank and Western creditors, Western governments were not oblivious to the domestic scepticism about the convoluted transition programme. This accounts for the immediate US reaction to the initial attempt to scuttle the presidential election through the court order secured by the ABN on the eve of the election (some commentators believe that the quick response dissuaded the regime from postponing the election).

The reactions to the annulment of the election were also immediate. The United States and most Western countries (notably Britain and France) immediately slammed limited sanctions on the country, although the hesitation of some like Germany to do so weakened their effects. Britain for example withdrew its official military team from the Nigerian War College, and placed restrictions on visas to government officials and military officers as well as members of their families. Other Western countries acting through the EU imposed similar sanctions, and bilateral aid agreements were suspended. The threats to impose further sanctions and other interventionist and provocative pronouncements, especially by the United States, were a major source of encouragement to the pro-12 June movement. At one stage there were strong rumours of a possible Noriega-type or Haiti-type direct intervention by the United States, and many ordinary followers of the movement pinned strong hopes on such an intervention, but by the end of October 1993 the Shonekan-led ING succeeded in persuading many countries to relax their tough stance against Nigeria (as reflected in the return of ambassadors withdrawn at the height of the crisis), but the return of the military, ending all hope of democratisation in the short run, isolated the country once more.

The Babangida regime had a twofold response to 'foreign intervention'. First it tried to arouse the deep nationalism and resentment of imperialist intervention for which Nigerians are well known, by constantly reiterating that the crisis was a Nigerian affair. As he said in his 26 June broadcast,

> 'The presidential election was not...imposed on us by the United Nations or...some global policemen of democracy. It was a decision embarked upon independently by the government of our country.[...] The action by...foreign countries is most unfortunate and highly regrettable. There is nowhere in the history of our country or indeed of the third world where these countries can be said to love Nigeria or Nigerians any more than the love we have for ourselves and for our country.'

However, as Babangida discovered, this strategy could only succeed if the government was popular. Secondly, the regime adopted the old cold war tactic of playing off one camp against the other. In the same broadcast, he appreciated the 'patience and understanding' of France, Germany and Russia and condemned those who regarded themselves as the policemen of democracy. This strategy also failed as the sustained harassment by the United States in particular overcame whatever support was forthcoming from these other countries.

FOREIGN POLICY

We close this chapter with a brief look at foreign policy in the Babangida years which, like other spheres in this period, was quite eventful. Although its cardinal points – national interest, Afrocentricity, goodneighbourliness and greater integration in the West African sub-region – remained basically unchanged, the period witnessed certain experiments and bold initiatives which reinforced the country's claim to being a power in Africa. The most notable among these were the attempt to organise a 'concert of medium powers' and the introduction of the Technical Aid Corps scheme under the foreign ministership of Bolaji Akinyemi, the 'economic diplomacy' initiative, the active response to the perceived threat from apartheid South Africa, the opening of diplomatic ties with Israel, and the deployment of a peacekeeping mission to war-torn Liberia.

Nigeria enjoyed some good moments under Babangida. In 1990 General Joseph Garba became president of the 44th session of the UN General Assembly, while Emeka Anyaoku emerged as secretary-general of the Commonwealth. The government also sponsored General Obasanjo's bid for the office of UN secretary-general. Despite being unsuccessful, it was a high point of the country's rising international profile. But, as with previous regimes, there was little or no coherence in the foreign policy initiatives. This was even more serious in the

Babangida years as the foreign policy arena greatly reflected the confusion and political turbulence in the domestic scene. For example, the minister of external affairs was changed five times (Akinyemi, General Ike Nwachukwu, Rilwanu Lukeman, again Nwachukwu and Matthew Mbu). As in previous chapters, we analyse here Babangida's foreign policy at three levels: the West African sub-continent, Africa continent-wide, and the larger international society.

At the West African sub-regional level, goodneighbourliness and ECOWAS remained the fulcrum of foreign policy. In pursuit of the former, borders closed for long periods under Buhari were reopened. Nigeria also mediated, with varying degrees of success, in the seemingly intractable Chadian crisis, the border clashes between Mali and Burkina Faso, and the disputes between the leaders of Togo and Ghana. But the decision to initiate the peacekeeping mission in Liberia under the aegis of ECOWAS stood out as the most remarkable and historic sub-continental peace initiative. It was influenced by a number of factors, including the close personal relations between Babangida and the then Samuel Doe, president of Liberia which led Nigeria to support Liberia in several ways before the war;[36] the evolution of a regional approach to solving regional problems which was welcomed by the UN, whose peacekeeping capacity was overstretched; the reluctance of the United States and other powers to intervene; and the potential threat of the Liberian civil war to the collective security of the sub-continent.

The last factor, which caused Ghana, Sierra Leone, Gambia, Guinea and other countries readily to support Nigeria's initiative, had to do with what was perceived as a grand design by Gadaffi's Libya to destabilise the sub-region and install puppet regimes in the different countries. Using Burkina Faso as a springboard, Gadaffi sponsored Charles Taylor's declaration of war in Liberia, which was to be only the first stage of a well-planned process (which quickly spread to Sierra Leone). The intricate involvements of Côte d'Ivoire, Sierra Leone and Guinea, Liberia's neighbours, in the war easily made it a sub-continental affair, and Nigeria's deployment of troops to help the Sierra Leonian government ward off the rebels associated with Taylor's NPFL in Liberia was part of its strategy to 'contain' the crisis (cf. Nwolise, 1992; Sesay, 1995, 1996; Osaghae, 1996). This was the background to the formation of the ECOWAS Monitoring

---

[36] Among others, the Nigerian government contributed US$2 million to establish a graduate school of international studies at the University of Liberia which was named after the Nigerian president, funded the construction of the trans-African highway linking Liberia with Sierra Leone, and supplied weapons to the Doe government in the war against Charles Taylor's NPFL long before ECOMOG was initiated.

Group (ECOMOG) after the failure of several attempts by ECOWAS leaders to reconcile Doe and Taylor. The complexity of the issues in the war – opposition to ECOMOG by Côte d'Ivoire and Burkina Faso, which tended to divide ECOWAS; the involvement of the United States, Russia, France and other foreign powers; Charles Taylor's NPFL's long-drawn-out opposition to Nigeria's intervention on account of Babangida's closeness to Doe; and the lack of clarity of ECOMOG's mission and mandate (peacekeeping, peacemaking or peace enforcement?) – strongly militated against ECOMOG's success.

The aspect of Nigeria's involvement in ECOMOG that interests us here is the fact that many Nigerians were hostile towards the ECOMOG initiative, which they saw as an extension of Babangida's personalisation of the country's affairs. But of greater concern was the wastage of the country's dwindling resources and the huge losses of soldiers and weapons in the protracted war. Nigeria was the chief financier of ECOMOG, although the United States backed Nigeria's initiative and at various points made financial and logistics contributions, including US$2.8 million in 1990. The exact size of Nigeria's total expenditure was not known, but was believed to have been a major waste-pipe for the country's revenue from 1990 – the windfall from oil sales during the Gulf war is believed to have been wasted on Liberia. Babawale (1995) estimates N470 million, following the original overall ECOMOG budget of N500 million, but other estimates put Nigeria's total expenditure at over N2.8 billion (*African Guardian*, 28 September 1992). Domestic hostility, the mismanagement of the country's resources in the name of ECOMOG and the apparent complication of the intractable civil war in Liberia due to ECOMOG's intervention cast a shadow over what was without doubt a pioneering and commendable foreign policy initiative (cf. Vogt, 1992).

On the larger plane, Nigeria did a lot to reactivate ECOWAS which went into a rapid decline in the early 1980s. It continued to carry the bulk of the organisation's budget (its average annual contribution was 33.3 per cent), maintain its secretariat, host its summits (in 1986, 1987 and 1991), chair the organisation when no other country was willing to do so and provide various forms of support to member states including, most notably, oil concessions and financial aid. Nigeria also championed the restructuring of ECOWAS in other important spheres. In 1990 a comprehensive trade liberalisation scheme involving a staggered relaxation of the restriction on the free movement of unprocessed goods, handicrafts and industrial goods was adopted. This complemented the minimum agenda for action, which entailed signing the second phase of the protocol on the free movement of persons, goods and services, as well as implementing the ECOWAS insurance scheme. As part of the moves towards monetary cooperation Ecobank and the West African Clearing House were established. Despite these strides, the growth of ECOWAS continued to be retarded by the separatism of the Francophone countries and suspicions of Nigeria's 'big brother' gestures.

At the African continental level, the OAU remained the major channel of the 'traditional' commitments to eradication of apartheid in South Africa, liberation of the entire continent from colonial rule, and the advancement of unity. Babangida became the OAU chairman in 1991 when Nigeria hosted the organisation's summit, although the extravagance of the hosting was condemned by a critical press. In 1986, Nigeria led thirty-two other countries in boycotting the Commonwealth games in Edinburgh, Scotland, in protest at Britain's reluctance to apply comprehensive sanctions against the apartheid regime, and continued to function as an honorary frontline state; and its financial contributions to the liberation movements were maintained from both private and official donations to the South African Relief Fund and Namibia Solidarity Fund. In 1989, for example, SWAPO was given US$1.5 million, the ANC US$1 million and the PAC US$600,000. Nigeria continued to chair the UN committee on apartheid, and Obasanjo's appointment to the Commonwealth's Eminent Persons Group was a recognition of its role in the liberation struggle. The release of Nelson Mandela from jail after twenty-seven years and the subsequent negotiations to end apartheid were celebrated in Nigeria as a major victory. The country continued to play a leading role in the search for a peaceful settlement; evidence of this was its inclusion in F.W. De Klerk's diplomatic shuttle across Africa during the negotiations.

In addition to liberation, Nigeria pursued the goal of African unity and development in other decisive ways. It sought to play mediatory roles in several internal disputes, including those in Angola and Uganda, although most of these were channelled through the OAU. It played crucial roles in the formation of, and signing of the treaty for, the African Economic Community in 1991, as well as the establishment of a conflict resolution department in the OAU. It also made donations in cash and kind to to several countries, largely to make good its image (for example, it assisted Zimbabwe when that country had to host the Non Aligned Movement summit). As OAU chairman in 1991, Babangida strongly articulated the demand for reparations to be paid to Africa by the former colonialists for the ravages of the slave trade and exploitation. But the reparations movement initially championed by M.K.O. Abiola turned out to be no more than a fleeting intellectual pastime. But Nigeria's most notable African policy innovation by far was the introduction of the Technical Aid Corps scheme (TAC) in 1987. Conceived along the lines of the peace corps in the United States, the scheme involved the secondment of Nigerian graduates and professionals – doctors, engineers, lawyers, teachers and others – to various African, Caribbean and Pacific countries, entirely at Nigeria's expense. The programme greatly boosted the country's status as a major contributor to African development.

Finally, at the global level, Nigeria maintained its pro-Western posture in trade and other socio-economic and political relations.[37] Its debt overhang and the SAP, whose success depended partly on external funds, reinforced this slant. Indeed, debt rescheduling, procurement of more credit lines and promotion of foreign investment were the main themes of the so-called 'economic diplomacy' which was vigorously pursued under Nwachukwu. Nigeria remained a committed member of OPEC, which continued to peg member countries' production quotas in its bid to shore up oil prices in the world market.

In 1987 however, largely to strengthen the use of the oil weapon by African countries, following the example of the Organization of Arab Petroleum Exporting Countries (OAPEC), and as part of 'economic diplomacy', Nigeria joined Algeria, Angola, Benin, Libya, Cameroon, Gabon and Congo to establish the African Petroleum Producers Association, APPA (Côte d'Ivoire, Egypt, Zaire and Equatorial Guinea joined in later years). The main objective of APPA was to promote cooperation among member states in hydrocarbon exploration, production, refining, petrochemicals, manpower development and acquisition and adoption of technology. APPA never became any serious strategic benefit to Nigeria, since member states found it difficult to reconcile their divergent interests. OPEC therefore remained the country's main collective platform for employing the oil weapon.

Nigeria also remained committed to the UN, the Commonwealth and the Non Aligned Movement through which positions on major global issues were articulated. As we saw, it became a full member of the Organization of Islamic Countries (OIC), but this had no significant impact on foreign policy, except for the emergence of Islamic financial institutions in the country. As for specific relations, the Babangida regime restored normal relations with Britain, strengthened existing relations with Germany and France, and established diplomatic links with Israel – a major achievement considering the historical opposition of conservative Northern Muslims to relations in that quarter.

---

[37] In 1993, 44.1 per cent of Nigeria's exports, mainly crude oil, went to the United States, 6.8 per cent to Germany and 5.9 per cent to France, while 14.0 per cent of imports was from Britain, 13.1 per cent from the United States, 10.1 per cent from Germany and 8.3 per cent from France.

Babangida's virtual dependence on Israeli security was crucial to the restoration of tries.

All this should not be taken to suggest that the international community was supportive of Nigeria in the Babangida years. The country's emergent image as a major channel in the world drug trade (cf. Klein, 1994) led, among other consequences, to the decertification of the country by the United States, resulting in a blocking of aid, and the placing of an embargo on direct flights between the United States and Nigeria. This was a major foreign policy problem, but a more serious problem with the international community, especially the United States and other Western powers, arose over the scuttling of the democratic transition process. The Western powers lent material and other capacity-building forms of support to the non-governmental organisations and pro-democracy movement which spearheaded the stirring of civil society and forced Babangida out of office – at one point, Vice-President Aikhomu referred to pro-democrats as lackeys of foreign powers, by which they were sponsored for 'subversive' activities. The anti-militarism of the Babangida years and after was also encouraged by the favourable and supportive international opinion and the direct criticisms and opposition to military regimes by Western powers.

7

THE ABACHA REGIME, 1993-1996

The Abacha regime is likely to go down in history as the most harassed government in Nigeria's post-independence history. The harassement which came from within and outside the country and involved intense opposition and hostility towards the regime from its very beginning gave it little or no room for any serious reflections on, or coherent response to, the complex problems facing the country. Admittedly the regime's own blunders – continued repression, the trial and conviction of officers accused of plotting to overthrow the regime, the killing of the Ogoni nine in defiance of world opinion – were partly to blame, but even these could be seen as part of its response to the hostile milieu and the survival imperative. The authoritarian prism through which most actions of the regime were regarded over-shadowed its underlying though poorly articulated nationalism and inward-looking character, which brought it close to the Buhari regime of old. The nationalist approach to the economic crisis which led, among other things, to the abrogation of liberalisation policies in 1994 and an adamant attitude to Western creditors; the attempts to 'sanitise' the country, which seemed to be targeted at the 'sacred cow' elites; and the involvement of key actors of the Buhari regime (including General Buhari himself) in strategic aspects of administration were some of the manifestations of this.

THE NATURE OF ABACHA'S INTERVENTION AND RULE

On 17 November 1993, General Abacha announced that he had accepted the 'resignation' of Ernest Shonekan and had 'dutifully' taken over as head of state to save the country from drifting further into collapse. The projection of the military coup as a voluntary relinquishment of power by the defeated regime was a deliberate ploy to make the new regime acceptable. An announcement of a coup would in all probability have turned the anti-military zeal of civil society against the regime, despite growing demands for the military to intervene because of the inability of the ING to deal with the worsened national crisis.

However, from the very beginning the regime faced hostility from the Western powers. The British foreign secretary, Douglas Hurd, stated that Britain would not tolerate a return to military rule and would consider the imposition of further sanctions. The US State Department condemned the take-over and warned that 'Further measures to frustrate democracy will result inevitably in increased confrontation with the international community.' At home there were mixed reactions. Given the obvious inability of the ING to deal with the deepening political and economic crisis and the fact that there had been clamours for the military to intervene, there was a muted welcome for the take-over, but many who welcomed it expected no more than a short-lived rescue operation. There were a few demonstrations against the coup by university students in Ibadan, Ife and Lagos, while sixty-seven senators issued a statement asking Nigerians to rise up against the military in defence of their rights. However, ordinary people simply adopted an expectant wait-and-see attitude, hoping that the new regime would be able to take the country out of the abyss.

The problems of credibility and acceptance which beset the regime were daunting. First it faced the difficult task of distancing itself from the Babangida regime (although it should be noted in passing that Abacha refrained from any direct criticism of it, and its alliance with key actors of the Buhari regime was part of this distancing game). So too were the ousting of the so-called Babangida boys from the military which began soon after Babangida stepped aside, the termination of the long-drawn-out transition programme and, for one year (1994), of the SAP, and the mostly cosmetic institutional changes. In terms of institutional changes, Abacha reverted to the appellation of head of state, and that *de facto* Number Two, General Oladipo Diya, was once again called Chief of General Staff (CGS); the apex ruling council was now called the Provisional Ruling Council (PRC)[1] and initially had civilian members; and agencies and programmes like MAMSER and the Better Life Programme (BLP) were rechristened: MAMSER became 'War Against Indiscipline and Corruption' (WAIC), while the BLP became the Family Support Programme (FSP) and, like its predecessor, was overseen at the federal level by the head of state's wife, and at the state and local levels by the wives of governors and chairmen. But by far the most serious institutional changes involved the abrogation of the transition programme and the dissolution of all democratic structures – political parties and all elected legislative and executive bodies at all levels of government.

---

[1] 'Provisional' was apparently chosen to suggest that the regime would not stay in power for too long.

Alongside building an autonomous image was the equally important task – perhaps more important – of building popular support and legitimacy. Here, although the overall civil society disposition was hostile to military rule, the regime had the advantage of open invitations by critical elites and sections of the press to the military to intervene and execute a 'quick-fix' operation to restore the country's fortunes. The invitations were critical because they came mostly from supporters of the restoration of 12 June who wrongly thought that, with Babangida out of the way, the top officers who survived Babangida's last-minute 'revenge' retirements, and whom the press had represented as supporters of restoration (including Generals Abacha and Diya who were said to have 'eased out' General Babangida), could intervene to install Abiola in power. Abiola himself praised General Abacha at a public reception in Kaduna in September 1993 for using his 'love of country, common sense, intellect and experience' to ease out Babangida, and believed he could use the same means to ease out Babangida's 'surrogates'. This was the underlying reason in the calls for military intervention by, among others, Adesuyi Haastrup, deputy governor of Osun state; Chukwuemeka Ezeife, governor of Anambra state; Gani Fawehinmi, frontline radical lawyer and pro-democracy activist; Bolaji Akinyemi, former external affairs minister (who wrote an open letter of invitation in the newspapers to General Abacha, then ING's secretary of defence), and Wole Soyinka (who defended the invitations on the grounds that the military were only being called to clear up the mess it created and not to rule). Making a point similar to Soyinka's, *The Guardian*, well respected for its critical views, called on the military 'as the only national institution that can act as the ... honest broker in the process of reconciliation' to convene a meeting of genuine national leaders to negotiate and form a government of national unity on the basis of the 12 June election (*The Guardian* editorial, 4 October 1993).

Another form of invitation involved consultations General Diya held with CD traditional leaders and other prominent political leaders before the coup. 'Since none of these openly opposed the action taken against the ING', Ihonvbere (1996: 195) has argued, 'it could well be assumed that they directly and/or indirectly supported the coup, and such tacit approval was later to constrain their ability to oppose the military.' These open and covert invitations did not go unchallenged. Most significantly the National Assembly, whose role in national affairs grew in prominence during the crisis, condemned them – the House of Representatives passed a resolution of 5 November in which they were condemned as self-seeking, unpatriotic and un-democratic.

But the most crucial invitation to the military in general, and to General Abacha in particular, was from Abiola himself. During his exile abroad he had been negotiating with Abacha and other segments of the military whom he believed could act to restore his 'mandate'; as he himself confessed, he only returned from abroad after 'clearing' his move with them. At the Kaduna reception referred to above, he openly invited the military to resolve the lingering political crisis. It is not known what deal he struck with the military men who took power on 17 November (he held meetings with Abacha immediately after the coup, and these were widely reported in the press), but there can be no doubt that he welcomed the new regime, and even – perhaps inadvertently – gave it a measure of legitimacy. By nominating Babagana Kingibe, his vice presidential running mate, and other close allies like Iyorcha Ayu and Solomon Lar to serve in the new government,[2] Abiola seemed to have transferred his 'mandate' to the new regime – as the regime claimed. In all likelihood Abiola expected that his gesture would be reciprocated by the regime handing over power to him after a brief stay, but if this supposition is correct, he failed to realise the full implication of the dissolution of all democratic structures. In particular, with the abolition of the two parties and the NEC and establishment of full-scale military rule, the foundations of Abiola's claim to victory had been destroyed. It was only after Abiola realised the 'grand deceit' that he reactivated his claims to powers, plunging the country into a new round of turbulence.

The open invitations became the focal point of the regime's defence of its intervention. In his broadcast to the nation at the height of the political crisis in June 1994 the head of state alluded to the fact that 'critical elements within the society openly invited the armed forces to intervene to secure the territorial integrity and sovereignty of the Nigerian state.[...] This administration came in to perform a mission of national salvation.' In a similar vein, Nwabueze (1994: 150) defends the regime 'because it was invited, overtly as well as covertly, by the very same people behind the popular resistance to military rule'. It is true that invitations were made, but the whole question of invitation raises certain critical issues. To begin with, the military had the option of refusing an invitation made by only a tiny section of the elite. After all, there were no significant invitations from the Northern and Eastern parts of the country and, as the House of Representatives resolution on the invitations said, they were undemocratic, unpatriotic and self-serving. Moreover, the invitations were

---

[2] Sixteen of the thirty-three ministers in Abacha's cabinet were vocal supporters of the restoration of 12 June.

for a brief stay or even for no more than an intervention to facilitate the restoration of democracy based on the 12 June presidential election. Yet what followed was full-fledged military rule based, like previous military regimes, on the Constitution (Modification and Suspension) Decree no. 107 of 1993 from which the ouster clauses of subsequent decrees derived. Points like these do not necessarily invalidate the invitation thesis, but they suggest the possibility of other reasons for the return of the military.

In any case, the regime clearly needed more than the invitations to make itself acceptable to the citizenry because, as has been pointed out above, there was a palpable anti-militarism in the civil society. It sought to use the composition of the cabinet and appointments to other top positions to mobilise popular support. Respected and popular leaders, most of them politicians, were appointed to the cabinet, which came to appear similar to Gowon's powerful and national war cabinet.[3] The composition of the cabinet, as the head of state said in a national broadcast on 17 August 1994, reflected the 'compromises and good faith received from all parties' in the task of resolving the political crisis.

Before the recomposition of the PRC in September 1994 and the cabinet reshuffle of January 1995, there were only two military ministers – the minister of defence (Abacha himself) and the Federal Capital Territory minister, Lt.-General Jeremiah Useni. Three civilian ministers also sat on the PRC: Onagoruwa (attorney general), Ibru (internal affairs) and Kingibe (external affairs). But once the regime consolidated its hold on power, many politicians and activists, who spent most of their time defending their roles in the increasingly alienated regime, were dropped – Babatope, Jakande, Rimi, Lar, Ayu, Gana, Okilo, Onagoruwa, Ciroma and Ibru. The appointment of hardliners like Walter Ofonagoro who became information minister, Tom Ikimi (foreign

---

[3] The civilians appointed ministers were Solomon Lar, Second Republic governor of Plateau state and member of former SDP (police affairs); Lateef Jakande, former populist governor of Lagos state and SDP presidential aspirant (works); Abubakar Rimi, former 'progressive' governor of Kano state (SDP, telecommunications); Jerry Gana, former MAMSER director and SDP presidential aspirant (information) Iyorcha Ayu, former senate president (SDP, education) Alex Ibru, publisher of *The Guardian* (internal affairs) Olu Onagoruwa, prominent lawyer and human rights and pro-democracy activist (attorney general and justice); Samuel Ogbemudia, former military and civilian governor of the old Bendel state (NRC, labour and productivity); Babagana Kingibe, former national chairman of the SDP and Abiola's running mate (foreign affairs); Ebenezer Babatope, 'progressive' politician and 12 June supporters (SDP, aviation); Melford Okilo, former governor of Rivers state (NRC, commerce and tourism); Bamanga Tukur, former NRC presidential candidate (industry and technology); Kalu I. Kalu, former finance minister and major architect of the SAP under Babangida (finance); and Adamu Ciroma, elder statesman and former NRC presidential aspirant (agriculture).

affairs), and Wada Nas (special duties) and the retention of others like Kingibe, who was moved to the powerful internal affairs ministry, signalled a major shift in the regime's orientation from soft to hard authoritarianism. According to *Africa Confidential*, the constant re-placement of service chiefs and retirement of senior officers were partly due to this tougher posture.[4] The regime's shift, as we analyse below, was largely due to the heightened hostility from the civil society, whose unrelenting protests in 1994 threatened its survival.

The regime's legitimation schemes also included, at the initial stages, the abrogation of liberalisation policies in 1994 (discussed below), and the promise to appoint civilian administrators and later deputy administrators in the states, as well as to convene a constitutional conference 'with full constituent powers' as demanded by pro-democracy activists and ethnic minority movements. The regime reneged on some of these promises, notably the appointment of civilian ad-ministrators. It also embarked on a corrective and anti-corruption crusade which steadily increased its popularity rating in spite of the pervasive hostility. The crusade, according to General Diya, the CGS, was aimed at cleansing society of indiscipline and entrenching probity, accountability and efficient management. It began with the setting up of panels to probe several 'sick' and 'corrupt' departments and agencies of government: the Customs, the Nigeria Ports Authority (NPA), the Central Bank of Nigeria (CBN); Nigeria Telecommunication Ltd (NITEL); the Nigeria Electric Power Authority (NEPA); the NNPC; the Nigeria Airports Authority (NAA); and, most important of all, the judiciary which had been badly battered in the final months of the Babangida regime. The reports of these panels were the basis of the 'purges' and restructuring carried out in the agencies (like the take-over of revenue collection in the ports by private agencies, the sacking of top officials in the NNPC, NPA, NEPA, NITEL and NAA; and the closing of business centres whose fraudulent activities denied NITEL revenue). State governments also set up panels to recover public funds and property believed to have been stolen by members of state executives and legislatures in the wake of the political crisis. Huge sums of money, vehicles and other property were recovered from former governors and other political functionaries.[5]

The report of the panel on the CBN (headed by Pius Okigbo, a respected economist), contained some of the most sensational findings.

---

[4] The service chiefs said to have been retired for being softliners were Vice Admiral Allison Madueke (chief of naval staff), Major-Generals Chief Alli and Alwali Kazir (chiefs of army staff) and Air-Vice-Marshal John Femi (chief of air staff).

[5] Some state military administrators (cf. Col. Obademi of Benue state) even went as far as to ban guilty functionaries from holding public office for life.

The panel probed the famous 'dedicated' and other special off-shore accounts operated by the Babangida regime, into which the proceeds from crude oil sales which had been earmarked for special projects were paid. The panel found that between September 1988 and 30 June 1994 a total of US$12.4 billion (including proceeds from the Gulf War windfall) was

> ... spent on what could neither be adjudged as genuine high priority, nor truly regenerative investment.[...] Neither the president nor the Governor of the CBN accounted to anyone for these massive and extra-budgetary expenditures.[...] These disbursements were clandestinely undertaken while the country was openly reeling from the crushing external debt overhang. (Okigbo panel, cited in *African Business*, London, January 1995: 24)

The panel observed that judicious use of the sum unaccounted for would have lightened the country's foreign exchange problems, changed the attitudes of creditors, and improved the investment climate. Its finding generated considerable excitement, since they confirmed the financial recklessness and lack of probity of the Babangida regime, especially after the CBN was placed under the direct supervision of the presidency. However, the Abacha regime failed to follow up on the finding – as it might have done by, for example, putting the former head of state and the former CBN governor on trial, as public opinion expected him to (this would undoubtedly have had a tremendous impact on the regime's popularity both within and outside the country). Many attributed this failure to military *esprit de corps* and the fact that the accounts were still being operated (the Okigbo Panel reported an increase in the volume of dedicated oil from 105,000 bpd to 150,000 bpd in 1994 – Economist Intelligence Unit, 1994: 23).

Despite the disappointment over the missing funds, the regime's corrective crusade received some acclaim as it extended its reach. What excited many people about the crusade, as could be gleaned from contributions to newspapers and magazines, was the unprecedented and 'fearless' manner in which it was executed. No one was spared, not even the powerful and wealthy elites from all sectors previously considered 'untouchable' and 'sacred'. These included the revered Sultan of Sokoto; Ibrahim Dasuki, who was sacked and arraigned before the failed banks tribunal (he was later acquitted); General Olusegun Obasanjo, former head of state and widely regarded as an elder statesman, and his former deputy Shehu Yar'Adua, who were tried and convicted for their alleged involvement in a coup to topple the regime; senior military officers who were tried for corruption, notably five who served as interim governors in the first few weeks of the new regime; top bankers and business men, and so on. In a sense the killing of Saro-Wiwa was consistent with this no 'sacred cow' policy, and there were persistent rumours that Babangida was going to be put on trial.

Most of the rich and powerful were affected by the Failed Banks Decree, under which directors, top management and debtors of collapsed and distressed banks (these were mostly ones which emerged in the SAP era) were tried by special tribunals for a broad range of fraudulent practices. Those found guilty were sentenced on conviction to long jail terms and asked to refund millions of naira. The former Sultan was put on trial over the N775 million unpaid loans from companies of which he was a director – Nigercafe and Foods (West Africa) Ltd. And Afro Continental (Nigeria) Ltd. – owed the liquidated Alpha Merchant Bank and Republic Bank. However, this was not the grounds for his dethronement and subsequent detention; according to the government, this had to do with acts of disrespect towards the head of state among others. (Alhaji Maccido, whom Dasuki had 'defeated' as the favoured candidate of the Babangida regime in the contest to become Sultan, was appointed to that position.)

Abacha's bold war on the rich and powerful won him muted popular acclaim – some contributors to newspaper opinion pages referred to him as the 'man of history' who had been 'sent by God' to work his vengeance on the corrupt and rich elites, the sources of whose wealth were hardly ever apparent. (Cf. 'Is Abacha a messiah or an evil genius?', *The Week*, 3 June 1996). Encouraged by the favourable press reports, the government decided also to set up failed parastatals tribunals to try those responsible for the huge losses suffered in the public sector. But it was difficult for the excitement and popular acclaim generated by this crusade to be transformed into popular support for the regime because it was an isolated event. The basic and more serious problems – political crisis accentuated by the regime's increasingly tough posture, unemployment, retrenchments, inflation, insecurity of life and property – remained, and were in many ways even getting worse. Besides, there was a lot of scepticism about the true intentions of the crusade. The failed banks decree for example, was believed to have been promulgated to recoup the huge sums deposited in the distressed banks by retired and serving military officers – it was indeed strange that although it was precisely retired military officers who formed a significant proportion of bank directors, entrepreneurs and 'money bags', only a few of them (notably General Salihu Ibrahim, retired chief of army staff, and retired General Halidu Hananiya) were arraigned under the decree. This view, however, is partly flawed by the fact that the decree which established the

National Deposit Insurance Corporation (NDIC), the body which investigated and prosecuted the operators of distressed banks, was enacted in 1989. Similarly, the failed parastatals decree was believed to have been aimed at discrediting Abiola and rich pro-democracy activists who were known to be major contractors. But even if the intentions were genuine, questions were raised over what became of previous probes and trials by military regimes (after all, were not former politicians who had been found guilty of corruption by tribunals appointed by the Buhari regime made ministers by the regime?).

Despite some of its fairly progressive steps, the regime continued to face hostility. This was due largely to the lingering economic decline and the political crisis, both of which were complicated by the determination of the Western powers to isolate the regime. These were the main factors for the turbulent uprising of the civil society. We shall consider these issues in turn.

CONTINUED ECONOMIC DECLINE

The regime inherited a most fragile economy made worse by the persistent riots, strikes and other acts of civil disobedience and the resulting state of anarchy which paralysed the country in the aftermath of the annulled 1993 election. The economic indicators for 1993/4 showed the decline. In 1993 real GDP growth rate was 2.6 per cent and fell to barely 1 per cent in 1994, from 8.2 in 1991, 4.7 in 1991 and 3.6 in 1992. Consumer price inflation was officially estimated at 57.2 per cent in 1993 and over 60 per cent in 1994, up from 44.6 per cent in 1992. Unemployment remained high as retrenchments continued in the public and private sectors. All over the country workers, especially primary and secondary school teachers, were owed huge arrears of salaries. Scarce foreign exchange and devaluation kept capacity utilisation low in the manufacturing and industrial sectors. Although oil prices showed marginal recovery, reaching US$16 pb in 1994, the oil sector remained in deep crisis because of the huge debts estimated at $800 million owed to the oil majors by the NNPC, and the reluctance of the majors to expand their investments. This led to a drastic fall in exploration activities: only 500 million barrels of new deposit were produced in 1993, compared to 1.5 billion in 1991, and by 1994 only fourteen drilling rigs in sixteen locations were active, compared to thirty-six active rigs in forty locations in 1991.

The crisis in the oil sector was compounded in January 1994 by the sacking of oil contractors/exporters and their replacement by relatively inexperienced entrepreneurs – mainly Lebanese businessmen and retired military officers. Total new investment, especially from foreign sources, remained low – indeed, massive capital flight and divestment by foreign companies remained the norm. Between 1993 and 1994 some major multinationals reduced their holdings in Nigeria: Standard Chartered Bank sold off about 28 per cent of its shares in First Bank (Nig) plc, thereby reducing its shares to less than 10 per cent; the Wellcome Foundation, a major British pharmaceutical company, sold off its 60 per cent equity in Wellcome (Nig) Ltd to Rumon Services; while Unilever divested its 40 per cent shares in UAC. Budget deficits remained high. In the midst of all this were the unrelenting demands for higher wages and better conditions of service by workers in all sectors, the paralysing strikes to back these demands, sporadic riots, and the generally tense political climate.

The regime responded to the desperate situation with a number of pragmatic measures whose mainstay was the abrogation of liberalisation policies as announced in the 1994 budget speech. Apart from the populist intentions, the decision to abandon market forces and return to a state-controlled economy was strongly influenced by Sam Aluko, the old nationalist and welfarist professor of economics who chaired the powerful Economic Intelligence Unit in the head of state's office, and the team of nationalistic and inward-looking ministers and top government officials, led by Lateef Jakande, minister of works, and Aminu Saleh. Jakande chaired the inter-ministerial task force appointed to oversee the implementation of the new economic policies. The power wielded by these 'economic nationalists' was shown in the sacking of Kalu I. Kalu as finance minister in October 1994 over his intransigent advocacy of liberalisation and criticism of some of the new policies – Anthony Ani was appointed in his place.

At the heart of the new economic regime was the pegging of the naira at an official rate of N22 to US$1, a decision welcomed by most ordinary people and by local manufacturers. But the policy was not well implemented and instead worsened the foreign exchange (forex) situation. For one thing, the supply of forex always fell far short of demand. For example, in September 1994, the Central Bank was able to supply less than $100 million as its auction sales whereas the total bids for forex were over $2.5 billion. The complicated system of forex allocation requiring all applications to pass through the Central Bank made it difficult for the scarce forex to be accessed by genuine manufacturers, industrialists and other end users. An attempt to 'sanitise' and prioritise the system by setting up a foreign exchange committee whose membership included representatives of the finance ministry, the chamber of commerce and the NLC yielded no better results, and ended up creating new rent-seeking opportunities. The resulting scarcity of forex led to sharp increases in the value of the dollar on the black market – the average price went up to N90, but once even hit N105. The government's unsuccessful attempts to wipe out the black market, which was declared illegal, only raised the prices higher.

Because manufacturers and importers were forced to obtain the bulk of their forex through the black market, these increases in the dollar price had a crushing effect on the prices of goods and services. But the system made millionaires of government officials involved in forex allocation, their agents, currency speculators and bankers who got forex at the official rate and sold to buyers at the black market rate. Other policies of regulation included pegging the interest rate at 21 per cent, freezing private domiciliary accounts, local sourcing of raw materials, reimposition of duties on selected goods, and increased government expenditure in the social sector, especially housing and rehabilitation of the infrastructure.

The abrogation of market reforms meant of course that the Abacha regime took on Western creditors – the IMF, the World Bank and the rest – headlong. This was at the expense of debt rescheduling and new trade credits, which the regime tried to circumvent by paying for most imports with cash and later adopting a refurbished counter-trade policy called commodity exchange. In 1994 the arrears on debt servicing stood at $2.5 billion, and it was estimated that if the policies were retained, they could climb to an all-time high of $10 billion. The resolution of the debt overhang seemed a distant hope as the Paris and London Clubs insisted on a return to market reforms and an IMF agreement as their condition for rescheduling. The reluctance of the formulators of Nigeria's economic policies to agree to these was aptly stated by Anthony Ani, the new finance minister, who appealed to the IMF to leave Nigeria alone: 'The IMF should not force any condition on Nigeria as we are finding [our own] solutions to our problems.' (*Daily Times*, 21 October 1994)

But mounting pressures from external creditors and the regime's attempt to impress them in other areas largely accounted for the massive increases in the prices of petroleum products in October 1994. As this proved insufficient to sway the creditors, the government was finally forced, in part by the poor achievements of the new policies and growing opposition to them by critical segments of the civil society, to reintroduce liberalisation policies in 1995. Devaluation was reintroduced and the naira was once again floated (although an official exchange rate of N22 to the dollar was retained) to bring it level with the black market rate of N82-85 to the dollar. The

Exchange Control Act was abolished, the Indigenisation Decree was further relaxed to enable greater participation by foreign investors, and new incentives to attract investors were announced. A new system of contract leasing was also introduced for the management of parastatals, from which the government was reluctant to disinvest.

Foremost among these were the sick refineries which were put up for contract leasing for ten years in the first instance. As this was not sufficient to attract investors the federal government was prodded by the IMF/World Bank to adopt a phased privatization scheme under which the refineries were to be managed by private oil companies in partnership with the federal government for a specified period (initially two years) after which government was expected to divest its holdings (*The Week*, 21 October 1996: 24-5). In other areas like interest rates (dual) exchange rate and removal of subsidies especially on petroleum products the federal government continued to reject IMF prescriptions. Its ability to do so however depended very much on favourable oil prices (which remained stable at US$19-22 pb in 1996) although it was obvious that little economic progress could be made as long as the political scene remained unstable.

The regime however demonstrated a remarkable level of fiscal discipline relative to the Babangida regime and managed to keep budget deficits low (this was however partly due to the fact that oil prices in the world market were ahead of budgetary estimates in 1995/6). The government maintained the policy of paying for imports directly in cash as much as possible, and sought to reduce the dependence of both the federal and state governments on external loans. In the face of increased hostility towards the regime by Western powers, the African Development Bank became an important source of alternative stabilisation funds for the country. However, disagreements with Western non-regional shareholders who attempted to take over control of the bank led the federal government to cancel most loans already secured. (*The Guardian*, 28 May 1996)

The results and consequences of the short-lived regulation regime were mostly negative, well-intentioned as its nationalist authors were. While Jakande and other government functionaries judged them successful, pointed to higher industrial and agricultural production, and claimed to have done more for the peoples' welfare than any other government since General Murtala Mohammed, both the Nigerian Economic Society and the NLC, among others, argued that the new policies worsened the misery of Nigerians. The manufacturers most directly affected by the measures (and who initially supported the pegging of the exchange and interest rates) warned of an imminent collapse of the economy, and pointed to low capacity utilisation (which had fallen to 20-25 per cent), closures and loss of jobs. Even the big companies – UAC, Lever Brothers, Cadbury and so on – who previously declared huge profits recorded shortfalls in production and demand because of inflation.

For the ordinary peoples at the receiving end the quality of life worsened still further. With inflation averaging over 150 per cent (contrary to official figures of 50-60 per cent) and real incomes declining, the costs of essential goods and services – food, rents, transport, health care, education – went far beyond the reach of most families and households. The introduction of value-added tax (VAT) in January 1994 led to further increases in prices. The situation then simply got out of hand with the massive increases in the prices of petroleum products which were far out of tune with income levels. Petrol went up from N3.25 a litre to N11 (N15 was first posted); diesel from N3 to N9 a litre (first N14), and kerosene from N2.75 to N6 (first N11). It was announced that the savings from these subsidy withdrawals, managed by a special trust fund comprising Nigerians of proven integrity, would be used to reactivate the social sector and infrastructural development; the Petroleum Trust Fund (PTF) with General Buhari as chairman and Tayo Akpata, a seasoned bureaucrat, as executive secretary was subsequently set up to manage the funds. But these savings could hardly compensate for the hyper-inflation and increased hardship which followed the increases and the reintroduction of liberalisation policies in 1995. In political terms, increased hardship further alienated the regime and strengthened opposition to it.

On balance, there was little hope of economic recovery. Even after market reforms were reintroduced at the beginning of 1995, and in spite of marked improvements in relations with creditors and the World Bank and fairly stable and high oil prices, the economy remained in dire straits. This was largely due to the self-inflicted political crisis and the regime's external problems. The tempo of the problems increased after the killings of the Ogoni nine in November 1995. Nevertheless, the federal government recorded huge surpluses from oil sales,[6] from domestic sources like VAT,[7] and from Central Bank interventions in the forex market. However, a large proportion of the increased revenue from local sources went into shoring up

[6] For example, the 1995 budget was hinged on $15 pb, but oil prices maintained a high $18 pb average which fetched a surplus of $239 million in the first quarter of the year.

[7] VAT turned out to be a goldmine: N6.58 billion was realised by October 1994, ten months after its introduction, far in excess of the total estimated revenue for the whole year. However, 90 per cent of revenue from VAT was to be allocated to the state governments.

the financial condition of the states and local governments, and rescuing them from their chronic insolvencies. In addition to expanding the stabilisation fund under which grants-in-aid were allocated to the constituent units, 90 per cent of the proceeds from VAT and the PTF went to the states and localities.

<h2 style="text-align:center">A RELUCTANT DEMOCRATIC TRANSITION?</h2>

Given the nature of the invitations extended to the military to intervene, and the circumstances in which the Abacha regime came into being, many expected it to stay briefly in power, execute a well-articulated democratic transition programme, and hand over power to civilians as quickly as possible. Or alternatively, it might complete the Babangida regime's aborted transition and hand over power to Abiola, the acclaimed winner of the 1993 election. But the regime did neither. The termination of the ING's amended transition programme and dissolution of all democratic structures in place at the time the regime took over implied that any programme of democratic transition had to begin again from scratch – new parties, a new electoral body and other institutions, a new constitution and so on. But the regime failed to articulate a clear programme of democratic transition in its early stages, thus generating considerable unease in civil society.

In his inaugural address to the nation, the head of state had promised to convene a constitutional conference with 'full constituent powers' in January 1994 which was seen by some pro-democracy activists as a good foundation for a lasting transition. In another national broadcast on 17 August 1994 at the height of a renewed wave of opposition to his regime, he referred to 'the unflinching commitment of this administration to an early return to civil democratic rule'. The question of how long the regime would stay was left unanswered, to be determined by the conference. But not only was the convening of the constitutinal conference (hereafter called confab) delayed (it began in July 1994 rather than January as announced), but the powers of the 'constitutional' (rather than 'sovereign national') conference eventually convened were more restricted than what the pro-democracy activists demanded. (For the differences between a constitutional conference, whose delegates do not possess final authority, and a sovereign national conference, see Nwabueze, 1994: 153ff; and Nwolise, 1994.) The confab was consequently opposed by a large section of the pro-democracy movement which, among other actions, mobilised people to boycott the election of delegates.

But even setting up the confab and articulating the so-called 'first phase' of the 'transition programme' were thought to have been done reluctantly in response to allegations by retired Brigadier David Mark, one of the so-called 'IBB boys', that the regime planned to stay in power for five years. In a sensational interview in *Newswatch* (4 April 1994) Mark, who claimed to have been one of those who carried out the 17 November coup, alleged that, contrary to the original plan of the coup plotters to stay in power for only one year, the regime had devised a plan to stay on for at least five years, and planned to use the constitutional conference to achieve this end. It was generally believed that it was to refute Mark's claims that a timetable for the 'first phase' of the transition was issued, stipulating the promulgation of a new constitution by the end of December 1994 and removal of the ban on politics on 17 January 1995. However, the confab – described by the head of state as 'the only viable option if we are to avoid the path of chaos and anarchy' – remained the fulcrum of the planned transition.

The process of convening the confab involved setting up a nineteen member National Constitutional Conference Commission (NCCC) to formulate an agenda for the conference based on contributions to a pre-confab debate organised throughout the country (the NCCC claimed to have received over 1,000 memoranda), and recommend a suitable method for selecting delegates. It arrived at thirty items, including a system of government, party system, electoral system, power sharing, revenue generation and allocation, leadership, federal character, civil service, ethnic nationalities, foreign policy, national identity and citizenship, defence and national security, and women in development. Despite opposition from pro-democracy groups and a low voter turnout (the total number of voters all over the country was about 300,000) 273 delegates were elected to join the ninety-six nominated by the federal military govement. The confab was headed by Mr Justice Adolphus Karibi-Whyte.

Given the controversial background to its setting up, the confab suffered from a crisis of credibility and confidence. Assertions like those made by the head of state in his 17 August broadcast, that 'this government made no contribution to the conference agenda and [did not] place any limitation on their discussion', and that 12 June was 'freely discussed', did little to convince cynics that the proceedings of the conference were not remote-controlled. The vacillations of the confab members on the exit date of 1 January 1996 for the regime and failure to complete its assignment in January 1995 as planned were commonly cited as evidence of this.[8]

---

[8] There were back-up allegations in the press that delegates enjoyed fabulous allowances and patronage. For example, *Newswatch* (23 January 1995: 12) reported that in December 1994 each delegate received N75,000 'Christmas bonus', while Muslim delegates were

Notwithstanding its precarious circumstances, the confab did address critical issues of governance, democracy and the 'national question', including 12 June, and sought solutions for them. In the sessions of the Assembly observed by this author, there was evidence that several membes took their task seriously. Delegates from minority oil-producing communities pressed for a new revenue allocation system that emphasised derivation; delegates from Igbo-speaking states sought to redress the marginalisation and neglect of their areas; Southern delegates made a case for a rotational presidency and power-sharing; and so on. Like the constituent assemblies before it, the confab also provided a forum for political associations to be formed in readiness for the lifting of the ban on politics. The various associations that came into being as a result of the conference included the Patriots, later called People's Democratic Alliance, led by Shehu Yar'Adua; the National Unity Club, formed by the 'progressives' including those in Abacha's cabinet; National Consensus, led by Olusola Saraki, Barnabas Gemade and Mahmud Yahaya; Liberal Alliance, led by Mukhtar Ahmed Aruna; New Generation Forum, a Middle Belt outfit, led by Ali Aku; Ndigbo, led by Alex Ekwueme; Middle Belt forum; and Southern minorities forum. Some of the political associations which competed for registration as political parties in 1996 had their origins in these groupings.

However, the greater significance of the confab lay in the decision it came up with in the draft constitution finally submitted after the long delays on 27 July 1995. Notable among the new instrumentalities recommended in this document were a system of rotational presidency, power-sharing based on a multiple vice presidency, a multi-party system, the establishment of a federal character commission, and a new system of revenue allocation placing greater emphasis on derivation. The PRC set up a committee to examine the draft, and by many accounts the military council found it unsatisfactory (cf. *New African* [London], October 1995), and threw it open to public debate. Some of the recommendations were modified, chief among which were the institution of a plural executive comprising president, vice president and prime minister, to facilitate the process of power-sharing among the six zones into which the states were grouped (the presidency of the senate and speakership of the House of Representatives were also to be zoned), and the limitation of the system of rotational presidency to an experimental period of thirty years.

---

sponsored for the lesser *hajj* in addition, and other sources talked of cash donations of N1 million and plots of land in Abuja. The appointment of former delegates to ministerial and other top government positions after the conference seemed to confirm these speculations and allegations.

The idea of rotational presidency – the most significant novelty of the new constitution – as an instrument of power sharing (it is also called the zoning formula) is not new in Nigeria. It was a major point of debate in the CDC in 1975 and was actually recommended by the sub-committee on executive and legislature, which divided the country into two groups of two zones each for the purpose of rotation. The recommendation was rejected for two major reasons: first, the president (and vice-president) were expected to be 'national' rather than sectional leaders, and secondly, given the uncertainty of civilian rule, the rotation of power to all zones could not be guaranteed (FGN, 1976: 67ff). The experience of the NPN, which adopted the zoning formula in the Second Republic, also showed that the 'rules of the game' were no guarantee that power would rotate; incumbent office-holders resisted all attempts to have them give way to candidates from other zones.

The Report of the Political Bureau also noted that many contributors to the national political debate of 1986/7 believed a system of rotational presidency to be necessary for political stability. It nevertheless rejected a constitutional entrenchment of the system on the grounds that 'it amounts to an acceptance of our inability to grow beyond ethnic or state loyalty' (FGN, 1987: 74). Was the adoption of the system by the confab then an acceptance of this inability? Seen against the backdrop of the strong feelings in the Southern parts of the country that the cancellation of the 12 June presidential election and its aftermath was a reflection of the unwillingness of conservative Northern leaders to let power shift to the South, the adoption of the rotational system can be seen as the best assurance for Southerners that they too could share in ruling the country. Its chief advocates in the confab were Southerners and some Middle-Belters – most Northern delegates opposed it, thereby seeming to confirm Southern fears.

Several interesting issues were raised by the adoption which we cannot examine here in any detail. Some are well articulated in the views of the CDC and the Political Bureau, but one point that has not received the attention it deserves is that the whole question of power-sharing and access to power in the federation has been provoked and complicated by persistent military rule. The late premier of the old Mid-Western region, Dennis Osadebey, pointed out that ethnic and regional balance (the main objective of rotation) was one of the 'unwritten ethics' of political office-holding and candidate selection for elections in the First Republic (Osadebey, 1978). There was a similar occurrence in the Second Republic – Awolowo's inability to find a Northerner to be his running mate in 1979 was believed to be a major reason for his failure in the presidential election.

Incessant military intervention and rule destroyed this balancing ethic, although this does not seem to have been deliberate. Coup planning and execution usually involves a close-knit core of officers, and 'federal balance' does not usually come into play – concern with balance would be likely to endanger the success of the coup and the lives of the plotters. It is perhaps for this reason that, with the exception of Ironsi's brief stay, all military regimes have had a preponderance of Northern officers, thus accentuating the problem of so-called Northern domination. As long as the threat of the military remains real, rotational presidency must be meaningless. Thus it is the military question that needs to be resolved – once and for all – since the imperatives of democratic governance are sufficient counterforces to political dominance if allowed to subsist.[9]

Despite completing its assignment and providing the basis for the long-awaited transition timetable, critics judged the confab to have failed because it did not stipulate a date for the regime to cede power. Nevertheless, the government announced that the submission of the draft constitution marked the end of the first phase of the transition. The ban on politics was then 'partially' lifted till 1 October 1995 when a 'comprehensive' transition timetable was to be announced. The programme released on that date is represented in Table 7.1.

Table 7.1. TIMETABLE FOR TRANSITION TO CIVILIAN RULE, 1995-98

1995: LAST QUARTER (OCTOBER-DECEMBER)

1. Approval of draft constitution;
2. Lifting of restrictions on political activities;
3. Establishment of National Electoral Commission (NECON);
4. Creation of Transitional Implementation Committee, National Reconciliation Committee, and Federal Character Commission;
5. Appointment of panel on creation of states, local government, and boundary adjustment.

1996: FIRST QUARTER (JANUARY-MARCH)

1. Election and inauguration of local government councils on a non-party basis;

1996: SECOND QUARTER (APRIL-JUNE)

1. Creation of new states and local governments;
2. Commencement of process of registering political parties;

1996: THIRD QUARTER (JULY-SEPTEMBER)

1. Registration of political parties;
2. Delineation of electoral constituencies;
3. Production of authentic voters register

---

[9] However, in the immediate short-run and to assuage the real fears exacerbated by the 12 June affair, a rotational presidency might be worth trying.

1996: FOURTH QUARTER/FIRST QUARTER 1997

1. Election of local government councils on party basis

1997: SECOND QUARTER

1. Party state primaries to select candidates for state assembly and governorship elections;
2. Screening and approval of candidates by NECON;

1997: THIRD QUARTER

1. State assembly elections

1997: FOURTH QUARTER

1. Election of state governors;
2. Sittings of state election tribunals and conduct of by-elections

1998: FIRST QUARTER

1. Inauguration of state assemblies and governors;
2. Party primaries to select candidates for National Assembly elections;
3. National Assembly election campaigns

1998: SECOND QUARTER

1. National Assembly elections;
2. Party primaries to select candidates for presidential election;
3. Commencement of nation-wide campaigns for the presidential election

1998: THIRD QUARTER

1. Presidential election

1 OCTOBER 1998

Swearing-in of newly elected president and final disengagement.

In its sequence and its staggered elections, the transition programme was similar to that of the Babangida regime, and there were certain detailed aspects that also resembled those of the previous transition. Most notable were the stringent requirements stipulated by the National Electoral Commission (NECON) for the registration of political parties.[10] Nevertheless, about twenty-three political associations, some of which had been waiting in the wings since the Babangida days, applied for registration. Of these eighteen completed registration formalities.

[10] These included payment of N500,000 registration fees, a minimum membership of 40,000 per state and 15,000 in Abuja administrative organisation and executive spread at local state and federal levels, as well as constitution, manifesto and articulation of issues. All these were to be done in two months, after which the electoral commission undertook a verification exercise assessed and ranked the parties, and recommended only those which scored above 50 per cent for registration. The following five scored highest and were accordingly registered: UNCP (75%), CNC (66%), NCPN (63%), DPN (57%) and GDM (54%).

The number later dropped to fifteen after mergers between some associations, as directed by the electoral commission. The merging process led to a temporary suspension of the verification exercise in August 1966. The fifteen associations are listed in Table 7.2. In September 1966, five of these were registered to put the transition programme on course: UNCP, CNC, NCPN, DPN and GDM. However, the new transition programme differed from Babangida's in important ways. It was less crowded, established fewer institutions, did not legally prohibit (this, however, was done through the exclusionary process of party registration, as is discussed below), and did not hinge on the learning of a new political culture (the CDS, which was the school of democracy, was scrapped in 1995) or the creation of a new political order (although from time to time key officials of the regime referred to the entrenchment of probity, discipline and accountability as a necessary condition for the success of the transition).

These differences could not eradicate the deep suspicions which characterised popular perceptions of the transition. These perceptions were based on a number of factors. First, in the background, there was the experience of the transition of the Babangida regime. Frequent interference in the transition process, as when a large number of candidates were disqualified from the local government elections in the first quarter of 1996, the cancellation of some of the results, and the enactment of a decree empowering the head of state to remove any local government chairman on grounds of national interest and security, gave grounds for scepticism. Second was the fact that the transition programme took so long in coming, and appeared to have been forced on the regime by the criticisms and opposition of pro-democracy activists and other elements of civil society as well as the international community, which became impatient at the regime's slow pace of democratisation. For similar reasons, the 1998 hand-over date was considered too long delayed. Third (already referred to) was the regime's increasingly hardline posture.

As the transition programme unfolded, suspicions grew. First was the process and outcome of party registration (see Table 7.2). The suspension of the verificatory exercise by the electoral commission in August 1996 (which was said to be on the regime's orders to allow the political associations to enhance their chances of registration by merging) was seen by many commentators as a way of strengthening the associations which the regime favoured. Second was the fact that the five associations eventually registered were closely identified with members of the regime and its supporters. Those suspected of belonging to opposition elements or likely to become 'too powerful' (PPP, SPP, ANC) were denied registration and proscribed (*The News*,

14 October 1996; *The Week*, 21 October 1996). This way, opponents of the regime and so-called old-brigade politicians were excluded from active participation without the dramatics of legal prohibition that characterised Babangida's transition. Thirdly, there were strong suspicions and rumours that the head of state planned to succeed himself by transforming himself into a civilian president via the ballot box. Not only had this mode of transition been well established in friendly West African states (Ghana, Burkina Faso, Niger, the Gambia) assisted by the Nigerian government, but certain actions of the regime were seen as indicative of this plan. The latter included the launching of *Vision 2010*, a long-term economic blueprint (which a 170-member body headed by Ernest Shonekan was set up to produce), the rising profile of General Abacha as a populist leader, and the spate of 'Abacha-must-stay' rallies and demonstrations in various parts of the country. As for *Vision 2010* in particular, the question was, how could a regime which planned to vacate office in 1998 initiate such a long-term project without involving the newly-registered political parties?

Table 7.2. POLITICAL ASSOCIATIONS WHICH APPLIED
FOR REGISTRATION IN 1996

All-Nigeria Congress (ANC)
Committee for National Consensus (CNC)
Democratic Party of Nigeria (DPN)
Grsssroots Democratic Movement (GDM)
National Centre Party of Nigeria (NCPN)
National Democratic Labour Party (NDLP)
National Democratic Party (NDP)
National Solidarity People's Alliance (NSPA)
Peoples Consensus Party (PCP)
Peoples Progressive Party (PPP)
Peoples Redemption Party (PRP)
Progressive Party of Nigeria (PPN)
Social Progressive Party (SPP)
Solidarity Group of Nigeria (SGN)
United Nigeria Congress Party (UNCP)

The regime was not unaware of the prevalent scepticism, and made conscious efforts to restore and increase the transition programme's credibility. In December 1995 the main transition institutions were established. These were NECON, headed by S.K. Dagogo-Jack and dominated, for the first time, by former politicians; the Transition Implementation Committee, headed by Mr Justice Mamman Nasir, formerly deputy chairman of the confab; the committee on states creation, headed by Arthur Mbanefo; the National Reconciliation Committee, headed by Alex Akinyele; the federal character commission, comprising state representatives, headed by Adamu Fika; and the National Committee on devolution of powers, headed by Abduraman Okenne. These institutions were expected to ensure the programme's successful implementation.

By October 1996, the regime had implemented some crucial transition policies, although in certain ways the transition programme still lagged behind. One of these was the registration of five political parties. Another was the appointment of new state administrators in August 1996, ostensibly to 'consolidate' the transition process. Third, and perhaps most important of all, was the creation of six new states and 138 local government areas on 1 October. This followed the report of the Mbanefo committee on states creation which received eighty-five requests for new states and 3,000 for new local governments, although the whole point of creating new states and localities (which critics argued had little relevance for the country's political and economic problems) was to garner more support for the regime. The new states retained the old principle of North-South balance and were spread equally across the six zones into which the country was divided for purposes of rotational presidency. They were Bayelsa from Rivers; Ebonyi from Abia and Enugu; Ekiti from Ondo; Zamfara from Sokoto; Gombe from Bauchi; and Nassarawa from Plateau (see Table 7.3).

CIVIL SOCIETY ERUPTION: NIGERIA ON THE MARCH AGAIN!

Opposition to the Abacha regime gathered momentum as the first anniversary of the annulment of the 12 June election drew near. It was clear by that time that the regime was not considering a restoration of the election. But the advocates of restoration were more determined than before to fight for it. The renewed struggle began in May 1994 when the National Democratic Coalition (NADECO), a loose coalition of old and new-breed 'progressives' mostly from the South-West of the country, joined by a common desire for the restoration of 12 June, issued an 'ultimatum' to the regime to hand over power to Abiola on 31 May. The successful completion of the transition in South Africa and the inauguration of President Nelson Mandela, which were widely publicised by the media in Nigeria, became a reference point of opposition and seemed to be the tonic needed to reinvigorate civil society. Vigorous campaigns were then launched by the 'opposition' press, the Campaign for Democracy (CD), and other pro-democracy groups, calling for the resignation of the military regime and restoration of the cancelled presidential election and there were increased pressures on Abiola to assert his 'mandate'.

Table 7.3. 1996: THIRTY-SIX STATES

30-state structure	*36-state structure*
Abia	Abia
	Ebonyi[*][†]
Adamawa	Adamawa
Anambra	Anambra
Akwa-Ibom	Akwa-Ibom
Bauchi	Bauchi
Benue	Gombe[*]
	Benue
Borno	Borno
Cross River	Cross River
Delta	Delta
Edo	Edo
Enugu	Enugu
Imo	Imo
Jigawa	Jigawa
Kaduna	Kaduna
Kano	Kano
Katsina	Katsina
Kebbi	Kebbi
Kogi	Kogi
Kwara	Kwara
Lagos	Lagos
Niger	Niger
Ogun	Ogun
Ondo	Ondo
	Ekiti[*]
Osun	Osun
Oyo	Oyo
Plateau	Plateau
	Nassarawa[*]
Rivers	Rivers
	Bayelsa[*]
Sokoto	Sokoto
	Zamfara[*]
Taraba	Taraba
Yobe	Yobe

* New state

† Carved out of Abia and Enugu states

On 30 May, after an earlier meeting of some former members of the National Assembly, fifty-four senators issued a statement signed by Ameh Ebute, former president of the Senate, demanding the immediate restoration of the democratic structures dissolved by the military regime and the declaration of the results of the annulled presidential election. These demands, according to the senators, were based on the 'point of law' that the 'tenure' of the Abacha regime had expired: 'The administration ... commenced on the 17th day of November 1993 purportedly upon the resignation of Chief Ernest Shonekan.[...] It should be noted that by virtue of section 206 of Decree no. 61'...the ING by virtue of which General Abacha succeeded Chief Shonekan expired on the 31st day of March 1994.' (Cited in *Tell*, 13 June 1994: 5) A similar statement was issued by a group of former members of the House of Representatives on 3 June. Ebute and some of the former legislators were promptly arrested. Then, on 11 June, Abiola declared himself president and was declared wanted by the police in Lagos.

What followed was an explosion of civil society which, against all expectations, surpassed in scope and intensity the riots and violent protests that followed the annulment of the election in 1993. One major factor in this was the tremendous support and encouragement the ostensibly pro-democracy groups and protests received from the international community, especially the United States. But the success of the pro-democracy campaigns hinged increasingly on the amount of foreign support they could muster – this was partly because the campaigns lacked the nationwide support required for successful action within the country. Foreign support included the granting of political asylum to 'dissidents', anti-military statements, imposition or threat of imposition of (more) sanctions, and direct and covert material support to the pro-democracy groups. For example, NADECO declared illegal by the Nigerian government – was granted recognition by a resolution of the US House of Representatives and by several Western governments which dealt directly with its leaders and granted them asylum, and received financial aid from the National Endowment for Democracy in the United States, among others (see statement by Bolaji Akinyemi, leader of NADECO abroad in *Newswatch*, 15 May 1995: 13). Non-governmental organisations like Randall Robinson's Trans-Africa, which played a crucial role in shaping US policies on apartheid South Africa, also supported the pro-democracy uprising and lobbied for the imposition of more sanctions.[11]

---

[11] On 7 June, for example, the US State Department issued a statement condemning the arrests of pro-democracy activists and referring to 'the growing scepticism and disillusionment of the people of Nigeria regarding the military's commitment to resolving

The domestic scene, especially Lagos and the South-western parts of the country, remained the main stage for civil society action. The new round of riots and protests provided an outlet for the frustrations of political impotence and economic misery. In Lagos and other cities the properties of prominent leaders believed to be opposed to the restoration of 12 June or supporters of the Abacha regime, or who were in any way 'responsible' for the economic hardship in the country were targeted by rioters. Thus Shonekan and Mrs Kuforiji Olubi (Lagos), Babatope (Ilesha), Lamidi Adedibu (Ibadan), Obasanjo (Abeokuta and Sango Otta), Ogbemudia and Anenih (Benin city) and Aikhomu (Irrua) had their homes vandalised. The protests however were sustained and derived their impact from the participation of various labour unions, which turned economic grievances into demands for political reforms or simply cashed in on the situation to raise the tempo of chaos. By mid-July at least ten unions were on strike, including the National Union of Petroleum and Natural Gas Workers (NUPENG), the Petroleum and Natural Gas Senior Staff Association of Nigeria (PENGASSAN), the Academic staff union of Universities (ASUU), the National Union of Banks, Insurance and Financial Institutions Employees, the National Union of Nurses and Midwives, the Nigerian Union of Teachers and the Senior Staff Consultative Association of Nigeria. The NLC also boarded the bandwagon, but the country-wide strike it called in July failed partly because it could not secure the support of the workers in most of the North and East of the country.

The strikes by NUPENG, led by Frank Ovie Kokori, and PENGASSAN, which were expressly declared to be political, had the most serious consequences because they paralysed the strategic oil sector. NUPENG made a statement defending its political stance: 'Our fate, destiny or life in general, is determined politically. Why then should we not be interested in the politics of our society?' (Wariebi Agamene, chairman of NUPENG, quoted in *African Guardian*, 25 July 1994) PENGASSAN, on the other hand, had underlying economic motives, but appeared to have been instigated by the oil companies which sought to use the union to press its demands from the federal government. Thus it cited as the main grounds for the strike mismanagement, waste in the oil sector (e.g. the hiring of 22 operational coastal tankers by the NNPC at the exhorbitant cost

---

the crisis created by the annulment of the June 12 presidential election'. This was followed by the reiteration of the sanctions imposed earlier in 1993. Then in a resolution on 19 July, at the height of the protests, the House of Representatives foreign affairs committee called, among other things, for the release of Abiola and other political detainees, and endorsed the imposition of sanctions on the military regime by the Clinton administration.

of $10 million per month), and the failure of the federal government to settle debts of over $700 million owed to the oil companies. However, the strike was political because, according to Milchrist Dabibi, the union's secretary-general, 'our travails in the oil industry and the nation generally are closely tied to the political crisis...government must resolve the crisis by respecting the sovereign will of the people as expressed in the last presidential election' (*African Guardian*, ibid.).

The strikes by the oil sector unions, which lasted till August, gave verve to the 12 June restoration protests, and made their impact felt all over the country. They paralysed the country and threatened the very foundation of the oil-based economy. The closure and sabotage of refineries, oil terminals and other installations led to acute shortages of petroleum products in the country, and badly affected oil exports. To meet domestic demands, the government resorted to importing petrol, which was assumed to be one reason for the sharp increases in the prices of petroleum products in October 1994. The position of oil exports was more precarious as production of crude oil quickly dwindled. The government had to act fast to save the economy (and indeed the country) from collapse – in addition to the oil strike, the banks were closed, work generally came to a halt, especially in Lagos, schools were closed, and the panic cross-country mass migrations to home states resumed as rumours and fears of war and political disintegration intensified.

Meanwhile Abiola, who had remained underground, made good his self-declaration as president by getting 'sworn in' in a brief ceremony at Rowe Park in Lagos.[12] He was later arrested, detained and taken to court on treason charges. The process of his trial and application for bail (conditionally granted at one stage but rejected by Abiola's lawyers who wanted free bail), which involved the high courts and courts of appeal in Abuja, Lagos and Kaduna, and got stalled at the Supreme Court, proved dramatic and controversial. The integrity of the judiciary was once again put to the test, as in 1993. The major bone of contention was the impartiality of the judges, which led to demands for the case to be tried in Lagos rather than Abuja or Kaduna in the North. The question of impartiality of the Supreme Court judges, who had an outstanding case in court with the *National Concord* newspaper owned by Abiola over accusations of receiving Mercedes-Benz cars as gratification from the Babangida regime, finally stalled the case, and left Abiola indefinitely in detention.

In its bid to arrest the drift towards anarchy and paralysis, the

---

[12] In his 'proclamation' Abiola called on the Abacha regime to resign, although he indicated his willingness to negotiate a smooth transition. He 'directed' sacked civilian governors to take over in the states and national and state assemblies to reconvene.

government cracked down heavily on pro-democracy groups and labour unions. The executive committees of NUPENG, PENGASSAN and NLC were dissolved and sole administrators appointed to run the unions (Asom Bur for NLC, Ahmed Jalingo for NUPENG and Lasisi Osunde for PENGASSAN). Their leaders, whom government accused of being opportunistic and having vested political interests,[13] were arrested and detained. So also were leaders of the Campaign for Democracy, which was behind the demonstrations in Lagos; NADECO (Anthony Enahoro, Cornelius Adebayo, Segun Osoba, David Jang, Dan Suleiman, Adeniji-Adele, etc), which was declared illegal, and other pro-democracy activists like Gani Fawehinmi. Many NADECO stalwarts seemed to be the targets of clandestine threats to their lives and property, of uncertain origin, and fled abroad. In its search for a resolution of the crisis, the government convened consultative meetings with various segments – traditional rulers, the armed forces, religious leaders, the private business sector, and political leaders (including those who had led NADECO at various times). On the other hand, it adopted a more hardline position by increasing militarisation, as has been referred to earlier. In addition, it issued eight new decrees underlining its toughened posture. These variously extended the period of detention without trial from six weeks to three renewable months, and another which proscribed three independent newspaper groups – publishers of *The Concord, The Guardian,* and *Punch.* By the end of August, it had succeeded in crushing the violent and economically damaging protests – in financial terms, the total cost of the protests from all sectors was estimated at over N167 billion.

The significance of the 1994 uprisings lay not so much in the demands for the restoration of 12 June as in their demonstration that 'the legitimacy and efficacy of military rule have always been vigorously contested' (Joseph, 1996: 193). But there is not a consensus in Nigeria on the military question. The unpopular pro-military or pro-regime activities of the ABN and its successors in the Abacha years[14] are easily dismissed as the work of opportunists or as contrivances to support and prolong the life-span of these regimes, but they do show that there are Nigerians who prefer military rule, largely because

---

[13] Frank Kokori, secretary-general of NUPENG, was said to have been an executive member of a banned political party and his opposition to the regime was attributed to his failure to secure employment as chairman of OMPADEC.

[14] These included the National Democratic Alliance which was formed by former ABN leaders, Jerry Okoro and Thomas Degarr; the Movement for Nigerian Unity which placed an advert in *West Africa* (1 August 1994) describing Abacha's government as the best way forward for the country; Pathfinders Nigeria; Defenders of Democracy; and Pragmatic Forum.

of the poor record of the civilian administrations. We return to this in the concluding chapter. But the most important pointer of the 1994 uprising was that the greatest impediments to the efficacy of civil society and democracy in Nigeria remained the deep ethnic and regional divisions within the country.

This was one of the major reasons for the failure to 'actualise' 12 June in 1993. As we saw, the sectional character of the demands for the actualisation led to the resurgence and strengthening of the irreconcilable 1965/6-type ethno-regional positions. These positions remained unchanged in 1994 as the protests, strikes and riots were concentrated and most effective in Lagos and the South-West of the country – it was the oil workers' strike that gave the uprising its national impact. While almost every segment of the Yoruba-West, including the conservative traditional rulers, rose to demand the restoration of 12 June and, later, the release of Abiola from detention (in fact there were calls on Yoruba ministers in the Abacha regime and delegates in the confab to resign), most civil society elements in the North and East of the country were resolutely opposed to its restoration. There were isolated pro-democracy activities in some minority states like Rivers, Edo and Delta whose citizens seized the opportunity to press their own demands for a more equitable federation, but that was all. Attempts by various Yoruba groups to reach out to these other groups were not very successful; NADECO, which increasingly became the main opposition movement both at home and abroad, was one of the products of such attempts, but although it had some notable non-Yoruba members[15], its leadership and membership profile was mainly Yoruba, and it functioned as the handmaid of *Afenifere*, the club of Yoruba 'progressives' led by Pa Adekunle Ajasin, who also chaired NADECO.

Occupational and class-based organisations did function to some extent to counteract some of the centrifugal forces, as could be seen in the frontline roles played by labour unions, professional associations, student organisations and other groups with more national orientation, but these were constrained by ethno-regional loyalties. One notable development which indicated the evolution of a more nationally-oriented civil society was the emergence of the church as a major pro-democracy group. Church leaders such as Archbishop Abiodun Adetiloye, head of the Anglican church in Nigeria, and Archbishop Olubunmi Okogie

---

[15] The non-Yoruba members of NADECO included Anthony Enahoro, Dan Suleiman, John Oyegun, Ralph Obioha who led the US branch, and in the initial stages retired Commodore Ebitu Ukiwe, Sam Mbakwe, retired Col. Joshua Madaki, Mohammed Arzika, Chukwuemeka Ezeife, Balarabe Musa, retired Rear Admiral Ndubuisi Kanu, Christian Onoh, and retired Group Captain David Jang.

of the Catholic Diocese of Lagos who was a long-standing human rights activist, as well as bodies like the Catholics Bishops' Conferences and the Christian Association of Nigeria (CAN), played leading roles in the pro-democracy civil society uprising. Significantly, Christians in the Northern states who led demands for a secular state, having been at the receiving end of the religious riots of the 1980s and 1990s, also rose in support of the pro-democracy movement. Apart from the Northern zonal and state branches of CAN through which this support was channelled, a new body – the Northern Christian Elders Forum – was formed to contest the more conservative positions of the larger Northern Elders Forum.

But ethno-regional cleavages were not, and have not been, the only impediment to civil society cohesion or, more specifically, to the pro-democracy movement. A more serious impediment was the character and calibre of the leaders of many organisations, who mostly came from the ranks of displaced predator elites. For example, the National Democratic coalition (NADECO) was a coalition of former politicians and retired military officers, some of whom had not only advocated and participated in military regimes, but had records of poor performance as elected politicians. As 'latter-day' converts to democracy, many were regarded with deep suspicion by other pro-democracy groups and as plain opportunists (one or two were said to have joined NADECO after their hopes of 'settlement' by the Abacha regime were dashed). The Campaign for Democracy (CD) explained its refusal to become part of NADECO on the grounds that most of its members were 'unprincipled opportunists who could not be trusted' (*Newsatch*, 15 May, 1995: 13). With such perceptions, which were shared by most of the other groups, it hardly needs to be said that concerted action would have been difficult.

Despite these weaknesses, the civil society demonstrated its strong potential for efficacy in 1994, but subsequently demands for the restoration of 12 June became less intense. Instead came demands for the release of Abiola and other political detainees as well as a quick hand-over of power to civilians. The fact that the clampdown on opposition elements within the country had forced many of them to flee abroad took the pro-democracy struggle to the international arena, and it was from there that much of the opposition to the Abacha regime came to be mobilised, with the active support of foreign governments. Within the country there were pockets of opposition activity, but this was mostly isolated and uncoordinated, and attempts by the CD and NADECO to organise protests along the lines of 1994 in subsequent years failed. There was an increase in terrorist and underground activities by clandestine groups: between June 1993 and June 1996 there were fourteen major bombing incidents, attributed to opposition groups, in different parts of the country. The crash of a presidential jet in January 1996 in which the son of the head of state and others died, was also attributed to opposition groups which the government accused at one stage of planning to attack the country. There was also an upsurge of assassinations, which forced more activists to flee abroad. Notable opposition figures whose sudden deaths were believed to be political assassinations were Alfred Rewane, Kudirat Abiola (wife of M.K.O. Abiola) and Suliat Adedeji. It was difficult to tell if these killings, which all took place in 1996, were inter-related or not, or which groups were behind them, but they were indications of a possible change in the orientation of resistance formations which, as the experience of countries like South Africa shows, could be expected in the face of repression.

Abroad, NADECO and other foreign-based groups such as the Association of Nigerians Abroad which had branches in most parts of Europe, the US-based Organization of Nigerians in the American, Organization of Nigerian Nationals, Nigerian Democratic Alliance, and the National Liberation Council of Nigeria/United Democratic Front, led by Wole Soyinka, led the campaign against the military regime. The campaign involved the lobbying of several governments, notably those of the United States, Britain, Germany, the Scandinavian countries and South Africa, to impose sanctions and exert other pressures on the regime. The UN's various agencies, the Commonwealth, international human rights organisations and international conferences were also used as platforms to press further for the isolation of the regime. The groups claimed responsibility for the isolation of Nigeria in the international community and the imposition of sanctions on the regime: 'The increasing international isolation of Nigeria, the FIFA boycott of Nigeria,[16] the Afro-American led initiative on Nigeria, and the South African initiative on Nigeria have all been possible because NADECO has kept the flame of democracy alive and burning (Bolaji Akinyemi on NADECO's success in *Newswatch*, 15 May 1995: 13).

There can be little doubt that NADECO and other foreign-based opposition groups were successful in getting the world to focus attention on the Nigerian situation, but their campaigns for sanctions were unpopular at home and cost them support among some home-based

---

[16] Nigeria had won FIFA's approval to host the junior world cup competition, but the event was cancelled at the last minute after it had spent heavily on preparations, as part of the isolation of the country from the international community. It was highly ironic that a country which strongly advocated sports sanctions against apartheid South Africa was itself now at the receiving end of this punishment.

activists and ordinary people who believed sanctions would make their already precarious economic situation still worse. In the circumstances, NADECO and other pro-democracy activists in exile were strengthened by the continued detention of Abiola and other pro-democracy activists and the country's poor human rights record, the delays in announcing a transition to civil rule programme, and the two so-called blunders committed by the Abacha regime in 1995: the coup trials and the killings of the Ogoni nine. The blunders brought down the full force of international condemnation on Nigeria.

In March 1995, the government announced that it had uncovered a coup plot to overthrow the regime. About forty-four people, both military officers and civilians, were subsequently tried by a special military tribunal headed by Brigadier-General Patrick Aziza, and sentenced to death or to long jail sentences. What attracted world attention to the coup trials was the inclusion of a former head of state, General Olusegun Obasanjo, and his former deputy, General Shehu Yar'Adua, among the accused. Some civilians, including journalists and pro-democracy activists,[17] were also tried and convicted. There were also allegations by the press and human rights activists that the coup was a ruse to eliminate the regime's 'enemies' in the army and silence opposition.

However, largely in response to pleas from the international community, including former US president Jimmy Carter and Archbishop Desmond Tutu, sent as the personal emissary of President Nelson Mandela of South Africa, as well as various groups within the country, the head of state commuted the sentences from death to life imprisonment and from life to shorter jail terms. The controversy generated by the trials unfortunately drowned the significance of the decision to commute the sentences, which is that it was the first time that coup plotters convicted by a military tribunal were not executed in the country. This was an important development since it not only gave hope that the Abacha regime was responsive to world opinion and pressure, but also marked the entry of human rights considerations into Nigerian military law. The further relaxation of military law in July 1996, allowing military officers to appeal in federal courts of appeal and the Supreme Court against judgements by military tribunals – a response to the recommendations of a UN committee investigating the human rights situation in Nigeria – was another positive step in this direction.

[17] The military officers were, in addition to Obasanjo and Yar'Adua, notably Colonels Lawan Gwadabe, Roland Emokpae and Bello Fadile. The civilians included journalists George Mba (*Tell,*), Kunle Ajibade (*The News*), Ms Chris Anyanwu (TSM) and Ben Obi (*Classique*), and Beko Ransome-Kuti of NMA, CD leader and pro-democracy activist.

But the trial, conviction and killing of the 'Ogoni nine' was a different matter altogether. As we saw in the last chapter, from 1990 Ken Saro-Wiwa led the Movement for the Survival of Ogoni Peoples (MOSOP) to demand compensation for the environmental hazards from oil exploration and production activities from the federal government and Shell, the oil major in Ogoniland, and political autonomy and other political rights for the minority Ogoni within the Nigerian federation. The suppression of the resultant Ogoni uprising by the federal and Rivers state governments and the violent tactics preferred by Ogoni youths who aligned with MOSOP led to divisions within the ranks of Ogoni elites and leaders between the 'radicals' led by Saro-Wiwa and the 'conservatives' led by Garrick Leton, former president of MOSOP, and some former members of the Babangida government. The struggle between these two groups underlay the murder of four leaders of the conservative camp – Albert Badey, Edward Kobani, Theophilus Orage snr, and Theophilus Orage jr – on 21 May 1994. Saro-Wiwa and nine other MOSOP leaders were subsequently tried and sentenced to death by the civil disturbances tribunal headed by Mr Justice Ibrahim Auta.

The high international profile of Saro-Wiwa and the drama of the trials centering around human rights issues drew attention to it from all over the world. The defence lawyers (and human rights activists) opposed the trials on a number of grounds: there had allegedly not been a thorough investigation before the trials began; a military officer, Lt. Col. Ibrahim Alli, sat on the tribunal; the defendants were tried in two different groups; the right of appeal was denied by the decree setting up the tribunal; the trial went ahead although a case was pending in the high court in which the defendants were challenging the impartiality of members of the tribunal; and the tribunal refused to allow the defence to present a videotape showing the military administrator of Rivers state, Col. Dauda Komo, accusing Saro-Wiwa of the murders before the trials, which meant that he was presumed guilty even before the trials began. At one stage the leading defence counsel Gani Fawehinmi and the second counsel Femi Falana withdrew from the case, and the tribunal had to appoint lawyers to replace them. In the end nine of the ten defendants, including Saro-Wiwa, were sentenced to death, while Ledun Mitee, vice president of MOSOP was acquitted. Within eight days of the judgement, the sentences were confirmed by the PRC (even before receiving the records of the trial, according to critics), and the nine Ogoni activists were executed on 10 November 1995.

The executions met with worldwide condemnation. Given Saro-Wiwa's profile as an author and minority rights and environmental protection activist, the trials had generated tremendous international interest. As with the coup trials, several entreaties were made to the regime to spare the defendants' lives, while international human rights organisations criticised what was regarded as the flawed judicial process of the trial. Once again President Mandela, whom NADECO and other human rights and pro-democracy groups had approached to help save the Ogoni nine, was in the forefront of these entreaties, and claimed to have received assurances from the Nigerian government that the case would be reconsidered. What made the killings even more extraordinary was that they were carried out on the very day the Commonwealth summit opened in Auckland, New Zealand.

Demonstrations were staged in many parts of the world to condemn the Nigerian government and Shell, which was accused of complicity in the killings. The Commonwealth suspended Nigeria from membership and made an accelerated return to civilian rule and human rights observance conditions for readmission, and the United States, European Community countries and South Africa recalled their ambassadors from Nigeria (Nigeria followed suit in retaliation). The UN General Assembly passed a resolution condemning the killings, and the Security Council considered imposing collective sanctions. Meanwhile, various sanctions were imposed by the United States, the EU, Britain, Germany, France, several other European countries, and Canada. These were largely limited sanctions which marked only a slight tightening of those imposed in 1993 – restrictions on visas for government officials and military officers and members of their families; an arms embargo and the cancellation of military cooperation and training; and sports sanctions (by EU countries). There were threats of more serious sanctions like freezing the country's assets and the accounts of government officials in Western banks, and oil sanctions, but it was difficult for consensus to be reached on this, especially given the precarious situation of oil in the world market (sanctions against Iraq, Libya and Iran had produced something of a crisis already). But much came to depend on how the regime would proceed and events unfold in an increasingly isolated Nigeria. Inside the country reactions to the killings were muted. The only notable attempt at a demonstration – by Gani Fawehinmi's National Conscience Party – was stopped by the police. However, the government made frantic efforts to limit the damage, including setting up a panel of eminent traditional rulers to consider how best the country could respond to its isolation. Emissaries were also sent abroad to 'explain' the government's case.

The Ogoni affair and its aftermath raised several pertinent questions. Why did the military regime defy world opinion which it had respected in the case of the coup trials? Why, of all days, were the Ogoni activists killed on the opening day of the Commonwealth summit? Why did the international community react (or over-react in some cases) with so much vehemence? As for the timing, killing the Ogonis on the opening day of the Commonwealth conference might not have been calculated to spite the organisation, but it showed how low the regime rated membership of it. Indeed, in order to assert the country's autonomy and finally cast off its colonial legacy, there had been strong demands to pull out of the organisation (cf. Akinyemi, 1989). After the ending of apartheid in South Africa, for which the Commonwealth had been a major forum for advancing Nigeria's commitment to that country's liberation, its importance appeared to be diminished even further. Nevertheless, largely to mitigate the country's isolation, efforts were made to normalise relations within the Commonwealth. These were mainly through negotiations with the Committee of Foreign Ministers (set up specifically to monitor developments in Nigeria), and some items on the transition agenda were seen as an attempt to meet conditions stipulated for re-admission. The reasons for the choice of date remained a matter for speculation.

As for the other questions, two observations are in order. First, it would appear that the government wished to deal decisively with the threat of opposition elements who were being actively encouraged by the international community. It was fairly obvious that being 'soft' on the Ogoni activists out of deference to international opinion would encourage the anti-government elements, which would become more powerful and daring and pose a threat to its own survival and an invitation to anarchy. In other words, the killings were part of the attempt to silence the opposition and assert control over the country. Secondly, the vehemence of the international reaction was the culmination of a gathering storm of hostility and opposition to the military regime. It is not unlikely that Nigeria would have been suspended from the Commonwealth anyway, given the trend of thinking up to the summit, which was that it should not be allowed to participate. The isolation that followed the killings and the threat of further sanctions had some positive effect, in that the regime became more sensitive to the democratic imperative, and initiated a review of the country's external relations.

FOREIGN POLICY

The hostility towards the Abacha regime and its harassment both domestically and externally accounted for its foreign policy being largely reactive and incoherent. The regime concentrated its energies mostly on consolidating its hold on the country and limiting the attempts by the international community to isolate it, and foreign policy was made to serve the need of this struggle for survival and consolidation. Thus the activities of foreign-based 'dissidents' and ways to combat them became a major determinant of foreign policy. The survivalist imperative also partly explains why the government pursued a foreign policy aimed at diverting attention away from the internal crises and tensions. Distractions came by way of the 'war' declared on Western imperialists who were accused of a conspiracy to destroy Nigeria, the clash with South Africa, and the border war with Cameroon over Bakassi. As in the previous chapters, we shall examine the Abacha regime's foreign policy at the various regional and global levels.

At the West African sub-regional level, ECOWAS remained the major focus, although it was less active than it had been in previous years. This was partly due to the francophone countries being more involved in the affairs of a parallel economic union – the West African Economic and Monetary Union (UMEOA) – formed in January 1994 following the devaluation of the CFA franc. From that time the francophone heads of states rarely attended the annual summits, and ECOWAS became increasingly an anglophone affair. But an even more important reason was that most countries in the region were greatly troubled by political instability and economic decline, and were preoccupied with solving these problems. Nigeria itself was in this situation, and between 1994 and 1995 the head of state was unable to attend ECOWAS summits and other crucial meetings. However, in July 1996 General Abacha became chairman of ECOWAS, and Nigeria seemed set once again to salvage the organisation. This was part of the regime's isolation-limiting policy, as well as the head of state's rising profile, which critics saw as part of the preparation for transformation to a civilian president.

ECOMOG remained the most important collective undertaking in which Nigeria was involved, but the intractability of the war in Liberia led to threats by Ghana, the other major participant in the peace-keeping mission, to pull out. Nigeria also considered pulling out, but the international acclaim from its involvement, which was a good counter-balance to its isolation, dissuaded the leaders from such a move. The ECOWAS summit at Abuja in July 1996 initiated a new peace offensive under which an interim government was formed and the warring factions agreed to disarm and prepare for elections. Outside ECOWAS Nigeria maintained its sub-continental 'superpower' role despite its increasing insolvency. Thus its troops remained in Sierra Leone where they assisted the government in warding off rebel attacks. The government pursued other collective development projects, one of which was the gas pipeline project jointly funded by Nigeria, Togo and Ghana, and involving the laying of pipes to supply gas from Nigeria to these other countries. The agreement was signed in September 1995.

Nigeria's relations with other countries in the region was also affected by the government's determination to contain opposition and dissident activities, as well as the responses of these countries to its isolation by Western powers. For example, relations with neighbouring Benin under Soglo were strained by that country's support for dissidents, and its rumoured agreement to have a US military base established there. Relations only improved after Matthew Kerekou, a long-standing friend of Nigeria, returned to power after defeating Soglo in the 1996 elections. There were also proposals by pro-government commentators to reduce assistance to countries like Mali and Sierra Leone which voted against Nigeria at major international forums. However, Nigeria made efforts to secure the support of other West African states in its struggles against the Western-led international community, including South Africa (especially when it boycotted the 1996 African football Cup of Nations hosted by that country). For this purpose, it relied partly on article 83 of the revised ECOWAS treaty which provided for the formulation and adoption of 'common policies on issues relating to international negotiations with third parties in order to promote and safeguard the interests of the region', but its efforts were unsuccessful.

The policy of good neighbourliness was largely shaped by the government's survivalist agenda. We have already referred to relations with Benin under Soglo, but there was a much more serious problem with neighbouring Cameroon which grew out of the long-standing dispute over the Bakassi peninsula. There were constant skirmishes and a few serious battles between the armies of the two countries, as well as a massive build-up of military units along the borders. Nigeria constantly accused Cameroon of being the aggressor, and of having French military backing. Various unsuccessful attempts were made to resolve the dispute, including mediation by the International Court of Justice. However, this worked in Nigeria's favour in so far as the lingering crisis helped to divert attention away from the problems at home.

At the African continental level, the end of apartheid and the entry of South Africa on to the scene as a major power brought changes which seriously affected Nigeria's policy towards the continent. With apartheid gone and the entire continent 'liberated' from the last vestiges of colonialism, the major plank which previously gave coherence to the country's policies had been removed. Even the OAU, which was a major channel of Nigeria's African policy, seemed to have lost its relevance, at least for the time being. In the process of charting a new African policy in the post-apartheid era, it seemed inevitable that Nigeria would sooner or later have to confront South Africa, as its rival for continental leadership. The opportunity came through South Africa's attempt to play a leading role in the resolution of the Nigerian crisis. Initially, Nigeria seemed ready to accept South Africa's intervention which, unlike that attempted by Western powers, was based on dialogue and mutual respect. Thus Mandela's emmissaries – Archbishop Desmond Tutu and Vice President Thabo Mbeki – achieved good results with the coup trial and detention of political activists where others largely failed. But even at that stage, strains could be observed in the relations between the two countries because of South Africa's open-door policy towards opponents of Abuja, especially the Nigerian pro-democracy groups. Relations deteriorated rapidly after the Ogoni killings, which Mandela considered a personal blow since he had received assurances that the activists would not be killed. His decision to champion the African arm of the international opposition while other African states maintained a low profile and had muted reactions to the executions, led to accusations by the Nigerian authorities that South Africa was a stooge of the Western powers. At the height of the bad relations, Nigeria withdrew from the 1996 African football Cup of Nations which South Africa hosted, on the grounds that the South African authorities had refused to guarantee the safety and security of its contingent. However, as the heat of the Ogoni affair subsided and allowed the Abacha regime some respite, steps were initiated to restore normal relations between the two countries. For its part, South Africa now distanced itself increasingly from the Nigerian 'dissidents' (as was evident in the last-minute cancellation of a major conference of Nigerian pro-democracy groups scheduled to be held in Johannesburg early in 1996) and charted a more African-contextualised rather than unilateral or Western-oriented policy towards Nigeria.

Finally, it was at the global level that the Abacha regime faced the greatest opposition and hostility from the very beginning. Its adamant nationalism and autonomy consciousness which, led to the abrogation of liberalisation policies in 1994 and a sustained anti-Western stance on many issues, reinforced this hostility. As we have seen, the United States and other Western powers actively encouraged and supported opposition groups in the country as well as those based abroad, and on some occasions issued statements which amounted to gross interference in the country's internal affairs. This reached its height with the Ogoni affair. The country's response to the Western actions was twofold. On the one hand, it invoked the non-interference clause of the UN and other international organisations to oppose undue interference, and sought to rally the support of other third world states, especially the 'pariah' states which were also at the receiving end of the 'Western conspiracy' – Iran, Libya, and Iraq. On the other hand, as during the civil war, the country searched for alternative allies in the old Eastern bloc and Arab countries. But the major channels of its global policies remained the UN, and for major economic policies it remained committed to OPEC, of which a former Nigerian foreign affairs and petroleum minister, Rilwanu Lukman, was secretary-general. With its suspension from the Commonwealth, it fell back on organisations like the moribund Non Aligned Movement. But in spite of all this, the country remained pro-Western, and the United States, Britain and Germany its major trading partners.

8

CONCLUSION

Writers on Nigeria in the mid-1990s have talked of the country's descent into decline or decay, especially in the 1980s and 1990s. These are typified by Lewis (1996) and Joseph (1996), both of whom locate the decline within the military regimes of these two decades, and identify the abortion of Babangida's 'bogus' transition and the execution of the Ogoni activists as its catalysts. Joseph however goes back in time to 15 January 1966, the day of the military's first intervention in the political process, as the beginning of Nigeria's entry into 'the dismal tunnel', and traces the decline through the successive military administrations.

The main explanation offered by both scholars is prebendalism, which involves the conversion and exploitation of state offices into instruments of private accumulation both for self and for constituent and kin groups. According to Joseph, this produces the 'rogue state', but there is no suggestion that it is peculiar to military regimes, since it was civilian politicians who fashioned the system under colonial rule and perfected it in the post-independence period, as the experiences of the First and Second Nigerian Republics showed. Nevertheless the military extended the system, because by the nature of its rule it was not an accountable body and could therefore not restrain the inevitable abuses of office (Joseph, 1996: 196). Nwabueze, as we saw earlier, describes the context within which the military operates as 'lawless autocracy'. These illuminating observations and perspectives on the country's decline provide a useful point of departure for this concluding chapter. Our analyses of the nature of governance, political conflicts, economic problems and so on in the preceding chapters lead to basically the same conclusions about what is called the country's decay, but they suggest that its nature and causes go beyond prebendalism which, as we tried to argue in Chapter 1, is a dependent rather than an independent variable. But, before we examine what explanations are crucial, we should first define what is meant by decline or decay. Has there really been a decline?

The notion of decline is best captured by Emeka Anyaoku's graphic description of the condition of the Nigerian state at the height of the devastating turbulence in 1994. He likened the country to 'a motor car with a capacity to run at 200 km. per hour which was moving at only 10 km. per hour and showing signs of a possible total breakdown'. However, the notion of decline can only be meaningful when related to a previous period of growth or development and stability. Can we say that Nigeria has had such a period? Unless we take the economic boom of the 1970s and early 1980s as an indication of development – which it is not – the country's history since colonial times does not suggest that it has. Perhaps, then, the country's 'glorious past' is used to refer to the vast potential for development and stability, rather than actual development and stability. As is well known, the country's large population, its wealth and resources, highly developed manpower and infrastructure, and a resilient democratic culture distinguished it from most other underdeveloped countries in Africa and the third world, and formed the basis for the hope at independence that the country would become a model new nation.

It is in this sense of *potential* that Anyaoku refers to a car with a *capacity* to run at 200 km. per hour (as opposed to one already running at that speed). This thesis of potential implies that decay, defined simply as stagnation or retarded growth, is not an emergent condition of the Nigerian state. Rather, it has been endemic. It is often forgotten that despite its enormous advantages over other third world countries, Nigeria is a typical peripheral formation whose autonomy of action and initiatives is limited by the circumstances of its location within the global economic system. Admittedly, it surpassed several other peripheral countries in challenging the domination of the global system by the Western capitalist nations, but its status as a rentier state made it different from the others in degree rather than in kind.

Given the foregoing, we may characterise the decline of the 1980s and 1990s as *accelerated decline* rather than a newly emergent condition. Indeed, the descent in this period was predictable. The oil boom of the 1970s had brightened the hopes that the country would come close to its potential. That it did not was largely the fault of the managers of the state who failed to make the best use of the boom, but it was also because the boom was artificial and could only continue for as long as the oil price remained high and stable in the world market; its rapid fall that began in the late 1970s therefore brought economic growth to an end. This was a major catalyst of decline, since oil prices never really recovered.

When we turn to the political arena, the notion of decline is not so obvious. Problems of stability and national cohesion have been endemic in the country, although the federal solution has been viewed favourably. But the focus of the decline thesis is on the descent to flagrant authoritarianism. As we said in Chapter 5, there has been a tendency to see the authoritarianism of the military regimes of the 1980s and 1990s as the opposite of the benevolence of previous regimes, which respected the country's time-honoured and abiding traditions of liberalism. This is then taken as one of the empirical measures of decline. The argument advanced earlier, which bears reiterating, is that all military regimes are without exception authoritarian, and if previous regimes appeared less so, this was largely because they did not have to face the desperate economic and political crisis, and the hostility, experienced by those of the 1980s and 1990s. But even so, they flagrantly abused fundamental human and group rights and ruled through draconian decrees[1] which, as Joseph observes, is the major reason for the legitimacy and efficacy of military rule being so vigorously contested. This was intensified in the 1980s and 1990s due to several factors, including the continued economic decline and hardship, the increased authoritarianism of the regimes, and the changing international climate which became intolerant of military governments.

The suggestion here is not that the country had been other than in a state of decay, but that the notion of a 'sudden' descent into decline is not supported by the evidence of history. Nevertheless, the decay was accelerated in the 1980s and 1990s when, as Anyaoku said, the car moving at 10 km. per hour threatened to give up. The hows and whys of this accelerated decay were examined in Chapters 5, 6 and 7, and need no repeating here, but they do suggest that prebendalism, poor governance, ethnicity and other internal factors by themselves do not explain it. Because the explanations offered by Joseph and Lewis omit the external factors and dimensions, they are incomplete. This omission could well have to do with the changed perception of the role of the United States and other Western powers, as well as the international organisations funded and controlled by them, as the agents and protectors of democracy and good governance in third world countries in the post-Cold War era of so-called democratic revolution. This role was defined within the context of the unprecedented economic and political decline of many of these countries, especially

---

[1] Authoritarian acts like the detention without trial of Wole Soyinka, Tai Solarin and Air Iyare, among others, by the Gowon administration, and the shaving of journalist Minere Amakiri's hair by the military governor of Rivers state in 1974 were true to type and not isolated incidents. The administration of General Mohammed trampled on cherished rights, but was forgiven for what was seen as a necessary and badly-needed instrument of cleansing.

in Africa, and gave new meaning to their colonial-type control which had been vehemently opposed and rejected in the anti-colonialism movement of the past. The West's new-found benevolence, however defined, could not disguise the self-serving policies of advanced capitalist countries which aimed at perpetuating the peripheralisation of the underdeveloped countries.

As I have argued elsewhere (Osaghae, 1995e), this self-serving attitude – which extended, as in the past, to attempts to install puppet regimes to support the democracy project in Africa – underlay the so-called political and economic reforms introduced at the behest of Western agencies. The acceleration of Nigeria's decay in the 1980s and 1990s cannot be analysed in isolation from the complex designs of the international community. This factor, as we have analysed above, comprises the decline in the oil price; the debt overhang which was the basis of the SAP, which in turn worsened the economic condition and led to a spate of political conflicts; the isolation of the military regimes for ostensibly refusing to return to democracy; and the support for opposition civil society groups and the imposition of sanctions in pursuit of these aims. These factors, which the military governments projected as a part of a grand conspiracy to destroy Nigeria, have to be sifted to distinguish those (like certain international non-governmental organisations) which genuinely aimed at restoring democracy and those which sought to block the country's efforts to assert its autonomy.

The reference to international factors is not an attempt to shift responsibility for the accelerated decay of the 1980s and 1990s. However, it was a fundamental factor in the decline of the Nigerian state and economy, and severely constrained the ability of the managers of the state to arrest the decline. As Nnoli (1989: 265) puts it, 'The truth is that during [the 1980s and 1990s], Nigerian governments became powerless to influence not only economic activities in the international system but also within the country.' This is not to ignore the central internal factors of prebendalism and so on, which hampered effective governance in the country and led some observers to give up on the state and project the civil society as deserving of support instead. Better management of the enormous oil revenue, especially during boom periods, would undeniably have gone a long way towards lifting the country out of the poverty which afflicted the vast majority of its people, international conspiracy or not. Nigeria was one of the few oil-rich countries which repeatedly experienced fuel shortages, and was unable to deploy its wealth rationally to improve the quality of life of its citizens. This, above all else, was the major indicator of the decay that characterised the country's post-independence history.

The way out of this decay, as suggested by our analysis, is twofold. First and more fundamental, Nigeria has to transform itself from a rentier state, subject to all the crisis of extraversion, to a productive state. This would involve a whole process of deperipheralisation to enable it to manage its affairs with a high degree of autonomy, and realise its manifest destiny in the conduct of its external relations. It is obvious that the process of reasserting Nigeria's autonomy and generation of productive forces would be enhanced by democratisation and entrenchment of the values of good and efficient governance. Which takes us to the second way out of the decline that has characterised Nigeria's post-independence history, which is via the internal level. Given the centrality of state power in Nigeria and the state's dominance of critical spheres of the society and economy, the way out of the decline at the domestic level lies in the resolution of key issues and problems in the political realm. These include (1) the national question: how effectively to structure the federation to accommodate the various groups and guarantee access to power and the equitable distribution of the country's resources; (2) the leadership question: the search for a visionary and nationally-oriented leadership; (3) the governance question: how to strengthen the institutions and processes of the state, and transform it from a 'soft' state to an effective state; (4) the political culture question: the search for a public realm morality to counter the embedded amorality which resulted in corruption, prebendalism, a crisis in legitimacy, and so on; and (5) the military question: how to end the military's dominance of the political process. These dimensions are closely related. Nevertheless, to the extent that prolonged military rule worsened the other problems, blocked the prospects of democratic rule and succeeded only in plunging the country into a political abyss from which recovery appeared supremely difficult, it is on the military question that we focus in conclusion.

Notwithstanding the self-serving motivations highlighted in this book, there was ample justification for the military interventions at the various times when they occurred. The subsequent military regimes proceeded on this basis to attempt to create, through the various political transition programmes, a political system approximating to their ideal state. The ostensible aim of this project was the enhancement of national cohesion and political stability. The various experiments did produce some positive results such as the federal character principle, local government reforms and, before it became an instrument of patrimonialism, the creation of more states, all of which were hailed as the creative genius of Nigeria's federalism under military rule. The military also saved the country at some points when its disintegration seemed imminent. But the negative consequences of its intervention and rule outweighed these positive results, and in any case have outlived their historical usefulness. The consequences for the military itself were devastating. These included a precipitate loss of *esprit de corps*; deep divisions along regional, ethnic and religious lines, as well as between the army, air force and navy; and the breakdown of discipline which increasingly came to characterise the top echelons of the military. Embedded traditions of hierarchy and unity of command gradually vanished as rival factions or camps, analogous to primitive political parties, emerged to struggle for supremacy. The decline that beset the military was manifest in various ways. There was the large-scale premature retirement of top officers between August 1993 and June 1996, when no less than 200 officers of the rank of colonel (or equivalent in other services) and above were retired, most of them below the age of fifty[2]; rapid changes were made in the command structure (between 1993 and 1996 the chiefs of the army, air and naval staffs were changed, in all, no less than ten times)[3]; a large number of retired military officers switched camps to join the burgeoning anti-military-rule segment of civil society; and rumours of coup plots, secret detentions and executions of officers and men of rival factions were rampant. While the military counted its losses and rapidly lost its credibility and superior claims to state control, the disorganisation served to heighten the authoritarianism of the successive regimes.

As credibility waned and opposition from civil society intensified, military leaders had to mobilise support from their military constituents to stay on. One of the ways in which they did this was to allude to a struggle between 'us' (the military) and 'them' (civil society). They told their military constituents that this called for a closing of ranks to save themselves from forfeiting their claim to being the custodians of the country. General Buhari reminded soldiers of the possibility of a Sudan-type 'civilian coup', and General Babangida admonished them to ensure that the military was not 'disgraced out of office'. The Babangida regime created a new institution – the Armed Forces Consultative Assembly – to ensure that the military 'spoke with one voice'. At its inaugural meeting on 5 July 1989, Babangida told the soldiers: 'We must not let *the military as an institution* be humiliated or disgraced out of office...' (*The Guardian*, 6 July 1989, emphasis added). The divide between the military and civil

---

[2] According to *Tempo* of 6 June 1996, out of over 173 generals – i.e. officers with the rank of brigadier and above – and equivalent ranks in the air force and navy retired since 1975, over 100 were retired in this period.

[3] Under the Babangida regime there was even a plan to decentralise the military command structure – to have army headquarters in Minna (capital of Babangida's home state, Niger), air force headquarters in Kano, and navy headquarters in Lagos. The plan did not materialise.

society was sometimes articulated in strong, uncompromising, warlike terms. In May 1992 Babangida seized upon the mounting opposition to his convoluted transition to civilian rule programme, which was presented as a military project and as an opportunity to attack pro-democracy elements, whom he regarded as 'forces of instability'. Declaring the battle open, he called the military 'practitioners in the management of violence' who would use all 'defensive and offensive' strategies, and if necessary shed 'the last drop of blood', to defend the programme.

The other consequences of incessant intervention and prolonged rule by the military are fairly obvious. The legitimacy of military regimes always depended on a number of factors, chief among which were demonstration of a superior public morality and ability in governance and public management, retention of a national orientation and absence of sectional interests, a short period in office and a commitment to returning power to civilians as quickly as possible, responsiveness to the demands of the civil society, and accountability. It also depended on developments in the wider international community, especially the pattern of progression towards or away from military rule, and the attitude towards military regimes. Despite their efforts, military regimes could not satisfy the imperatives of domestic legitimacy; only the Mohammed/Obasanjo regime successfully handed over power to civilians. They were as corrupt as civilian politicians, if not more so; they became instruments of sectional interests; they sought to perpetuate themselves in power; and they were accountable only to themselves. These were the bases for opposition to military rule and the agitations for democracy which intensified in the 1980s and 1990s.

But the resolution of the military question is not as simple as such an outline might suggest. This is partly because military rule in Nigeria mirrored the divisive conflicts in the political society. Thus, while the majority of the people were opposed to its continuation, others actively supported it. Many people also remained sceptical of politicians and their ability to perform well in office. Their disappointing responses to the annulment of the 1993 presidential election discouraged some pro-democracy elements, who saw the struggle as leading to the empowerment of equally unacceptable members of the political class. But a general consensus is not necessarily a condition for resolving the military question. After all, the military itself has been the major obstacle to efforts by constitution-makers to outlaw the unconstitutional succession to power: ultimately the military is its own major defender,[4]

---

[4] The military lost much of its support in the 1980s and 1990s when it took on the rest of society as a self-serving institution. The changing character of military regimes and especially the resort to hard-line tactics was interpreted by civil liberties and pro-democracy organisations as amounting to, in the words of Clement Nwankwo, leader of the Con-

and it will never forget its ability to settle matters through the barrel of a gun.

Be this as it may, one of the major gains of the anti-military uprising of civil society in the 1980s and 1990s, especially the strengthening of an independent press, was the emergence of a new code of public conduct which had transparency, accountability and national sentiment at its core. The demands of this new code reinforced the struggle against the military. If it is sustained, it can become the basis for consolidating civilian democracy by minimising the war-like approach to elections, pervasive corruption and other problems which provide the justification for military rule. It will also help to resolve the core problem of Nigerian politics, which is leadership. This has all along been wrongly approached as a function of the personal attributes of particular leaders, but such a notion has favoured military rulers who, unlike elected civilian leaders, could act arbitrarily to establish supposedly strong governments. Good leadership requires excellent personal qualities like love of country, moral uprightness, vision and decisiveness, but these are not sufficient to guarantee that the good leader will still not be corrupt or incapable of good management. Constitutionalism and the resurgent rule-setting and watchdog role of the civil society can be counted on to check the arbitrariness of state management and enhance the quality of leadership.

---

stitutional Rights Project (CRP), a declaration of war by government on its own people. The significance of this development lay in the fact that it marked the resolve of civil society to reject the military's self-appointed custodian role once and for all. This was a recurrent theme of the political struggles waged by various segments of civil society in the period under review, which for the first time seriously attempted to link democratic enthronement and consolidation in the country with a permanent retreat of the military from politics.

REFERENCES

Abba, A. *et al.* (1988) *The Nigerian Economic Crisis: Causes and Solutions* (Zaria: Academic Staff Union of Universities).

Adamolekun, L. (1985) *The Fall of the Second Republic* (Ibadan: Spectrum).
——— (1989) 'The 1979 Constitution and Intergovernmental Relations' in P.P. Ekeh *et al.*, eds, *Nigeria Since Independence: The First 25 Years,* vol. V: *Politics and Constitutions* (Ibadan: Heinemann).
——— and Kincaid, J. (1991) 'The Federal Solution: Assessment and Prognosis for Nigeria and Africa', *Publius: The Journal of Federalism*, vol. 21, no. 4.

Adamu, M. (1978) *The Hausa Factor in West African History* (Zaria: Ahmadu Bello University Press and Ibadan: Oxford University Press).

Adeboye, T.O. (1989) 'A General Survey of the Economy' in M.O. Kayode and Y.B. Usman, eds, *Nigeria Since Independence: The First 25 Years,* vol. II: *The Economy* (Ibadan: Heinemann).

Adejumobi, S. (1995) 'Structural Reform and its Impact on the Economy and Society' in S. Adejumobi and A. Momoh, eds, *The Political Economy of Nigeria Under Military Rule: 1984-1993* (Harare: SAPES Books).

Adekanye (Adekson), J. (1979a) 'Army Recruitment in Colonial Plural Society', *Ethnic and Racial Studies*, vol. 2, no. 2.
——— (1979b) 'Dilemma of Military Disengagement' in O. Oyediran, ed. *Nigerian Government and Politics under Military Rule, 1966-79* (London: Macmillan).
——— (1981) *Nigeria in Search of a Stable Civil-Military System* (Boulder: Westview Press).
——— (1989a) 'Politics in a Military Context' in P.P. Ekeh *et al.*, eds, *Nigeria Since Independence: The First 25 Years, vol. v: Politics and Constitutions* (Ibadan: Heinemann).
——— (1989b) 'The Quota Recruitment Policy, Its Sources and Impact on the Nigerian Military' in P.P. Ekeh and E.E. Osaghae, eds, *Federal Character and Federalism in Nigeria* (Ibadan: Heinemann).
——— (1990) 'Elections in Nigeria: Problems, Strategies, and Options', *Nigerian Journal of Electoral and Political Behaviour*, vol. 1, no. 1.

Ademoyega, A. (1981) *Why We Struck: The Story of the First Nigerian Coup* (Ibadan: Evans).

Adeniran, T. (1991) 'The Two-Party System and the Federal Political Process', *Publius: The Journal of Federalism*, vol. 21, no. 4.

Adepoju, A. (1981) 'Military Rule and Population Issues in Nigeria', *African Affairs*, vol. 80.

Adisa, J. (1994) 'Urban Violence in Lagos' in E.E. Osaghae *et al.*, *Urban Violence in Africa* (Ibadan: IFRA, University of Ibadan).

Afigbo, A.E. (1991) 'Background to Nigerian Federalism: Federal Features in the Colonial State', *Publius: The Journal of Federalism*, vol. 21, no. 4.

Agbaje, A. (1990) 'Travails of the Secular State: Religion, Politics and the

319

Outlook on Nigeria's Third Republic', *Journal of Commonwealth and Comparative Politics*, vol. 28, no. 3.

—— (1992) 'Adjusting State and Market in Nigeria: The Paradoxes of Orthodoxy', *Afrika Spectrum*, vol. 27, no. 2.

Agbese, P.O. (1991) 'Demilitarization and the Prospects for Democracy in Nigeria', *Bulletin of Peace Proposals*, vol. 22.

—— (1992) 'Moral Economy and the Expansion of the Privatization Constituency in Nigeria', *Journal of Commonwealth and Comparative Politics*, vol. 30, no. 3.

Aikhomu, A.A. (1994) 'Federal-State Relations under the Military, 1985-1992', *Nigerian Journal of Federalism*, vol. 1, no. 1.

Ajayi, J.F.A. and B. Ikara eds. (1985) *Evolution of Political Culture in Nigeria* (Ibadan University Press).

Ake, C. (1985a) 'The State in Contemporary Africa' in Ake, ed., *Political Economy of Nigeria* (London and Lagos: Macmillan).

—— (1985b) 'The Nigerian State: Antinomies of a Peripheral Formation' in Ake, *Ibid.*

Akeredolu-Ale, E.O. (1975) *The Underdevelopment of Indigenous Enterpreneurship in Nigeria* (Ibadan University Press).

Akinola, A.A. (1989) 'A Critique of Nigeria's Proposed Two-Party System', *Journal of Modern African Studies*, vol. 27, no. 1.

—— (1990) 'Manufacturing the Two-Party System in Nigeria', *Journal of Commonwealth and Comparative Politics*, vol. 28, no. 3.

Akinyemi, A.B. (1974) *Foreign Policy and Federalism: The Nigerian Experience* (Ibadan University Press).

—— (1979) 'Mohammed/Obasanjo Foreign Policy' in O. Oyediran, ed., *Nigerian Government and Politics under Military Rule, 1966-79* (Lagos: Macmillan).

—— (1989) 'The Colonial Legacy and Major Themes in Nigeria's Foreign Policy' in A.B. Akinyemi *et al.*, eds, *Nigeria Since Independence: The First 25 Years*, vol. X: *International Relations* (Ibadan: Heinemann).

Alagbe, K.O. (1986) 'A Critical Appraisal of Fundamental Human Rights in Nigeria: A Case Study of the Buhari Administration', unpublished B.Sc. thesis, University of Ibadan.

Albert, I.O. (1994) 'Violence in Metropolitan Kano: A Historical Perspective' in E.E. Osaghae *et al. Urban Violence in Africa: Pilot Studies* (Ibadan: IFRA, University of Ibadan).

—— (1995) 'University Students in the Politics of Structural Adjustment in Nigeria' in T. Mkandawire and A. Olukoshi, eds, *Between Liberalization and Oppression: The Politics of Structural Adjustment in Africa* (Dakar: CODESRIA).

Aluko, O. (1981) *Essays on Nigerian Foreign Policy* (London: Geo. Allen and Unwin).

Aluko, S.A. (1965) 'How Many Nigerians? An Analysis of Nigeria's Census Problems, 1901-63', *Journal of Modern African Studies*, vol. 3, no. 3.

Amuta, C. (1992) *Prince of the Niger: The Babangida Years* (Lagos: Tanus Communications).

Andrae, G., and B. Beckman (1986) *The Wheat Trap: Bread and Under-development in Nigeria* (London: Zed).

Aniagolu, A.N. (1993) *The Making of the 1989 Constitution of Nigeria* (Ibadan: Spectrum).

Anifowoshe, R. (1982) *Violence and Politics in Nigeria: The Tiv and Yoruba Experience* (New York: Nok).

Apter, A. (1987) 'Things Fell Apart? Yoruba Responses to the 1983 Elections in Ondo State, Nigeria', *Journal of Modern Africa Studies*, vol. 25, no. 3.

Arikpo, O. (1967) *The Development of Modern Nigeria* (Harmondsworth: Penguin).

Asiodu, P.C. (1979) 'The Civil Service: An Insider's View' in O. Oyediran, ed. *Nigerian Government and Politics Under Military Rule, 1966-79* (London: Macmillan).

Ate, B.E. (1991) 'The Political Imperative of Structural Adjustment in Nigeria' in L.A. Deng *et al.*, eds. *Democratization and Structural Adjustment in Africa in the 1990s* (Madison: African Studies Programme, University of Wisconsin).

Awa, E.O. (1964) *Federal Government in Nigeria* (Berkeley: University of California Press).

Awolowo, O. (1947) *Path to Nigerian Freedom* (London: Faber and Faber).

Ayandele, E.A. (1967) *The Missionary Impact on Modern Nigeria, 1842-1914: A Political and Social Analysis* (New York: Humanities Press).

Ayeni, V., and K. Soremekun, eds. (1988) *Nigeria's Second Republic: Presidentialism, Politics and Administration in a Developing State* (Lagos: Daily Times).

Ayoade, J.A.A. (1986) 'Ethnic Management in the 1979 Constitution', *Publius: The Journal of Federalism*, vol. 16.

Azikiwe, N. (1945) *Political Blueprint for Nigeria* (Lagos: African Book Company).

———— (1965) 'Essentials For Nigerian Survival', *Foreign Affairs*, vol. 43, no. 3.

Babalakin Report (1991) *Report of the Judicial Commission of Inquiry into the Affairs of the Federal Electoral Commission (FEDECO) 1979-83* (Lagos: Federal Government Printer).

Babawale, T. (1995) 'Nigeria's Foreign Policy' in S. Adejumobi and A. Momoh, eds. *The Political Economy of Nigeria Under Military Rule: 1984-1993* (Harare: SAPES Books).

Bach, D.C. (1989), 'Managing a Plural Society: The Boomerang Effects of Nigerian Federalism', *Journal of Commonwealth and Comparative Politics*, vol. 27, no. 2.

Ballard, J.A. (1971) 'Administrative Origins of Nigerian Federalism', *African Affairs*, vol. 70, no. 281.

Bello, A. (1962) *My Life* (Cambridge University Press).

Bienen, H. (1985) *Political Conflict and Economic Change in Nigeria* (London: Frank Cass).

Biersteker, T.J. (1987) *Multinationals, the State, and Control of the Nigerian Economy* (Princeton University Press).

Bolaji, L. (1980) *Shagari: President by Mathematics* (Ibadan: Automatic Printing Press).

Campbell, B. (1989) 'Indebtedness in Africa: Consequence, Cause or Symptom of the Crisis?' in B. Onimode, ed., *The IMF, the World Bank and the African Debt*, vol. 2: *The Social and Political Impact* (London: Institute for African Alternatives/Zed).

Clarke, P.B. and I. Linden (1984) *Islam in Modern Nigeria: A Study of a Muslim Community in a Post-Independence State, 1960-1983* (Mainz: Grünewald).

CLO (1994) *Terror in Ogoni* (Lagos: Civil Liberties Organization Action Report).

Coleman, J.S. (1958) *Nigeria: Background to Nationalism* (Berkeley: University of California Press).

Crampton, E.P.T. (1975) *Christianity in Northern Nigeria* (London: Geoffrey Chapman).

Crowder, M. (1962) *The Story of Nigeria* (London: Faber and Faber).

Dare, L. (1989) 'The 1964 Elections and the Collapse of the First Republic' in P.P. Ekeh *et al.*, eds, *Nigeria Since Independence: The First 25 Years, vol. 5: Politics and Constitutions* (Ibadan: Heinemann).

Dent, M. (1989) 'Federalism in Africa, With Special Reference to Nigeria' in M. Forsyth, ed., *Federalism and Nationalism* (Leicester University Press).

Diamond, L. (1982) 'Cleavage, Conflict and Anxiety in the Second Nigerian Republic', *Journal of Modern African Studies*, vol. 20, no. 4.

—— (1983) 'Social Change and Political Conflict in Nigeria's Second Republic' in I.W. Zartman, ed., *The Political Economy of Nigeria* (New York: Praeger).

—— (1984) 'Nigeria in Search of Democracy', *Foreign Affairs*, spring.

—— (1988a) 'Nigeria: Pluralism, Statism and the Struggle for Democracy' in L. Diamond *et al.*, eds, *Democracy in Developing Countries* (Boulder: Lynne Rienner).

—— (1988b) *Class, Ethnicity and Democracy in Nigeria: The Failure of the First Republic* (Syracuse University Press).

Dudley, B.J. (1968) *Parties and Politics in Northern Nigeria* (London: Frank Cass).

—— (1973) *Instability and Political Order: Politics and Crisis in Nigeria* (Ibadan University Press).

—— (1982) *An Introduction to Nigerian Government and Politics* (London: Macmillan).

Dusgate, R.H. (1985) *The Conquest of Northern Nigeria* (London: Frank Cass).

Eberhard, W. (1973) 'Problems of Historical Sociology' in R. Bendix *et al.*, eds, *State and Society: A Reader in Comparative Sociology* (Berkeley: University of California Press).

Edozien, E.C. and E. Osagie, eds. (1982) *Economic Integration of West Africa* (Ibadan University Press).

EIU (1994) *Nigeria: 4th Quarter 1994* (London: Economist Intelligence Unit).

Ekeh, P.P. (1975) 'Colonialism and the Two Publics in Africa: A Theoretical

Statement', *Comparative Studies in Society and History*, vol. 17, no. 1.

——— (1989a) 'Nigeria's Emergent Political Culture' in P.P. Ekeh *et al.* eds. *Nigeria Since Independence: The First 25 Years,* vol. V: *Politics and Constitutions* (Ibadan: Heinemann).

——— (1989b) 'The Structure and Meaning of Federal Character in the Nigerian Political System' in P.P. Ekeh and E.E. Osaghae, eds, *Federal Character and Federalism in Nigeria* (Ibadan: Heinemann).

——— (1994) 'The Public Realm and Public Finance in Africa' in U. Himmelstrand *et al.*, eds. *African Perspectives on Development: Controversies, Dilemmas and Openings* (London: James Currey).

——— and E.E. Osaghae, eds. (1989) *Federal Character and Federalism in Nigeria* (Ibadan: Heinemann).

Ekekwe, E. (1986) *Class and State in Nigeria* (London: Longman).

Ekwe-Ekwe, H. (1990) *Conflict and Intervention in Africa: Nigeria, Angola, Zaire* (London: Macmillan).

Ekoko, A.E., and L.O. Amadi (1989) 'Religion and Stability in Nigeria' in J.A. Atanda, G. Asiwaju and Y. Abubakar, eds, *Nigeria Since Independence: The First 25 Years,* vol. IX: *Religion* (Ibadan: Heinemann).

Elaigwu, J.I. (1979) 'The Military and State-Building: Federal-State Relations in Nigeria's 'Military Federalism' 1966-76' in A.B. Akinyemi *et al.,* eds, *Readings on Federalism* (Lagos: NIIA).

——— (1986) *Gowon: The Biography of a Soldier-Statesman* (Ibadan: West Books).

——— (1988) 'Nigerian Federalism Under Civilian and Military Regimes', *Publius: Journal of Federalism,* vol. 18, no. 1.

——— (1991) 'Federalism and National Leadership in Nigeria', *Publius: Journal of Federalism,* vol. 21, no. 4.

——— (1993) *The Shadow of Religion on Nigerian Federalism, 1960-93* (Abuja: NCIR Monograph Series, no. 3).

——— and V. Olorunsola (1983) 'Federalism and the Politics of Compromise' in D. Rothchild and V. Olorunsola, eds, *State Versus Ethnic Claims: African Policy Dilemmas* (Boulder: Westview Press).

Eleazu, U. (1977) *Federalism and Nation-Building: The Nigerian Experience* (Ilfracombe: Stockwell).

Emenuga, C. (1993) 'Nigeria: The Search for an Acceptable Revenue Allocation Formula' in *The National Question and Economic Development in Nigeria* (Ibadan: Nigeria Economic Society).

Enwerem, I.M. (1995) *A Dangerous Awakening: The Politicization of Religion in Nigeria* (Ibadan: IFRA).

Essien-Udom, E.U. (1965) 'Politics and Vision in Relation to Present-day Nigeria', *New Nigerian,* vol. 1, no. 3.

Ezera, K. (1964) *Constitutional Developments in Nigeria* (Cambridge University Press).

Fadahunsi, A. (1993) 'Devaluation: Implications for Employment, Inflation, Growth and Development' in A.O. Olukoshi, ed., *The Politics of Structural Adjustment in Nigeria* (London: James Currey).

Falola, T., and J. Ihonvbere (1985) *The Rise and Fall of Nigeria's Second Republic, 1979-1983* (London: Zed).

Faruqee, R. (1994) 'Nigeria: Ownership Abandoned' in I. Husain and R. Faruqee, eds, *Adjustment in Africa: Lessons from Country Case Studies* (Washington DC: World Bank).

Fashoyin, T. (1993) 'Nigeria: Consequences for Employment' in A. Adepoju, ed., *The Impact of Structural Adjustment on the Population in Africa* (London: James Currey).

Fatton, R. jr. (1995) 'Africa in the age of Democratization: The Civic Limitations of Civil Society', *African Studies Review*, vol. 38, no. 2.

FGN (1967) *Nigeria 1966* (Lagos: Federal Government Printer).

―――― (1976) *Report of the Constitution Drafting Committee*, 2 vols (Lagos: Federal Government Printer).

―――― (1981) *Report of the Tribunal of Enquiry on Kano Disturbances* (Lagos: Federal Government Printer).

―――― (Dasuki Report, 1984) *Local Government: Report by the Committee on the Review of Local Government Administration in Nigeria* (Lagos: Government Printer).

―――― (1987a) *Report of the Political Bureau* (Lagos: Federal Government Printer).

―――― (1987b) *Government's Views on the Findings and Recommendations of the Political Bureau* (Lagos: Federal Government Printer).

―――― (NEC) (1989) *Report and Recommendations on Party Formation* (Lagos: NEC).

Forrest, T. (1993) *Politics and Economic Development in Nigeria* (Boulder: Westview Press).

Gambari, I. (1989) 'Nigerian Foreign Policy at the Cross roads: Concepts, Critical Issues and Management of External Affairs Under the Buhari Administration' in A.B. Akinyemi *et al.*, eds, *Nigeria Since Independence: The First 25 Years, vol. X: International Relations* (Ibadan: Heinemann).

Gana, A.T. (1989) 'Nigeria, West Africa and the Economic Community of West African States' in A.B. Akinyemi *et al.*, eds, *Nigeria Since Independence: The First 25 Years,* vol. X: *International Relations* (Ibadan: Heinemann).

Garba, J.M. (1989) *The Time Has Come...Reminiscences and Reflections of a Nigerian Pioneer Diplomat* (Ibadan: Spectrum).

Gboyega, E.A. (1979) 'The Making of the Nigerian Constitution' in O. Oyediran, ed. *Nigerian Government and Politics Under Military Rule* (London: Macmillan).

―――― (1981) 'Intergovernmental Relations in Nigeria: Local Government and the 1979 Nigerian Constitution', *Public Administration and Development*, vol. 1.

―――― (1983) 'Local Government Reform in Nigeria' in P. Mahwood, ed., *Local Government in the Third World* (New York: John Wiley).

―――― (1987) *Political Values and Local Government in Nigeria* (Lagos: Malthouse Press).

―――― (1995) 'The Civil Service Reforms: A Critique' in S. Adejumobi and A. Momoh, eds, *The Political Economy of Nigeria Under Military Rule: 1984-1993* (Harare: SAPES Books).

Gbulie, B. (1981) *Nigeria's Five Majors: Coup d'Etat of 15th January 1966, First Inside Account* (Onitsha: Africana Educational).

Gibbon, P., Y. Bangura and A. Ofstad, eds, (1992) *Authoritarianism, Democracy, and Adjustment: The Politics of Economic Reform in Africa* (Uppsala: Nordiska Afrikainstitutet).

Graf, W.D. (1988) *The Nigerian State: Political Economy, State Class and Political System in the Post-Colonial Era* (London: James Currey).

Hutchful, E. (1986) 'New Elements in Militarism: Ethiopia, Ghana, and Burkina Faso', *International Journal*, vol. 41.

Hyden, G. (1980) *Beyond Ujamaa in Tanzania: Underdevelopment and Uncaptured Peasantry* (London: Heinemann).

Ibrahim, J. (1989) 'The Politics of Religion in Nigeria: The Parameters of the 1987 Crisis in Kaduna State', *Review of African Political Economy*, vol. 45/46.

—— (1991) 'Religion and Political Turbulence in Nigeria', *Journal of Modern African Studies*, vol. 29, no. 1.

Idang, G.J. (1973) *Nigeria: Internal Politics and Foreign Policy, 1960-1966* (Ibadan University Press).

Igbokwe, J. (1995) *Igbos: Twenty-Five Years after Biafra* (Lagos: Advert Communications).

Ihonvbere, J. (1991) 'A Critical Evaluation of the Failed 1990 Coup in Nigeria', *Journal of Modern African Studies*, vol. 29, no. 4.

—— (1996) 'Are Things Falling Apart? The Military and the Crisis of Democratization in Nigeria', *Journal of Modern African Studies*, vol. 34, no. 2.

Ikime, O. (1977) *The Fall of Nigeria* (London: Heinemann).

—— ed. (1980) *Groundwork of Nigerian History* (Ibadan University Press).

Ikporukpo, C.O. (1986) 'Politics and Regional Policies: The Issue of States Creation in Nigeria', *Political Geography Quarterly*, vol. 5, no. 2.

Isamah, A. (1994) 'Unions and Development: The Role of Labour Under Structural Adjustment Programmes' in E. Osaghae, ed., *Between State and Civil Society in Africa: Perspectives on Development* (Dakar: CODESRIA).

—— (1995) 'Labour Response to Structural Adjustment in Nigeria and Zambia' in T. Mkandawire and A. Olukoshi, eds, *Between Liberalization and Oppression: The Politics of Structural Adjustment in Africa* (Dakar: CODESRIA).

Isekhure, N. (1992) *Democracy in Crisis (Edo State Electoral Tribunal in Perspective)* (Benin City: Jodah Publications).

Iwayemi, A. (1979) 'The Military and the Economy' in O. Oyediran, ed., *Nigerian Government and Politics under Military Rule, 1966-79* (London: Macmillan).

Jakande, L.K. (1979) 'The Press and Military Rule' in O. Oyediran, ed., *Nigerian Government and Politics Under Military Rule, 1966-79* (London: Macmillan).

Jinadu, A. (1985) 'Federalism, the Consociational State, and Ethnic Conflict in Nigeria', *Publius: The Journal of Federalism*, vol. 15.

―――― (1995) 'Electoral Administration in Africa: A Nigerian Case Study Under the Transition to Civil Rule Process' in S. Adejumobi and A. Momoh, eds, *The Political Economy of Nigeria Under Military Rule: 1984-1993* (Harare: SAPES Books).

Joseph, R.A. (1981) 'The Ethnic Trap: Notes on the Nigerian Campaign and Elections, 1978-79', *Issue*, vol. 11, no. 1/2.

―――― (1987) *Democracy and Prebendal Politics in Nigeria: The Rise and Fall of the Second Republic* (Cambridge University Press).

―――― (1996) 'Nigeria: Inside the Dismal Tunnel', *Current History*, vol. 95, no. 601.

Kano State Government (1981) *Report of the Maitatsine Disturbances Tribunal of Inquiry* (Kano: Government Printer).

Kayode, M.O. and Teriba, eds (1977) *Industrialization in Nigeria* (Ibadan University Press).

Kirk-Greene, A.H.M. (1971) *Crisis and Conflict in Nigeria*, 2 vols (Ibadan: Oxford University Press).

Klein, A. (1994) 'Trapped in the Traffick: Growing Problems of Drug Consumption in Lagos', *Journal of Modern African Studies*, vol. 32, no. 4.

Koehn, P. 'Competitive Transition to Civilian Rule: Nigeria's First and Second Experiments', *Journal of Modern African Studies*, vol. 27, no. 3.

Kukah, M.H. (1993) *Religion, Politics and Power in Northern Nigeria* (Ibadan: Spectrum).

Kurfi, A. (1983) *The Nigerian General Elections, 1979, and the Aftermath* (Lagos and Ibadan: Macmillan).

Laitin, D. (1982) 'The Sharia Debate and the Origins of Nigeria's Second Republic', *Journal of Modern African Studies*, vol. 20.

Legum, C. (1987) 'Nigeria' in C. Legum, ed., *Africa Contemporary Record: Annual Survey and Documents 1985-1986* (New York: Africana).

Lewis, P.M. (1994) 'Endgame in Nigeria? The Politics of a Failed Transition Programme', *African Affairs*, vol. 93.

―――― (1996) 'From Prebendalism to Predation: The Political Economy of Decline in Nigeria', *Journal of Modern African Studies*, vol. 34, no. 1.

Luckham, R. (1971) *The Nigerian Military: A Sociological Analysis of Authority and Revolt, 1960-67* (Cambridge University Press).

Mackintosh, J.P. ed. (1966) *Nigerian Government and Politics* (London: George Allen and Unwin).

Mahwood, P. (1980) 'The Government of Nigeria: Structural Change as a Response to Pluralism' in S. Ehrlich and G. Wootton, eds, *Three Faces of Pluralism* (Farnborough: Gower).

Mainasara, A.M. (1982) *The Five Majors: Why They Struck* (Zaria: Hudahuda Press).

Marenin, O. (1987) 'The Anini Saga: Armed Robbery and the Reproduction of Ideology in Nigeria', *Journal of Modern African Studies*, vol. 25, no. 2.

Miners, N.J. (1971) *The Nigerian Army 1958-1966* (London: Methuen).
Mkandawire, T. (1995) 'Adjustment, Political Conditionality and Democratization in Africa' in E. Chole and J. Ibrahim, eds, *Democratization Processes in Africa: Problems and Prospects* (Dakar: CODESRIA).
Mohammed, S. and Edoh, T. *A Republic in Ruins* (Zaria: Ahmadu Bello University Press).
Mohammadu, T., and Haruna, M. (1979) 'The Civil War' in O. Oyediran, ed. *Nigerian Government and Politics Under Military Rule* (London: Macmillan).
——— (1989) 'The Making of the 1979 Constitution' in P.P. Ekeh *et al.*, eds., *Nigeria Since Independence: The First 25 Years, vol. v: Politics and Constitutions* (Ibadan: Heinemann).
Muffett, D.J.M. (1982) *Let the Truth be Told* (Zaria: Hudahuda Press).
Mustapha, A.R. (1992) 'Structural Adjustment and Multiple Modes of Livelihood in Nigeria' in P. Gibbon *et al.*, eds, *Authoritarianism, Democracy, and Adjustment: The Politics of Economic Reform in Africa* (Uppsala: Nordiska Afrikainstitutet).
Naanen, B. (1995) 'Oil-Producing Minorities and the Restructuring of Nigerian Federation: The Case of the Ogoni People', *Journal of Commonwealth and Comparative Politics*, vol. 33, no. 1.
Nafziger, E.W. (1992) 'The Economy' in H.C. Metz, ed., *Nigeria: A Country Study* (Washington, DC: Library of Congress).
NEC (National Electoral Commission, 1990) *The 1987-1988 Local Government Elections in Nigeria*, 2 vols (Lagos: NEC).
Ngou, C.M. (1989) 'The 1959 Elections and Formation of the Independence Government' in P.P. Ekeh *et al.*, eds, *Nigeria Since Independence: The First 25 Years*, vol. V: *Politics and Constitutions* (Ibadan: Heinemann).
Nicolson, I.F. (1977) *The Administration of Nigeria, 1900-1960* (Oxford: Clarendon Press).
Nnoli, O. (1978) *Ethnic Politics in Nigeria* (Enugu: Fourth Dimension).
——— (1989) 'Nigeria's Foreign Policy and the Struggle for Economic Independence' in A.B. Akinyemi *et al.*, eds, *Nigeria Since Independence. The First 25 Years*, vol. X: *International Relations* (Ibadan: Heinemann).
——— ed. (1981) *Path to Nigerian Development* (London: Zed).
——— ed. (1993) *Deadend to Nigerian Development* (Dakar: CODESRIA).
Northern Regional Government (1953) *Report on the Kano Disturbances: 16th, 17th and 19th May 1953* (Lagos: Government Printer).
Nwabueze, B.O. (1982) 'The Problems of Federalism in Nigeria', paper presented at a special seminar at the Institute of African Studies, University of Ibadan, February.
——— (1983) *Federalism Under the Presidential Constitution* (London: Sweet and Maxwell).
——— (1994) *Nigeria '93: The Political Crisis and Solutions* (Ibadan: Spectrum).
Nwokedi, E. (1994) 'Nigeria's Democratic Transition: Explaining the Annulled 1993 Presidential Election', *Round Table*, no 330.
Nwolise, O.B.C. (1992) 'The Internationalization of the Liberian Crisis and its Effects on West Africa' in M.A. Vogt, ed., *Liberian Crisis and*

ECOMOG: A Bold Attempt at Regional Peace- Keeping (Lagos: Gabumo Publishers).

—— (1994) 'The Constitutional Conference in Perspective', paper presented at the launching of the War Against Indiscipline and Corruption, Ibadan.

Nzimiro, I. (1979) *The Nigerian Civil War: A Study in Class Conflict* (Enugu: Fourth Dimension).

Obasanjo, O. (1981) *My Command: An Account of the Nigerian Civil War, 1967-70* (London: Heinemann).

—— (1985) 'Nigeria: Which Way Forward?', keynote address, annual conference of the Agricultural Society of Nigeria held at Ibadan.

—— (1990) *Not My Will* (Ibadan University Press).

Ochoche, S.A. (1987) 'Political Manipulation and Scheming by the Kaduna Mafia' in B.J. Takaya and S.G. Tyoden, eds, *The Kaduna Mafia* (Jos University Press).

Odetola, T.O. (1978) *Military Politics in Nigeria* (New Brunswick, NJ: Transaction Books).

—— (1980) *Military Politics in Nigeria: Economic Development and Political Stability* (New Brunswick, NJ: Transaction Books).

Ofoegbu, R. (1979) 'Foreign Policy under Military Rule' in O. Oyediran, ed., *Nigerian Government and Politics Under Military Rule, 1966-79* (London: Macmillan).

Ohiorhenuan, J.F.E. (1989) 'The State and Economic Development in Nigeria Under Military Rule, 1966-79' in T.N. Tamuno and J.A. Atanda, eds, *Nigeria Since Independence: The First 25 Years*, vol. IV: *Government and Public Policy* (Ibadan: Heinemann).

—— and G. Onu (1989) 'The Political Economy of Federal Character: The Case of the Iron and Steel Industry' in P.P. Ekeh and E.E. Osaghae, eds, *Federal Character and Federalism in Nigeria* (Ibadan: Heinemann).

Ojigbo, L.O., ed. (1983) *How Shagari was Confirmed President: The Legal Decisions of the Meaning of '2/3rd of 19'* (Lagos: Tokion, for NPN).

Ojo, A. (1989) 'The Republican Constitution of 1963', in P.P. Ekeh *et al.*, eds, *Nigeria Since Independence: The First 25 Years*, vol. V: *Politics and Constitutions* (Ibadan: Heinemann).

Okolie, A.C. (1995) 'Oil Rents, International Loans and Agrarian Policies in Nigeria, 1970-1992', *Review of African Political Economy*, vol. 22, no. 64.

Okolo, A. (1989) 'Nigeria and the Superpowers' in A.B. Akinyemi *et al.*, eds, *Nigeria Since Independence: the First 25 years*, vol. X: *International Relations*, (Ibadan: Heinemann).

Okonjo, I.M. (1974) *British Administration, 1900-1950* (New York: Nok Publishers).

Okpaku, J., ed. (1972) *Nigeria: Dilemma of Nationhood: An African Analysis of the Biafran Conflict* (New York: Third Press).

Okpu, U. (1977) *Ethnic Minority Problems in Nigerian Politics, 1960-1965* (University of Uppsala).

—— (1989) 'Ethnic Minorities and Federal Character' in P.P. Ekeh and E.E. Osaghae, eds, *Federal Character and Federalism in Nigeria* (Ibadan: Heinemann).

Olagunju, T. (1992) 'The Party System and the Creation of Two Political Parties' in O. Uya, ed., *Contemporary Nigeria: Essays in Society, Politics and Economy* (Buenos Aires: Artes Graficas Editoriales Publiciterias).

———, T., A. Jinadu and S. Oyovbaire (1993) *Transition to Democracy in Nigeria, 1985-1993* (Ibadan: Safari and Spectrum).

Ollawa, P.E. (1981) 'The Nigerian Elections of 1979: A Further Comment', *Journal of Commonwealth and Comparative Politics*, vol. XIX, no. 3.

——— (1989) 'The 1979 Elections' in P.P. Ekeh *et al.*, eds, *Nigeria Since Independence: The First 25 Years*, vol. V: *Politics and Constitutions* (Ibadan: Heinemann).

Olowu, D. (1990) 'Centralization, Self-Governance and Development in Nigeria' in J.S. Wunsch and D. Olowu, eds, *The Failure of the Centralized State: Institutions and Self-Governance in Africa* (Boulder: Westview Press).

Olugbade, K. (1992) 'The Nigerian State and the Quest for a Stable Polity', *Comparative Politics*, vol. 24, no. 3.

Olukoshi, A.O. ed. (1991) *Crisis and Adjustment in the Nigerian Economy* (Lagos: JAD).

——— ed. (1993) *The Politics of Structural Adjustment in Nigeria* (London: James Currey).

——— (1995a) 'The Political Economy of the Structural Adjustment Programme' in S. Adejumobi and A. Momoh, eds, *The Political Economy of Nigeria Under Military Rule: 1984-1993* (Harare: SAPES Books).

——— (1995b) 'The Politics of Structural Adjustment in Nigeria' in T. Mkandawire and A. Olukoshi, eds, *Between Liberalization and Oppression: The Politics of Structural Adjustment in Africa* (Dakar: CODESRIA).

——— (1995c) 'Bourgeios Social Movements and the Struggle for Democracy in Nigeria: An Inquiry into the "Kaduna Mafia" ' in M. Mamdani and E. Wamba-dia-Wamba, eds, *African Studies in Social Movements and Democracy* (Dakar: CODESRIA Books).

Olukoshi, A.O., and C.N. Nwoke (1994) 'The Theoretical and Conceptual Underpinnings of Structural Adjustment Programmes' in Olukoshi *et al.*, eds, *Structural Adjustment in West Africa* (Lagos: Pumark, for NIIA).

Oluleye, J.J. (1985) *Military Leadership in Nigeria, 1966-1979* (Ibadan University Press).

Omorogiuwa, P.A. (1987) 'Economic Costs of the Political Transition Programme (1987-1992) in Nigeria', paper presented at the National Workshop on the Political Transition Programme, Department of Political Science, University of Benin, November 1987.

Omoruyi, O. (1989) 'Federal Character and the Party System in the Second Republic' in P.P. Ekeh and E.E. Osaghae, eds, *Federal Character and Federalism in Nigeria* (Ibadan: Heinemann).

Onimode, B. (1982) *Imperialism and Underdevelopment in Nigeria* (London: Zed).

——— (1988) *A Political Economy of the African Crisis* (London: Zed).

Osadebey, D.C. (1978) *To Build a Nigerian Nation: An Autobiography* (Lagos: Macmillan).

Osaghae, E.E. (1986a) 'Do Ethnic Minorities Still Exist in Nigeria?', *Journal of Commonwealth and Comparative Politics*, vol. 24, no. 2.

———— (1986b) 'On the Concept of the Ethnic Group in Africa: A Nigerian Case', *Plural Societies*, vol. XVI, no. 2.

———— (1987) 'The African Food Crisis and the Crisis of Development in Africa: A Theoretical Exploration', *Africa Quarterly*, vol. XXIV, nos 3-4.

———— (1988) 'The Complexities of Nigeria's Federal Character and the Inadequacies of the Federal Character Principle', *Journal of Ethnic Studies*, vol. 16, no. 3.

———— (1989a) 'The Character of the State, Legitimacy Crisis, and Social Mobilization in Africa: An Explanation of Form and Character', *Africa Development*, vol. XIV, no. 2.

———— (1989b) 'Federal Character: Past, Present and Future' in P.P. Ekeh and E.E. Osaghae, eds, *Federal Character and Federalism in Nigeria* (Ibadan: Heinemann).

———— (1990a) 'Social Mobilization as a Political Myth in Africa', *Africa Quarterly*, vol. 30, nos 3/4.

———— (1990b) 'Considerations on the Confederation Debate in Nigeria', *Plural Societies*, vol. XX, no. 1.

———— (1991a) 'Ethnic Minorities and Nigerian Federalism', *African Affairs*, vol. 90.

———— (1991b) 'The Political Transition Process and the Prospects for Democracy in Nigeria' in L. Akinyele *et al.*, eds, *Economic and Democratic Reforms in Nigeria's Development* (Ibadan: SID & Friedrich Ebert Foundation).

———— (1992) 'The First and Second Republics: An Analysis of Change and Continuity' in L.C. Fejokwu *et al.*, eds, *Political Leadership Handbook and Who's Who* (Lagos: Polcrom).

———— (1993) 'From Benevolence to Greater Benovolence: The State and the Politics of Structural Adjustment in Rural Africa', *Africa Quarterly*, vol. 33.

———— (1994) 'Inter-State Relations in Nigeria', *Publius: The Journal of Federalism*, vol. 24, no. 4.

———— (1995a) 'The Nigerian Federal Experience: What Lessons for South Africa?' in H. Kotze, ed., *The Political Economy of Federalism in South Africa* (Stellenbosch: Centre for International and Comparative Politics, University of Stellenbosch).

———— (1995b) 'The International Experience of Opposition Politics: Lessons for South Africa? – The Nigerian Experience' in H. Kotze, ed., *Parliamentary Dynamics: Understanding Political Life in the South African Parliament* (Stellenbosch: Centre for International and Comparative Politics, University of Stellenbosch).

———— (1995c) *Structural Adjustment and Ethnicity in Nigeria* (Uppsala: Nordiska Afrikainstitutet Research Report no. 98).

——— (1995d) 'The Ogoni Uprising: Oil Politics, Minority Agitation, and the Future of the Nigerian State', *African Affairs*, vol. 94.

——— (1995e) 'The Study of Political Transitions in Africa', *Review of African Political Economy*, vol. 22, no. 64.

——— (1996a) 'Human Rights and Ethnic Conflict Management: The Case of Nigeria', *Journal of Peace Research*, vol. 33, no. 2.

——— (1996b) *Ethnicity, Class, and the Struggle for State Power in Liberia* (Dakar: CODESRIA Monograph Series 1/96).

———, Isumonah, A., and I.O. Albert (1994) *Liberalization Policies and Changing Legitimacy Structures in Nigeria*, research report submitted to the NISER/SSCN project on the Impact of Liberalization Policies in Nigeria.

Oshionebo, B. (1995) 'The Civil Service Reforms: Changes and Challenges' in S. Adejumobi and A. Momoh, eds, *The Political Economy of Nigeria Under Military Rule: 1984-1993* (Harare: SAPES Books).

Osoba, S.O. (1987) 'The Transition to Neo-Colonialism' in T. Falola, ed., *Britain and Nigeria: Exploitation or Development?* (London: Zed).

Osuntokun, J. (1979) 'The Historical Background of Nigerian Federalism' in A.B. Akinyemi *et al.*, eds, *Readings on Federalism* (Lagos: Nigerian Institute of International Affairs).

Othman, S. (1984) 'Classes, Crises and Coup: The Demise of Shagari's Regime', *African Affairs*, vol. 83, no. 333.

——— (1989) 'Nigeria: Power for Profit – Class, Corporatism, and Factionalisation in the Military' in D.B.C. O'Brien, J. Dunn and Rathbone, eds, *Contemporary West African States* (Cambridge University Press).

Otite, O. (1990) *Ethnic Pluralism and Ethnicity in Nigeria* (Ibadan: Shaneson).

Otubanjo, F. (1989) 'Introduction: Phases and Changes in Nigeria's Foreign Policy' in A.B. Akinyemi *et al.*, eds, *Nigeria Since Independence: The First 25 Years*, vol. X: *International Relations* (Ibadan: Heinemann).

Oyediran, O., ed. (1980) *Nigerian Legislative Houses: Which Way?* (Ibadan: University of Ibadan Consultancy Unit).

——— ed. (1981) *The Nigerian 1979 Elections* (London: Macmillan).

——— (1981) 'The Road to the 1979 Elections' in O. Oyediran, ed., *The Nigerian 1979 Elections* (Lagos: Macmillan Nigeria).

——— (1988) *Essays on Local Government in Nigeria* (Lagos: Project Publications).

——— (1989) 'The 1983 Elections' in P.P. Ekeh *et al.*, eds, *Nigeria Since Independence: The First 25 Years*, vol. X: *Politics and Constitutions* (Ibadan: Heinemann).

——— (1990) 'Democratic Electoral Process: Can Nigeria Make it this Time Around?' *Nigerian Journal of Electoral and Political Behaviour*, vol. 1, no. 1.

——— and A. Agbaje (1991) 'Two-Partyism and Democratic Transition in Nigeria', *Journal of Modern African Studies*, vol. 29, no. 2.

——— and A. Gboyega (1979) 'Local Government and Administration' in O. Oyediran, ed., *Nigerian Government and Politics under Military Rule, 1966-79*, (London: Macmillan).

Oyediran, O. and O. Olagunju (1979) 'The Military and the Politics of

Revenue Allocation' in O. Oyediran, ed., *Nigerian Government and Politics under Military Rule* (London: Macmillan).

Oyewole, A. (1987) 'Failure of the First Experiment: A Viewpoint' in S.E. Oyovbaire, ed., *Democratic Experiment in Nigeria: Interpretative Essays* (Benin City: Omega Publishers).

Oyovbaire, S.E. (1985) *Federalism in Nigeria: A Study of the Development of the Nigerian State* (London: Macmillan).

―――― (1987) 'The Context of Democracy in Nigeria' in S.E. Oyovbaire, ed., *Democratic Experiment in Nigeria: Interpretative Essays* (Benin City: Omega Publishers).

―――― (1989) 'Military Rule and the National Question in Nigeria' in P.P. Ekeh and E.E. Osaghae, eds, *Federal Character and Federalism in Nigeria* (Ibadan: Heinemann).

Paden, J. (1973) *Religion and Political Culture in Kano* (Berkeley: University of California Press).

―――― (1986) *Ahmadu Bello, Sardauna of Sokoto: Values and Leadership in Nigeria* (Zaria: Hudahuda).

Panter-Brick, K., ed. (1978) *Soldiers and Oil: The Political Transformation of Nigeria* (London: Frank Cass).

Phillips, A. (1988) *Essentials of the 1988 Civil Service Reforms in Nigeria* (Ibadan: NISER).

―――― (1991) 'Four Decades of Fiscal Federalism in Nigeria', *Publius: The Journal of Federalism* (special issue on Federalism in Nigeria), vol. 21, no. 4.

Post, K.W.J., and M. Vickers (1973) *Structure and Conflict in Nigeria 1960-65* (London: Heinemann).

Reno, W. (1993) 'Old Brigades, Money Bags, New Breeds, and the Ironies of Reform in Nigeria', *Canadian Journal of African Studies*, vol. 27, no. 1.

Robertson, Sir James (1974) *Transition in Africa: From Direct Rule to Independence: A Memoir* (London: C. Hurst).

Schwarz, F.A.O. (1965) *Nigeria: The Tribe, The Nation or the Race* (Cambridge, MA: MIT Press).

Scott, J. (1985) *Weapons of the Weak: Everyday Forms of Peasant Resistance* (New Haven: Yale University Press).

―――― (1990) *Domination and the Arts of Resistance* (New Haven: Yale University Press).

Sanusi, J.O. (1988) 'Deregulating the Nigerian Economy: Achievements and Prospects', *Economic and Financial Review* (Central Bank of Nigeria), vol. 26, no. 4.

Sesay, M.A. (1995) 'Collective Security or Collective Disaster: Regional Peace Keeping in West Africa', *Security Dialogue*, vol. 26, no. 2.

―――― (1996) 'Civil War and Collective Intervention in Liberia', *Review of African Political Economy*, vol. 23, no. 67.

Shyllon, F., and O. Obasanjo (1980) *The Demise of the Rule of Law: Two Points of View* (Ibadan: Institute of African Studies, Occasional Publications no. 33).

Sklar, R.L. (1963) *Nigerian Political Parties: Power in an Emergent African Nation* (Princeton University Press).

———— (1965) 'Contradictions in the Nigerian Political System', *Journal of Modern African Studies*, vol. 3, no. 2.

Smith, R.S. (1988) *Kingdoms of the Yoruba* (Madison: University of Wisconsin Press).

Soremekun, K. (1987) 'Oil and the Military' in A.O. Sanda *et al.*, eds, *The Impact of Military Rule on Nigeria's Administration* (Ile Ife: Faculty of Administration, University of Ife).

———— and C.I. Obi (1993) 'Oil and the National Question' in *The National Question and Economic Development in Nigeria* (Ibadan: Nigeria Economic Society).

Soyode, A. (1989) 'Indigenization' in T.N. Tamuno and J.A. Atanda, eds, *Nigeria Since Independence: The First 25 Years*, vol. iv: *Government and Public Policy* (Ibadan: Heinemann).

St Jorre, J. de (1972) *The Nigerian Civil War* (London: Hodder and Stoughton).

Stremlau, J. (1977) *The International Politics of the Nigerian Civil War* (Princeton University Press).

Suberu, R. (1991) 'The Struggle for New States in Nigeria, 1976-1990', *African Affairs*, vol. 90, no. 361.

———— (1995) 'The Politics of State Creation' in S. Adejumobi and A. Momoh, eds, *The Political Economy of Nigeria under Military Rule: 1984-1993* (Harare: SAPES Books).

Synge, R. (1993) *Nigeria: The Way Forward* (London: Euromoney Books).

Takaya, B.J. (1987) 'Ethnic and Religious Roots of the Kaduna Mafia' in Takaya and Tyoden, eds, *The Kaduna Mafia* (Jos University Press).

———— and S.G. Tyoden (1987) *The Kaduna Mafia: A Study of the Rise, Development and Consolidation of a Nigerian Power Elite* (Jos University Press).

Tamuno, T.N. (1970) 'Separatist Agitations in Nigeria Since 1914', *Journal of Modern African Studies*, vol. 8, no. 4.

———— ed. (1984) *The Civil War Years* (Zaria: Nigeria Since Independence History Project, vol. III).

———— ed. (1989) *Nigeria Since Independence: The First 25 years*, vol. X: *The Civil War Years* (Ibadan: Heinemann).

———— (1991) *Peace and Violence in Nigeria* (Ibadan: Panel on Nigeria Since Independence History Project).

Toyo, E. (1984) 'The Causes of Depression in the Nigerian Economy', *Africa Development*, vol. IX, no. 3.

Tseayo, P. (1975) *Conflict and Incorporation in Nigeria: The Integration of the Tiv* (Zaria: Gaskiya).

———— (1980) 'The Emirate System and Tiv Reaction to 'Pagan' Status in Northern Nigeria' in G. Williams, ed., *Nigeria: Economy and Society* (London: Rex Collings).

Turner, T., and A. Baker (1984) 'Soldiers and Oil: The 1983 Coup in Nigeria', McGill University Centre for Developing Area Studies Discussion Paper no. 28.

Ukwu, I.U., ed. (1987) *Federal Character and National Integration in Nigeria* (Kuru: Nigerian Institute for Policy and Strategic Studies).

Umar, M.S. (1989) 'Islam in Nigeria: Its Concept, Manifestations and Role in Nation-Building' in J.A. Atanda, G. Asiwaju and Y. Abubakar, eds *Nigeria Since Independence: The First 25 Years*, vol. IX: *Religion* (Ibadan: Heinemann).

Usman, Y.B., ed. (1979) *Studies in the History of the Sokoto Caliphate* (Zaria: Ahmadu Bello University Press).

―――― (1986) *Nigeria Against the IMF: The Home Market Strategy* (Kaduna: Vanguard Publishers).

―――― (1987) *the Manipulation of Religion in Nigeria, 1977-1987* (Kaduna: Vanguard Publishers).

―――― and Y. Bangura (1984) 'Debate on the Nigerian Economic Crisis', *Studies in Politics and Society*, no. 2.

Uwazurike, P.C. (1990) 'Confronting Potential Breakdown: The Nigerian Redemocratization Process in Critical Perspective', *Journal of Modern African Studies*, vol. 28, no. 1.

Uya, O.E., ed. (1992) *Contemporary Nigeria: Essays in Society, Politics and Economy* (Buenos Aires: Artes Graficas Editoriales Publiciterias).

Vogt, M.A. (1992) *Liberian Crisis and ECOMOG: A Bold Attempt at Regional Peace-Keeping* (Lagos: Gabumo Publishers).

Whitaker, C. (1970) *The Politics of Tradition: Continuity and Change in Northern Nigeria, 1946-66* (Princeton University Press).

Williams, G. (1980) *State and Society in Nigeria* (Idanre: Afrografika).

Williams, D.C. (1992) 'Accommodation in the Midst of Crisis? Assessing Governance in Nigeria' in G. Hyden M. Bratton, eds, *Governance and Politics in Africa* (Boulder: Lynne Rienner).

Willink Report (1958) *Report of the Commission Appointed to Enquire into the Fears of the Minorities and the Means of Allaying Them* (London: HMSO).

Wilmot, P. (1989) *Nigeria's Southern Africa Policy, 1960-1988* (Uppsala: Nordiska Afrikainstitutet, Current African Issues, no. 8).

Yahaya, A.D. (1989) 'Local Government: The Military Initiative' in P.P. Ekeh *et al.*, eds, *Nigeria Since Independence: The First 25 Years*, *vol. v: Politics and Constitutions* (Ibadan: Heinemann).

Yahaya, S. (1993) 'State Versus Market: The Privatization Programme of the Nigerian State' in A.O. Olukoshi, ed., *The Politics of Structural Adjustment in Nigeria* (London, Ibadan & Portsmouth, NH: James Currey and Heinemann).

INDEX